Walter Davis

The early records of the town of Lunenburg, Massachusetts

Walter Davis

The early records of the town of Lunenburg, Massachusetts

ISBN/EAN: 9783337281632

Printed in Europe, USA, Canada, Australia, Japan

Cover: Foto ©ninafisch / pixelio.de

More available books at **www.hansebooks.com**

THE

EARLY RECORDS

OF THE

TOWN OF LUNENBURG

MASSACHUSETTS

INCLUDING THAT PART WHICH IS NOW FITCHBURG

1719 — 1764

A COMPLETE TRANSCRIPT OF THE TOWN MEETINGS AND SELECT-
MEN'S RECORDS CONTAINED IN THE FIRST TWO BOOKS
OF THE GENERAL RECORDS OF THE TOWN

ALSO A COPY OF ALL THE VITAL STATISTICS OF THE
TOWN PREVIOUS TO THE YEAR 1764

COMPILED BY

WALTER A. DAVIS, CITY CLERK

FITCHBURG
PUBLISHED BY AUTHORITY OF THE CITY COUNCIL
1896

FITCHBURG, MASS., Jan. 29, 1895.

TO THE HONORABLE CITY COUNCIL OF THE CITY OF FITCHBURG.

Gentlemen: The undersigned petition your Honorable Body, and respectfully represent that the preservation of the records of the town of Fitchburg, prior to its incorporation as a city, and also such records as may be obtainable of the town of Lunenburg and its early proprietors, prior to the formation of the town of Fitchburg, is a matter of great importance; and therefore they respectfully pray that the city council of the city of Fitchburg may take such measures as shall be deemed expedient to secure and preserve an additional copy or copies of said records, to be deposited in such fire-proof situation, other than the city hall, as may be authorized by your council.

A. NORCROSS,　　　　*Committee of*
ARTHUR H. LOWE, } *Fitchburg Historical*
J. F. D. GARFIELD,　　*Society.*

IN BOARD OF ALDERMEN, Feb. 5, 1895.

Referred to committee on education. Sent down for concurrence.

WALTER A. DAVIS, *Clerk.*

IN COMMON COUNCIL, Feb. 5, 1895.
Concurred.

JOHN R. OLDFIELD, *Clerk.*

CITY OF FITCHBURG.

IN CITY COUNCIL, Feb. 19, 1895.

The joint standing committee on education, to whom was referred the petition of the Fitchburg Historical Society, relative to the preservation of early records of Fitchburg, and so much of Lunenburg as relates to Fitchburg, have attended to the business committed to them, and present the following report, and would recommend the adoption of the following order:

ORDERED, That the sum of $500 (five hundred dollars) be, and the same hereby is, appropriated for the purpose of copying and printing the early records of the town of Fitchburg prior to its incorporation as a city, and so much of the records of the town of Lunenburg as pertains to Fitchburg prior to its separation from Lunenburg, the work to be done under the supervision of the city clerk, who shall have authority to employ such assistance as he may need in doing the work, the amount to be charged to account of incidentals.

C. A. CROSS,
SAMUEL ANDERSON,
JAMES A. AUSTIN,
GEORGE F. COMLEY,
WILLIAM V. LOWE,
Committee on Education.

IN BOARD OF ALDERMEN, Feb. 19, 1895.

Report read, accepted, and order adopted. Sent down for concurrence.

WALTER A. DAVIS, *Clerk.*

IN COMMON COUNCIL, Feb. 19, 1895.

Adopted in concurrence.

JOHN R. OLDFIELD, *Clerk.*

MAYOR'S OFFICE, FITCHBURG, MASS., Feb. 21, 1895.

Approved.

EDGAR S. MOULTON, *Mayor.*

A copy of record. Attest:

WALTER A. DAVIS, *City Clerk.*

CITY CLERK'S OFFICE,

FITCHBURG, MASS., Nov. 1, 1895.

In compliance with the preceding vote, I immediately corresponded with the Selectmen and Town Clerk of Lunenburg, with a view to obtain the books containing the earlier records of the town, viz.: What was embraced between the years 1728 and 1764, or previous to the incorporation of Fitchburg as a town.

The value of these records cannot be estimated in dollars and cents, and the wisdom of the city council in taking measures to preserve them will become apparent as time advances.

It is intended that the following pages shall be an exact transcript of the original record, and every portion of the original is copied as far as possible.

The pagination of the original volumes is inserted in our text in brackets.

After considerable search and diligent inquiry, I succeeded in securing the book containing the proprietors' records. As there is so much matter, I have concluded to have them printed in a separate book, and consequently it will appear later.

These old records contain much information as to the names and possessions of the first settlers, together with an accurate idea of the power exercised by the old town governments, and furnishes much food for the student of social science.

This work was undertaken not in the interest of the historian, so much as for the use of the city; for its more familiar acquaintance with, and its surer preservation of, its own annals, and the bringing together in one place of so much of the Lunenburg records as are connected with, and are a part of, this city.

The idea of copying and printing the old records originated with the Fitchburg Historical Society and was urged by their secretary, James F. D. Garfield, to whom I am indebted for many suggestions and references. Many cities and towns are having the same work done, and while it may take some time to do it and do it well, the value of the copy will be enhanced by having it accurately done.

The vital statistics in this book have been copied from a volume owned by the town of Lunenburg, which was carefully transcribed by John R. Rollins in or about 1849. Minutes have been noted down of such suggestions as he has made. These vital statistics have not been copied beyond 1764, except to complete the record of families, and to add such vital statistics as belonged in Fitchburg and were not recorded here. In the Lunenburg records these are included in the same volume with the town records. In the Fitchburg records, to be published later, they may be separated.

It is to be hoped that the work of copying the remaining records will continue, and that soon the time will come when all the vital statistics will be printed each year.

I desire to express my appreciation to Selectmen Hildreth and Jones and Town Clerk Stillman Stone of Lunenburg, for the many courtesies extended to me.

Walter A. Davis.

City Clerk.

SURVEY AND ALLOTMENT

OF THE

NEW SOUTH TOWN WEST OF GROTON CALLED TURKEY HILLS.

[1] An Acco^t of the Gen^{ell} Courts Comm^{tees} Proceedings In Granting And Lotting out the Lands in the South Town Ship Westward of And Contiguous To ye Town of Groton in the County of Midd^{sx} Called Turky Hills By Virtue of ye Grant or Order of ye Gen^{ell} Court.

At a Great & General Court or Affembly for His Majefties Province of ye Mafsachusets Bay Held Novr 4. 1719

In ye Houfe of Reprefentatives The Vote for Granting Two New Towns Was brought Down from the Board with Amendments Which Wear Read & Agreed to, And ye Vote is as follows: Viz Voted that Two Towns Each Containing a Quantity of Land not exceeding Six Miles Square to be Laid out in as Regular Forms as ye Lines Will Allow, to be Settled in A Defenfible Manner On ye Wefterly Side of Groton Weft Line, And that William Tailer, Samuel Thaxter, Francis Fullam Capt John Shiply & Mr Benjamin Whittemore be a Comm^{tee} fully Impowered to Allott and Grant out ye Land Contained in Each of ye said Towns (a Lot not to Exceed Two Hundred & Fifty Acres) to Such P^{r}Sons & Only Such as Will Effectualy Settle ye Same Within ye Space of three Years Next Enfuing ye Laying out & Granting Such Lotts by S^d

Comm:tee: Who Are Inftructed & Directed to Admitt Eighty Families or perfons at Least Who Shall pay to y:e: S:d: Comm:tee: for y:e: Ufe of y:e: Province the Sum of Five pounds for Each Allottm:t: Which Shall be Granted & Allotted as afforef:d: And that Each P:r:Son to Whom Such Lot or Lotts Shall be granted & Laid out Shal be Obliged to build a Good Dwelling Houfe theron & Inhabit it, & alfo to break up & Fence in three Acres of Land at y:e: Leaft Within y:e: Term of three Years, and y:t: there be Laid out & Referved for y:e: firft Settled Minifter a good Convenient Lot alfo A Lot for y:e: School, And A Minifterial Lot & A Lot for Harvard Colledge of Two Hundred & fifty Acres Each & y:e: Settlers be Obliged To build A Convenient Houfe for y:e: Worfhip of God in Each of S:d: Towns within The Term of four years, & to pay y:e: Charge of Necefary Surveye & y:e: Comm:tee: for their Service in & About y:e: premifes. And that y:e: Comm:tee: Give Publick Notice of y:e: Time & place When they Will Meet to Grant Allottm:ts:

                                              Confented to, SAM:LL: SHUTE
Copy Examined

[2] Whereas We John Farnworth Jonathan Boyden Jonas Prefcott Jun:r: John Ames And Benjamin Prefcott Ware Chofen & Impowered by the Town of Grotton to Confer with the Honourable the Great Genarall Courts Committee Concerning the Weft Line of the Townfhip of Grotton, & Settle the Same With them, As by A Vote Or Act of the Inhabitants of f:d: Town At there Meeting on the 4:th: Day of February 1719/20 Doth or May More at Large Appear.

Now Let All Men Know, by these Prefents That We (The Committee Before Named) having Confidered of the Premifes, & Taken Upon us the Charge of the S:d: Buisnefs, Do Hereby Conclude Concurr & Agree [ ] Honourable Committee of the Genarall Court affore f:d:, that th[Corner of the Town Shipp of Grotton be A Small Tree With a heap of Stones About it, Standing & Being on the Easterly side of Niftaqualothe* hill, (So Called) by

*Probably the same as Nissitissit. [W. A. D.

Whereas we John Farnworth, Jonathan Boydon, [...]
[...] John Ames, and Benjamin Prescott were chosen [...]
by the Town of Groton, to Confer with the Honourable the
Generall Courts Committee Concerning the [...] Line of the Town of
Groton, & Settle the Same with them, as by a Vote or Act of the [...]
of s'd Town at there Meeting on the 4th Day of February 1719/20
[...] or may more at Large appear: —
Now Let all men Know by these Presents, That we (the Committee
before Named) haveing Considered of the Premises, & taken upon us
Charge of the s'd Premiss, Do Hereby Conclude Concurr & agree [with the]
Honourable Committee of the Generall Court aforesaid, that the
Corner of the Township of Groton be a Small Tree with a heap of
Stones about it, standing & being on the Easterly side of Nishaque [...]
hill (so Called) by Dunstable Line and that the Southwest Corner [...]
Township, be a stake and heap of stones being forty Poles South of [...]
heap of stones about half a mile Southward of Catacoonamog Pond
Called and westward of a Brook Called Pennitt Brook, Made in the P[resence]
of [...] William Elyer, Mr Benjamin Whitemore, & Mr [...]
and that a Strait Line be Made from one of the s'd Corner [...]
Which Line Being so Made Shall be the West Line of Groton
Witness our Hands the Second Day of April Anno Dom 1720

John Farnworth
John Ames
Jonathan Boydon
Benja Prescott

Survey and Allotment of Turkey Hills.

Dunftable Line, and that the Southwest Corner of s⁴ Townfhip, be a Stake and heap of Stones being Forty Poles South of a Smal Heap of Stones about half a mile Southwad of Cataconamog Pond (So Called) and westward of a Brook Called Benith* Brook Made In the Prefents of Francis Fullam Efqʳ Mr Benjamin Whitamore & Mr Jo[†] and that A Strait Line be Made from one of the S⁴ Corne[   ] Which Line Being So Made Shall be the West Line of Groton

Witnefs our Hands the Second Day of Aprill Anno Dom 1720.

                JOHN FARNWORTH
                JOHN AMES
                JONATHAN BOYDON
                BENJA PRESCOTT

[3] An Acc.ᵗ of Time & Expences in yᵉ Survey of yᵉ New South Town West of Groton Called Turky Hills

	£.	S.	d
To mʳ Benjᵃ Whittemore, And Francis Fullam Who began S.ᵈ Service On Monday yᵉ 21ˢᵗ of Dec.ʳ 1719. And Ended Said Whittemore Service yᵉ 31ˢᵗ of yᵉ Same Month Ten Days	5	00	00
And S.ᵈ Fullams Ended yᵉ firſt Day of Jan.ʳʸ Eleven Days	5	10	00
Capt Shiply from yᵉ 22ᵈ of S.ᵈ Month of Dec.ʳ to ye Laſt 9 Days	4	10	00
‡ yᵉ Surveyer M.ʳ Sam.ˡˡ Jones Who began S.ᵈ Service yᵉ 21ˢᵗ of Dec.ʳ 1719 & Ended yᵉ 31 of yᵉ Same Month Ten Days	4	10	00
To 4 Chainmen &c. Viz Liut. Jon.ᵗʰ Boyden, Wᵐ Whitney Finchas Parker, & Thom.ˢ Tarbul, Who began their Service the 22ᵈ of S.ᵈ Dec.ʳ & Ended yᵉ 30ᵗʰ Day of yᵉ Same Eight Days Each	8	00	00

*Probably Bennet Brook, a name which it still bears. [W. A. D.
†Brackets signify that a portion of the original has been destroyed. [W. A. D.
‡This character is undoubtedly meant for the word "Item." So says Dr. Samuel A. Green, Librarian of the Massachusetts Historical Society of Boston. [W. A. D.

Whittemors To y̌ᵉ General Expenc as Reckned at Concord
Expenc Mʳ Whittemore p⁴ £1-7-2   1 7 2
　　　　　More p⁴ by Mʳ Whittemore on yᵉ
Road 3/₁₀ᵈ   00 3 10
More p⁴ by Capᵗ Shiply £00 - ₁₅ⁿ = 00 at pages.
More ₀₀ᵊ - ₁₂ⁿ - 6   01 7 6
To yᵉ wᶜʰ General Expenc Sd ffullam p⁴ £1-7-1 1 7 1
Fullams More Expenc Going & Returning
　　　　　home 3-6 [
Expenc More to Bisket & Cheefe to Carry
　　　　　into ye Woods in Sᵈ Service [
&c 　　To A Journy to Bofton to Search
　　　　　yᵉ Records of Pʳticuler Grant [
& Expenc in Sᵈ Journy ₅ⁿ. And ₁ᵈ/₆ᵈ p⁴ for
a Copy [

[4] The Commᵗᵉᵉ for yᵉ New Towns Westward of
　　　Groton Met on the 5ᵗʰ of April 1720.
April PʳSent Collᵒ Tailer, Capᵗ Shiply, Mʳ Benjᵃ
5ᵗʰ　Whittemore Francis Fullam Who was then
1720. Appointed Clerk to Sᵈ Commᵗᵉᵉ
The Commᵗᵉᵉ Confidering yᵉ Propofal of A Commᵗᵉᵉ
Appointed by The Town of Groton On yᵉ 4ᵗʰ of Febʳ
Laft paft to Confer, & Settle Groton West Line With yᵉ
Courts Commᵗᵉᵉ Prefented by Enˢ John Farnfworth One
of Sᵈ Commᵗᵉᵉ for Groton, Who Declared That yᵉ Small
Tree with A heap of Stones About it on yᵉ Eafterly Side
of Niftiqualit Hill is No Other, but yᵉ Same Heap of Stons
Where yᵉ General Courts Commᵗᵉᵉ Began their Survey,
And it being So Accepted & Underftood fᵈ propofals Are
Accepable, & yᵉ Sᵈ Line to be Run & finaly Settled Ac-
cording
　　Then yᵉ Commᵗᵉᵉ agreed to Meet at Concord the 11ᵗʰ
of May Next And yᵗ ffullam in yᵉ Name of yᵉ Commᵗᵉᵉ
Write to yᵉ Selectmen or petʳˢ of Lancafter to Meete yᵉ
Commᵗᵉᵉ at Concord On Sd Day to Settle [   ] the Line
The Expense then p⁴ at Angers by yᵉ Commᵗᵉᵉ
　　was　　　　　　　　　　　　　　　　　£00 - 17 - |
And On yᵉ Road by ffullam ₈ᵈ　　　　　　 00 - 00 - |

Survey and Allotment of Turkey Hills. 11

4. Coll? Tailers Attendenc One Day   00 - 10 - [
4: Cap! Shiply Attendanc & Travil 3 Days   [
4: M! Whittemores Attendanc One Day   00 - 10 - [
4. Francis Fullams Attendanc One Day   00 - 10 - 00
Expenc p^d by Cap! Shiply On y^e Road 3/   00 - 03 - 00
More Expenc by Mr Whittemor on y^e Road
$\tfrac{v}{0} - \tfrac{s}{0} - 6$ 00 - 00 - [
                                            ────── [
                        Totall   04 = 01 = [

The Comm^tee also Agreed to Meete at Concord, To goe to Groton to p^rfect [   ] y^e Survey of y^e Lines, And Settle y^e Line With Groton, On Saterday y^e 16th [   ] Day of April 1720.

Memorandom y^t y^e North Town is Made D^r [   ] one half part of y^e Charge & Expence of S^d Meeting being [   ] The South Town is D^r for ye Like Sum being— — — [

[5] P^rSuant to the Vote of ye Comm^tee Entred on y^e
    Other Side April 20th 1720 Mr Whittemor &
April   Fullam Sett out to Groton On Saterday y^e
5th   16th Day of April 1720. Ther Staid Sabath.
1720   On Monday ye 18th proceed With Cap!
Ended   Shiply, Mr Jones, ye Surveye, & Chainmen &
         prop^r affistance With Groton Comm^tee viz
En^s Farnsworth, Liu^t Prefcot & Mr Boyden, To ye Heap of Stones at Groton Nor west Corn^r. Thenc began our Work

To Mr Whittemores from ye 16, to ye 23^d of
    April 7 Days   3 10 00
To Cap! Shiply from ye 18th to the 23^d 6 Days   3 00 00
To Francis Fullam from ye 16th to ye 23^d
    7 Days   3 10 00
To Mr Jones Surveyer from ye 18th to ye 23^d
    6 Days   2 14 00
To Liu! Jon^th Boyden 4 Days & ½   1   2 [
To Wm Laurane, And Nath^ll Wood 4 Days &
    half Each   2   5 [
To Tarbul & finehas Parker 5 Days Each   2 10 [

To Mr Green One Day 00 5 [
Expences p^d at Greens in S^d Survey by Capt 1 00 10
Shiply £1-00-10
by Mr Whittemore £1 = 00-10- More Expenc
on y^e Road ³/₆ 1 4 4

	By Fra : Fullam	£1 = 00-10			
	More at Pages	0 - 00- 6			
Fullams	At Concord p^d	0 - 01- 3			
Expenc	for Bifket, Cheefe &	)0 - 6- 7			
	Jenger to Carry. Totall	1 - 9- 2	1	9	2

22 10 10

Memorand^m y^t of y^e Sum Total of £22 : 10 : 1̇0 as Above
The North Town is Made D^r for One half be-
ing £11 5 5
And y^e South Town is D^r for ye Like Sum of £11 5 5

[6]   CONCORD, MAY THE 11TH 1720.

The Comm^{tee} Appointed, & fully Impowered by ye Great & Gene^{ell} Court Or Affembly of His Majefties Province of ye MaffachuSett Bay in New England At Their feffion, On ye 7th of Decr 1719 To Allott & Grant out ye Lands Contained, in Each of ye Two TownShips Laft Granted by ye Court Each Containing The Quantity of Six Miles Sqare Lying Weftward of, & Contiguous to ye Town of Groton &c.

Mett at Concord in ye County of Middlesex On Wednesday the Eleventh Day of May 1720. At ye Houfe of Mr Jonth Hoberd, In Order to Grant out Said Townships, Agreeable to ye Order & Direction of ye General Court (The Whole of S^d Comm^{tee} Viz.

Wm Tailer & Sam^{ll} Thaxter Efq^r Capt John Shiply Mr Benjamin Whittemore & Fra : Fullam P^{r}Sent)

And Accordingly Proceeded to Grant out said Lands to ye P^{r}Sons Whofe Names Are Under Written On ye Other Sides, On ye following Conditions & provifions And Not Other wife.

Survey and Allotment of Turkey Hills.

1ˢᵗ That Each & Every PʳSon to Whom A Lot is or Shall be granted (No Allottmᵗ or Share to Exceed yᵉ Quantity of 250 Acres) Shal be Obliged at yᵉ Entring his Name With yᵉ Commᵗᵉᵉ to pay Down yᵉ Sum of fifty Shillings in part, And at yᵉ Drawing of his Lott, or When yᵉ Same is Laid out, The Sum of fifty Shillings More in full of yᵉ five pounds for yᵉ ufe of yᵉ Province. And if any PʳSon Who Enters his Name, & pays yᵉ first fifty Shillings Shall Neglect or Refufe to pay yᵉ Laft fifty to Compleat yᵉ five pounds As Ordered by the General Court, When his Lott is Laid out & Redy for Draft, Every Such PʳSon Shal forfit his first payment And yᵉ Lott be free to be Granted to An Other proper perfon as yᵉ Commᵗᵉᵉ Shal See Meet.

2ᵈ That Every PʳSon to Whom a Lott is, or Shall be Granted Shall be, & is herby Obliged To build A good Dwelling Houfe on his Sᵈ Allottmᵗ And also to break up, & Sufficiently fence in three Acres of Land at yᵉ Leaft Within yᵉ Space of three years After yᵉ Sᵈ Lotts are Laid out & Drawn, And Do also pay & Do Each of their full proportions Towards yᵉ Building & Finifhing of A Convenient Houfe for yᵉ Publick Worfhip of God, in Such Town Where his Lott Shall fall, Sᵈ Houfe to be Finifhed in four Years According to yᵉ Order of yᵉ General Court, And Do also pay yᵉ Necefary Charge of yᵉ Surveys And yᵉ Commᵗᵉᵉ for their Servic in And & bout yᵉ Premifes.

3ᵈ

[7] 3ᵈ That Every Grantee to Whom A Lott is or Shal be Granted Shall be & is hereby Enjoyned Effectualy To Settle & Inhabit yᵉ Same In his Own Proper PʳSon, And Not have Liberty in Any Way What So Ever to Sell or Alienate or Any Ways to Difpofe of His Interest or Allottmᵗ in Either of Said Towns to Any PʳSon What So Ever Untill the Whole Conditions Enjoyned by yᵉ General Court be fully Complied With, & Pʳformed, Without yᵉ Leave & Approbation of The Commᵗᵉᵉ Or the Majer part of them. Nor to Any PʳSon, or pʳSons But Such As They Shall Approve And to be Accepted by yᵉ Commᵗᵉᵉ

Survey and Allotment of Turkey Hills.

		£	s	d
1	John Fletcher — of Concord — — —	2	10	00
2	Nath^{ll} Harris — of Needham — — —	2	10	00
3	Mofes Smith — of Needham — —	3	00	00
4	Roberd Harris — of Needham —	2	10	00
5	Abra^m Woodward — of Brookline — — —	2	10	00
6	Aron Smith — — of Needham — —	2	10	00
7	Timothy Harris — of Roxbury — — —	2	10	00
8	Ephraim Sautle — — of Groton — — —	2	10	00
9	Mr Whittemor for his Son Nath^{ll} Concord —	2	10	00
10	Jonth Hubard — — of Concord — — — —	2	10	00
11	Jofeph Hubbard — — of Concord — — — —	2	10	00
12	Dan^{ll} Davis — — — of Concord — — — —	2	10	00
13	Jonth Hartwell — — — of Concord — — —	2	10	00
14	Mr Wm Keene — — — of Concord — — —	5	00	00
15	Elias Barron — — — of Concord — — — —	2	10	00
16	En^s John Warrin for his son John of Marlborough — — —	2	10	00
17	Jonth child of W — — — — — — —	2	10	00
18	Jacob Fullam of Weston — — — — — —	2	10	00
19	John Whitny of Watertown — — — — —	2	10	00
20	William Wood of Concord — — — — — —	2	10	00
21	Liu^t Jones for his Son Joliah of Weston —	2	10	00
22	Eleazer Green of Groton — — — — — —	2	10	00
23	Ephraim Peirce for His Son Ephraim of Groton	2	10	00
24	Nath^{ll} Holden of Groton — — — — —	2	10	00
25	Zachariah Sautle for his Son David of Groton —	2	10	00
26	Wm Whitny for his Son W^m of Groton	2	10	00
27	Isaac Stone of Groton — — —	2	10	00
28	Nath^{ll} Woods of Groton — — — —	2	10	00
29	Nath^{ll} Woods Ju^r of Groton — — —	2	10	00
30	Nathan Haward of Concord	2	10	00
31	Edwd Emerson Efq^r for his Son Edward-Newbery	2	10	00
		80	10	00

Survey and Allotment of Turkey Hills. 15

		£	s	d
[8] Brought Over From ye Other Side		80	10	00
32:	John Calfe of Boston — — — — —	2	10	00
33:	Thomas Hale for His Son Jofhua of Newbery — — —	2	10	00
34:	Dan^{ll} Thirfton for His Son Jonth of Newbery — — —	2	10	00
35:	Phillip Goodridge of Newbery — — — —	2	10	00
36:	Jonth Poore of Newbery — — — — —	2	10	00
37:	Wm Blount for his Son David Blount of Andover —	2	10	00
38:	Henry Chandler Ju^r of Andover — — —	2	10	00
39:	Thos Pearly for Phillip Amey of Boxford	2	10	00
40:	Jer. Perly for John Amey of Boxford — —	2	10	00
41:	Jonth Woodman for his Son Stephen Woodman Bradford	2	10	00
42:	Thos Tailer of Reading — — — — —	2	10	00
43:	Nath^{ll} Stow for His Son Nath^{ll} Stow of Reading	2	10	00
44:	Walter Bees of Lancafter — — — —	2	10	00
45:	Wm Wheeler of Concord — — — — —	2	10	00
46:	Peter Harwood of Concord for His Son Nath^{ll}	2	10	00
47:	Thos Woolly — Concord —	2	10	00
48:	Sam^{ll} Hartwell for His Son Isaac Concord	2	10	00
49:	Jofeph Ball for his Son Jofeph Watertown	2	10	00
50:	John Haftings Watertown	3	00	00
51:	Ebenezer Chadwick Weston	2	10	00
52:	Jofeph Allen for his Son Weston	2	10	00
53:	Jonth Boyden for his Son Jofiah Groton	2	10	00
54:	Benja Prefcot Groton	2	10	00
55:	Phinehas Parker Groton	2	10	00
56:	Thos Tarbul Groton	2	10	00
57:	Jofeph Gilson for his Son Jonas Groton	2	10	00
58:	Wm Laurance Groton — — — —	2	10	00
59:	Jam^s Goold Salem — — —	2	10	00
60:	Mr Sam^{ll} Page of Turky Hills &	2	10	00
61:	S^d Sam^{ll} Page for his Son Jofeph	2	10	00
62:	Capt Jam^s RichardSon Wooburn &	2	10	00
63:	for his Son Wm Wooburn	2	10	00

Survey and Allotment of Turkey Hills.

64:	Jon.ᵗʰ Whitny of Concord		2	10	00
65:	Isaac Whitny of Concord		2	10	00
66:	Shadrik Whitny Concord		2	10	00
67:	Thoˢ Kembal Ju.ʳ		2	10	00
68:	M.ʳ W.ᵐ Clark Bolton		2	10	00
69:	Jon.ᵗʰ Shiply Groton	paid page 15	00	00	00
70:	John Burrill Esq.ʳ	" " "	00	00	00
71:	Jon.ᵗʰ Dows Esq.ʳ	" " "	00	00	00
72:	Jer Allen Esq.ʳ — — — —		5	00	00
73:	Nath.ˡ Whitny Ju.ʳ of Weston		2	10	00
74:	Edw.ᵈ Hartwel of Lancaſter Paid page 15		00	00	00
75:	Amos Brown of Stow	" " "	00	00	00

                                                          181 00 00

[9]	Brought Over from y.ᵉ Other Side		181	00	00
76	M Eleaze.ʳ Flagg Wooburn Paid page 15		00	00	00
77	Cap.ᵗ Rich.ᵈ Kembal for his Son Joseph of Bradford		2	10	00
78	M.ʳ James Burbeen for his Son James paid page 15		00	00	00
79	Finehas Richardson paid page 15		00	00	00
80	Lin.ᵗ Thoˢ Perly paid page 15		00	00	00
	Totall		183	10	00

                                                           £ s d

May 11.ᵗʰ 1720. The Comm.ᵗᵉᵉˢ Attendence, Travil & Expences in Granting out y.ᵉ South Town Lotts For w.ᶜʰ S.ᵈ Town is D.ʳ

To Coll.ᵒ Tailer Two Days & half	1	00	00
To Coll.ᵒ Thaxter Two Days Attendance & Travil One Day	1	4	00
To Cap.ᵗ Shiply Two Days Attendanc & Travil	00	16	00
To Liu.ᵗ Whittemor One Day & half at 8ˢ	00	12	00
To Francis ffullam One Day & half	00	12	00
Expence p.ᵈ by Cap.ᵗ Shiply	00	04	00
Expence then p.ᵈ at M.ʳ Hubbards Two pounds Seven Shillings And Sixpence	2	7	6
p.ᵈ by M.ʳ Whittemore at Concord £00 - 00 - ¹⁰⁄ᵈ	00	00	10
	6	16	4

Survey and Allotment of Turkey Hills. 17

S.ᵈ South, & North Towns Contr.ˢ Creditt

Concord	By Bills of Credit Then Rec.ᵈ		
May 11ᵗʰ 12ᵗʰ	of yᵉ Grantees of both Towns		
& 13ᵗʰ	Three Hundred & Twenty		
1720	pounds	320 00 00	

Viz of yᵉ South town Grantees One Hundred &
Seventy One pounds & Ten Shillings — 171 10 00
And of yᵉ North Town One Hundred & forty
Eight pounds Ten — 148 10 00
— 320 00 00

of yᵉ Which Sum there Was then p.ᵈ by y.ᵉ
Com.ᵗᵉᵉ for past Expences A Necefary
Charges of Surveys Sixty Six pounds One
Shi.ˡˡ & a peny — 66 01 01
as is More p.ʳticularly Sett Down in yᵉ North
Town Acco.ᵗˢ pag 10ᵗʰ

The Remainder Sent To y.ᵉ Province Treafʳ viz
By yᵉ Hon.ᵇˡᵉ Coll.ᵒ Tailer Eighty Two pounds — 82 00 00
By Coll.ᵒ Thaxter Seventy Two pounds Twlve
Shillings — 72 12 00
By Fra: Fullam Ninty Nine pounds Seven Shil-
lings — 99 07 00

[10]   South Town D.ʳ   £ s. d
Sept 10ᵗʰ To M.ʳ Whittemore Who began his
Service yᵉ 10ᵗʰ Day of Sep.ᵗʳ 1720
1720   And Ended yᵉ 17ᵗʰ of yᵉ Same
Month 7 Days at 8.ˢ p.ʳ Day — 2 16 00
To Cap.ᵗ Shiply 6. Days — 2 8 00
To Fra: Fullam began Monday yᵉ 12ᵗʰ Ended
Saterday 17ᵗʰ 6 Days — 2 8 00
M.ʳ Sam.ˡˡ Jones Surveyer from y.ᵉ 10ᵗʰ to y.ᵉ
17 Day 6 Days & half — 2 12 00

chain- Wᵐ Laurane four Days & half at
        4.ˢ — 00 18 00
men   Finehas Parker & Nath.ˡˡ Woods 3
        Days & half at 4.ˢ — 1 08 00

Expenc p^d at Groton p^d by Capt Shiply Eight
Shillings & $^d_{11}$ 0 . 8 11
p^d by m^r Whittemore 16^s & $^d_1$ 00 16 01
p^d By Fra: Fullam Eleven Shillings & one peny 00 11 01

Sep^t 22^d Mr Whittemore A Day to Dorches-
1720   ter & Expence   00 9 6

                   14 15 7

Septr 26   At A Meeting of y^e Comm^{tee} Appointed by y^e
1720   Great & General Court or Affembly of y^e
     Province of y^e Mafsachusetts &c. for ye Two
New Towns Laft Granted Westward of Groton &c. At
Cambridge the 26 Day of Sep^{tr} 1720

   P^{r}Sent Wm Tailer Efq^r Capt Shiply Benjamin Whittemore and Fra: Fullam,

   1. Agred That ye Comm^{tee} or Majer part of them Do
forthwith proceed to Allott out both ye New Towns if
Time Will permit But First the South Town, No Lott to
be Lefs then forty & five Acres And that to be ye Stand-
ard of ye beft Land, & if Need Require to Add five or
More Acres to Make Each Lott Equal in ye Judgm^t of y^e
Comm^{tee} The Lotts to be Laid in Half mile Ranges Where
ye Land Will Allow it So to be

   And y^t ther be Laid out Convenient Ways Not Lefs
then Six Rods Wide, And that ye School Lott be Laid out
as Near ye Center of ye houfe lotts as May be. That y^e
Minifterial Lott be alfo Laid as Near ye Center of ye houfe
Lots as May be &c. That ye Lot for ye firft Settled
Minifter be Laid as Conveni^t To ye Meetinghoufe place as
May be. That ye Colledg Lott be Laid out as Convenient
as May be Without Incomoding ye Houfe Lotts In One
Intire peice Two Hundred & fifty Acres together

Survey and Allotment of Turkey Hills. 19

	£	s	d
[11] South Town D⸺			
Sept 26 To: Coll⸺ Tailer One Day		8	00
1720 4: Cap⸺ Shiplys Attendanc & Travil 3 Days ⸺	1	4	00
4: M⸺ Whittemore One Day	00	8	00
4: Fra: Fullam One Day	00	8	00
To Coll⸺ Tailers Expenc then at Cambridge 6/3ᵈ	00	06	3
To Capt Shiplys Expenc in yᵉ Journy $_{10}^{s}$ $_{11}^{d}$	00	10	11
M⸺ Whittemores Expence $_{7}^{s}$ 5	00	07	5
Fra Fullams Expence $_{6}^{s}$/3ᵈ	00	06	3
	03	18	10

	£	s	d
Octobʳ 3ᵈ Survey in Loting out yᵉ South Town			
1720 Westward of Groton From Monday yᵉ 3ᵈ of Oct⸺ 1720. To Saterday yᵉ 22ᵈ of the Same Month.			
Mʳ Whittemore 17 Days at 8ˢ	6	16	00
Capt Shiply 16 Days — — —	6	08	00
Fra: Fullam 14 Days	5	12	00
Mʳ Samᵘ Jones. 18 Days	7	4	00
Liuᵗ Jonᵗʰ Boyden 10 Days	2	00	00
Finehas Parker 13 Days	2	12	00
Thomas Tarbel 16 Days	3	4	00
Wᵐ Lauranc 11 Days	2	4	00
Expences then pᵈ by Capt Shiply $_{2}^{£}$/4ˢ : 7ᵈ	2	4	7
Mʳ Whittemore pᵈ $_{2}^{£}$. $_{1}^{s}$. 11 penc. More 0-$_{7}^{s}$. $_{1}^{d}$	2	9	00
Fra Fullam then pᵈ £2 : 3 : 3. More on yᵉ Road $_{9}^{d}$ &	2	4	00
More for horfe Keeping 13 Days $_{3}^{s}$/9ᵈ	0	3	9
Expenc pᵈ Wᵐ Lauranc for 19 pound & half of Beefe at 2½ pʳ pound	1	4	[
pᵈ at Pages	———	[	
Total	48	08	[

[12] BOSTON MARCH 24ᵀᴴ 1720/1

March 24 At A meeting of yᵉ Commᵗᵉᵉ for yᵉ New Towns 1720/21 West of Groton PʳSent Collᵒ Thaxter, Mʳ Whittemor & Fra: Fullam.

In Anſwer to yᵉ Petetion of Timothy Harriſs of Rowley, Samˡˡ Hale of Bradford, Richᵈ Kimbel for his Son Joseph of Bradforde & Samˡˡ Tennys of Bradford. Dated March 22ᵈ 1720. Requeſting to be Lett into The South Town West of Groton to Take Up Lotts there if it Might be but if Not yᵗ they Might be Admitted into yᵉ North TownShip the Pʳforming yᵉ Conditions that Others Do.

Voted P̃ yᵉ Commᵗᵉᵉ that yᵉ A Bove Named Timᵒ Harriss, Samˡˡ Hale, Richᵈ Kembel for his Son Joſeph & Samˡˡ Tennys Requeſt Be So farr Granted yᵗ they be Admitted in to yᵉ North Town if They Cannot be Admitted in to yᵉ South, Which is almoſt full, Upon the paymᵗ of their Money as Others.

And yᵗ Any Two of yᵉ Commᵗᵉᵉ be impowred to Lay out yᵉ Lotts in Caſe Anything Extrᵃ prevent yᵉ Attendance of three.

The Lotts to be Drawn On Tueſday yᵉ 23ᵈ Day of May Next at Concord, The Commᵗᵉᵉ to Meet there on the 22ᵈ in yᵉ Evening.

Mʳ Wᵐ Clark Admitted
Samˡˡ Kendal of Wooburn Admitted pᵈ   2 10 00
Nathˡˡ Whitny Juʳ of Weston Admitted pᵈ   2 10 00
The Above Named Rich Kembal Hath pᵈ for
    himſelf   2 10 00
And for Mʳ Samˡˡ Tenny   2 10 00
Mʳ Joſeph Plympton of Medfield for his Son pᵈ   2 10 00

Ten pounds of yᵉ Mony in mʳ Whittemores hands
And in fullams Hand Recᵈ of Sᵈ Whitny   £02 - 10 - 0
More by Sᵈ ffullam of Mʳ Wᵐ Clark   02 - 10 - 0
More by Sᵈ ffullam of Mʳ Jer. Allen   05 - 00 - 0
                        10 = 00 - 0

Survey and Allotment of Turkey Hills. 21

		£	s	d.
[13] March 31 1721	March 31, 1721 Expenc p^d by Francis Fullam at bofton When Mett With Coll^o Tailer, Coll^o Thaxter & y^e Comm^{tee}	00	01	6
	More to y^e Secretary for A Copy of y^e Court Order 4/6	00	4	6
	p^d by Capt Shiply for Writing One Shilling	00	1	00
		00	07	00

		£	s	d
from April 10th 1721	April 10th 1721. South Town D^r In Lotting S^d Town To Mr Whittemor Who began ye 10^t & Ended ye 21 Day of ye Same Month 10 Dayes at 8^s	4	00	00
	To Capt Shiply. 9 Days	3	12	00
	To Fra: Fullam begining y^e 10th & Ending y^e 21st 10 Days	4	00	00
	To m^r Surveyer Jones 10 Days	4	00	00
chain-men	To Thomas Tarbel. 9. Days. at 4^s p Day	1	16	00
	4: Parker & Lauranc. 8. Days Each	3	4	00
	Expences p^d by m^r Whittemor £01-12-10	1	12	10
	p^d by Capt Shiply £01=12-00	1	12	00
	p^d by Fra: Fullam £1-12-00	1	12	00
	totall	25	15	10

[14] An Account of y^e Mony Rec^d at Concord &c by y^e General Courts Comm^{tee} of the Several Grantees of y^e South Town Called Turky Hills, When, & Since they Drew Their Lotts the 23^d Day of May. 1721.

		£	s	d
John Fletcher in part — — —	Lot No: 81 — — —	2	10	0
Nath^{ll} Harris in full — — — —	No: 71 — — —	4	5	0
Moses Smith in full — — — —	No: 64 — — —	3	15	0

Survey and Allotment of Turkey Hills.

Roberd Harris in full — — —	No: 23 — — — 4	5	0
Abra<u>m</u> Woodward in full — —	No: 82 — — — 4	5	0
Aron Smith in full	No: 46 — — — 4	5	0
Tim<u>o</u> Harris in full	No: 31 — — — 4	5	0
Ephr<u>m</u> Sautle in full	No: 33 — — — 4	5	0
Jon<u>th</u> Huburd in full	No: 51 — — — 4	5	0
Joseph Hubard in full	No: 24 — — — 4	5	0
Dan<u>ll</u> Davis in full	No: 61 — — — 4	5	0
M^r W<u>m</u> Keen in full	No: 56 — — — 1	15	0
Jon<u>th</u> Hartwel in full	No: 73 — — — 4	5	0
Elias Barron in full	No: 32 — — — 4	5	0
En<u>s</u> John Warrin in full	No: 18 — — — 4	5	0
John Child in full	No: 10 — — 4	4	6
Jacob ffullam — in full	No: 80 — — 4	5	0
Nath<u>ll</u> Whittemor in full	No: 57 — — — 4	5	0
John Whittny — in full	No: 76 — — 4	5	0
W<u>m</u> Wood — in full	No: 79 — — 4	5	0
Liu<u>t</u> Jones — in full	No: 34 — — 4	5	0
Eleaz<u>r</u> Green — in full	No: 20 — — — 4	5	0
Ephr<u>m</u> Peirce — in full	No: 65 — — — 4	5	0
Nath<u>ll</u> Holden in full	No: 42 — — — 4	5	0
Zachariah Sautle in full	No: 28 — — — 4	5	0
Ephr<u>m</u> Peirce in Room of Wm Whitny in full	No: 68 — — — 4	5	0
Isaac Stone in full	No: 29 — — — 4	5	0
Nath<u>ll</u> Wood of Groton in full	No: 58 — — — 4	5	0
Nath<u>ll</u> Wood Ju^r in full	No: 53 — — — 4	5	0
Nathan Haward in full	No: 38 — — — 4	5	0
Edw<u>d</u> Emerfon Efq^r in full	No: 78 — — — 4	5	0
John Calf. in full	No: 21 — — — 4	5	0
Tho<u>s</u> Hale in full	No: 22 — — — 4	5	0
Dan<u>ll</u> Thirston in full	No: 50 — — — 4	5	0
Phillip Goodridg in full	No: 70 — — — 4	5	0
Jon<u>th</u> Poor in full	No: 54 — — — 4	5	0
W<u>m</u> Blount in full	No: 55 — — — 4	5	0
Henry Chandler in full	No: 13 — — — 4	5	0
Thos Perly in full	No: 84 — — — 4	5	0
Jer: Perly for John Amy in full	No: 67 — — — 4	5	0
	165	4	6

Survey and Allotment of Turkey Hills.

[15]

	No:	£	s	d
of Jon.th Woodman — in full	No: 17 — — — 4		5	00
of Thomas Tailer — in full	No: 4 — — — 4		5	00
Tho.s Kembal Ju.r in full	No: 16:— — — 4		5	00
Nath.ll Stow in full	No: 19 — — — 4		5	00
Walter Bees in full	No: 49 — — — 4		5	00
W.m Wheeler in full	No: 47 — — — 4		5	00
of Peter Harwood for his Son Nath.ll in full	No: 59 — — — 4		5	00
Tho.s Wooly in part $\frac{s}{50}$ Reft to be p.d in 3 weeks	No: 74 — — — 2		10	00
Sam.ll Hartwell for his Son in full	No: 26 — — — 4		5	00
Jofeph Ball in full	No: 45 — — — 4		5	00
John Haftings in full	No: 63 — — — 3		15	00
Ebenez.r Chadwick in full	No: 15 — — — 4		5	00
Jofeph Allen in full	No: 30 — — — 4		5	00
Jon.th Boyden in full	No: 35 — — 4		5	00
Benja Prescot in full	No: 72 — — — 4		5	00
Finehas Parker in full	No: 12 — — — 4		5	00
Tho.s Tarbul in full	No: 11 — — — 4		5	00
En.s Jofeph Gilson in full	No: 43 — — — 4		5	00
W.m Laurane in full	No: 44 — — — 4		5	00
Jam.s Goold in full	No: 5 — -- 4		5	00
M.r Sam.ll Page for Two Lotts in full	No: 41 & 52 — 8		10	00
Cap.t James Richardson in full & for his Son W.m Richardson in full	No: 66 — — 4		5	00
	No: 36 — -- 4		5	00
Jon.th Whitny in part	No: 25 — — — 2		11	00
Isaac Whitny in full	No: 62 — — — 4		5	00
Shadrik Whitny in full	No: 6 — — — 4		5	00
M.r Wm Clark in full	No: 48 — — — 4		5	00
Jon.th Shiply in full	No: 60 — — -- 6		15	00
John Burrel Efq	No: 3 — -- — 6		15	00
Jon.th Dows Efq.r in full	No: 27 — — — 6		15	00
Ier: Allen Efq.r paid page 8	No: 40 — — —			
Nath.ll Whitny Ju.r in full	No: 77 — — — 4		5	00
Edw.d Hartwell in full	No: 37 — — — 6		15	00
for Amos Brown of Stow p.d by Jabez Fairbank of Lancafter in part	No 2		5	

24   Survey and Allotment of Turkey Hills.

Maj.^r Eleaz.^r Flag in full	No: 8 — — — 6	15 00
Capt Richd Kembal for his son Joseph in full	No: 75 — — — 4	5 00
of Mr Jam.^s Burbeen for his Son Jam.^s in full	No: 9 — — — 6	15 00
Lin.^t Thos Perly in full	No: 7 — — — 6	15 00
John Perham of Littleton in full	No: 14 — — — 6	15 00
Finehas Richardson in full	No: 69 — — — 6	15 00

Highest no. 84 — 81 drafts.
Gone Nos 1 — 39 and 83

[16]
May 23.^d May ye 23, 1721 the Comm.^{tee} At-
1721   tendanc Travil & Expenc When
The Lotts Were Drawn at Concord, for wch y.^e South Town D.^r

	£	s	d
To Coll.^o Tailer Two Days	00	16	00
To Coll.^o Thaxter Two Days & half	01	00	00
To m.^r Whittemore Two Day:	00	16	00
To Capt Shiply Two Days	00	16	00
To Fra: Fullam Two Days	00	16	00
Expenc p.^d at Hubbards at Concord £1-14=00	1	14	00
More To Capt Shiply Two Days to Marlborough & Expenc	1	2	00
To Fra: Fullam Two Days y.^e Same Service & Expenc	1	00	00
total	08	00	00

[17] Page 17 left blank.

[18] Page 18 left blank.

[19]
June 8.th South Town Is D.^r To Francis Ful-
1721   lam for One Day of my Self &
Horse, To Concord to Notifie Mr Whittemore, & Mr Jones, and Sending to Capt Jonas Prescot, & Writing to Capt Ward to Attend ye General Courts Comm.^{tee} As Ordered at Cambridge by Said Comm.^{tee}   00 10 09
To ffullams Expenc then p.^d 9.^d

Survey and Allotment of Turkey Hills.   25

To m.^{r} Whittemore half A Day ye Same Time at Concord	00	5	00
& Whittemores Expenc then p.^{d}	00	2	00
More to m.^{r} Whittemore Attendenc On ye General Courts Comm^{tee} at Cambridge as by them Ordered Two Days	1	00	00
Necefary Expenc In S.^{d} Journy p.^{d} by Whittemor	00	06	00
total	2	03	9

Decr 5 & 6th The Comm^{tee} Appointed by y^e Great & General 1721. Court or Affembly of His Majefties Province of y^e Maffachusetts Bay in New England at their fseffion Novr 4th 1719.

For y^e Granting & Allotting out y^e New Towns Westward of and Contiguous to y^e Town of Groton.

Mett at Concord in y^e County of Middlesex on y^e 5$^{th}_\&$ Sixth Days of Decr 1721.

P^{r}Sent Coll.^{o} Tailer, Coll.^{o} Thaxter Capt Shiply Mr Whittemor, & Fra: Fullam.

Orded, y.^{t} Mr Sam.^ll Jones as Surveyer With Sutable affiftance and Chainmen Under Oath Do With What Speed they Can Take an Exact Account of y^e Juft Quantity of Acres of Medows (Not alredy Laid out into Lotts) in ye South Town Westward of Groton in Order to A Division of the Medows in Juft proportion to ye Several Grantees in Said Town Also y^t there be a Second Divifion of Upland Laid out to Each Grantee With What Speed May be Each Division to Contain fifty or Sixty Acres as ye Comm^{tee} Shall Think best And ye Land Will bare. The Rev.^{d} m.^{r} Sam.^ll Stow Upon his Motion to ye Comm^{tee} Had Leave to Purchase A Lott in ye South Town he Settling ye Lot himSelf or by Such P^{r}Son as ye Committee Shall Approve Who Shall performe Conditions As Other of ye Grantees in f.^{d} Town Are Obliged to do.

[20] South Town D[r] to y[e] Comm[tee] for Time Travil & Expene

	£ s d
Dec[r] 5 &	
6th To Coll[o] Tailer 3 Days at Holdins	
1721. in Concord & Travil	01 10 00
To Coll[o] Thaxter 4 Days	2 00 00
4. Cap[t] Shiply 3 Days with his Travil	1 10 00
To m[r] Whittemore Two Days £	1 00 00
To Fra Fullam Two Days Attendenc	1 00 00
Expences then p[d] at Concord	
By Coll[o] Thaxter at Holdins £1-2-6 More at Hobbards 8/6	2 11 00
More p[d] by Coll[o] Thaxter T[r] Traveling Expene	00 9 6
Then More p[d] by Fra Fullam 4[s]/	00 4 00
Total	10 4 6

	£ s d
Feb 12th South Town D[r]	
1721/2 To m[r] Benja Whittemore Who with Surver Jones Sett out (to Take An Acco[t] of y[e] South Town Medows as Ordred) The 12th Day of feb[r] 1721/2 & Ended March 1st	
S[d] Whittemore 10 Days	5 00 00
Cap[t] Shiply 8 Days	4 00 00
M[r] Sam[ll] Jones Ten Days	4 00 00
chain Liu[t] Boyden 8. Days at 4s	1 12 00
men Jofeph Page 5. Days	1 00 00
Expene then p[d] by M[r] Whittemore	1 5 1
And by Cap[t] Shiply y[e] Like Sum of	1 5 1
More Two Days Travil out & home of S[d] Whittemore and M[r] Jones being Drove off by ftreff of Wether	1 10 00
More Expene p[d] by f[d] Whittemore	00 8 1
And by Cap[t] Shiply More p[d]	00 4 5
	20 4 8
Ag[st] 25, 30th To Benja. Whittemor for Time & Expene About y[e] affair of Lancafter T[r] Order South Town D[r]	———— 1 6 8
	21 11 4

This Whole Side 31-15-10

[21] South Town   D⁛
To Coll⁚ Tailer With y⁾ Comm^tee at Cambridge
    Ap⁷ 19th 1723 on y⁾ Afairs of S⁴
April 19th   Town One Day 10ˢ   00 10 00
1723
         To m⁷ Whittemor ₀₀⁼ ₁₀₋₀₀, & Ex-
pence One Shilling & four pence   00 11 4
To Fra: Fullam One Day   00 10 00
To Expence then p⁴ by Coll⁚ Tailer at Cam-
bridge 00-12-6   00 12 6
                                         ─────────
                                          2 3 10

The One half of this Charg being £1-⅛-¹¹ᵈ to 01 1 11
be p⁴ by y⁾ North Town. y⁾ Other half by ─────────
y⁾ South Town being y⁾ Totall   01 1 11

June 25th   CONCORD, JUNE 25ᵀᴴ & 26   1723
1723   At A meeting of the Comm^tee Apoynted by y⁾
    Great & General Court for y⁾ Granting y⁾ Two
Town Ships Westward of & Contiguous to The Town of
Groton
    P⁷Sent Coll⁚ Thaxter, Lin⁷ Whittemore And Fra
Fullam.
    Pinehas Richardson Moved to y⁾ Comm^tee that Sam^ll
Bennett Might be Admitted, in his Roome he having Sold
his Lott to him in Turky Hills if the Committee Approve
therof.
    Ephraim Sautle Desires Leave to Sell his Lott in ye
South Town to Timothy Gibfon for his Son Timothy.
    Wm Richardson Requefts y⁾ Favour. to be Entred to
Lott N⁰ 66. And y⁴ his Brother James be Admitted &
Entred to Lott N⁰ 36 and That Sam^ll Farnsworth May
be Admitted Inftead of f⁴ Wm Richardson upon Lott
N⁰ 66.
    Nath^ll Stow Defires His Brother Tho⁵ Stow May be
Entred And Admitted in his Room to Act & Settle
    Advifed & Propofed by y⁾ Grantees of y⁾ South Town
That the Medows in S⁴ Town, As Soon as May be With
Conveniancy, May be Laid out & proportioned to y⁾
Grantees in One Division
                                         2ᵈˡʸ

28   Survey and Allotment of Turkey Hills.

[22] 2dly That the Second Division Now to be Laid out (Each Divifion to Containe Sixty Acres) be Laid out, as Soone as May be With Conveniancy, And that yᵉ Commᵗᵉᵉ Endeaver as Near as They Can to Ballanc yᵉ Lotts & Divisions.

Voted by The Commᵗᵉᵉ That Sᵈ Divisions be Made Accordingly Any Two of yᵉ Commᵗᵉᵉ being PrSent.

At yᵉ Request of Mr Wm Keen the Commᵗᵉᵉ Voted to Admitt David Perlin of Concord to Settle on yᵉ Lott of Said Keen in yᵉ South Town Sᵈ Perlin having bought Sᵈ Lott of Sᵈ Keen With yᵉ Commᵗᵉᵉˢ Allowanc

		£	s	d
Jun 25th & 26th 1723	South Town Dr To: yᵉ Commᵗᵉᵉ for their Attendenc, Travil & Expences			
	To: Collᵒ Thaxter 3 Days	1	10	00
	To: mr Whittemore Two Days	1	00	00
At Concord	To: Fra: Fullam Two Days	1	00	00
Expence then Paid by Collᵒ Thaxter		00	6	00
Genᵉˡˡ Expenc pᵈ by mr Whittemor at Concord		1	9	3
Expenc pᵈ by Fullam 00–4–10		00	4	10
And by Whittemore 00–3–7		00	3	7
	Totall	5	13	8

		£	s	d
[23] Janry 3d 1723/4	South Town Dr To yᵉ Commᵗᵉᵉ for Time & Expenc in Laying out 2d Divifion Lands in Said Town from Janry 3. 1723/4 Ending yᵉ 22d of yᵉ Same Month			
To Fra: Fullam 15 Days & half at 10/8		7	15	00
To mr Whittemore 15 Days fifteen Days		7	10	00
To Capt Shiply 14 Days at 10/8		7	00	00
To mr Samˡˡ Jones Surveyer 13 Days		5	4	00
Expence then pᵈ at Pages at Turky Hills by yᵉ Comᵗᵉᵉ		2	10	5
More pᵈ by mr Whittemor		3	5	2
More then pᵈ by fra fullam at Reads 1/6 at Holdens 2/		0	3	6
		33	8	01

Survey and Allotment of Turkey Hills.

		£	s	d
Feb^r 1st 1723/4	More to S^d Com^{tee} from Feb^r ye first 1723/4 & Ending ye 29 For Laying out 2^d Divisions in S^d Town			
To: Capt Shiply 24 Days		12	00	00
To: m^r Whittemore 25 Days		12	10	00
To: Fra Fullam 23 Days		11	10	00
Surveyer Jones 24 Days		9	12	00
To Jacob Fullam 17 Days		3	8	00
chainmen To John Shiply Ju^r 15 Days		3	00	00
Mr Joseph Page 9 Days & half		1	18	
To Mark Bignal 4 Days		00	16	00
Mr Sam^ll Bennett 3 Days		00	12	00
Jonas Gilfon 8 Days		01	12	00
John Wood 7 Days		1	8	00
Walter Bees 1 Day 4^s & 3^s/ for Oats		00	7	00
Totall Expense.		92	01	01

[24]

		£	s	d
Feb^r 1st To ye 29th 1723/4	South Town D^r for Necefary Expenc in ye Survey of the 2^d Divifion Lands from ye firft Day of Feb^r 1723/4 To ye 29th of ye Same Month.			
Expence p^d at m^r Pages Turk Hills Five pounds Nine Shillings		5	09	00

		£	s	d
March 6 1723/4	South Town D^r To Capt Shiply for One Day & half Attendanc at Concord & half A Day for Travil March 6 &c 1723/4 to Make Some Recknings And Acounts About ye Surveys of ye 2^d Divifions Lands	1	00	00
To m^r Whittemore One Day & half		00	15	00
To Fra Fullam One Day & half		00	15	00
Expence then Paid at Concord by m^r Whittemore		00	18	4
More from March 9 to ye 17th Capt Shiply & m^r Surveyer Jones 8 Days each		07	4	00
To Jofeph Page 3 Days & half. Jonas Gilson 2 Days Mark Bignal One Day		01	06	00
Expences p^d at pages fourteen Shillings & four pence		00	14	4

30   Survey and Allotment of Turkey Hills.

		£	s	d
March 30th 1724	More from Monday March 30th 1724 to Thursday ye 2^d of April following.			
To: Capt Shiply 3 Days		1	10	00
To: m^r Whittemore 3 Days		1	10	00
To: Fra: Fullam 3 Days		1	10	00
Expenc then p^d by Capt Shiply				
Expenc then p^d by m^r Whittemore				
Expenc then p^d by Fra: Fullam Ten Shillings & Eight pence		00	10	8
		23	2	4

		£	s	d
[25] South Town	D^r			
April y^e 8. 1724	To m^r Whittemore for More Service Begining y^e 8th of April 1724, and Ending y^e 13th Day of y^e Same Month: 5 Days	2	10	00
To: Capt Shiply 4 Days		2	00	00
To: Fra: Fullam 5 Days		2	10	00
Expenc then p^d by Mr Whittemore £1-4=9 to Hubard £1-5-0		2	9	9

		£	s	d
April 20th 21st 1724:	More At Concord Two Days April 20th & 21st 1724 To Ballane Lotts			
Capt Shiply Two Days & half		1	5	00
To m^r Whittemore Two Days		1	00	00
To: Fra Fullam Two Days		1	00	00
Expence then p^d by Mr Whittemore Comm^{tees} Charge £1-6-7		1	6	7

		£	s	d
Jan^{ry} 26 1725/6	More to Fra Fullam for a Journy to Dorchefter & Bofton to Coll^o Tailer About Calling A Meeting for ye South Town Man Horfe & Necefary Expence in S^d Journy	00	16	00
	Total	14	17	4

Survey and Allotment of Turkey Hills. 31

CONCORD FEB^{RY} 23^D & 24TH 1725/6

Feb^r 23 &   At A Meeting of ye Comm^{tee} Appointed by y^e
24—   Gen^{ell} Court for ye New Towns West of Groton
1725/6   P^{r}Sent Coll^o Tailer, Coll^o Thaxter Capt Shiply Liu^t Whittemore & Fra: Fullam.

    To Confider ye Affairs of ye Settlem^t of y^e South & North Towns Weftward of And Contiguous to y^e Town of Groton

    1: Voted by y^e Comm^{tee} That y^e Clark procure Books for y^e Entrys of The proceedings of y^e Comm^{tee} for Each of y^e Towns South, & North

    2: Voted by y^e Comm^{tee} That Notyfication be forthwith Isued $\tilde{p}$ Order of y^e Comm^{tee} for A Meeting of y^e P^{r}Sons Admitted to Lotts or Intereft in y^e South Town, To Meet at Groton at y^e Houfe of Liu^t Jonth Hobbard On Wednefday y^e 16th Day of March 1725/6

                                                firft

[26] 1: To Inform y^e Comm^{tee} How Far they have proceeded in the Settlm^t of ye Allottments in S^d Town in Complyane With ye Order of ye Comm^{tee}

    2dly To Inform ye Comm^{tee} What they Would have them Do Concerning The Lotts in S^d Town that Are Under Some Difficulty & Dispute

              CONCORD FEB^{RY} 23 & 24. 1725/6

Feb^r 23 &   South Town D^r to ye Comm^{tee} for Travil At-
24, 1725/6   tendane at S^d Meeting & Expence

To: Coll^o Tailer 3 Days	1	10	00
To: Coll^o Thaxter 4 Days	2	00	00
To: Capt Shiply Two Days & half	1	5	00
To: Mr Whittemore 2: Days	1	00	00
To: Fra Fullam 2: Days	1	00	00
To Fra Fullam One Day to Bofton for Advertifm^{ts} & Difpereing them for S^d March Meeting Agreed on—00-$\frac{8}{10}$-00	00	10	00

FEB^R 24TH 1725/6

Expence p^d by Liu^t Whittemore at Balls $\tilde{p}$ Order of the Comm^{tee} Was £3 = 15 - 11	3	15	11
More Expene p^d by Coll^o Thaxter With Coll^o Tailer	3	18	6
Total	14	19	5

[27] At A Meeting of yᵉ Genᵉˡˡ Courts Commᵗᵉᵉ With yᵉ Proprieᵗʳˢ of yᵉ South Town West of Groton Called Turky Hills.

PʳSent Collᵒ Tailer, Collᵒ Thaxter, Capᵗ Shiply, Liuᵗ Whittemore and Fra: Fullam.

At yᵉ Houſe of Liuᵗ Jonᵗʰ Hubbard at Groton in yᵉ County of Middleſex On Wednesday yᵉ 16ᵗʰ Day of March 1725/6 at Ten in The Morning

Mett in Order to Informe yᵉ Commᵗᵉᵉ How far they Have proceeded in yᵉ Settlemᵗˢ of yᵉ Allottments in Complyance With The Order of the Commᵗᵉᵉ

And Also to Inform yᵉ Commᵗᵉᵉ What they Would have them Do Concerning The Lotts in Sᵈ Town yᵗ are (at Preſent) Under Some Dificulty & Diſpute.

The Information yᵉ Settlers then Gave yᵉ Commᵗᵉᵉ Was that there was then 26 Houſes Raiſed & Ten of them Settled & Inhabited

1 Voted by yᵉ Commᵗᵉᵉ That No pʳSon Whatso Ever Shall Have Liberty to Box Any Pine Trees Growing on yᵉ Comons in yᵉ South Town.

2 That Fra: Fullam Capᵗ Shiply & Liuᵗ Whittemore, Or Any Two of them With Sutable Aſſiſtance Do Lay out yᵉ Aquivalent Land as Soon as May be.

GROTON MARCH Yᴱ 16: 1725/6

	£	s	d
March¹⁵16 South Town is Dʳ To yᵉ Commᵗᵉᵉ 17. & *18* for their Attendence Travil & Expe			
1725/6 To: Collᵒ Tailer 4 Days	2	00	00
To: Collᵒ Thaxter 5 Days	2	10	00
To: Capᵗ Shiply 2 Days & half	1	5	00
To: mʳ Whittemor 3 Days	1	10	00
To: Fra: Fullam 4 Days yᵉ 15ᵗʰ: 16ᵗʰ, 17ᵗʰ & 18ᵗʰ of March	2	00	00
Expene pᵈ by Mʳ Whittemore	7	19	11
More Expene pᵈ by Collᵒ Thaxter	1	3	00
More pᵈ by Collᵒ Tailer	00	16	00
Totall	19	03	11

Survey and Allotment of Turkey Hills.   33

[28]   At A Meeting of yͤ Commᵗᵉᵉ of yᵉ South Town
Bolton   West of Groton Called Turky Hills In order
Decemʳ   to Settle Some Accounts Relating To Sᵈ Town
7ᵗʰ   &c.
1726   PʳSent Collᵒ Tailer Collᵒ Thaxter Capt Shiply
         Liuᵗ Whittemore, & Fra: Fullam

Decʳ 7ᵗʰ   South Town is Dʳ to yᵉ Comᵗᵉᵉ for
1726   Attendanc Travil & Expenc To
           Attend Sᵈ Meeting   £   s   d
To: Collᵒ Tailer Day   00 00 00
To: Collᵒ Thaxter Day   00 00 00
To: Capᵗ Shiply 3 Days   00 00 00
To: Mʳ Whittemore 2 Days £1 = 00 = 00 &
    Expenc   01 12 00
To: Fra: Fullam 2 Days & Expenc   1   4 00

                              Totall   2 16 00

[29]   The Commᵗᵉᵉ for yᵉ South Town West of Groton
Sepᵗ 28ᵗʰ   Mett at Cambridge The 28ᵗʰ Day of Sepᵗ
1724   1724.
         PʳSent Collᵒ Tailer, Collᵒ Thaxter, Capᵗ Shiply
Liuᵗ Whittemore And Fra Fullam
         To Make up Some Accoᵗˢ for past Service & Sur-
veys &c.   £   s   d
Then pᵈ by Collᵒ Thaxter to Mʳ Samˡˡ Jones
    Surveyer In full to that Time for his Ser-
    vice in South Town Thirteen pounds &
    One Shilling   13   1 00
More to Fra: Fullam in full to yᵗ Day for Sᵈ
    Town   11 13   6
More to Capᵗ Shiply in part   12 00 00
More to mʳ Whittemore in part   3   1   4
More then Due to mʳ Whittemore, to Ballance   11   7   9
More then pᵈ Mʳˢ Anger for Victuals Drink &
    horsmeat   2   1   6

                              Total   53   5   1

34　　　*Survey and Allotment of Turkey Hills.*

APRIL 25TH 1726

April 25 1726　An Acco.t of y.e Charges & Expence of y.e Viewing y.e Equivalent Land for Turk hills or South Town Agreeable to y.e Order of y.e Gen.ell Court

	£ s d
To: Cap.t Shiply Who began S.d Service April 26.th 1726, & Ended May y.e 2.d 7 Days	3 10 00
To m.r Benj.a Whittemore beging April 25.th & Ended May y.e 3.d 9 Days	4 10 00
To m.r Sam.ll Jones Surveyer 9 Days	4 10 00
To: m.r Edw.d Hartwell 6 Days at 5.s	1 10 00
chainmen To: Jon.th Shiply 7 Days	1 15 00
To: Cap.t Willard for his Man 6 Days	1 10 00
Expence in S.d Service then p.d by m.r Whittemore	4 2 9
	21 7 9

[30] CAMBRIDGE SEP.T 28.TH 1724. SOUTH TOWN D.R To y.e Com.tee for Attendance, Travil, & Expence, viz

	£ s d
To: Coll.o Tailer One Day Ten Shillings	00 10 00
To: Thaxter Two Days One pound	01 00 00
To: Cap.t John Shiply Two Days & half	01 05 00
To: m.r Benjamin Whittemore One Day	00 10 00
To: Fra: Fullam One Day Ten Shillings	00 10 00
Expence then p.d at Cambridge for Victuals Drink & horfmeat by Coll.o Thaxter Two pounds One Shilling & Six pence	02 01 06
	05 16 06

[31]　Page 31 left blank.

[32]　TURKY HILLS SOUTH TOWN APRIL 12.TH 1727.

April 12.th 1727.　At A Meeting of y.e Com.tee Appointed & Impowred by the Great & General Court At their at Bofton, Dec.r 7.th 1719 To Allott & Grant out the Lands Contained in the South Townfhip Granted Weftward of & Contiguous to y.e Town of Groton in y.e County of Middlefex.

Survey and Allotment of Turkey Hills. 35

Pr:Sent y:e Hon:bla Coll:o Tailer & Sam:ll Thaxter Esq:rs Cap:t John Shiply, Lin:t Benja: Whittemore & Fra: Fullam Esq:r

S:d Committee being Mett at y:e House of Cap:t Josiah Willard In S:d Turky Hills After Due Warning Given, As Weil at y:e Requeft of y:e Settlers As to be Informed What progrefs Was Made in Setling Each Lott, as Injoyned by y:e General Court, & S:d Comm:tee.

And finding that Several of y:e Lotts in S:d Town Are Not Settled as injoyned by y:e General Court, And their Comm:tee And Several that to this Day have Never Done Any Labour at all on Them, but y:t y:e pr:fons Who Drew them Have hitherto Kept the Lotts from Others Likly to Settle them, And have Only Traded them from One Man to Another for Exceffive Gaine & Prices, Which Practice is Directly Contrary to y:e Written Conditions & Provisos Upon Which Each Pr:Son had his Lott of y:e Comm:tee Which practice Tends Greatly to Retard y:e Settling S:d Town, And Opreffion of thofe Who muft finaly Do it.

Voted p' y:e Comm:tee that Lott N:o 19. Lott N:o 45. Lott N:o 25 and Lott N:o 44. In y:e S:d South Town Are Declared forfitted, And Shall forth with be Granted to Such Sutable Pr:Sons as Will forthwith Settle them Effectualy No Lott to be Sold for More then fifty pounds Nor for Lefs then forty pounds.

The Comm:tees Attendenc, Travil, & Expenc at S:d Meeting

	£	s	d
To: Coll:o Tailer 5 Days	2	10	00
To: Coll:o Thaxter 6 Days	3	00	00
To: Cap:t Shiply 4 Days	2	00	00
To: m:r Benja Whittemore 5 Days	2	10	00
To: Fra: Fullam 5 Days To Turky Hills & Concord	2	10	00
To Expenc then p:d by Coll:o Thaxter with Coll:o Tailer	3	14	00
More by m:r Whittemore p' Order	8	8	00
More To m:r Whittemore A Day to bring y:e Turky hill petition In Order for y:e Above Meeting	0	10	00
	25	12	00

[33] SOUTH TOWN TURKY HILLS APRIL 28TH 1727.

To Francis Fullam Efq:" Clerk of y^e Comm^tee for Said Town, —

We y^e Subscribers Have proceeded to Sell y^e four for-fitted Lotts in S^d Town; And y^e Conditions And Delivery Wear in y^e Words Following. (viz)

By Order of y^e Reft of y^e Comm^tee of the Hon^rd General Court for South Town So Called. We grant you, A: B = Pofsefsion of Lott N^o: — With all y^e Rights thereto be Longing in this Said Town, On Conditions & Not Otherwife That you Do forth with fullfil y^e General Courts Act by building a good Dwelling Houfe Breaking up, & fencing in Three Acres of Land theron &c And by Doing And fullfilling all Other Duties According to ye Directions of ye S^d Courts Comm^tee in & A bout ye Same, On penaly of forfitting ye Same into ye Hands of ye Comm^tee Again.

April We Sold & Gave Pofsefsion of Lot N° 25. To
26th   Capt Joliah Willard for ye Sum of Fifty
on S^d Day pounds. Wittnefs—Sam^ll Jones & Ephr^m Sau-
tle We Sold and Gave Pofsefsion of Lott N° 19 to Josiah Baylee for ye Sum of fifty pounds. Wittnes m^r Sam^ll Jones, Mr Ephraim Sautle

April 27th We Sold & gave Poffeffion of Lott N° 44: To Jofhua Hutchins for The Sum of forty pounds. Wittnefs Sam^ll Jones Dan^ll Auftin

April 28th We Sold And gave Poffefsion of Lott No 45 to Jon^th Whitny Ju^r for ye Sum of forty pounds Wittnefs Sam^ll Jones & Ephraim Sautle

BENJ^A WHITTEMORE
JOHN SHEPLE

The Amounts of ye S^d Sums is One Hundred & Eighty pounds £180. For Which ye S^d Benjamin Whittemore Makes HimSelf Debter to the Comm^tee Rec^d for Entry May 2^d 1727. BENJ^A WHITTEMORE.
P' FRA: FULLAM *Clerk.*

Survey and Allotment of Turkey Hills. 37

	£	s	d
The Charge of y^e Sale of S^d forfitted Lotts			
To: m^r Benja: Whittemore 3 Days & half	1	15	00
To: Capt Shiply 2 Days & half	1	5	00
To: m^r Jones 3 Day & half	1	8	00
To: m^r Sautle 2 Days & half.	00	10	00
Expenc then p^d by m^r Whittemor £1=11=7			
& A Day to Make Return 10s	2	1	7
	6	19	7

[34] Page 34 left blank.

[35] CONCORD NOV^r Y^e 6TH & 7TH, 1727.
At A Meeting of y^e General Courts Comm^{tee} for y^e South Town Called — Turky Hills West of Groton

P^rSent The Honble Coll^o Tailer, Capt John Shiple, Liu^t Benj^a Whittemore & Fra: Fullam.

Novr 6 & Voted by ye Comm^{tee} That ye Propriet^{rs} of y^e
7   Lott Lands in Said Turky Hills be Directed;
1727. This Winter Without further Delay to proceed to The Erecting, building, & finifhing of A Sutable & Convenient Meeting houfe For ye Publick Worship of God in S^d Town, Not Lefs than forty and Five feet in Length, And thirty And five feet in Width, Nott Lefs then Eighteen feet, Nor More then Twenty feet between Joynts, And to be Sett on ye Same Spott of Ground as Ordered by ye Comm^{tee} Lying between The Houfe of Benoni Boynton and Horfmeat Medow in S^d Town.

And that Mefurf Sam^{ll} Page, Capt Jofiah Willard Edward Heartwell Benoni Boynton & Isaac Farnfworth be Defired to be And Act as A Sub comm^{tee} to Accomplifh S^d Work as before Directed Subject NevertheLefs to ye Order & Directions of ye General Courts Comm^{tee}

And that there Shall be A Meeting of ye Gen^{ell} Courts Comm^{tee} With ye propriet^{rs} of Turky Hills (at Turky Hills) Some Time this Winter as Soon as May be In Order to Raife A Sutable Sum of Mony to Carry on S^d Work

Survey and Allotment of Turkey Hills.

Concord South Town Dr	£	s	d
To Attendenc Travil & Expenc at S:d Meeting			
Nov.r 6th & To: Coll:o Tailer Two Days & Ex-			
7 pence	1	3	00
1727 To: Cap:t Shiple Two Days	1	00	00
To: Liu:t Benj:a Whittemore One Day & half	00	15	00
To: Fra: Fullam One Day & half	00	15	00
To Expences then paid by m:r Whittemor r:p order	2	12	1
Octo:r 31 To: Fra: Fullam for A Journy to			
1727 Dorchefter to Agree on S:d Meet- ing Man, Horfe & Expenc	00	12	6
	6	17	7

[36] At A Meeting of the Comm:tee for y:e South
Bofton   Town West of Groton Called Turky Hills
Nov.r 30th P:rSent Coll:o Tailer, Coll:o Thaxter, Cap:t
&   Shiple & Fra: Fullam
Dec:r 1:st & 2:d The following Requeft of y:e Selectmen of
1727.   Wooburn was Read as followeth

WOBURN NOV:R Y:E 24TH 1727

To y:e Hon:ble W:m Tailer Sam:ll Thaxter & Fra: Fullam Esq:rs M:r Benj:a Whittemore And Cap:t John Shiple Gen:t

Thefe Are to Requeft of you, Either by your Selves or Some That you Shall Appoint to Meet us at y:e Houfe of M:r Edward Hartwell of Turky Hills On Wednesday y:e Sixth Day of Dec:r Next at Eight of y:e Clock in y:e fore- noon to perambulate y:e Lines between the Two Thoufand Acres belonging to y:e Town of Woburn And y:e Lands be =longing to Turky Hills

Signed r:p JOSEPH WRIGHT
            SAM:LL WALKER   } Selectmen of
            SAM:LL RICHARDSON   } Wooburn
            ROBERT CONVERSE

Dec:r 1:st & In Anfwer to y:e Above Requeft The following
2:d 1727 Power Went forth

Survey and Allotment of Turkey Hills. 39

BOSTON DEC^r 1st 1727

To Capt John Shiply Capt Joſiah Willard, Lin^t Edward Hartwell And m^r Benoni Boynton

Gen^{tn} The Selectmen of Wooburn Having Requeſted The Gen^{ell} Courts Comm^{tee} Either by them Selves, or Such P^rſons as they should Appoint to Meet at ye houſe of m^r Edward Hartwell of Turky Hills On Wedneſday ye Sixth Day of Decem^r 1727 at Eight of ye Clock in ye Morning to P^rambulate ye Lines between ye Two Thouſand Acres belonging to ye Town of Woburn And ye Lands belonging to Turky Hills.

The Comm^{tee} Mett at Boſton ye Day A bove And agreed To Deſire & Impower You the Above Named John Shiply Joſiah Willard, Edward Hartwell & Benoni Boynton to Meet ye S^d Selectmen & Run ye P^rambulation Lines as Above

Pr Ord^r of ye Comm^{tee} FRA FULLAM *Clerk*

[37] South Town D^r to ye Comm^{tee} for Attendanc Travil & Expenc

		£	s	d
Boſton To: Coll^o Tailer Day		00	00	00
No^{vr} *30th* To: Coll^o Thaxter Day		00	00	00
—&— To: Capt Shiply 3 Days & half.		1	15	00
Dec^r *1st_& 2^d* To: Fra: Fullam 3 Days		1	10	00
1727 Expenc then p^d by Fra: Fullam		1	1	2
More p^d by Capt Shiply		1	3	00
To: m^r Whittemore One Day		00	10	00
		5	19	2

At ye Town Ship Called Turky Hills December 7th 1727 We the Subscribers, John Shipley Benoni Boynton With Several of the Inhabitants or Propriat^{rs} of Turky Hills, S^d Shiply And Boynton being Appointed by by ye Gen^{ell} Courts Comm^{tee} to P^rambulate with Woburn Gentlemen Such as S^d Woburn Should Send, Which Was Sam^{ll} Walker And Sam^{ll} Richardson Round Woburn farme Lying in ye TownShip Above Said And We Mett On y^e

Survey and Allotment of Turkey Hills.

Sixth Currant & Did P^rambulate On ye Eaft Side & North Eand And ye Bounds On ye Eaft Side Are as Followeth

We began at An Old Whit Oak Above Capt Willards Saw mill, & ye firft Mark was S^d Oak, And we Run Northerly ye Next Was a Pitch Pine, Chefnut Whit Oak, Piller of Stones, Cheftnutt, Red Oak & Burch Together, Chefnut Piller of Stones at ye North Eaft Corner. Alfo many Other Trees Marked on S^d Line though Not Named.

Then We Turned & Run ye North Line, firft A Burch then A Chefnut, A Maple Two Chefnuts Marked facing, Pople, Blak Oak, Piller of Stons, Chefnut Chefnut, Blak Oak, Whit Oak, Bafswood Trees Standing in a Hallow Whit Oak Chefnut, Blak Burch, Chefnut, Blak Oak, Piller of Stones, Whit Oak, chefnut Black Oak, Whit Oak, Walnut, Blak Oak, Walnutt, chefnut Walnut a Walnut at ye Northweft Corn^r of S^d Farme, And there be Several More Marks on S^d Line though Not Named. And We p^rambulated On ye Wefterly Side of ye Pond Called Unkechewalom. We began at A Marked Chefnut by S^d Pond that is between S^d Farme & Turky Hill Land & Run North wefterly About Eighty pole to A Chefnut Tree Then We Turned & Run South Weft^rly to a Piller of Stons y^t is a Corn^r between Woburn farm and Dorchefter farm, & A Side bounds to Turky hills, And to Confirm our perambulation We have Enterchangably Signed ye Day Above Said

JOHN SHEPLE	SAM^LL WALKER	Comm^tee
BENONI BOYNTON	SAM^LL RICHARDSON	
The propriators Wear	J Jofeph Burnap Was prefent	
Ifaac Farnfworth	And Aflifted in S^d Perambulation	
Jofhua Hutchins		

[38] To ye Comm^tees Attendence, Travil & Expenc *June 12th* When Ordered to Attend ye General Court On *& 13th* ye Petetion of Jon^th Whitny June ye 12th & *1727* 13th 1727

To: Coll^o Tailer Day	00	00 00
To: Coll^o Thaxter Day	00	00 00
To: Capt John Shiply 3 Days	1	10 00
To: Liu^t Benj^a Whittemore 3 Days	1	10 00

Survey and Allotment of Turkey Hills. 41

To: Fra: Fullam One Day & half	00	15	00
To: Expenc, & Writings then Given in by Fra Fullam	00	10	00
Expenc then Paid by m!̣ Whittemore P̣ Order & For Writings &c	3	16	7
	8	1	7

Decr 19th More to ye Comm^{tee} for their Attendenc Travil
1727 & Expenc To Wait On ye General Court as by them Ordred Dec: 19th 1727

To: Coll? Tailer	00	00	00
To: Coll? Thaxter	00	00	00
To: Cap! Shiply 4 Days & Expenc	2	12	00
To: Liu! Whittemore 3 Dayes	01	10	00
To: Fra: Fullam 3 Days & Expence	1	16	00
To: Expenc then p!̣ by m!̣ Whittemor	00	18	00

Jan^{ry} ye 4th More to ye Comm^{tee} for their Attendanc Travil
1727/8 & Expenc To Wait on ye General Court as Ordered Jan:ry 1727/8

To: Coll? Tailer	00	00	00
To: Coll? Thaxter	00	00	00
To Cap! Shiply 11 Days	5	10	00
To: m!̣ Benja: Whittemore 9 Days	4	10	00
To: Fra: Fullam 9 Days	4	10	00
Expenc then p!̣ by Cap! Shiply	2	7	00
Expenc then p!̣ by m!̣ Whittemor	1	18	00
To: Expenc then p!̣ by Fra: Fullam for his horfe keeping to m!̣ Edmunds	1	01	00
To pocket Expenc & Writings	2	17	00
To: A Day to Bofton to fetch y^e papers & Expenc	00	11	6
Feb:ṛ total	38	2	1

[39] WESTON APRIL 2ᵈ, 1728 SOUTH TOWN Dr   £   s   d

April 2ᵈ   To yᵉ Comm^tee for their Attendanc
1728   Travil & Expenc to prepare Ac-
             counts to Lay before yᵉ General
Court as Ordered
To Capt Shiply Two Days £1 = 00-0 & Expenc   1 00 00
To mr. Whittemore One Day   00 10 00
To Fra: Fullam One Day & Expence   00 14 00

April   More To mr. Whittemore One Day
1728   to Wefton on fᵈ Servic   00 10 00
          Ditto To Fra Fullam One Day With
mr. Whittemor   00 10 00
          More to Expenc by Sᵈ fullam   00 03 00
May yᵉ 3ᵈ Ditto Sᵈ Whittemore One Day at
1728   Wefton on fᵈ Service   00 10 00
            Ditto to faid Fullam One Day &
Expenc   00 13 0

CONCORD MAY yᵉ 16:ᵀᴴ & 17ᵀᴴ 1728

South Town is Dr. To yᵉ Com^tee for Attendance Travil & Expenc to prepare Accounts to Lay before yᵉ Gen^ell Court

To Coll^o Tailer for South Town Acco^ts One
    Day at 10ˢ   00 10 00
Ditto: To Coll^o Thaxter One Day & half   00 15 00
To: mr. Benj^a Whittemore One Day   00 10 00
To: Fra: Fullam One Day   00 10 00
Expenc then pᵈ by Coll^o Tailer at Concord
    charged to yᵉ South Town   00   5   3
Ditto there pᵈ by Coll^o Thaxter   00   5   3
Ditto: by Mʳ Whittemor   00   5 10
Ditto then pᵈ by Fra: Fullam   00   5 10
                                             ―――――――――
                                              7 17   2

Survey and Allotment of Turkey Hills.

June 5 1728 More to m^r Whittemore One Day at Wefton to prepare Accounts to Lay before y^e Gen^{ell} Court as Ordrd With ffullam One Day at $\frac{s}{10}$ five shill^s to y^e South Town And 5^s to y^e North Town		
Ditto to Francis Fullam One Day at $\frac{s}{10}$ Expence 4^s for y^e wch y^e North Town D^r for 7^s & y^e South Town for	00	05 00
	00	7 00
	8	9 02
South Totall	08	09 02

[40] Left blank.

[41]
[42]
[43]   Pages 41, 42, 43, 44, cut out.
[44]

[45] Left blank.

[46] Left blank.

[47] Left blank.

[48]

THE BOUNDS OF Y^E SOUTH TOWN MEDOW LOTTS

Two Lotts of Medow No: 9 & 10

Two Meadow Lotts Ajoyning to Lott No: 5: In the Second Divifion Near Bennetts Both Makes up: 10: Acres and are Bounded As Followeth. Northerly on the Above S^d: 5th Lott Westerly on Said Bennitts Lot No: 69: in the First Divifion & Southerly Bounded on Meadow Lot, No: 8: Near the uper End of Cataconamog meadow & Easterly Bounded by Marks & Upland thefe are the most Northerly Meadows in Cataconamog Meadows, & Belong to Lotts No: 5: and : 6: in Second Divitions — — —

The lines here printed in italics are in the original written in the margins. [W. A. D.

Meadow N^o : 8 :—5 Acres

Meadow Lot, N^o: 8: In Cataconamog Bounded Northerly on the 10 acre of Meadow above S^d Westerly on Bennitt or the 69th Lot, in First Divifion, Southerly on the three Acres above ye Bever Dam, Easterly by Marks and Upland — —

Meadow No 7 5 Acres

Meadow Lot, No: 7: In Cataconamog Bounded Westerly on Marked Trees, Partly Southerly on Meadow Lot N^o : 6: and Easterly by marks by the Upland Northerly by marked Trees at the Angles — —

Meadow N^o : 6:

Meadow Lot N^o : 6: Bounded Westerly by Marks on the Upland 19 : Rods - Southerly by the Meadow N^o: 5: in s^d Cataconamog Meadows Easterly by Upland, Northerly by Meadow Lot N^o : 7: in Cataconamog meadows

Meadow N^o —5— 5 Acres

Meadow Lot N^o: 5: in Cataconamog Bounded Northerly on Meadow Lot N^o : 6: Easterly on the Marks by the Upland, 16: Rods Southerly by Meadow Lot N^o : 4: and Southwesterly by Marks About 20: Rods

Meadow No —4— 5 Acres

Meadow Lot N° 4: in Cataconamog Meadows Bounded Norwesterly on Meadow Lot N^o: 5: Easterly on the Upland: 10: Rods and Partly Southeasterly on Meadow Lot N^o: 3: & Southerly on Marks about 33 Rods

Meadow N^o : 3: 5 Acres

Meadow Lot N°. 3. in Cataconamog above Mr Bormans Farm Bounded Westerly on the above Mentioned Meadow N^o: 4: Bounded Northerly & Easterly on Upland, & Southerly on Marks 39 Rods this Contains about Six acres by Reafon of the widnefs of the Brook that Runs through the Same —

Medow N⁰ 2 5 Acres
Meadow Lot N⁰ 2: in Cataconamog Meadow, Bounded Norwesterly on Marks Near 19. Rods Easterly on medow Lots N⁰ 4. & 5. Southerly on Staks & Westerly on Lot N⁰ 1. on Mafsapog Brook

5 Acres
Medow Lot No 1: in Cataconamog on Both Sids Mafapog Brook Bounded Northerly 34 Rods by upland & marks & westerly it Bounds: 20: Rods by marks & Southerly about 34 Rods by marks in Meadow Lands and Easterly it Bounds on Meadow Lot No: 2:

[49] *N⁰: 1: above Mafsapog Where the Brook Comes into the Meadow 5: Acres*
An account of the Meadows above Mafsapog Pond Begining at N⁰ 1: Where Unchawalam Brook Comes into the Meadow by A Small White Oak Marked & from thence it Bounds South & Southwesterly on Marks & on Upland Near Forty two Rods to a Ded Pine Tree thence it Bounds Partly East 23 Rods to a Stake from thence it Bounds North on Meadow Lot N⁰ 2. & Norwesterly 20 Rods on Upland to the Small White Oak Where we Began — —

Meadow N⁰ —2: 5 Acres
Meadow Lot N⁰ 2. Bounds South Westerly on meadow Lot No 1. — Norwesterly it Bounds on Upland 28 Rods and Noreasterly it Bounds on Meadow Lot N⁰. 3. & Southeasterly it Bounds about 27 Rods Rods on Upland. — —

Meadow N⁰: 3: 5 Acres & 20 Rods
Meadow Lot No. 3. is 4 acres & 20 Rods Bounded South easterly on the: 2ᵈ: or N⁰ 2. Norwesterly on Marks & upland, Noreasterly on Marks & Common Swamp. & South easterly on Marks & Common Swamp alfo one acre more Lying at a Small Diftance Easterly from it Being 20 Rods Long & Eight Rods Wide at the North end

is Two Stakes one at Each Corner & at the South End a Ded Popler Stump & a Small Marked Tree at the Southeast Corner

Meadow N^o: 4: 5 Acres
Meadow Lot N° 4. on the Northerly Side Mafsapog Pond Bounded North & Norwesterly 25 Rods on Marks & Upland Northeasterly it Bounds on Mr Gutrog 34 Rods Southerly Near the S^d Pond 33 Rods Westerly on Marks 28 Rods.

Meadow N^o: 1: 5 Acres
Meadows Below Mr Bormans Farm on Cataconamog Brook N°. 1. on the East Side the Brook Begining at Mr Bormans Farm Down to the Pond the Brook Being the South & Southwesterly Bounds, and the Upland the North and Easterly Bounds — — —

Meadow N° 2: 5 Acres.
Meadow Lot No 2. Below Mr Bormans Farm & is Bounded on the Brook Northerly, & Easterly, & Westerly on Marks 28 Rods & Southerly it Bounds on Meadow Lot N^o: 4: 30 Rods.

Meadow No. 3. 5 Acres
Meadow Lot No. 3. Bounds Norwesterly 25 Rods on Common Upland to a Stake, & Westerly it Bounds on Marks Southerly on Upland, Easterly on Meadow Lot N° 4.

Meadow N° 4—5 Acres
Meadow Lot N° 4 Bounds Westerly on Meadow N° 3. Northerly on Meadow No 2. & Easterly & Southerly it Bounds on Upland

[50] Meadow N° 5 5 Acres
Meadow Lot N° 5. Lyes Below the Ridge hill on the Southerly Side & adjoyning to Cataconamog Pond

Survey and Allotment of Turkey Hills. 47

Bounds Northerly by the Pond North easterly by the Brook. Southeasterly by Meadow Lot No 6 and Southwesterly by the Ridge hill or upland.

Meadow No. 6 5 Acres.
Meadow Lot N⁰ 6 Near Cataconamog Pond Bounded Norwesterly by meadow Lot N⁰ 5. North or North easterly by the Brook & Southeasterly by meadow Lot N⁰ 7 and Southeasterly by Upland. 18. Rods

Meadow No 7—5 Acres.
Meadow Lot No 7. Bounds Westerly on Lot N⁰ 6— & Northerly on the Brook Southeasterly on the Marks by the Upland & Southwesterly by Marks A Pich Pine & A Maple Marked

Meadow N⁰. 1. 5 Acres
Medow, Turkey hill Medow, Lotts which are. 4. No. 1. Bounded Easterly by the 47th Lot in the First Division and Upland South & Southwesterly by Marks & by the Bever Dam & Marked Trees and the Upland, & North westerly it Bounds on meadow Lot No. 2. — —

Medow N⁰. 2. 5 Acres
Medow Lot N⁰ 2. Bounds Partly Southeasterly by Meadow Lot N⁰ 1. & Westerly it Bounds on Marks by the Upland Northerly by Lot of Medow N⁰. 3. & Northeasterly it Bounds on Lot N⁰ 47 in the First Divifion

Medow No 3. 5 Acres
Medow Lot No 3. Bounds Southeasterly by Meadow Lot N⁰ 2. Westerly by Marks by the Upland Norwesterly by a Medow Lot N⁰ 4: Noreasterly by the First Division — — —

Medow No 4, 5 Acres.
Medow Lot No. 4. Southeasterly by Medow Lot N⁰ 3. & Westerly by Marks, & Norwesterly by marks, & Noreasterly by Lot No 46. in the First Divifion.

Medow No 1. 5 Acres.

Medow Lotts in Horsmeet Medow No 1. Bounded Nor easterly on L! Perleys or N? 7. in the first Divifion & Easterly on S.ᵈ 7ᵗʰ Lott South on Medow No 2. West on old m.ʳ Hills Medow in the 15ᵗʰ Lot

Medow No. 2 5 Acres.

Medow Lot No. 2. in horfmeet Bounded on the North by medow Lot No 1. on the East by the 7ᵗʰ Lot in First Division, on the South by Medow No 3. on the West by the 15ᵗʰ Lot in yᵉ First Divifion

Medow Nᵒ. 3. 5 Acres.

Medow Lot, No. 3. in Horsmeet Medow Bounded North by Medow Lot No. 2. Easterly by Lot No 7. in the first Divifion Southerly by the Ministeriall Lot. & West by Old m.ʳ Hills Lot No: 15ᵗʰ in first Divifion

Medow Nᵒ 1. 5 Acres.

Medow Lot the First above the Bever Dam in Bever Pond medows is Bounded Easterly on Groton Line Southwesterly on the upland & Norwesterly on a Line Crofs the Medow & North & Noreasterly it Bounds on a Poin Ridge by the Side of S.ᵈ Medow — —

[51] *Three Acres and 60 Rods.*

And their is on the Same Stream Below the Line of the above f.ᵈ Medow or the 5 acres 3 acres & 60 Rods Before the Stream Crofses Groton Line

Medow No: 1: 5 Acres

Medow Lot Nᵒ: 1: in Clay Pitt Medows Bounded as Followeth Southeasterly on Marks & Southwesterly on Severall Marks by the upland, and Northwesterly on Medow Lot No 2. & Easterly & NorEasterly on Marks by the Upland

Medow No. 2. 5 Acres.

Medow Lot No: 2, in Clay Pitts Medow, Bounded Partly South East on Medow Lot No: 1: and Southwesterly it bounds on Common Upland 18 Rods & Norwesterly it Bounds on Medow Lot No 3. & Easterly on Common Land

Medow No: 3: 5 Acres

Medow Lot No: 3: Bounded South easterly on Medow Lot No 2: and South westerly it Bounds on Marks by the Upland; and Norwesterly it Bounds on Lot N°. 4, and Easterly it Bounds on Common Land.

Medow N^o: 4: 5 Acres

Medow Lot N^o: 4: Bounded Southeasterly on Lot N^o: 3: South westerly on Marks by Common Upland, & Norwesterly it Bounds on Medow Lot N^o: 5: & Easterly it Bounds on Common Land.

Medow No: 5: 5 Acres

Medow Lot N^o: 5: Bounded South easterly on Medow Lot No: 4: and Common Land, South westerly on Marks 4 Rods wide at this end and Norwesterly it Bounds on Medow No: 6: and Easterly it Bounds on Common Upland 29 Rods.

Medow No: 6: 5 Acres

Medow Lot No: 6: in Clay Pit Medow Bounded Southeasterly on Medow No: 5: & Southwesterly it Bounds on Marks about 10 Rods & Norwesterly it Bounds on Lot N^o: 7: of medow, and Easterly it Bounds on Common Land about 10 Rods Wide

Medow No: 7: 5 Acres

Medow Lot N^o: 7: in Clay Pit Medow Bounded South easterly on Medow No: 6: and South westerly it Bounds on Marks Better then Ten Rods and Norwesterly it Bounds on Medow Land in Lot No: 40: in the First Divifion & Easterly on Upland

Medow No: 1: 5 Acres

Medow Lot N^o: 1: in ye Most Southerly Parts of

Mulpus Medows, Bounding Norwesterly on Daniel Thursting, & Easterly on Upland, & Southerly on Beefes 2 Acres an quarter of medow to Make Up his Medow Part and Westerly on Upland

Medow No: 2: 5 Acres
Medow Lot No: 2: Bounded Southerly by Lot of Medow No: 1 and Westerly on Daniel Thurstings Medow Land & Northerly on Medow No: 3: and Easterly by Upland

Medow No: 3: 5 Acres
Medow lot No: 3: Bounded Southerly by Lot of Medow No 2: & Common Land and Westerly on Marks by the Upland & Northerly by Medow lot No: 4 —

[52] *Medow No: 4 5 Acres*
Medow Lot No 4: Bounded Southerly on Medow N° 3: and Southwesterly Marks and Northerly by Medow No. 5: & Southerly by Common Land — — —

Medow Lot No: 5 6 Acres
Medow Lot No: 5 Bounded 20 Rods on or Near the Brook; South Easterly 14 Rods by Common Land & Southerly on Medow No: 4: and Northerly on Medow No: 6: at the west end it is but about 4 Rods wide this Medow Takes in at the East End A Pine Island of Near an Acre

Medow No: 6: 5 Acres.
Medow Lot No 6: Bounded Southerly by Medow No: 5: South westerly by Marks & Northerly on Medow N°: 7: and Easterly it Bounds on the Brook

Medow No: 7: 5 Acres
Medow Lot No: 7: Bounded Southerly on Medow N°: 6: Southwesterly on Marks, & Northerly it Bounds on Medow No: 8: and Easterly on the Brook

Medow No: 8—5 Acres.
Medow Lot No: 8: Bounded Southerly by Medow No: 7: & Westerly by Marks & Upland & Northerly

Partly on Medow No: 9: and the Brook, and Noreasterly on the Brook.

Medow No: 9: 5 Acres
Medow Lot No: 9: Bounded Southerly on Medow No: 8: Westerly on Marks, & Northerly on Medow No: 10: & Easterly on the Brook —

Medow No: 10: 5 Acres
Medow Lot No: 10 - : on the West Side the Brook Below the Falls is Bounded South on Medow No: 9: West on Marks & Upland and North on Marks and East on the Brook —

Medow No: 11: 4: Acres
Medow Lot No: 11: on the West Side the Brook, up to the Falls, Bounded South by the Medow Line No: 10: & West by Upland, & North on the Falls. & East on the Brook, & this Contains 4 Acres.

Medow No: 1: 5 Acres
Medow Lot N°: 1: on the East Side the Brook, Beginning by the Falls and So Counting Down the Brook, Bounding West on the Falls & the Brook, North on the Marks, and the Upland, & East on Marks & Upland, South on Medow No: 2:

Medow No 2: 5 Acres.
Medow Lot N° 2: Bound North on Medow No: 1: & Marks Westerly on the Brook & Southerly on S.ᵈ Brook, & Easterly on Medow No: 3: & a Pine Ridge & Marks

[53] *Medow No: 3: 5 Acres.*
Medow No = 3 = Bounded Southerly on the Brook, & West on Medow No = 2 = & Norwest on Upland & Swamp, & East on Medow No: 4 = , and Marks

Medow No: 4 5 Acres
Medow Lot No: 4: Bounded Southwest on the Brook & South on the Medow No: 5: & Southeasterly on Upland, & Northerly on A line & West & Nor west on Marks.

Medow No: 5: 5 Acres
Medow Lot No: 5: Bounds on Upland Down the Brook on Both Sids Till it Comes Near the East line of Lot No: 52 in Second Divifion

Medow No: 1 5 Acres.
Medow Lot No: 1: above the Falls, in Mulpus Medows this was Guest at, and is Bounded Southerly at the Falls & Upland, and Westerly on Fisk, & Joseph Page. & Northerly on Marks & Easterly on the Upland.

Medow No = 2 = 5 = Acres.
Medow No: 2: in uper Mulpus on the Easterly Side of the Brook Cheafly & Bounded South on Upland & North East on Upland, North on Marks, & West on Medow No: 3:

Medow No: 3: 5 = Acres
Medow Lot No: 3: Bounded South on the Brook, & Westerly on Medow No: 4: & Northerly on Upland, & Easterly on Medow No: 2:

Medow No = 4 = 5 = Acres
Medow Lot No: 4: Bounded Southward on the Brook, & west on medow No: 5: and North on upland, & East on Medow No: 3:

Medow No: 5: 5 = Acres
Medow Lot No: 5 = Bounded South westerly Partly on the Brook and Westerly on Medow No: 8: & North easterly on Upland & : 10 : Rods East on Medow No: 4: this Lott of Medow Lies on Both Sids the Brook

Medow No: 6: 5 = Acres.
Medow Lot No 6: Lies on the East Side Mulpus Brook Bounded Easterly on the Upland, & Northerly on Marks, and Westerly on a Strait Line Near the Brook.

Medow No: 1: 5 Acres.
Medow Lot No: 1: In Perhams Medow or Rock Medow. Begining at the Lower end of the Bever Dam.

Survey and Allotment of Turkey Hills. 53

Bounding Southerly by Marks by said Dam. and Westerly by Marks on the Upland, and Nor[ ] it Bounds on Medow, No: 2: and Easterly it Bounds On Marks by the Upland.

[54] *Medow No: 2: 5= Acres.*

Medow Lot No: 2: in s.d Medow Bounds South on Medow No: 6: and West on Marks & North on Medow No: 3: and Easterly on Marks and Upland — —

Medow No: 3: 5 = Acres.

Medow Lot No: 3: in Perham's or Rock Medow, Bounds Southerly on Medow Lot No: 2: and Nor westerly it Bounds by Marks by the Upland and Northerly it Bounds cheatly on Marks in the Medow Land & Southeasterly it Bounds it Bounds on the Upland and Marks.

Medow No: 7: 5: Acres.

Medow & Swamp Lot No: 7: on the East Side Mulpus Brook Against & Bound Northward or Lot No: 10: in Second Divifion Upland and Easterly on Upland, & Southerly on Upland about: 8: Rods, & Westward it Bounds on Lot of Medow & Swamp No: 8:

Medow No: 8: 5 Acres.

Medow & Swamp No: 8: Bounds Northerly on Lot No: 11: in Second Devifion Upland Easterly it Bounds on Medow: No: 7: and South on Medow No: 6: and west on Undivided medow Land

Medow No: 8: 5 acres.

Medow Lot No: 8: on the Westerly Side Mulpus Brook, in Uper Mulpus Medows, a Triangler Lot and is Bounded Northerly on Lot No: 9: of Medow, and Southeasterly on Medow Lot No: 5: and South westerly on + Mark Trees and upland,

Medow No: 9: 5 Acres.

Medow Lot No: 9: Bounded Southerly on Medow No: 8: and Westerly it Bounds marks, Northerly, on Medow No: 10: and Easterly on Upland.

8

Medow No: 10: 5 Acres.

Medow Lot No: 10: with allowance for a Pine Ridg in it and is Bounded Southerly by Meadow Lot No: 9: and Westerly by Marks, and Northerly by Meadow Lot No: 11: & Eastward it Bounds on upland.

Medow No: 11: 5: Acres.

Medow Lot No: 11: Bounded Southward on Medow Lot No: 10: and Westward on Marks, & Nor west on Medow Lot No: 12: & Eastward Partly, on Medow No: 6: and Partly on Upland.

Medow No: 12: 5 Acres.

Medow Lot No: 12: Bounded Southward on Medow No: 11: And Westward on Marks & Northward on Medow Lot No: 13: and Eastward on Medow No: 6:

Medow No. 13: 5 Acres.

Medow Lot No: 13: Bounded Southward on Medow Lot No: 12: and Westward on Marks, & Northward on Medow: 14: & Eastward on Medow No: 6:

[55] *Medow No: 14: 5 = Acres.*

Medow Lot No: 14: Bounded Southerly on Medow No: 13: and Westward is Bounded on Marks. Northward it is Bounded on Medow No: 15: and Eastward it is Bounded on Medow No: 6: —

Medow Lot No: 15: 5 Acres.

Medow Lot No: 15: Bounded Southward on Medow No: 14: and Westward on Marks, & is about 28 Rods Shorter then the 14: Medow Lot, & it is 22 Rods Wide, and Bounds Northerly by a Strait Line by Common Land to a Larg White Pine Tree Taking in Two Points of Upland, & Bounds Easterly on Medow No: 6:

Thirteen Medow Lotts & one Acre and half is cont] the Bounds of other Lotts.

[56] Page 56 left blank.

[57] Page 57 left blank.

[58] HOLDING THE SOUTH TOWN LOTS.

Name				
John Fletcher	81	84	15	West uper Mulpus
Nath[ll] Harris	71	66	5	Lower end of Mulpus
Moses Smith	64	19	3	above Borman's farm
Roberd Harris	23	36	11	West of uper Mulpus
Abr[m] Woodward	82	51	3	in horfmeet
Aron Smith	46	52	11	in Lower Mulpus
Tim[o] Harris	31	37	12	west of uper Mulpus
Ephr[m] Sautle	33	34		Medow in first Divifin
Jon[th] Hubbart	51	62	2	in Turkey hill Medow
Joseph Hubbart	24	30	2	in Perl hill Medow.
Daniel Davis	61	13	5	in Uper Mulpus
W[m] Keen	56	10	7	E: of Uper Mulpus
Jon[th] Hartwell	73	89		Medow in the Lott
Elias Barron	32	35	8	W: of uper Mulpus
John Warrin	18 Not yet	74 Done	2	in perrams medow
John Child	10	29	4	E: Side of uper mulpus
Jacob Fullam	80	2[d] Divifion 87		South of Mulpus Medow Joyns thereto
Nath[ll] Whittemore	57	6	6	in Cattaconamog
John Whitney	76	22	1	in Perrams Medow
W[m] Wood	79	3[d] Divifion		South of Cap[t] Perleys Lott 45 Acres 1 in horfmeet
L[t] Josiah Jones	34	75	3	in Perhams Medow
Eleaz[r] Green	20	33	2	E: of uper mulpus
Eph[m] Peirce	65	86	1	above Mafapoge
Nath[ll] Holdin	42	3		Medow in the Lot
Zacheriah Sautle	28	26	1	W: of Uper Mulpus
Ephr[m] Peirce W:W:	68	87	5	in Cattaconamog
Isaac Stone	29	76	9	west of Uper Mulpus
Nath[ll] Woods	58	11	8	in uper mulpus
Nath[ll] Woods Jun[r]	53 2[d] divifin	37	3	in Turkey hill Medow
Nathan Hayward	38	73	9	above Bormans Farm
Edward Emerfon Efq[r]	78	21	4	E: lower Mulpus
John Calf	21	27	3	E: lower Mulpus
Tho — Hall	22	38	1	S. of lower Mulpus
Daniel Thurstin	50	46		medow in the Lott
Phillip Goodridg	70	85		Medow in the Lott
Jonathan Poore	54	79	7	in Cattaconamog
Will[m] Blunt	55	81	3	Behind Turkey hills
Henry Chandller	13	50	4	Behind Turkey hills
Cap[t] Tho Perley	84	58	1	On Mafapoge Brook
Jeremiah Perley	67 Changed	80 91	4	in Cattaconamog
Jonathan Woodman	17	40	2	in Cattaconamog.
Thomas Tailler	4	28	7	west of Lower Mulpus
Thomas Kimball	16	24	3	Cata: above Bormans

[59]

			] Poor
			] Captn Jofiah Willard
		Jury Chandler	Daniel Austing
	]	Capt Thomas Perley	Samll Austing
	]	Jeremiah Perley	Benjamin Goodridg
	]	Jonathan Woodman	Jonathan Woodman
	]	Thomas Tailer	Samll Johnfon
	]	Thomas Kimball	Thomas Kimball
	]	Nathll Stow	Jofiah Bailey
	]	Walter Bees	Walter Bees
	]	William Wheeler	William Wheeler
	]	Petter Heywood	Petter Harwood
]	14	Thomas Woolley	Abnathan Jones
]	26	Samll Hartwell for Isaac	Jofiah Willard Efqr
] N{o}	45	Joseph Ball	Jon{a} Whitney Junr
]t N{o}	63	John Hastings	John Hastings
] Lot N{o}	15	Ebenezer Chadwick	Thomas Hill
] Lot N{o}	30	Joseph Allien	John Brewer
] Lot N{o}	35	Lt Jonathan Boyden	Feffeis in Trust for Maddam Willard
] Lot N{o}	72	Benja Prefcot	Timothy Gibfon Junr
] Lot N{o}	12	Phineas Parker	Finehas Parker
]e Lot N{o}	11	Thomas Tarbell	Wm Larrance
]fe Lot N{o}	43	Joseph Giffon	Jonathan Whitney
]fe Lot N{o}	44	William Larrance	Jofhua Hutchens
] Lot N{o}	5	James Gold	Samll Jonfon
] N{o}	41	Jofeph Page	Jofeph Page
] N{o}	52	Samll Page	Samll Page.
] N{o}	66	James Richardson	Samll Farnsworths hiers
]t N{o}	36	Willm Richardson	David Gold
] Lot N{o}	25	Jonathan Whitney	Jofiah Willard
] Lot N{o}	62	Isaac Whitney	William Wallis
]fe Lot N{o}	6	Shadrach Whitney	John Haywood
] Lot N{o}	48	Mr Willm Clark	Mr Willm Clark

[60]

Houfe Lot N{o} 60	[	
Houfe Lot N{o} 3	John Burrill Efq{r}	]
Houfe Lot N{o} 27	Jonathan Dows Efq{r}	Jon{a} Do[
Houfe Lot N{o} 40	Jeremiah Allien Efq{r}	Jeremiah Allien Efq{r}
Houfe Lot N{o} 77	Nathll Whitney Junr	Richard Estey
Houfe Lot N{o} 37	Edward Hartwell	Benjamin Cory
Houfe Lot N{o} 2	Amos Brown	Hilkiah Boynton
Houfe Lot N{o} 8	Majr Elea Flagg	the heirs of sd Maj Flag.
Houfe Lot N{o} 75	Capt Richard Kimball	John Wood
Houfe Lot N{o} 9	James Burbeen	James Burbeen
Houfe Lot N{o} 7	Lt Thomas Perley	James Colbern
]fe Lot N{o} 14	John Perram	Samll Page
] Lot N{o} 69	Phineas Richardfon	Samll Benith

Survey and Allotment of Turkey Hills.

]infter   1   Hous Lott
]terial   39   Hous Lott
] Lot No   85   Wm Tailer Efq^r   Wm Tailer Efq^r
] Lot No   86   Sam^ll Thaxter Efq^r   Sam^ll Thaxter Esqr
] Lot No   87   Fra: Fullam   Edward Heartwell
] Lot No   88   Capt John Shiply   Ephraim Peirce
] Lot No   89   Benj^a Whittemor   Jon^th Willard

[61]

[62]

South Town House Lots	No.	The Names of thofe That first Drew them	The Names of those That Now hold them
Houfe Lot No	81	John Fletcher	Eben^r Wheeler & Jon^th Ball
Houfe Lot No	11	Nath^ll Harris	by ye Heirs of Sam^ll Farnsworth
Houfe Lot No	64	Mofes Smith	John Grout
Houfe Lot No	23	Robert Harris	Mr Andrew Gardner
Houfe Lot No	82	Abraham Woodward	Isaac Farnsworth
Houfe Lot No	46	Aron Smith	Mofes Goold
Houfe Lot No	31	Timothy Harris	Nath^ll Harris
Houfe Lot No	33	Ephraim Sautle	Timothy Gibfon
Houfe Lot No	51	Jonathan Hubbart	Sam^ll Page
Houfe Lot No	24	Jofeph Hubbert	Robert Paul
Houfe Lot No	61	Daniel Davis	Benoni Boynton
]fe Lot No	56	Willm Keen	Jacob Stiles
] Lot No	73	Jonathan Hartwell	Edward Hartwell
] Lot No	32	Elles Barron	Arch^a Mackfeddres & John Scot
] Lot No	18	John Warrin	Sam^ll Warren
]ufe Lot No	10	John Child	John Child
Houfe Lot No	80	Jacob Fullam	Benoni Boynton
Houfe Lot No	57	Nath^ll Whitemore	Jofiah Willard
Houfe Lot No	76	John Whitney	John Whitney
Houfe Lot No	79	William Wood	Jonathan Willard
Houfe Lot No	34	Lt Jofiah Jones	Lt Jofiah Jones
Houfe Lot No	20	Eleazer Green	John Hill
Houfe Lot No	65	Ephraim Pierce	David Peirce
Houfe Lot No	42	Nath^ll Holdin	John Fisk
Houfe Lot No	28	Zachariah Sautle	Nathan Towns
Houfe Lot No	68	Ephraim Peirce W: W:	Ephraim Peirce Junr
Houfe Lot No	29	Isaac Stone	John Goodridg
Houfe Lot No	58	Nath^ll Woods	Nath^ll Woods
Houfe Lot No	53	Nath^ll Woods Junr	Jonas Gilfon
Houfe Lot No	38	Nathan Hayward	Nathan Hayward
Houfe Lot No	78	Edward Emerfon Efq^r	Edward Emerfon Efq^r
Houfe Lot No	21	John Calf	John Calf
Houfe Lot No	22	Thomas Hale	Thomas Hale
Houfe Lot No	50	Daniel Thurstin	Daniel Thurstin

LUNENBURG TOWN RECORDS

# THE EARLY RECORDS

OF THE

TOWN OF LUNENBURG.

A TABLE.

The first Town meeting for Choice of Town officers—
Page, 1, 2
Money granted for y^e minifters Sallery and for Building
of a meeting House p. 3

Thunder Bolts 1749.

Annual meeting— P.—4
Annual meeting— P—5
A Reccord of High wayes P.—6, 12, 21, 22, 30,
33, 34, 35, 38, 41, &c. 42.

Page Norcross

money granted for mending High wayes. Isaac Farnsworth to to make a book of records. Eighty pounds
to be paid M^r. Gardner p 7
Com^{tte} chofen to build Seets and pulpit. money granted
therefor. money granted for building a Pound. To
build Pews a Com^{tte} chofen to State places. a Com^{tte}
chofe to Reckon with m^r Gardner—— p. 9:8

Thunder Struck before Noon.

Annual meeting p. 9
except accounts. 20 pounds ordered for m^r Gar^{dner} 9.

A TABLE.

Capt Hartwell chofe to Joyn with ye heirs of Kiby in a petition to Court.

Choice of Jury men   p. 10

Regester for ye County Treafurer for ye County
Jury men Isaac Farnfworth chofe to wait
on ye Court to get ye Land Taxt— — —   P. 11—

Voted m^r Gardner a Difmiffion
and ye Select men power to pay and   12
do anything elfe to perform it

a road from Northfield Road to the meeting house thro' ministerial land—

Annual Meeting   13

Money granted to by weights and measures and to pay ye Towns Debts   p 12 & 15

Granted to m^r Gardner a Pew ye com^{tte} for pews to appoint a minifteral Pew——   p. 15

a Record of Mr Gardner's Receipts and Request for a Dismifsion, & Discharge—   p. 16

Com^{tte} chofe to provide Preaching money Granted to pay Heywood— — — —   p 17

agreed to hire m^r Stearns 2 months Longer & Granted 50 £ for to Suply ye Pulpit   p 17

Com^{tte} to hire a School mafter: ministerial and School Land to be put on Record: ye Com^{tte} for hyring a minifter be Difmif.^d & a book to be provided for ye Selectmen   18

Choice of minifter: money Granted for Settlement & Sallery &c: P. 19.

Granting money: Choice of Town Officers & Excepting of High ways—   20-21-2

Mr Stearns ordination: Galleries in ye meeting Houfe to be finished forthwith— — —   23.

money Raised to pay Col.^l willard for Entertaining ye ordination Councell— — — — —   23

A TABLE.

200 £ Mr Stearns Settlement ½ on Poles & ye other half on Estats— — — — — — 24

Mr Gardner, School for 3 months— — — 24
Preambelating Lins with Lancefter 24

Annual meeting. Granting money— — 25-6

Co^{ll} willard ajant to get ye Land Taxt 26

Confcerning a School ajants for a new County 40 £
Granted for High ways— — — 27

Laying Rates Granting money. Power to ye ajants for a new County altered. 28

Annuel meeting Granting money Excepting High wayes Selling Town Rode To pay for others.— — — 29, 30

Granting money Isaac Farnfworth to get ye money Due to building ye meeting House Juftice Hartwell to Take a Leas of ye Ground where ye meeting Houfe Stands. Two Tything men Chofen.— — — 31

Northfield road road by the bury-g place part discontinued. } 33

---

[1] In Council August 2, 1728. ordered that Capt Josiah Willard a Principle Inhabitant of the Town of Lunenburg be and hereby is Impowered and Directed to Afsemble the freeholders and other Inhabitants of Said Town to Convene as Soon as may be to Elect and Chuse Town Officers there to Stand untill the Anniversary Meeting in March next.
    Sent Down for Concurrence.
      J. WILLARD *Secry*.

 In the House of Reprefentatives August 2, 1728
  Read and Concured
     Wm DUDLEY. *Spek^r*.

   Confented to, Wm BURNET

A True Coppy Examined   ῤ J. WILLARD *Secry*.

By virtue of the above written order I have warned the freeholders and other Inhabitants of Said Town To Assemble at y⁵ House of Ensigne Jonathan Willards on y⁵ 19 day of August 1728

JOSIAH WILLARD—

Recorded by me   ISAAC FARNSWORTH, *Town Clerk.*

[2] At a Legal meeting of y⁵ freeholders and other Inhabitants of y⁵ Town of Lunenburg (by an order from y⁵ General Court) Afsembled August 19 : 1728.—
voted and Chose Cap⁺ Josiah Willard moderator.

Lt James Colburn
Cap⁺ Josiah Willard   } Chofen
m⁺ Hilkeah Boynton   } Select
m⁺ Ephraim Pearce   } men
m⁺ Sam¹¹ Page

Isaac Farnsworth   } Chofen
Noah Dodge   } Constables

Jofhua Hutchens   } Chofen
Jonathan Willard   } Survayers
Nathan Haywood   } of high wayes.

Eleazer Houghton   } Chofen
Sam¹¹ Johnson   } Tything men

L⁺ – Edward Hartwell } Town Treasurer.

James Jewell   }
John Fisk   } Chofen
Jeremiah Norcross } Hoggreaves

Jacob Stiles   } Chofen
Jonathan Whittney } fence viewers.

Recorded ꝑ me   ISAAC FARNSWORTH *Town Clerk*.

[3] At a Legal meeting of the Inhabitants and freeholders of y⁵ Town of Lunenburg Afembled—September y⁵ 24: 1728 Cap⁺ Josiah Willard was Chofen moderator.

Ily voted and Granted y⁵ Sum of Eighty Pounds money to be Levied on y⁵ whole of y⁵ Lands within Said Townfhip for y⁵ minifters Sallery for y⁵ Term of Six years next Comming.

2ly voted and Granted ye Sum of Two Hundred Pounds money to be Levied on Each Right or full Grant Equally to be proportioned for ye building and finishing of a meeting house in Said Town so far as it will do or anfwer there for.— — —

3ly. voted that Capt Josiah Willard and m^r Hilkiah Boynton wait on ye General Court for a Confirmation of ye aforefaid articals and also to obtain a Reccord of Said Town—

Recorded by me.   ISAAC FARNSWORTH *Town Clerk*.

At a Legal meeting of ye freeholders and Inhabitants of ye Town of Lunenburg Afsembled Janewary ye 27: 1728/9— — — —

Voted and Chose Capt Josiah Willard Agant for ye Town of Lunenburg aforefaid to Joyn with Such other men as ye Several neighbouring Towns Shall appoint to Consider what may be best in order to devide ye County of middlsex into two Counties.

A True Record ISAAC FARNSWORTH, *Town Clerk*.

[4] At a meeting of ye freeholders and other Inhabitants of ye Town of Lunenburg Afsembled March ye 31: 1729. Capt Josiah Willard was Chofen moderator

Sam^{ll} Jonson
Ephraim Pearce
Capt Josiah Willard   } Chosen Select men.
Noah Dodge,
Edward Hartwell

Hilkiah Boynton } Constable

Sam^{ll} Jonson } Town Treasurer

Josiah Willard
James Colburn   } Chofen Colectors
Joshua Hutchens

John Grout
nathan Heywood } Tything men.

John Heywood } Survayers of high
Jonathan Willard } —wayes—
Nath!! Harwood }

Sam!! Jonson } Fence viewers
Noah Dodge }

John Grout }
Jeremiah Norcross } Hoggreaves
Benjn Corey }

Recorded by me ISAAC FARNSWORTH *Town Clerk*

[5] At a Legal meeting of the freeholders and other Inhabitants of ye Town of Lunenburg Afsembled March ye 11. 1729/30. Capt Josiah Willard was Chofen Moderator.

Capt Josiah Willard }
Lt Edward Hartwell } Chosen
Isaac Farnsworth } Select   Sworn as
Ephraim Wetherbe } men   afsefsors
Jonathan Willard }

Isaac Farnsworth } Chosen Town Clerk & Sworn.

Daniel Austen } Chofe Constable & Sworn.

Edward Hartwell } Chofen
Josiah Willard } Survayers of high wayes—
Sam!! Jonson }

Jonas Gillson }
David Gould } Tything men

Jacob Gould }
Joseph Page } Fence viewers. Sworn.

William Jones }
Joshua Goodridge } Hogg reives.
Nath!! Harwood }

Ephraim Wetherbe } Colector Chofen & Sworn.

Sam!! Johnson } Town Treasurer.

At^s   ISAAC FARNSWORTH *Town Clerk*

[6] LUNENBURG, Feb: ye 13: 1729/30.

An account of ye Town wayes Laid out by ye Select men of ye Town above Said Beginning at ye meeting House in Said Town and Running through Burbeans house Lott 64 Rods 4 Rods wide as it is now marked out and through Pools house Lott 120 Rods 4 Rods wide adjoyning on Burbeens Land to ye way which is Called Northfield Rode, and also ye northfield rode as it is Laid by ye General Courts Com^{tte} from or near Pearl hill Brook to where ye way is turned into Jonathan Whittneys Lot, and then Going through Said Whittney Lott 24 Rods, 4 Rods wide where it is now marked out. and Runing through Thurstins Lott 50 rod 4 Rods wide where it is now marked out. and then Running through Eleazer Boyntons meddow 31 rods one rod one half wide as it is marked out and Through Beeths Land 96 rod 4 rods wide. and through Moses Willards Land 26 rods 4 rods wide with high way marks to where it Coms into ye rode or way Left by ye General Courts Com^{tte} and then running a Crofs the Corner of ye Land Laid to Archiball Mackfatrich to Groton Line.: ye ways as above mentioned is accepted and confiermed by ye Town at ye Annuell meeting in March held ye Eleventh day in ye year 1729/30

An account of ye wayes or Town Rode Laid out by ye Select men of Lunenburg beginning at Lancester Line and making high way marks on ye westerly Side thereof to Lunenburg meeting house the Said way to be 4 rods wide as it is now Laid out. an account of ye said way going through mens Lotts where there is no alowance made by ye General Courts Com^{tte} Going through Ebenezer Richardson Land 100 rods Through Benjamin Coorys Land. 80 rods throug John Heywoods Land 64 rods Through Nathan heywoods And John heywoods Land 132 rods. Through Edward Hartwells Land 165 rods Through Goodridges Land 212 rods through harreses Land 50 rods through Gipsons Land 12 through Ephraim Pearces Land 94 rods &c. which rode is accepted alowed and Confiermed by ye Town at ye meeting above Said.

Recorded by me   ISAAC FARNSWORTH *Town Clerk.*

[7] At a Legal meeting of y[e] freeholders and other Inhabitants of y[e] Town of Lunenburg afsembled May y[e] 18. 1730 Cap[t] Josiah Willard was Chofen moderator.

then voted that there be granted y[e] Sum of Twenty Shillings to be paid by Each full Grant for y[e] mending of high wayes

2ly. Voted and ordered that Isaac Farnsworth Town Clerk for y[e] time being be Impowered to Record all Such votes and orders that are proper to be Recorded (which hath ben here to fore past) fairly in a Town Book.

3ly. Voted that Eighty Pounds be paid to m[r] Gardner out of y[e] money Granted by y[e] General Court upon y[e] Lands for y[e] Support of y[e] Gospell for y[e] prefent year.

Recorded by me   ISAAC FARNSWORTH Town Clerk.

At a Legal meeting of y[e] freeholders and other Inhabitants of y[e] Town of Lunenburg afsembled Feb[r] y[e] 8: 1730/31 Then Cap[t] Josiah Willard was Chofen moderator

1ly. voted and agreed to build a body of Seets and a pulpit in y[e] meeting houfe.

2ly. voted and Chofe Isaac Farnsworth Jonathan Willard and Benj[a] Goodridge. to be a Com[tte] to build y[e] Seets and Pulpit afore faid.

3ly. voted and Granted y[e] Sum of Thirty Pounds money upon y[e] house Lotts to be Equally Proportioned and paid for the building of a body of Seets and a pulpit in y[e] meeting houfe.

4ly. voted and Granted y[e] Sum of five Pounds Twelve Shillings and Six pence money to pay m[r] Sam[ll] Page for building a Pound and for y[e] Land y[e] pound Stands on and a way to pafs and Repafs to it.

5ly. voted to build Pews in y[e] meeting house. so many as there is Conveniant Room for—

—6ly—

[8] 6ly. voted that Cap[t] Josiah Willard L[t] Edward Hartwell m[r] Sam[ll] Page m[r] Ephraim Wetherbe and L[t] James Colburn be a Com[tte] to State Places for building of Pews in y[e] meeting house and order who Shall or may have them according to y[e] Direction of y[e] Town and it is further voted y[t] y[e] Rule y[e] Com[tte] Shall go by Shall be according to y[e] Inhabitants Improvements

and Stations and having Some Referance to Pay. it is also voted and agreed that ye perſons preferred to have Pews Shall build them on their own Coſt and Charge

7ly. Voted and Choſe Capt Josiah Willard Lt Edward Hartwell Isaac Farnsworth James Colburn and Ephraim Wetherbe to be a Com^{tte} to Reckon with Mr Gardner to See what ye Town are Indebted unto him Since his ordination and make Return thereof to ye next Town meeting.

Recorded by me   ISAAC FARNSWORTH *Town Clerk*

[9] At a Leg^{ual} meeting of ye freeholders and other Inhabitants of ye Town of Lunenburg Aſsembled March ye 1: 1730/31 Capt Josiah Willard was Choſen moderator.

Capt Josiah Willard
Mr Sam^{ll} Page
Mr Ephraim Wetherbe
Lt Edward Hartwell
Dr Sam^{ll} Johnson
} Choſen Selectmen. and aſeſsors.

Isaac Farnsworth } Choſen Town, Clerk, and Sworn.

Nathan Heywood } Choſen Conſtable. and Sworn.

Isaac Farnsworth } Choſen Colector, and Sworn

Ephraim Wetherbe
Daniel Austen
} Choſen Tythingmen. and Sworn.

Edward Hartwell
Ephraim Pearce
Josiah Willard
Sam^{ll} Johnson
} Choſen Survayers of highwayes.

John Grout
Jonathan Page
} choſen fence viewers. and Sworn

Benj^a Cory
Jonas Gillſon
Jonathan Page
} Choſen Hoggreives and Sworn.

Sam^{ll} Johnson } Choſen Town Treasurer & Sworn

Voted y^t ye Town accept of ye accounts brought in by ye Com^{tte} appointed to Reckon with Mr Gardner

Voted and ordred that Twenty Pounds in bills of Credit y^t is Raifed upon ye unimproved Lands in Said Town to be paid to ye Rev^nd Andrew Gardner for his fettlement here in Said Town Provided Mr Gardner doth Give a full Discharge of ye whole of his Settlement in all Particulars as he shall Claim as a promise from ye Town aforef^d

I^s FARNSWORTH *Town Clerk—*

[10] At a Legual meeting of ye Inhabitants and freeholders of ye Town of Lunenburg Afsembled July 5: 1731 Lt Edward Hartwell was Chofen moderator—then voted and Chofe Ll^t Edward Hartwell Agant for ye Town of Lunenburg to Joyn with ye Gardean or heirs of James Kibby (or who foever shall Claim by from or under him) in a Petition to ye General Court for an Equivilent in ye Province Land for y^t which is thought by Some to Lye within our Town Provided they will Relinquish their Claim in Said Town.

At^s — ISAAC FARNSWORTH *Town Clerk*

At a Legual meeting of ye freeholders and other Inhabitants of ye Town of Lunenburg afsembled July 26: 1731

Then voted and Chose Mr Edward Hartwell Grand Jury man to Sarve on ye Grand Jury for ye year Enfuing

At^s ISAAC FARNSWORTH *Town Clerk*

At a Leg^ual meeting of ye freeholders and other Inhabitants of ye Town of Lunenburg afsembled August ye 20th 1731:

Then voted and Chofe Mr Jonathan Willard Grand Juryman To Sarve on ye Grand Jury at a Superiour Court of Judicature Court of Afsize and General Goal Delivery, To be holden at Worcester for ye County of Worcester on the Fourth Wednfday of September next 1731 and no Longer.—

Voted and Chofe Mr Ephraim Wetherbe Petty Juryman to Sarve on ye Petty Jury at Court, Time, and Place afore Said. and no Longer.

At^s ISAAC FARNSWORTH *Town Clerk*

[11] At a Legual meeting of yᵉ Inhabitants and freeholders of yᵉ Town of Lunenburg afsembled September yᵉ 2 : 1731.

Then voted and Chofe Isaac Farnsworth modderator Voted and Chofe John Chandler Junʳ Esqʳ to be Regefter of Deeds for yᵉ County of Worcefter.—

Then voted and Chofe Mʳ Jonathan Houghton To be Treasurer for the County of Worcester.

Atˢ   Iˢ Farnsworth *Town Clerk*

At a Legual meeting of the Inhabitants and freeholders of yᵉ Town of Lunenburg Afsembled October yᵉ 25 : 1731 Voted and Chofe Mʳ Ephraim Wetherbe Petty Jurey man To Sarve on yᵉ Jury of Trials at an Inferiour Court of Common Pleas to be holden at Worcester for yᵉ County of Worcester on Tuesday yᵉ Seccond Day of November next Ensuing yᵉ Date hereof &c.

At A Legual meeting of the Inhabitants and free holders of yᵉ Town of Lunenburg Afsembled December yᵉ 6:ᵗʰ 1731

Mʳ Samˡˡ Page was Chofen Modderator.—

1ly. Voted and Chofe Isaac Farnsworth To wait on yᵉ General Court in behalf of yᵉ Town with a Petition that the Land In Said Town may be Taxed for yᵉ Support of yᵉ Gospel—Both Improved and unimproved farms Grants and Devifions, &c :

And for anything Elfe that Shall be Thought Proper

Atˢ   Iˢ Farnsworth *Town Clerk*

[12] At a Legual meeting of the Inhabitants and freeholders of the Town of Lunenburg Afsembled Febʳ yᵉ 7ᵗʰ 1731/2 Voted and Chofe Josiah Willard Efqʳ modderator Then voted and Granted yᵉ Reverand Andrew Gardner a Dismifsion from his Paftoral or minifterial office in Said Town According to his Request

2ly. Voted. and ordred that yᵉ Select men or their Suckfefsers be vested with Power for and in behalf of the Town to Pay Mʳ Gardner all and what foever yᵉ Town are Indebted unto him and also do and Perform any thing or things Else Reffering to his Dismifsion from his Paftoral office and obligation in Said Town as Soon as can be Conveniantly Performed

At: I. FARNSWORTH *Town Clerk*

An account of a High way or Town Rode Layed out by ye Select men of ye Town of Lunenburg March ye 4th 1731/2 Beginning at a Rhode Called northfield Rhode. marked on ye Eafterly Side of Said Rhode four Rods wide firft Running through Jofiah Bayley Land on ye fore Side of his new dwelling Houfe, then Running through Jeremiah Norcrofs,es Land, Running by ye fore Side of Said Norcrofs,es Houfe, Then Running Through ye Land of Sam^{ll} Davis at one Corner of his Lot.

Then Running Through ye minifterial Land. Then Running Through Jonathan Pools Land to ye Corner of a Rhode Laid out to ye meeting Houfe Through Ephraim Wetherbes Land.

The above Said Rhode Excepted and allowed by ye Town at their Annual meeting in march held ye 6 day: 1731/2

Recorded here in ye Twelveth Page of ye Book being an empty fpace for want of room in ye Thirteenth Page.

ISAAC FARNSWORTH *Town Clerk*

[13] At a Legual meeting of ye Inhabitants and freeholders of ye Town of Lunenburg Afsembled March ye 6: 1731/2

Dec. Sam^{ll} Johnson was Chosen modderator

Benj^a Goodridge
James Colburn
John Heywood   Chofen
Hilkiah Boynton   Select men and Sworn
Daniel Austen   as Afsefsors

Isaac Farnsworth } Chofen Town Clerk and Sworn

Mr Edward Hartwell } Chofen Town Treasurer. and Sworn

Mr Sam^{ll} Page } Chofen Collector. and Sworn

Jeremiah norcrofs } Chofen Conftable: and Sworn

Jonathan Houghton } Chofen County Treasurer.

William Jones
Eleazer Houghton } Chofen Survayers of high ways
Nath!! Harwood   and Sworn.

Jonathan Willard }
Hilkiah Boynton } Chosen Tything men. and Sworn.

Sam!! Davis   } Chofen Fence viewers. and Sworn.
Benj:a Coorey. }

David Pearce }
Nath!! Page   } Hogg reives. and Sworn.
Benj:a Fofter }
John Hill   }

Voted that y:e Hoggs in Said Town Shall run at Large.

M:r Sam!! Page } Chofen Pound Keeper.

At:s   ISAAC FARNSWORTH *Town Clerk*

[14] At a Legual meeting of y:e Inhabitants and freeholders of y:e Town of Lunenburg Afsembled March y:e 13 1731/2

Voted and Chofe M:r Hilkiah Boynton Modderator

1ly. Voted and Granted y:e Sum of Six Pounds money for the Buying of Weights and Measures for Standards for Said Town

2.ly Voted and Granted y:e Sum of Eight Shillings for building of a pair of Stocks.

3ly. Voted and Granted y:e Sum of four Pounds four Shillings to pay M:r Edward Hartwell for Sarvice done for Said Town

4ly. Voted and Granted y:e Sum of Six Shillings to pay M:r Jonathan Willard for Sarvice done for Said Town

5ly. voted and Granted y:e Sum of Ten Shillings to pay M:r Ephraim Pearce for Sarvice done for Said Town

6ly. voted. and Granted y:e Sum of Twenty Shillings to pay M:r Ephraim Wetherbee for Sarvice done for Said Town

7ly. voted and Granted ye Sum of thirteen Shillings to pay Mr Sam^ll Page for Sarvice done for Said Town

8ly. voted. and Granted ye Sum of Three Shillings to pay Mr. Daniel Austin for Sarvice done for Said Town

9ly. voted. and Granted ye Sum of Six Shillings to pay Mr Hilkiah Boynton for Sarvice done for Said Town

10ly. voted. and Granted ye Sum of nine Shillings to pay M^r nathan Heywood for Sarvice done for Said Town

11ly. voted. and Granted ye Sum of Six pounds Thirteen Shillings and one penney to pay Isaac Farnsworth for Sarvice done for Said Town

HILKIAH BOYNTON moderator

[15] At a Legual meeting of the Inhabitants and freeholders of the Town of Lunenburg Afsembled Sep^tr ye 18th: 1732

Voted and Chofe Mr Sam^ll Page Modderator

1ly. voted and Granted ye Sum of Thirty Two Shillings To pay Co^ll Jofiah Willard for Eight dayes Sarvice Done for Said Town at Laying of Rates and Laying out High wayes for time past —

2ly. voted and Granted ye Sum of Sixteen Shillings to pay Mr Sam^ll Johnson for Sarvice done for Said Town Time 4 dayes

3ly. voted and Granted ye Sum of Twenty Two Shillings to pay Mr Jeremiah Norcrofs for Sarvice Done for Said Town

4ly. voted and Granted ye Sum of five Pounds to pay Isaac Farnsworth for his Collecting or Gathering of Rates for ye year 1731

5ly. voted and Granted ye Sum of Three Pounds to pay Mr Ephraim Wetherbe for his Collecting or Gathering Rates for year 1730.

6ly. voted and Granted ye Sum of Three Pounds Eighteen Shillings for ye ufe of Mr Nathaniel Page for fencing in the burying Place

At^s ISAAC FARNSWORTH Town Clerk

At a Legual meeting of ye Inhabitants and freeholders of ye Town of Lunenburg Afsembled October ye 30.th 1732 voted, and Chofe Mr Hilkiah Boynton Modderator

voted To ye Rev.nd Mr Andrew Gardner a Place in ye meeting houfe at ye Right hand of ye Great Doors to build a Pew

voted that this meeting be ajourned to fryday next at one of ye Clock in ye afternoon:

Voted. That ye Com.^{tte} appointed for Stating Places for Pews in ye meeting houfe be Directed and ordered to State, order and appoint, a place for a menifterial Pew adjoyning to ye foot of ye Pulpit Stairs at ye Right hand of ye Pulpit.

      At.^s — Isaac Farnsworth *Town Clerk.*

[16] (A Record of) a Receipt Given By the Rev.nd Mr Andrew Gardner of Lunenburg in full Difcharge to ye Town for his Settlement and Sallery there.

Then Received of the Select men for the Town of Lunenburg the Juft Sum of three Hundred Ninety and four Pounds Twelve Shillings and three Pence which is in full for my Settlement and Sallery there: I say Received p.^r me

      Andrew Gardner *Paftor*

Lunenburg October ye 27: 1732

 A True Record From ye originall Att.^s

    Isaa Farnsworth *Town Clerk*

(A Record of) a Requeft from ye Reverand Mr Andrew Gardner. To his Church in Lunenburg for his Difmifsion.

To the Brethren of ye Church of Christ in Lunenburg—

Beloved Brethren. I cannot but Think from what I have heard, and alfo from what I have obfarved of ye tranfactions and behaviour of this People Relating to me and my affairs that there is not that affection born towards me that there should be from a People to their Gospell minifter—or that there is where a People are Likely duly to profit under their minifter ye Confideration whereof has been very Grevious and difcouriging to me and there fore think it beft to Sepperate I do therefore propofe a Sepperation and if affeectual Care be Taken y^t my dues be honeftly Paid me: ye first minifters Lott with its appurtenances put upon Record and Attefted and a Sufficiant Pew at ye Right hand of Going in at ye Great dooers of ye meeting House I shall be free to be Difmifsed from my Paftoral Relation and office obligation to you as Soon as it Can Regularly be performed.

from your Loving Paftor who wifheth you ye Divine Direction and blefsing and defires your Prayers for ye Same to him.

Lunenburg Sep^{tr} 18. 1730   ANDREW GARDNER *Paftor*

according to Church warning then ye Church met at ye meeting houfe and received his acquittance from his Paftoral Relation to us as Atteft his hand.

ANDREW GARDNER, *Paftor*

Lunenburg november ye 3: 1732
A True Record from ye originall
          ISAAC FARNSWORTH *Town Clerk*

[17] At a Legual meeting of the Inhabitants and freeholders of ye Town of Lunenburg afsembled Nou^r ye 10th : 1732

Voted. and Chofe Capt Edward Hartwell modderator

Voted. that Dec. Sam^{ll} Johnson Dec. Ephraim Pearce and Mr Isaac Farnsworth be a Com^{tte} to Provide a minifter from time to time to Supply ye Town with Preaching till further order, and to aggree with him in ye Towns behalf what he Shall have for his Sarvice.

Voted. and Granted ye Sum of Sixteen Shillings to pay Mr John Heywood for Going to Court to anfwer to ye Towns Prefentment
       At^t ISAAC FARNSWORTH *Town Clerk*

At a Legual meeting of Inhabitants and freeholders of ye Town of Lunenburg Afsembled Decemb^r ye 4:th 1732

Voted. and Chofe Co^{ll} Jofiah Willard modderator

Voted. and aggreed that ye Com^{tte} appointed. hire Mr Stearns Two months Longer after ye Term is out which ye Com^{tte} appointed to Supply ye Town with Preaching hath hired him.

Voted. and Granted ye Sum of Fifty Pounds to Defray ye Charge of Supplying ye Pulpit in Said Town

Recorded P^r me   ISAAC FARNSWORTH *Town Clerk*

[18] At a Legual meeting of ye freeholders and other Inhabitants of ye Town of Lunenburg Afsembled December ye 11 : 1732

Voted and Chofe Capt Edward Hartwell modderator

voted. that Col^l Jofiah Willard Capt Edward Hartwell and Mr Benjamin Goodridge be a Com^ttee to Provide a School and School Mafter for to teach Children and youth to Read and write & if the Com^ttee See Good to hire a Gramer School mafter, they Shall have ye Liberty. Provided they Pay ye over Plus Charge of what ye Keeping of a Gramer School would be more y^n ye charge of Keeping an Englifh School :—

Voted, that ye Com^ttee appointed to Lay out the first Devifion Seccond Devifion or meddow Lott or any Part thereof to any y^t shall need, be alfo a Com^ttee to take a Survay & Lay out ye minifterial and School Land with Mr Nathan Heywood Survayer and make and Return a Plan thereof to ye Propriators Clark in order to have ye Same put upon ye Propriators Book of Reccords, and make Return to the Town of ye Charge thereof. — — —

Voted y^t ye Bill of ye Com^ttee appointed to hire a minifter from time to time be alowed which is £3-10-0-

Voted. y^t ye Com^ttee for hyring a minifter be Difmifsed from their further Sarvice in y^t affair.

Voted. that there be a book Provided for ye Select men to Record ye Town Rates in and how they are ordred out in order to Prevent miftakes

At^t Isaac Farnsworth *Town Clerk*

[19] At a Legual meeting of ye freeholders and other Inhabitants of ye Town of Lunenburg Afsembled February ye 12th 1732/3.

Then voted and Chofe Deacon Sam^ll Johnfon Modderator

Voted that ye Town meeting be Ajourned to fryday ye 23 day of february Currant at Two of ye Clock in ye afternoon. at which time ye Town being meet and formed Proceeded to Bufinefs.

1ly. Voted and Chofe Mr David Stearns to be our Gospel minifter to Carry on ye work of ye miniftrey in Said Town.

2ly. Voted and Granted y̌ Sum of Three Hundred Pounds for y̌ ufe of Mʳ David Stearns for his Settlement in y̌ work of y̌ miniſtrey in Said Town.

3ly. Voted and ordred that Two Hundred of y̌ above Said Three Hundred Pounds be paid to Mʳ David Stearns y̌ first year of his Settlement and y̌ other Hundred y̌ Seccond year of his Settlement which in y̌ whole makes up y̌ above Said Sum of Three Hundred Pounds.

4ly Voted and Granted y̌ Sum of one Hundred and Twenty Pounds in Bills of Credit to be Paid Mʳ David Stearns in y̌ first year of his Settleing and y̌ Sum of Five Pounds more of Like money to be added yearly till in y̌ whole it amounts to y̌ Sum of one Hundred and Fourty Pounds y̌ money to be quallified according to y̌ Prefent value and to be Paid yearly for his Sallery in Proportion as afore fᵈ

5ly. Voted and Chofe y̌ Two Deacons namely Mʳ Ephraim Pearce & Mʳ Samˡˡ Johnfon, and Jofiah Willard Efqʳ to be a Comᵗᵗᵉ to wait on y̌ Reverand Mʳ David Stearns with y̌ Towns Propofals.

Atˢ·   Isaac Farnsworth *Town Clerk*

[20] At a Legual meeting of y̌ Inhabitants and freeholders of y̌ Town of Lunenburg Afsembled march y̌ 5ᵗʰ 1732/3

Voted and Chofe Mʳ Benjamin Goodridge Modderator

1ly. voted and Granted y̌ Sum of Three Pounds Ten Shillings To pay Deacon Samˡˡ Johnfon and Isaac Farnfworth for Going to Hire a minifter for Said Town

2ly. voted and Granted y̌ Sum of Nine Shillings to Pay Mʳ Jeremiah Norcrofs for warning nine Town meetings

3ly. Voted and Granted y̌ Sum of Three Pounds Seven Shillings and Eight Pence to Pay Mʳ Andrew Gardner for Keeping the Minifters and Deligates on y̌ Bufinefs of y̌ Town

4ly. voted and Granted y̌ Sum of Five Pounds to pay Mʳ Samˡˡ Page for his Collection. of Rates for y̌ year 1732.

5ly. voted and Granted y̆ᵉ Sum of Twelve Shillings to pay Mṛ Samˡˡ Page for Keeping Six Horſes on yᵉ Towns occaſion

6ly. voted and Granted yᵉ Sum of Thirteen Shillings to pay Mṛ Nathan Heywood for Keeping of School in Said Town

7ly. Voted and Granted yᵉ Sum of Eight Shillings to pay Mṛ Benjamin Goodridge for Keeping of School in Sᵈ Town

8ly. voted and granted yᵉ Sum of Three Pounds to pay Mṛ Hilkiah Boynton for Keeping of School in Said Town

9ly. voted and granted yᵉ Sum of Three Pounds to pay Mṛ Joſiah Willard Junʳ for Keeping of School in Said Town

10ly voted and Granted yᵉ Sum of fourty Shillings to pay Mṛ Benjamin Goodridge for Services done for Said Town

11ly. voted and Granted yᵉ Sum of Twenty Two Shillings to pay Mṛ James Colburn for Sarvice done for Said Town

12ly. voted and Granted yᵉ Sum of Twenty Shillings to pay Mṛ Daniel Auſten for Sarvice done for Said Town

13ly. voted and Granted yᵉ Sum of Fourteen Shillings to pay Mṛ John Heywood for Sarvice done for Said Town

14ly. voted and Granted yᵉ Sum of Thirty Six Shillings to pay Mṛ Hilkiah Boynton for Sarvice done for Said Town

15ly. voted and Granted yᵉ Sum of Six Shillings to pay Mṛ Daniel Auſten for his hors to Worcester on yᵉ Town occaſion

yᵉ other buſineſs of yᵉ above Said meeting Entred on yᵉ other Page

[21] March yᵉ 5ᵗʰ 1732/3 Annual meeting

Mṛ Benjamin Goodridge.
Mʳ James Colburn.   Choſen
Mʳ John Grout.   Select and Sworn Aſseſors
Mṛ Jonas Gillſon.   men
Mṛ Hilkiah Boynton

Isaac, Farnſworth, Town Clerk. and Sworn
M.˗ James Colburn. Town Treaſurer and Sworn
M.˗ John Gront. Choſen Conſtable & Sworn
M.˗ William Jones. Choſen Collector & Sworn

M.˗ Sam.ˡˡ Page
M.˗ William Jones   } Choſen Survayers of
M.˗ Joſhua Goodridge   } High wayes Sworn

M.˗ Sam.ˡˡ Johnſon } Choſen Tythingmen
M.˗ Jonathan Page   }

M.˗ Joſiah Bayle   }
M.˗ Eleazar Houghton } choſen Fence viewers

M.˗ Sam.ˡˡ Farnſworth }
M.˗ Jonathan Whitney }   Farnsworth
M.˗ Jonathan Gould   } Choſen Hoggreives: Gould Sworn

Voted that y.ᵉ Hogs Shall Go at Large in S.ᵈ Town
M.˗ Ephraim Pearce Choſen Sealer

      At.ˢ ˗ Isaac Farnsworth *Town Clerk*

An account of High wayes Excepted at y.ᵉ above Said meeting one High way Laid out from Will.ᵐ Wallaces land to y.ᵉ Rode that Goeth from Lunenburg to Groton: which Road begins at the Corner of y.ᵉ Said Wallace's Land, Lying Two Rods Eastwardly and Two Rods Westwardly from a white oak Tree mark,t being y.ᵉ Said Wallaces Corner and So runing by y.ᵉ Line between y.ᵉ Said Wallaces Land, & Mitchel Land on a Strait Line taking of Two Rods from Each mans Land for Said High way, till it Comes to Nath.ˡˡ Pages Land and
            and

[22] And so Runing between the Said Mitchels Land and y.ᵉ Said Pages Land taking Two Rods wide from Each mans Land till it comes to a Stake there making an angle & then Coming into y.ᵉ Said Mitchels Land and then mark,t on the Northerly Side to a Pine Tree Mark,t in Jonathan Pages Land and So Runing Through y.ᵉ Said Pages Land till it Comes to M.˗ Clarks Land four Rods wide and mark,t on y.ᵉ Easterly Side till it Comes to a White oak Stump Standing in or near the Roade that Leads from Lunenburg to Groton. Also Laid out a High way from where y.ᵉ Rode began at Jonathan Whitneys

Land & So Runing as ye General Courts Committe Laid it out between Thirftons Land and Jacob Goulds Land and So between Thirftons and George Wheelers Land. Alfo Laid out a bridle way across Eleazar Houghtons Land and William Wallaces Land faid way begining at ye Countrey Rode and Runing by ye South Wefterly Side of Col.! Willards fence and So to ye End of ye fence and then up the Ridge to a Tree mark,t on ye Eafterly Side of Said way and So mark,t and So mark,t ye Same Side of Said way till it comes to David Pearces Land. Also we have Taken a view of ye High way that Runs acrofs Jonathan Whitneys Land by his Defire and we think it as Conveniant for ye way to Go Round ye Said Whitneys Land Saving four Rods at ye Southerly Corner which he offers to Give ye Town for a High way. Provided that they will Throw up the other way: which Land fo Left out, begins at a Great White oak Stump, and fo runs on a Strait Line to ye Caufeway: or whether ye Town will Give faid Whitney Six Pounds for ye way as it now Ly-eth. (Voted y^t ye alteration be alowed.) Alfo ye High way being a Little altered between Leiu^t. Colburns Land and Hilkiah Boyntons Land by Reafon of ye Said Boy-tons Setting his Houfe in ye High way through a mistake and hath fince purchafed fome Land of ye faid Colburn for to be added to faid way in Stead of what Land ye faid Boynton hath Taken up: we there fore ye faid Colburn and Boynton defire ye Town to Confierm ye Land which is Left out of ye faid Colburns Land for part of ye High-way aforefaid.

(Excepted by ye Town)

    At^s.   Isaac Farnsworth *Town Clerk.*

[23] At a Legal meeting of ye Inhabitants and free-holders of ye Town of Lunenburg Afsembled March ye 19th 1732/3

Voted and Chofe Isaac Farnfworth Modderator

1ly. Voted that ye Third Wedenfday in April next which will be on ye Eighteenth day of faid month fhall be ye Day for ordaining ye Rev.nd M^r. David Stearns in ye work of ye miniftrey in faid Town

2ly. Voted that Co^{ll} Jofiah Willard Shall make Sufficiant Provifion for ye ordination Counccll: minifters and Schollers and Mr Stearnf-es Relations, and ye Charge thereof fhall be Paid on Demand.

3ly. Voted y^t ye Galleries in ye meeting Houfe fhall be forth with finifhed and ye Stears. built up into ye Galleries.

4ly. voted y^t Jonathan Willard Benj^a Goodridge and Isaac Farnfworth Shall be a Com^{tte} To Carry on ye work aforeSaid. at ye Towns Charge

      ISAAC FARNSWORTH *Town Clerk*

At a Legall meeting of ye freeholders and other Inhabitants of ye Town of Luncnburg Afsembled May ye 22th 1733—

Voted and Chofe Lt Jonathan Willard—Modderator

Voted y^t Co^{ll} Willards account for Entertaining ye ordination Counfell and others be alowed which is Twenty Three Pounds Eighteen Shillngs and Two Pence.

Voted and Granted ye Sum of Twenty Three Pounds Eighteen Shillings and Two Pence as above f^d to pay Co^{ll} Jofiah Willard for Entertaining ye ordination Councell and others as heretofore hath ben voted.

Voted that ye money Granted as above faid be Raifed ye one Half on Pools and ye other half on Eftates

   At^t.   ISAAC FARNSWORTH *Town Clerk*

[24] At a Legal Town meeting of freeholders and other Inhabitants of ye Town of Luncnburg affembled Sep^{tr} ye 13th 1733 Mr Hilkiah Boynton Chofen Modderator.

1ly at ye above Said meeting it was agreed and voted that ye one half of ye Two Hundred Pounds Granted to ye Revnd Mr David Sterns for part of his Settlement in Said Town for ye firft Payment) Shall be Laid on Poles and ye other half on other Ratable Estate.

2ly. voted at Said meeting that Mr Jacob Gould Shall have Two Pounds Eight Shillings Paid by Said Town for putting Pillers under ye Galleries and making Ladders and for putting up Rails in ye meeting Houfe in ye Galleries.- Hilkiah Boynton Modderator

    At^t ⌐ ISAAC FARNSWORTH *Town Clerk*

At a Legall meeting of y⁽ᵉ⁾ Inhabitants and freeholders of y⁽ᵉ⁾ Town of Lunenburg affembled December y⁽ᵉ⁾ 31: 1733

Voted and Chofe Co⁽ll⁾ Jofiah Willard Modderator

1ly. Voted to hire a School mafter Three months from : y⁽ᵉ⁾ Time y⁽ᵉ⁾ School mafter begins his School. ——

2ly. Voted that y⁽ᵉ⁾ School Shall be kept at y⁽ᵉ⁾ Houfe of M⁽r⁾ Gardners y⁽ᵉ⁾ Three months aggreed on to keep a School:

3ly. Voted and Chofe M⁽r⁾ Andrew Gardner to be y⁽ᵉ⁾ School mafter to keep y⁽ᵉ⁾ School y⁽ᵉ⁾ Term of Three months as afore faid in faid Town or Such other as he Shall Provide therefor.

At⁽s⁾   ISAAC FARNSWORTH *Town Clerk*

Lunenburg December y⁽ᵉ⁾ 25⁽th⁾ 1733. Then Edward Hartwell Efq⁽r⁾ and M⁽r⁾ Benj⁽a⁾ Goodridge by order of y⁽ᵉ⁾ Select men of Lunenburg. Met y⁽ᵉ⁾ Com-tte appointed by Lancefter Select men at y⁽ᵉ⁾ Houfe of Thomas Houghtons in Lancefter to preambulate y⁽ᵉ⁾ Lines between y⁽ᵉ⁾ Town of Lancefter and ye Town of Lunenburg as y⁽ᵉ⁾ Law Directs. and alfo performed y⁽ᵉ⁾ Bufinefs: as by Return made to me may appear.

ISAAC FARNSWORTH *Town Clerk.*

[25] At a Legall meeting of y⁽ᵉ⁾ Inhabitants and Freeholders of y⁽ᵉ⁾ Town of Lunenburg Afsembled March 4⁽th⁾ 1733/4

voted and Chofe Cap⁽t⁾ Jonathan Hubbard Modderator

Co⁽ll⁾ Jofiah Willard
M⁽r⁾ Benj⁽a⁾ Goodridge   } Chofen
Dec. Sam⁽ll⁾ Johnfon   } Select
Cap⁽t⁾ Jonathan Hubbard   } men
M⁽r⁾ John Grout

Isaac Farnfworth } Chofen Town Clerk & Sworn

Isaac Farnfworth } Chofen Sealor of Weights & Meafures & Sworn

M⁽r⁾ James Colburn } Chosen Town Treafurer & Sworn

William Jones } Chofen Collector

Nathaniel Harwood } Chofen Conftable

Dea. Sam.ll Johnfon }
Dea. Ephraim Peirce } Chofen Survayers of Highways & Sworn
and Jonas Gillfon

Hilkiah Boynton }
Ephraim Wetherbe } Chofen Tything men & Sworn

Jacob Gould }
John Farmer } Chofen Fence viewers

Sam.ll Davis }
Sam.ll Commings } Hogg Reives
Jofeph Dodge }

Voted that Hoggs Shall Run at Large in S.d Town

M.r Sam.ll Page } Chofen Pound Keeper

The other Buifnefs acted and Done on y.e above faid Day is Recorded on y.e other Side of y.e Leaf

[26] March y.e 4 : 1733/4

Voted. and Granted y.e Several Sums to y.e Several Perfons heafter named. for Sarvices Done for Said Town.

1ly. Granted. To Col.ll Jofiah Willard Three Pounds Ten Shillings

2ly. Granted. To Edward Hartwell Efq.r Two Shillings —

3ly. Granted. To M.r Sam.ll Page Ten Shillings —

4ly. Granted. To Isaac Farnfworth Four Shillings —

5ly. Voted. To Give Isaac Farnfworth Twenty Five Shillings for Taking Care of the meeting Houfe for y.e year Paft and y.e year to Come — — — —

6ly. voted & Granted y.e Sum of Twenty Four Shillings To Jofiah Willard Jun.r for Sarvice Done for Said Town —

7ly. Granted To Benj.a Goodridge Thirty Four Shillings

8ly. Granted. To Hilkiah Boynton Twenty Two Shillings.

9ly. Granted. To Jacob Gould Six Shillings and Three pence.

10ly. Granted. To John Grout Twenty Five Shillings —

At.t   ISAAC FARNSWORTH *Town Clerk* —

ye Town of Lunenburg aforef^d to Do and act any thing or things Respecting ye making of a New County out of ye northerly Parts of ye Countyes of Middlefex and Worcefter as they in their wifdom Shall think moft Proper and Conducing to ye welfare thereof. ——

At^t ISAAC FARNSWORTH *Town Clerk*—

[29] At a Legal meeting of the freeholders and other Inhabitants of ye Town of Lunenburg Afsembled at ye Publick meeting Houfe in Said Town on March 3.th 1734/5

Voted and Chofe Col^l Jofiah Willard Modderator

Col^l Jofiah Willard
Edward Hartwell Esqr
Mr Nathan Heywood
Lieu^t James Colburn
Isaac Farnfworth
} Chofen Select And Taken ye oath men of afsefsors

Isaac Farnfworth Chofen Town Clerk Sworn
John Heywood Chofen Conftable, & Sworn
Isaac Farnfworth Chofen Survayer of Hemp & flax & Sworn

Lieu^t Jonathan Willard
Mr Jofiah Bayle
} Chofen Survayers of High ways Sworn

Decon. Sam^{ll} Johnfon
Decon. Ephraim Peirce
} Chosen Tything men

Mr Ephraim Wetherbe
Mr Amos Robinson
} chofen Fence Viewers Sworn

Major Jonathan Hubburd Chofen Town Treasurer Sworn

Major Jonathan Hubburd Chofen Collector.

Mr Jeremiah Norcrofs
Mr Benjamin Bellows
} Chosen Hoggreives. Sworn.

Voted that Hoggs Run at Large. in S^d Town

Then voted that ye Bufinefs and other Articles Contained in ye warrant for ye above f^d meeting be Adjourned to ye Third monday in march Currant at ye Publick meeting Houfe in Lunenburg at Eight of ye Clock in ye forenoon.

ISAAC FARNSWORTH *Town Clerk*

[30] Brought over — — — — — — — —
John Fisk Chofen Conftable & Sworn.

Isaac Farnfworth Chofen Seeler of Waits & meafures

Voted that ye Rode Called northfield Rode Runing through ye Town be Sold To pay for Sum other Rode or Rods that is or Shall be Laid out in Said Town not yet paid for Excepting Four Rods wide yet to Lye and Continue for a Town Rode or High way. (and that Co^ll Jofiah Willard Edward Hartwell Esqr and Major Jonathan Hubburd be a Comitte fully Impowered to Sell and Give Title of ye Same to Such perfon or perfons as Shall appear to buy ye Same &c: ——

Voted that ye Rode Laid out through Jeremiah Norcrofs Land Sam^ll Davifs Land ye menifterial Land and Amos Robinfons Land be accepted which is as followeth. begining at a heap of Stones at ye north eaft Corner of Jofiah Bayley Land and So runing as ye mark Directs firft to a Chefnut y^n to a Beach y^n to a Chefnut marked y^n to a Chefnut Logg. with an heap of Stones thereon y^n to a Black oak before Jeremiah Norcrofses Door & from thence to a Chefnut Tree upon Sam^ll Davifes Land marked 162 Rods &c: from y^t Chefnut Tree to a white oak marked y^n to another white oak 44 Rods on Sam^ll Davifes Land then runing acrofs ye minifterial Land untill it Comes to Amos Robinfons Land and Runs forty one Rods and there Comes in to ye other Rode or High way by ye Corner of Said Robinfons Fence ye Rode Lying on ye South westerly Side of ye marks through ye Said Lands. Also a Rode begining at ye Corner of William Joneses fence & So Runing upon John Scotts Lott to a heap of Stones upon a Rock near ye Brook So Extending acrofs y^e Brook to Two Trees marked and then Runing upon y^e East Side of John Scotts Lott into north field Rode marked on y^e westerly Side of Said Rode. Laid out February 24th 1734/5 by Jofiah Willard Benjamin Goodridge and Jonathan Hubbard Select men of Lunenburg. — — — — —

Granted y^e Sum of $\frac{5-8-0}{4}$ to pay Benj^a Goodridge for making Rates & Laying out High ways

Granted y^e Sum of 1-2-0 to pay John Grout for making Rates & Laying out Highwayes

Granted to Juſtice Hartwell 4 Sh. for Renewing Bounds with Groton Selectmen

Granted to Ephraim Pierce 4 Sh. for Renewing Bounds as aforeſ:ᵈ

Granted to Nathan Heywood 6 Sh. for yᵉ aforeſ:ᵈ Sarvice — — — —

Granted to Amos Robinson 1 = 5 = 0 to take Care of yᵉ meeting Houſe Church Baſon & Cloth and keep all Clean and in good order — for yᵉ year—1735 — — —

      Isaac Farnsworth *Town Clerk.*

[31] At a Legall meeting of yᵉ freeholders and other Inhabitants of yᵉ Town of Lunenburg Aſsembled March yᵉ 17ᵗʰ 1734/5

Voted & Choſe Coˡˡ Joſiah Willard Modderator

Granted yᵉ Sum of Fourty Pounds for Building of Stairs up into yᵉ Galleries in yᵉ meeting Houſe & for Building or making of Seats in the Galleries

Granted yᵉ Sum of Eight Pounds nine Shillings & Six pence to pay Mʳ Ephraim Wetherbe for what he hath Expended in building yᵉ meeting Houſe in Said Town over & above his Proportion.

Voted that Isaac Farnſworth be fully Impowered for and in behalf of yᵉ Town of Lunenburg to wait on yᵉ General Court with a Petition Praying for Direction and order to make Such grantees or owners of Houſe Lotts in Sᵈ Town who has not paid their part & proportion to build yᵉ meeting Houſe in Said Town forth with to pay yᵉ Same: or to use & take Such other method as he Shall think proper.

Voted that Edward Hartwell Esqʳ be Impowered for and in behalf of yᵉ Town to Take a Leaſe of Mʳ Ephraim Wetherbe of yᵉ Ground where yᵉ meeting Houſe Stands So Lond as a meeting Houſe for yᵉ Publick worſhip of God Shall Stand there

Voted that yᵉ Select men be a Comitte fully Impowered to make Due Proviſion and provide for a School in Said Town according to yᵉ beſt manner for yᵉ Towns Safety & Interſt.— —

  Atˢᵗ Isaac Farnsworth *Town Clerk* –

At a Legall meeting of ye freeholders and other Inhabitants of ye Town of Lunenburg Afsembled at ye Publick meeting Houfe in Said Town Sep.^tr ye 15.th 1735 —
Voted and Chofe Edward Hartwell Efq^r Modderator—
Voted & Chofe Jofiah Bayle & John Divel Tything men
Voted that ye Town wayes for ye Future be mended by a Town Rate
Voted & Granted ye Sum of Forty Pounds for ye mending of Town wayes for this prefent year.
Voted y^t any Inhabitant have Liberty to work out their proportion of ye Forty pounds before Grantend for ye mending of Town ways at Three Shillings Pr Diem a man: and alfo Three shillings p^r Diem for a pair of oxen & Cart.

ISAAC FARNSWORTH *Town Clerk* —

[32] At a Legall meeting of ye Freeholders and other Inhabitants of ye Town of Lunenburg Afsembled Jan^r 26,^th 1735/6
Voted and Chofe Co^ll Jofiah Willard modderator
Nothing done at Said meeting

At a Legall meeting of ye Freeholders and other Inhabitants of ye Town of Lunenburg Afsembled March ye 1th 1735/6
Voted and Chofe Isaac Farnfworth Modderator —
Voted and Chofe

Co^ll Jofiah Willard
Isaac Farnsworth } Select   Sworn as Afsefsors
Dr Sam^ll Johnfon } men
Mr John Heywood
Dr Ephraim Pierce

Isaac Farnfworth } Chofen Town Clerk & Sworn

Mr Benjamin Goodridge } Chofen Conftable & Sworn

Mr Jonathan Whitney } Chofen Conftable & Sworn

Major Jonathan Hubburd } Chofen Town Treafurer & Sworn

Isaac Farnſworth—Choſen Survayer of Hemp & flax
& Sworn

Benjᵃ Goodridge—Choſen Collector & Sworn

James Colburn ⎫ Choſen Tything men
David Pierce ⎭ Pierce Sworn

Jonathan Willard ⎫ Willard Sworn
Joſiah Bayle ⎭ Survayers of High wayes

John Gibſon ⎫
Joſhua Goodridge ⎭ Fence Viewers : Sworn

Eleazar Houghton ⎫ Houghton Sworn
Amos Robinson ⎭ Hogreaves

[33] Hilkiah Boynton ⎫ Field Drivers.
Benjamin Cory ⎭

Isaac Farnſworth ⎫ Sealer of Waits & meaſures

Voted. that Joseph Turner be Diſcharged of his Rates Two years past

Voted. that Ezekel Wyman take Care of yᵉ meeting Houſe & keep it Clean, take Care of yᵉ Church Baſon & Cloath for Baptiſm and Bring water therefor when Deſired for 25 Sh.

Granted yᵉ Sum of £-ˢ-ᵈ 1-10-0 to Isaac Farnſworth for Sarvice Done for Said Town

Granted yᵉ Sum of 0-12-0 to James Colburn for Service Done for yᵉ Town

Granted yᵉ Sum of 0-6-3 to Isaac Farnſworth for Laws Bought for yᵉ Town

Granted yᵉ Sum of-0-15-0 to Isaac Farnſworth to pay for mending yᵉ meeting Houſe glaſs.

Benjᵃ Goodridge ⎫ Choſen a Comᵗᵗᵉ to Seat yᵉ meet-
John Heywood ⎪ ing Houſe in Sᵈ Town upon their
Jonathan Whitney ⎬ own Coſt and Charge, according
Hilkiah Boynton ⎪ to yᵉ Inſtructions that Shall be
Nathaniel Harwood ⎭ Given them from yᵉ Town — —

Voted that yᵉ Inſtructions yᵉ Comᵗᵗᵉ appointed to Seat yᵉ meeting Houſe in Said Town Shall be according to yᵉ Inhabitants Pay or Rates accounting or Looking Back Four years —

2ly voted that yᵉ afore Sᵈ Comᵗᵗᵉ for Seeting yᵉ meeting Houſe in Said Town Do and perform yᵉ Buſineſs thereof on or before yᵉ first Day of April next.

Voted that all that part or Bredth of Northfield Rode So Called Runing through part of y⁰ Town Except Four Rods wide of Said Rode yet to Lye and Continue for a Rode &c be Discontinued from being a Rode or part of a Rode as afore fd

and also all that part or Bredth of yᵉ Rode from Jonathan Willards Runing to Andrew Flemings Except four Rods wide as aforefaid. and Except that part of Sd Rode that Lyes by yᵉ Buring place. yt to Lye and Contain its full Bredth as before : yᵉ other part of yᵉ Said Rode Excepting as before Excepted be hereby Discontinued from being a Rode or part of a Rode as afore fd ——

[34] Brought over.

Voted and Chofe Major Jonathan Hubbard Mr Jeremiah Ballard and Mr Ephraim Pierce to be a Comitte fully Impowered for and in behalf of yᵉ Town to make Sale of all yt part or Bredth of Northfield Rode So Called as within mentioned & Difcribed & Discontinued and alfo yᵉ Rode from Jonathan Willards Runing to Flemings in Said Town that is Difcontinued as within is Difcribed, to Such perfon or Perfons as Shall appear to buy yᵉ Same, and Give and Pafs Good and abfolute Deeds in yᵉ Law to yᵉ Purchafer thereof; and yᵉ aforefd Comttᵉ is hereby ordered and Directed upon Sale of Such Land, forth with upon Sale thereof to Return yᵉ money yᵉ Land Shall be Sold for into yᵉ Town Treafure — — — — — —

£12 0 0 Granted yᵉ Sum of Twelve Pounds to pay Jeremiah Norcrofs for a Town Rode Laid out acrofs his Land in Said Town

3 = Granted yᵉ Sum of £3-0-0 to pay Samll Davif for a Town Rode Laid out acrofs part of his Land in Said Town —

3 = 10 = 0 Granted yᵉ Sum of Three Pounds Ten Shillings to pay Amos Robinfon for Land taken for a Town Rode &c —

Voted that Major Jonathan Hubburd be Difcharged from his Collection yᵉ year Paft and that he be alowed Five Pounds out of his Collection which he hath in his hands for his Sarvice therein.

A Record of a Receipt Given By the Rev'd M'r Andrew
Gardner of Lunenburg in full Discharge to y'e Town for his
Settlement and Salary there.

Then Received of the Select men for the Town of
Lunenburg the Sum of three Hundred [——] Ninety and
four Pounds Twelve Shillings and three Pence which is in
full for my Settlement and Salary there. I Say Received p'r me
　　　　　　　　　　　　　　　Andrew Gardner Pastor

Lunenburg October y'e 27. 1732.

　　A True Record from y'e originall Att's
　　　　　　　　　　　Isaac Farnsworth Town Clerk

A Record of a Requeall from y'e Reverand M'r Andrew
Gardner To his Church in Lunenburg for his Dismission.

To the Brethren of y'e Church of Christ in Lunenburg
Beloved Brethren. I Cannot but Think from what I have
heard, and also from what I have observed of y'e transactions
and behaviour of this People Relating to me and my affairs
that there is not that affection born towards me that
there should be from a People to their Gospell minister,
or that there is where a People are likely duly to profit
under their minister, y'e consideration whereof has been
very Grevious and discouriging to me, and therefore
think it best to seperate. I do therefore propose a
Seperration and if effectual Care be Taken y't my dues
be honestly paid me, y'e first ministers lott with it's
appurtenances pitt upon Record and Attested, and a Sufficiant Pew at y'e Right hand of Going in at y'e Great doors
of y'e Meeting House I shall be free to be Dismissed from
my Pastoral Relation and official obligation to you as
Soon as it Can Regularly be performed.
from your Loving Pastor who wisheth you y'e Divine
Direction, and blessing, and desires your Prayers for
y'e Same to him.　　　Andrew Gardner Pastor

Lunenburg Sep't'r 18. 1730
according to Church warning then y'e Church met at y'e
meeting House and received his acquittance from his Pastoral Relation to us as Attest his hand Andrew Gardner Pastor
Lunenburg November y'e 3. 1732
A true Record from y'e originall　Isaac Farnsworth Town Clerk

Voted and Chofe Major Jonathan Hubbard Benj^a^ Goodridge and Isaac Farnfworth to be a Com^tte^ to Examine and Settle accounts with William Jones Collector for time past and James Colburn a Former Treasurer for Said Town

0-10-0 Granted ye Sum of Ten Shillings to pay Benj^a^ Goodridge for Sarvice Done

A Town or By Law. Whereas of Late years there hath been brought into our Town many Cattle and Horfes not properly belonging to ye Inhabitants thereof, and Turned out into ye woods in ye Town whereby ye feed has ben So Eaten up that ye Cattle & Horfses belonging to ye Inhabitants of ye Town are in Dainger of Suffering, if ye matter as afore f^d^ be not Speedaly Redrefsed.

For Redrefs whereof. — — — — — — — — — —

Voted that whatfoever Perfon or Perfons from and after ye first day of April next one Thousand Seven Hundred and thirty Six Shall bring take or Receive into our Town Directly or Indirectly by any wayes or means what Soever any Cattle or Horfes of Either Sort being not of their own property or Estate Shall for Every ox, Cow, Stear, or Heifer, [35] Hifer-Hors, mare, or Colt. brought in taken or Received as afore faid. forfit and pay to ye ufes of ye Poor of the Town ye Sum of Ten Shillings to be Recovered in manner as by Law is Directed &c. Except oxen for Labour or Cows that Give milk—them. to be taken into the Town by any of ye Inhabitants thereof for their ufe and Benifit. &c — — —

Voted and accepted of a Town way or Rode Laid out by order of ye Select men of ye Town of Lunenburg May ye 29th 1735 begining at ye South west Corner of Old Mr Whites Houfe Lot on which he now Dwells and So runing Between Said Whites Land and Elifha Smiths Land on Said Smiths Land Two Rods wide Down to ye Lower or Easterly End of ye Said Smiths Land then Runing on Said Smiths Land Two Rods wide as ye High way marks Directs Down to Mullipus Entervail marked on ye Southerly Side of ye Rode, and then Runing acrofs a narrow peice of Entervail of Aberaham Sanderson Two Rods wide marked on ye Easterly Side of ye Rode, to ye Corner of John Trulls Land and Said Sanderfons upland, and then Runing on Said Trulls Land and Sanderfons Land Two Rods wide a Rod on Each mans Land to Townfhend Line. &c

the Bufinefs on ye four Laft pages Done at ye Annual meeting in March 1735/6

Att: ISAAC FARNSWORTH *Town Clerk*

At a Legal meeting of ye freeholders and other Inhabitants of Said Town Afsembled April y^e 5th 1736

Voted & Chofe Co!! Jofiah Willard — Modderator

Granted y^e Sum of Twenty Pounds to make up Mr Stearns Sallery for y^s Prefent year with what is Laid in y^e penny acre Rate.

Granted to Justice Hartwell for his Sarvice y^e Last year & Laying out y^e minefterial Land £3 = 15 = 6

Granted to Jona^{th} Willard for Laying out of minifterial Land, 6 Sh.

Granted y^e Sum of £3—4—0 to Nathan Heywood for Survaying y^e minifterial Land. & Sarvice y^e year past

voted that y^e Com^{tte} appointed to Reccon with Lt Colburn & Mr Jones make their Report to y^e Select men.

voted & Chofe ye Select men for this prefent year a Com^{tte} to provide for ye keeping of a School in Said Town for ye Prefent year. & to Hire School Dames as they Shall se meet.—and otherwife as ye Law Requires —

[36] Brought over —

The Report and Return of ye Comitee Chofen to Seat ye meeting Houfe in Said Town is accepted as by ye Said Comittes Paper of Seeting, in ye Town Clerks office—may appear —

voted and Granted all that Room behind ye Seets in ye Front Gallery in ye meeting Houfe in Lunenburg to Jonathan Wood. Sam^ll Reed. Phinehas, Osgood. Ezekel Wyman. David, Page. Stephen Boynton. John Fitch. Jonathan Abbit, for to Build a Long Pew or Seet for them felves and wives for Ever. (To Set in) &c. Provided ye Perfons aforenamed Build ye Said Seat within Four months from ye Date of this Grant.

Att: ISAAC FARNSWORTH *Town Clerk—*

At a Legal meeting of ye freeholders and other Inhabitants of ye Town of Lunenburg Afsembled June ye 21th 1736

This Meeting void —

Voted and Chofe Edward Hartwell Esqr Modderator

voted y^t ye Committe Chofen to Sell a Part of northfield Rode So Called Runing Through part of ye Town be Difmift from y^r office and Truft in ye Premifes & alfo from Selling any part of ye Rode from Jonathan Willards Runing to Flemings &c.

Voted that

be a Committe fully Impowered for & in behalf of ye Town of Lunenburg

At a Legal meeting of ye freeholders and other Inhabitants of ye Town of Lunenburg Afsembled November ye 22^d 1736

Voted and Chofe Jofiah Willard Esqr modderator

Granted. ye Sum of Twenty Pounds for ye ufe of ye School in S^d Town — —

voted that Major Hubburds Houfe in Said Town be one of ye Places afsigned and appointed for ye Keeping of a School in Said Town.

voted that ye Houfe of Mr Benj^a Bellows in S^d Town be afsigned and appointed (for a Place) to Keep School in Said Town or on non procurement thereof: then Such other Place as near to ye meeting Houfe as may be in S^d Town as Shall be provided by ye Com^tte appointed for Providing for a School in f^d Town.

        ISAAC FARNSWORTH *Town Clerk*

[37] At a Legal meeting of ye freeholders and other Inhabitants of y^e Town of Lunenburg Regularly Afsembled March y^e 7th 1736/7

voted & Chofe Jofiah Willard Esqr Modderator

Jofiah Willard Esqr
Benj^a Goodridge
Ephraim Wetherbe   } Chosen Select men
John Grout
Major Jonathan Hubburd

Benj^a Goodridge } Chofen Town Clerk

Edward Hartwell Esq.r \
Benj.a Goodridge } Chofen Afsefsors \
John Grout

James Colburn \
Jacob Stiles } Chofen Conftables

Major Jonathan Hubburd } Chofen Town Treafurer

Major Jonathan Hubbard } Chofen Collector

Dr Sam.ll Johnfon } Chofen Survayor of hemp & flax

Dr Sam.ll Johnfon } Chofen Sealor of weights & meafures.

Benj.a Fofter \
John Divel } Chofen Survayors of High wayes \
Jeremiah Ballord

Noah Dodge \
Jonas Gillfon } Chofen Fence viewers

Jeremiah Ballord \
Daniel Auften } Chofen Tything men

Jacob Gould \
Moses Willard } Chofen Hogg reives

Voted that Hoggs Shall Run at Large in Said Town

Nathan Heywood \
John Scott } Chofen Field drivers \
Ezekiel Wyman

Ephraim Wetherbe Chofen to Sweep y.e meeting Houfe in S.d Town to Carry Water for Baptizen for y.e year Enfuing for £1-5-0 — — — — —

[38] Brought over.

Granted to Isaac Farnfworth £4 = $\frac{8-d}{4-10}$ for Sarvice done for S.d Town

Granted to John Heywood - 0-18-0 for Sarvice done for S.d Town

Granted to Dr Sam.ll Johnfon - 0-10-0 for Sarvice Done for S.d Town

Granted to Dr Ephraim Pierce - 0-08-0 for Sarvice Done for S.d Town.

Voted y.t That part of y.e Town Rode (Runing from north field Rode, So Called to William Jones,es) that Turns in to y.e Land of John Scots and Runs acrofs y.e north Eaft Corner of his now Dwelling House Lot be Discontinued and Ceafe to be a Rode or part thereof –

ye other part of Said Rode Remain a Rode notwithstanding. Runing on ye East Side of Said Scotts Land from north field Rode So Called over to Wm Jones Houfe

Voted that ye other affairs and Bufiness of this meeting as Contained in ye warrant for ye Sam be adjourned to ye Fourth Monday of May next.

ISAAC FARNSWORTH *Town Clerk*

At a meeting of the freeholders and other Inhabitants of the town of Lunenburg June the 27th 1737

Voted and Chofe Major Jonathan Hubburd Modderator

Voted that ye School be Moved to four places in Said town

Voted that John Heywood John Grout and Nathniel Harwood be a Committe to hire a School Master and to provide places for ye School to be keept in this prefent year

Voted that the Committe be paid for their time in spent in hireing a School Master

[39] At A meeting of the freeholders and other Inhabitants of the town of Lunenburg Afsembled July the 11th 1737

Voted and Chofe Mr Nathan Heywood Modderator

Voted that the School be keept in four places for the Space of one year Next Enfuing

Voted that Mr John Grout Mr Jacob Gould and Mr David Paree be a Committe fully Impowered to hire a lawfull School Mafter for the town of Lunenburg and to provide four Conveniant places for the School to be Keept in where it May Beft Conven the Inhabitants the time of keeping in Each place to be proportioned according to ye Number of Schoolers for the Space of one year Next Ensuing

Voted that Mr Samvel Page Edward Hartwell Efq^r Mr James Colburn Benj^a Goodridge and Mr John Heywood be a committe to Examine the Town tearsurers accounts and others that has any of yᵉ town money in their hands and Report thereof to the town and to Confer and agree with the Revend Mʳ David Stearns about yᵉ Quallification of yᵉ money in order for his Discharging the town of his Sallarys by Giveing Receipts in full

Voted and Granted the Sum of fifty pounds for yᵉ ufe of yᵉ School

Voted that this meeting be adjourned to the frift Monday of August Next at four of yᵉ Clock in yᵉ afternoon at yᵉ meeting houfe

August yᵉ first 1737 Mett by adjornment and upon hearing the report of the Committe Voted and Granted the Sum of fifteen pound to the Revᵈ Mʳ David Stearns an equeilent for the moneys not Beeing so Good as when he was fettled for yᵉ year 1736

Voted and Granted yᵉ Sum of ten pound to pay yᵉ towns Debts

Voted and Granted the Sum of fourty pound to Mend Highways withall

At a meeting of the freeholders and other Inhabitants of the town of Lunenburg Afsembled November the fourteenth 1737

Voted & Chofe Edward Hartwell Esqʳ Modderator

Voted and Granted the Sum of twenty five pounds to make up Mʳ Stearns Sallary for the year A. D 1737

Voted that the High way Rate be worked out at five Shillings ₽ Day from the first of May to the first of September and from the first of September to the first of may at three Shillings ₽ day and two Shillings ₽ day for a pair of oxen and one Shilling per Day for a Cart at any time of year

Recorded ₽ Benjᵃ Goodridge *Clerk*

[40] At a meeting of the freeholders and other Inhabitants of yᵉ Town of Lunenburg Regularly Afsembled March yᵉ Sixth A D 1737/8

Voted & Chofe Edward Hartwell Esqʳ Modderator

Edward Hartwell Esqr ⎫
Benj^a Goodridge ⎪
Mr Jeremiah Ballard ⎬ Chofen Selectmen
Mr Samvel Johnfon ⎪
Mr James Colburn ⎭

Benj^a Goodridge Chofen Town Clerk

Jeremiah Ballard ⎫
John Divol ⎬ Chofen Surveyors of highways
Benj^a Forftor ⎭

Maj Jonathan Hubburd Chofen town Treafurer

Eleazer Houghton ⎱
Jofiah Bayley ⎰ Chofen Conftables

Samvel Johnfon Chofen Surveyor of Hemp & flax

William Snow ⎱
Joseph Fuller ⎰ Chofen Tydingmen

Amos Robinfon ⎱
Benj^a Bellows ju ⎰ Chofen fence viewers

Jonathan Smith ⎱
John Fitch ⎰ Chofen Hogg reives

Samvel Johnfon Chofen Sealer of weights and meafures.

John Heywood Chofen Sealer of Leather

Jonathan wood ⎱
Samvel Cummings ⎰ Chofen feilder drivers

[41]

Voted and Granted to Edward Hartwell Esq	-0-12-0
Granted to Benj^a Goodridge	1- 6-0
Granted to Major Jonathan Hubburd	0-16-0
Granted to Mr Ephraim Wetherbe	0- 8-0
Granted to Mr Hezekiah Wetherbe	0 4-0
Granted to Mr John Grout	1- 4-0
Granted to Mr Benj^a Bellows ju^r for Sweeping the meeting houfe for ye year enfuing	1- 5-0

Voted that ye way from John Divols houfe Lott Between Jofhua Goodridges and John Fitchs Land to ye way that Comes Lancafter and gos to ye meeting in Lunenburg be Excepted and Confrimed a privet way as it was laid out and marked by ye General Courts Committe five rod wide

Voted that this meeting be adjorned till ye Last tusday in April Next at one of ye Clock in ye afternoon at ye meeting houfe

Voted that this meeting be further adjorned untill y⁽ᵉ⁾ third munday of May next at two of Clock in y⁽ᵉ⁾ afternoon at y⁽ᵉ⁾ meeting houſe this further adjornment was enterd In a rong place by a mistake.

At a meeting of the freeholders and other Inhabitants of the town of Lunenburg Aſsembled the twenty-fifth Day of April A D 1738
Voted and Choſe M⁽ʳ⁾ Samvel Johnſon Modderator
Voted that Hoggs run at Large in Said town for y⁽ᵉ⁾ preſent year
☞ Voted that thoſe perſons that Give ways through their land to the town Shall not pay any thing to the Buying of other ways in Said town untill Such time as the town has Bought So many as Shall amount to an Equal proportion of what Shall be Given Such ways to be Eſtimated by the Select men that lay out the Same and Excepted by the town in the town meeting when the ways are excepted
Voted and Granted the Sum of fourty pound to mend town ways withall

Recorded P⁽ʳ⁾ BENJ⁽ᵃ⁾ GOODRIDGE *Clerk*

[42] At a meeting of y⁽ᵉ⁾ freeholders and other Inhabitants of y⁽ᵉ⁾ Town of Lunenburg held by adjornment on y⁽ᵉ⁾ third Monday of May A D 1738 from an adjornment on y⁽ᵉ⁾ Laſt tuesday of April last past then Voted that a town way be Excepted from y⁽ᵉ⁾ way Between the meeting houſe and Co⁽ˡ⁾ Joſiah Willards houſe Begining at y⁽ᵉ⁾ End of the lane as it is now fenced and runs by the fence on y⁽ᵉ⁾ Southerly Side of Said Lane untill it comes to M⁽ʳ⁾ Seccartary Willards land two Rod wide. 108 Rod. then Runs acroſs M⁽ʳ⁾ Secar Willards Land one hundred and twenty Rod on Said Willards land and is marked on trees on y⁽ᵉ⁾ Southerly Side of Said way which is two Rod wide then truns into Jonathan Abbotts land and runs acroſs one Corner of Said Abbotts land fifty one Rod two Rod wide to a two Rod way Between the firſt and Second Range of Lotts in woburn farm and is marked upon trees on y⁽ᵉ⁾ Southerly Side and from Said way one hundred and Sev-

enty Six rod acrofs M[r] Ephraim Wetherbes Land to a two Rod way Between y[e] Second and Third Rang of lots in Woborn farm and from Said way on M[r] Jofeph Fullers land one hundred and twenty four Rod untill it Comes to M[r] Jacob Stileses land then runs Between Said fullers and Stiles land a rod on Each mans land twenty Six Rod till it Comes to y[e] pond and is marked on trees on y[e] Southerly Side then runs fifty two rod by the Side of y[e] pond on Said Stiles land then makes an Angle at a Certain tree marked and on y[e] Southerly Side of Said Stilese Barn one hundred & twenty two Rod till it Comes to a heep of Stones which is the Corner of Samvel Commins and John Haftings jun land and is marked on trees on the Southerly Side and is two rod wide then runs between Said Commins and Haftings land a rod on Each mans land

Alfo voted that a town way Be accepted Begining at a two rod way at or neer the line Between M[r] Seacretary Willards land and the land of Co[ll] Jofiah Willards runing across a corner of M[r] Secr. Willards land and runing acrofs the land of M[r] Jeremiah Ballard by the Eafterly Side of M[r] Secr Willards Land untill it comes neer the Brook then Crofsing the Brook neer the place where y[e] path now goes and leaving a corner of said Ballards land on the west Side of Said way untill it comes to a two rod way Between y[e] first and second rang of Lotts in woburn farm the Said way is two rod wide and markd on trees on the Eafterly Side

At a further adjornment of S[d] meeting on Monday the twenty third day of october A. D. 1738

Voted that a town way Be accepted from the End of the way that runs acrofs M[r] Ballards Land acrofs the land of M[r] Thomas Cartter and then acrofs the Land Belonging to one Woodard untill it Comes to the Land of Benjamin Goodridge and then runs acrofs Said Goodridge-s Land untill it Comes to his Houfe S[d] way is is two rod wide and marked on trees on y[e] Eafterly Side of Said way

[43] At a meeting of the freeholders and other Inhabitants of the the town of Lunenburg Aſsembled May the 22nd 1738

Voted and Chooſe Major Hubburd Moddrator

Voted that the Seats in the Gallary be moved forward so that there may be two Seats more Built Behind round the Gallary

Voted that the Seats be raised higher that are to be Built

Voted alſo that the alley Between ye Seats Below in the meeting House be made into Seats.

Voted that Mr Samvel Johnſon Mr Jeremiah Ballard Mr Samvel Page Be a Committe to lett out S^d work

Recorded p̃ BENJ GOODRIDGE *Clerk*

At a meeting of the freeholders and other Inhabitants of the town of Lunenburg Aſsembled Sept ye 12th 1738

Voted that ye town will provide a School maſter for the firſt six months and School Dames for ye other six months for the year enſuing

Voted that ye School be Keept in three places the firſt six months

Voted that ye School be Keept in Six places the laſt six months

Voted that Mr Jeremiah Ballard Mr John Heywood Mr John Grout Mr Samvel Page and Mr Jacob Gould be a Committe to Regulate ye Same

Voted that the Sum of Sixty pound be raiſed and granted to Support the School with all for ye year enſuing

Voted that Seven pound be Granted to Build ye Seats Behind In ye Gallary .

At a meeting of the freeholders and other Inhabitants of the town of Lunenburg aſsembled october ye 23th 1738

Voted and Chooſe Mr Samvel Johnson modderator

Voted y^t the Sum of fifteen pound Be Granted to ye Revd Mr David Stearns an addition to his Sallary for ye year 1737

Voted that ye Sum of fifteen pound be granted to y^e

Revd Mr David Stearns an addition to his Salary for the year 1738
Recorded p̃ Benj.^a Goodridge *Clerk*

[44] At a meeting of the freeholders and other Inhabitants of the town of Lunenburg Afsembled March the thirteenth A D 1738/9.
Voted and Choofe Major Jonathan Hubburd Modderator

Edward Hartwell Esqr
Benj.^a Goodridge
Mr Ephraim Wetherbe   Choofen Select men
Mr Samvel Johnfon   and
Mr John Heywood   Sworn Afsefsors

Benj.^a Goodridge Chofen town Clerk and Sworn
Major Jonathan Hubburd Chofen town Treafurer
Jonas Gillfon   } Chofen Constables and Benj.
Benj.^a Bellows Junr } Bellows Sworn.

Edward Hartwell Esqr
Samvel Johnson   Chofen Surveyers of
Benj.^a Goodridge   High ways
James Litch
Jeremiah Norcrofs
Samvel Page
                                                   Sworn
Samvel Johnson Chofen Sealer of waights & Meafures &
Eleazer Houghton Chofen Sealer of Leather
Ezekeil Wyman }
John Heywood } Chofen tying men
Jonathan Willard }
Jeremiah Norcrofs } Chofen fence veiwers
Ezekeil Wyman }
David Page   } Chosen Hogg reives
Jofiah Bayley Chofen Surveyer of Shingles

Voted that Samvel Johnson Benj.^a Goodridge and John Heywood be a Committe to fill up all the Vaccant Room in the meeting Houfe with Seats in ye Best manner that can be with Convenince

Voted that ye Sum of fourteen pound be Granted to Sattisfy the Coft occationed thereby

Voted Samvel Johnfon be a perfon apointed to buy a burying Cloth

[45] Voted that the Sum Seven pound ten Shillings be Granted to Buy a burying Cloth withall
Voted and Granted to Edward Hartwell Esqr ye Sum of -1-4-0
Voted and Granted to Benj^a Goodridge ye Sum of 1-0-0
Voted and Granted to James Colbourn ye Sum of 0-8-0
Voted and Granted to Samvel Johnſon ye Sum of 0-6-0
Voted and Granted to Jeremiah Ballard ye Sum of -0-8-0
Voted and Granted to Joſiah Baylay ye Sum of -0-3-6
Voted that ye Town way Be Discontinued where it went neer Thomas Harkneſs-s Land on flatt hill and that ye way Be allowed where it is now Laid out in Lieu thereof

Voted that a Town way be Excepted two Rods wide Begining at a heap of Stones and a Stake on the Eaſterly Side of the Road in Dea Ephraim Parces Land and runs acroſs a little Strip of Said parces Land two Rod wide to ye land of John Gibson and then runs two Rod wide through Said Gibſons land to ye Said Ephraim parces Second Diviſion and then runs through Said Parces 2^d Diviſion two Rods wide to Eleazer Houghton Second Diviſion and then runs through Said Houghton Second Diviſion to David Parces Land two Rod wide then through Said David Parces Land two Rod wide to ſaid Gibſons Second Diviſion and to David Carliles Land and all ye Said way is Deſcribed by marked trees which are on ye weſterly and Southerly Side of ye Said way.

And also there is another Short way of two Rod wide Laid out from this S^d way in ye Said Houghtons Second Deviſion to ye farm where Mr James Litch and Robert Ruſſell now Dwells upon for their Convenince to Bring them in to this Road as it is Deſcribed by marked trees

Voted that a bridle way of one rod wide be Excepted from Jethro Wheelers land on ye eaſt Side of Joſeph Dodges land that was to ye way by John Swans houſe

At a meeting of the freeholders and other Inhabitants of the town of Lunenburg afsembled May the Twenty first A D 1739

Voted and Choofe Mr John Heywood modderator

Voted that the Sum of fifty pound Be Granted to mend Highways withall to Be worked out in the way and manner of a former vote of this town

At a meeting of ye freeholders and Inhabitants of the town of Lunenburg afsembled augufl the fourtenth A. D 1739

Voted and Choofe Maj Jonathan Hubburd Modderator

Voted and Granted the Sum of five pound to bye Meafures withall and if f.^u Sum be to much the over plus to go into the treafury and if any be wanting to take it out of the treafury

these meetings Recorded ̄p̄ Benj.^a Goodridge *Clerk*

[46] At a legal meeting of the freeholders and other Inhabitants of the town of Lunenburg afsembled November the ninth one thousand Seven Hundred and thirty nine

Voted and Choofe Mr Samvel Johnfon Modderator

Voted and Chofe Mr Nathan Heywood and Mr Jonathan Smith to Enfpect the Killing of Deer at an unfeafonable time of the year as the Law Directs

Voted that the heads pay two third parts of the Afsfsments and the Eftates the other third part thereof

Voted and Chofe Mr William Jones to hire a lawfull School mafter for the town of Lunenburg for three months to Begin at Janvary next

Voted that the School be Keept at Mr Ephraim Parce's old Houfe six weeks

Voted that the School be Keept at the Houfe of Mr. John Jenifones or at Judge Dowses Houfe the other Six weeks

Voted and Granted the Sum of twenty pounds In Bills of the old tenor for the poor

Recored ̄p̄ Benj.^a Goodridge *Clerk*

106   *The Early Records of the Town of Lunenburg.*

[47] At a legal meeting of the freeholders and other Inhabitants of the town of Lunenburg Afsembled March the third 1739/40

Voted and Chofe Edward Hartwell Esqr modderator

Edward Hartwell Esqr
Mr Benjn Goodridge — Chofen
Mr John Grout — Select men
Mr Ephraim Wetherbe — and Sworn afsefsors
Capt Jonathan Bradftreet

Benj^a Bellows Junr Chofen Town Clark and Sworn

John Divol Chofen Conftable Benj^a Bellows Jur Sworn in his Rome

Jacob Gould Chofen Conftable & Sworn

Mr John Grout Chofen town Treafurer and Sworn

David Parce
Sam^{ll} Comings — Chofen Suveyers of
Ezekil Wyman — high Ways
John Scot — Parce Wyman & Comings Sworn
Hilkiah Boynton

Samvel Johnfon | Sealer of Waights and Meafurs

Benj^a Gould
Jonathan Abbot
Hezikah Wetherbe — hogg Reives & Sworn
John Gibfon

Daniel Aften
Jeremiah Norcrofs — Tything men

Elezer Houghton | Sealer of Leather

Jacob Stiles | Chofen
Jofeph fuller | fence viewers & Sworn

Benj^a Bellows Ju^r to profecute Such Perfons as Shall
Jonathan Smith   Kill Deer Contatry to Law and Sworn

Edward Hartwell Esqr be a committe to Examin the
Benj^a Goodridge   town Treafurers accompt and
Jacob Stiles   to Give him a discharge for
                          ye payments he has advanced
                          and make report thereof to y^e
                          town

[48] Voted that the Bridle way be discontinued that runs Acrofs Elezer Houghton Land

Voted that this meeting be Ajorned tell the third monday of May next at two of the Clock in ye afternoon at the meeting houfe in Lunenburg

    Ats. BENJ^A BELLOWS J^{UR} *town Clark*

at a metting march ye 3th 1740

Voted and Excepted of a way Laid out two Rod Wide through John Wyman and Ezekil Wymans Land a rod on Each mans one Hundred thirty four rod then runing Acrofs Ezekiel Wymans feild thirty Seven Rod then runing acrofs Stephen Boynton feild twenty rod to ye two Way betwen ye firft and Scond Rang of Lotts in Woborn fairm then Acrofs S^d two rod way thence between Holts Lotts one hundred and Sixty rod to ye miniftreal Land then acrofs ye miniftrail Land to ye Way by Amos Robingfon

    Attest BENJ^A BELLOWS J^{UR} *town Clerk*

May y^e 19th 1740 met by adjornment and upon Hearing the Report of the Commettee Chofen to Recken With Maj Jonathan Hubburd Town Treafurer and thay Report to the town that on the day above S^d that thay Reckned With him and find that he has Rec^{ed} of the towns money the Sum of £797-$\frac{sh}{17}$-$\frac{d}{1}$- out of Which he has Paid by Order the Sum of £795-$\frac{sh}{15}$-$\frac{d}{0}$ and thare Remains in his Hands the Sum of $\frac{£}{2}$-$\frac{sh}{2}$-$\frac{d}{1}$-

We find allfo in Conftable HarWoods hands the Sum of 2-6-3 and alfo in Conftable Whetneys hands y^e Sum of 1=11=6 and alfo in the hands of Maj^r Hubburd Collecter the Sum of 20=14=10 and in the hands of L^{tt} James Colburn Conftable the Sum of 8=9=2 and in the hand of Jacob Stiles Conftable y^e Sum of 1=17=8 and in the hands of Benj^a Goodridge Conftable the Sum of 16=5=9 and in the hands of Conftable Bayley the Sum of 21=9=3 and in the hands of Benj^a Bellows Conftable the Sum of 16=13=3

Voted and Granted to Maj Jonathan Hubburd for two years Collection $\frac{£}{10}$-$\frac{sh}{0}$-$\frac{d}{0}$.

Voted to M.[r] Benj.[a] Goodridge for one years Collection 5=0=0=

Voted to Edward Hartwell Esq.[r] for Sarvices done for the town 1=18=0

Voted to M[r] Benj.[a] Goodridge for Sarvis done the Town 1=18=0

Voted to M.[r] John Heywood for Sarvis done the Town 0=8=0

Voted to Benj.[a] Bellows Jun.[r] for Sarvis done the Town 3=0-0

Voted to Maj.[r] Jon[th] Hubburd for Being Treafurer 5 years 2=0=0

Voted that L.[tt] Ephraim Wetherbe & M[r] John Heywood & M.[r] Mofes Willard be a Commettee to Provide a Lawfull School & School Mafter for the this Prefent year.
Attest.

    BENJ.[a] BELLOWS JU.[r] *Town Clerk*

[49] At a Meeting
 of the freeholders and
 other Inhabitance of   } June y.[e] 2th 1740
 the town of Lunenburg

Voted and Chofe Maj.[r] Jonathan Hubburd modderator

Voted that thay Abate 1—7—11 of Benjamin Goodridge Rates Whoe was Conftable for the year 1736

Voted that thay Abate 1—17—8 of Jacob Stiles Rates Whoe was Conftable for y.[e] year 1736

Voted that thay Abate 4-16-3 of Joliah Bayley Rates Whoe was Conftable for the year 1738

Voted that thay Rafe thirty Pounds for Defraing the School

Voted to the Re[nd] M.[r] David Stearns the Sum of thirty Pounds to make up his Salery for the year 1739 & the year 1740

Granted fourty Pounds to mend Hieways with all

  Attest   BENJ.[a] BELLOWS JUN.[r] *town Clerk*

At A Meeting of the Freeholders and Other Inhabitance of the Town of Lunenburg held on the 29th of September A D 1740.

Voted and Chofe M̃ʳ Benjᵃ Goodridge Modrator

1ly Voted that thay Build two School Houfen in Said town one to be by Decon Ephraim Pearce the other to be on the Eaft Side of Mʳ Jeremiah Norcrofses as Near as may be to the Road—

2ly Voted that the School Houfen be twenty three feet in Lenth and Eighteen feet in Wedth and Seven feet Stud

3ly Voted that Mʳ William Jones & Mʳ Jeremiah Norcrofs & Mʳ Jofiah Bayley be a Committee to Buld the North End School Houfe

4ly that Decon Ephraim Pearce & Mʳ John Divol & Mʳ John Gipfon be a Committee to Buld the South End School Houfe

5ly Voted that the School Houfen be Borded and Shingled and the Loar floor be Laid Down and the Chimney be Built and the Houfen under Pend & A partion maid & doors maid and Hung

6ly Voted that thay Rafe one Hundred and twenty Pounds to Buld the the School Houfen & to Defray the Charge of the School

Attest. Benjᵃ Bellows Junᴿ *Town Clerk*

[50] At a Legual Meeting of the freeholders and other Inhabitance of the Town of Lunenburg Held on the firft monday of November A D 1740)

Voted and Chofe Majʳ Jonathan Hubbard Moddrator

firft Voted to Buld but one School Houfe in Said Town & that to Stand as near the Said meeting Houfe as the town Shall appoint and that all the Inhabitance of the Said town that Lives above two Miles diftance from the Place Whare the Said School Houfe Shall be Built the two miles all ways to be Eftimated as the Roads go and that all the Inhabitance that Live above two miles as above Said Shall from time to time & at all times hereafter have the Whole of each of thare Refpective Share Sum or Sums that thay Shall hereafter pay towards any School Rate or tax Whatfoever repaid to them again out of the Town Treasurie to Provide Schooling And School houfen for them Selves thay dividing into

Companies and making it to Appear to the Select men that thay have Laid out So much money for the End aforefaid and alfo that all the Schools Within the Said Town at the Same Time Shall be free for any of the Inhabitance to Send Whare they Pleafe and alfo that the town meeting Wich Was on ye twenty ninth day of Laft September and Every Article and Claufe therein mentioned Shall be repealed and annulled to all Intents and Porposes Whatfoever

2ly Voted that the School Houfe Be Set in the Corner of Mr Thomas Prentices Land Whare the Lain turns to y^e to Capt Bradftreets Houfe out of the Road

3ly Voted that thay Rafe one Hundred Pounds of the old tenner for the Use of Town

4ly Voted that the Town meeting be Warned by the Conftables going about and notifying the People by Word of mouth for the futer

5ly Voted that the Afsefsors Lay two thirds of the tax on the Heads and one third on the Eftates

6 Voted that the Town Treafurer Call in the Town Debts Dirict

Attest BENJ^A BELLOWS JUN^R *Town Clerk*

[51] At a legall meeting of the freeholders and other Inhabitants of the town of Lunenburg Afsembled March the Second A D 1740/1

Voted and Chofe Maj^r Jonathan Hubbird Modderator

Edward Hartwell Esqr ⎫
Benj^e Goodridge ⎪
Mr Thomas Prentice ⎬ Chofen Selectmen
Mr Nathaniel Harwood ⎪
Mr Samvel Johnfon ⎭

Benj^a Goodridge town Clerk & Sworn

Mr Thomas Prentice.-town Treafurer & Sworn

Mr John Gibfon ⎱
Mr William Jones ⎰ Chosen Conftables & Sworn

Mr Jofeph Fuller ⎫
Mr Mofes Mitchael ⎪
Mr Ephriam Parce ⎬ Chofen Surveyers of
Mr Amos Robbingfon ⎪ Highways
Mr Jacob Gould ⎭

Mr John Grout } Chosen tying men
Mr Jeremiah Norcross

Mr Benj^a Bellows junr Chosen Sealer of weights & Meafures & Sworn

Mr Jeremiah Norcrofs }
Mr John Jenifon } Chosen fence Viewers

Mr Eleazer Houghton Chosen Sealer of Leather

Mr William Snow }
Mr Abraham Sanderfon } Chosen Hogreves & Sworn
Mr Nathanael Page }

Mr Ezekiel Wyman }
Mr Samvel Reed } Deer officers

2ndly Voted that the town way be Excepted as it is Laid through Jofhua Goodridges Land In Exchange for ye town way where it was formerly laid through S^d land the new way to be four rod wide and is Defcribed by markt trees on the Eafterly Side thereof and and the former way is discontinued accordingly also

turn over

[52] Alfo Excepted a town way from Andrew Mitchaels Houfe two rod wide being one rod on william wallases Land and one rod on Mitchaels Land till it comes to the Highway Laid to Said Wallases Land.

Voted and Granted to Mr Samvel Johnfon ye Sum of 0-14-0

Voted and Granted to Mr John Grout the Sum of 0-8-0

Voted and Granted to Mr Ephriam Whetherbe ye Sum of 0-6-0

Voted and Granted to Edward Hartwell Esqr ye Sum of 1-2-0

Voted and Granted Capt Jonathan Bradftreet ye Sum of 0-4-0

Voted and Granted to Mr Benj^a Bellows jun^r ye Sum of 2-0-0

Voted and Granted to Benj^a Goodridge ye Sum of 1-0-0

Recorded ℗ Benj^a Goodridge *Clerk*

At a legall meeting of the freeholders and other Inhabitants of the town of Lunenburg Afsembled May the twenty fifth 1741
voted and Chofe maj^r Jonathan Hubbaird Modderartor.

1th Voted that the Select men provide a place to keep the School in

2^{ndly} Voted and Granted the Sum of Six pound to Build a pound withall

3^{rdly} Voted that major Hubburd and Mr Benj^a Bellows jr Be a committe to Lett out ye pound to be Built

4^{thly} Voted that Hoggs run at Large this prefent year

Recorded p̄ Benj^e Goodridge cler

[53] Lunenburg March 9th 1740
Then Received of Mr Thomas Prentice Town Treaf^r The Sum of one Hundred Sixty one Pounds Two Shillings and Three Pence which Is In full for my Salary for the years 1739 and 1740

Received p^r me David Stearns

Lunenburg

March 9th 1740 1 The Subfcriber Hereby acknowledge That I Have Received of the Town of Lunenburg The full of my Salary from the time of my Settling with them for ye work of ye miniftry To the Prefent Day

Received p^r me David Stearns

Received alfo the full of what was granted to me for Settlement

Received p^r me David Stearns

Janvary the fourth 1741 then the Selectmen and treafurer Reckned with Mr James Colbuorn Constable for the year 1737 and find that he has paid the whole of his Rates for said year

At the time Reckned with Benj^a Goodridge Conftable and Colector for ye year 1736 and Conftable and Colector for ye year 1736 and conftable for ye year A. D 1738 and find that he has paid the full of his Collections for both ye years aforefaid

[54] At a Legall meeting of the freeholders and other Inhabitants of the town of Lunenburg Afsembled the Eleventh Day of January A D 1741/2
1ly Voted and Chofe M.r Samvel Johnfon Moddrator for the Government of S.d meeting
2ndly Voted and Granted the Sum of Eighty pound In the old tennor for the ufe of the School
    Recorded p̄ Benj Goodridge
        town Clerk

At a Legual meeting of the freeholders and other Inhabitants of the town of Lunenburg afsembled March the 15th A D 1741/2
Voted and Chofe M.r John Grout moderator for the Government of the meeting

Benjamin Goodridge ⎫
M.r John Grout ⎪ Chofen Selectmen
Cap.t Jonathan Braudftreet ⎬ and Sworn
M.r John Heywood ⎪ Afsefsors
M.r William Jones ⎭

Benj.a Goodridge Chofen town Clerk and Sworn
M.r Thomas Prentice Chofen town treafurer and Sworn
M.r Joshua Goodridge ⎫
M.r Jonathan Page ⎬ Chofen Conftables and Sworn
M.r William Jones ⎫
M.r John Gibfon ⎪
M.r Benj.a Bellows Jun.r ⎬ Chofen Surveyers of Highways
M.r Thomas Brown ⎭

M.r Benj.a Bellows junr Chofen Sealer of weights and meafures
M.r Eleazer Houghton Chofen Sealer of Leather
M.r Jacob Stiles ⎫
M.r Jofeph Fuller ⎬ Chofen tying men
M.r Jeremiah Norcrofs ⎫
M.r Amos Robinfon ⎬ Chofen fence Viewers
M.r Jofeph Fuller ⎫
M.r Nathanel Page ⎬ Chofen Deer reves
[55] M.r David Goodridge ⎫
M.r Patrick White ⎬ Chofen Hogg reves and
    Sworn
Voted and Excepted of a town way as Reported of by the Seelect men begining in the former way in Joseph

Fullers Land and turning into Said Fullers feild by a white pine tree in his fence and runing through said Fullers Land in al one hundred and Seven rods two rods wide then through Ephraim Wetherbes Land one hundred and five rod then on Thomas Carters Land fifteen rod then through S^d Wetherbe-s Land ninty rod then through Said Carters Land twenty one rod to the road that Leads from Benjamin Goodridge = s to the meeting houfe in S^d town the said road is Laid out two rod wide and is Defcribed by certain marks and the Several owners of the said Land say they will freely give the Land for the said way whare they are Laid out purfuant to the town vote Concerning thofe that shall Give there Land to town ways &c provided the said town shall Discontinue ye former Road where this new road is Laid out in Leiu of that.

Voted and Excepted alfo of one other town way as Reported of by the Selectmen viz beginning at Mr William Clarks Land and runing through his Land Sixty two rod two rod wide through William Moffetts Land sixty nine rod two rod wide through Nathanel Harwood Land Seventy seven rod two rod wide through Mr Allens Land ninty rod two rod wide through Thomas Littles Land one hundred and fifty two rods two rod wide then through Mofes Willards Land by Groton line a few rods two rod wide and the said way is Defcribed by markt trees on the Right hand as the way Leads to Groton the above named William Clark Esqr Jeremiah Allen and Mofes Willard we have not seen but the other Gentlemen that owns the Land where the ways are Laid out are free and willing to give the Land for the Same perfuant to the vote of the town Concerning Highways &c

Alfo voted and Excepted of another town way as Reported of by the Selectmen viz Begining at the Houfe of Mr Hezekiah Wetherbe and runs ten Rod on S^d Wetherbe,s land as the Lane runs South on Land of Daniel Auftin Eighty two Rod Southerly by markt trees and on Common Land forty eight rod by markt trees on land of Jofeph Page one hundred and Eighty Rod by markt trees Eafterly and Southerly all which way is two rod wide

The Early Records of the Town of Lunenburg. 115

and is Given by the owner of the land according to the vote Concerning town ways &c

Voted that way Be Discontinued from the white pine tree where the new way turns into Mr Jofeph Fullers feild where it runs acorfs fullers Wetherbes Abbotts and Willards Land till it comes into ye road between Capt Broadftreets caufeway and ye corner of Jonathan Hubburd ju land &c

Turn over

[56] Voted and Granted to Mr Thomas Prentice 1-16-0

Voted and Granted to Mr Samvel Johnfon 1-6-0
Voted and Granted to Benj^a Goodridge 2-18-0
Voted and Granted Mr Nathanel Harwood 0-16-0
Voted and Granted to Edward Hartwell Esqr 2-16-10
Voted that the Selectmen provid a School Mafter and places to Keep School in for the year enfuing

Recorded p^r BENJ^a GOODRIDGE *town Cler*

At a legual meeting of the freeholders and other Inhabitants of the town of Lunenburg Afsembled May the ninteenth A. D. 1742

Voted and Chofe Mr John Heywood modderrator

Voted and Granted the Sum of twenty pounds to mend High ways withall

Voted that men be allowed two Shillings per Day from this Day to the Laft Day of September for this prefent year and one shilling and sixpence from then to the first day of March next and that nine pence be allowed for a pair of oxen a day and three pence for a Cart

Voted that the Repairing of the meeting houfe be Committed to Mr Samvel Johnfon and that he Bring an account of the Coft thereof to the next town meeting

Voted that Swine go at Large this prefent year

Recored p^r BENJ GOODRIDGE *Cler*

At a legual meeting of the freeholders and other Inhabitants of the town of Lunenburg Afsembled September the 13th A. D. 1742

Voted and Chofe Major Jonathan Hubburd Modderrator

Voted and Granted John Jenifon 1 = 15 = 0 old tennour

Voted and Granted forty two pound ten shillings for the Rev⁴ Mʳ Stearns es Sallary for yᵉ year 1742

Voted and Granted yᵉ Sum of three pound fifteen Shillings to the Rev⁴ Mʳ Stearns to make good his Sallary for the year 1741

Voted and Granted the Sum of two pound ten Shillings to Benjᵃ Goodridge and John Grout to pay Capᵗ Stevens for Service done.

Recorded ᵖᵉ Benjᵃ Goodridge *Clerk*

[57] At Legual meeting of the freeholders and other Inhabitants of the town of Lunenburg Afsembled Janvary the thirty first 1742/3

Voted and Chofe Mʳ John Heywood Modderator

Voteded and granted to Mʳ Nathanael Page the Sum of five Shillings for Building the pound in Sᵈ town

Voted and Granted to Mʳ Samvel Johnfon for repairing the meeting house the Sum of eight Shillings

Voted and Granted to Mʳ Benjamin Bellows juʳ for a lock and key for the pound one Shilling and eight pence

To Mʳ Thomas Prentice Town Treafurer for the town of Lunenburg or his Succefsor in faid office Sʳ this may Certify to you that we have afsefsed the Sum of Sixty pound seven Shillings and nine pence on the Inhabitants of the town of Lunenburg and have Delivered one Lift to Joshua Goodridge Constable of thirty three pounds and three pence and to Jonathan Page Conftable a Lift of twenty Eight pound Seven Shilling and Six pence which Sums you are to Demand and Receive and to pay out as follows (viz)

To the Rev⁴ Mʳ David Stearns the Sum of
$\frac{c}{42}$ = 10-0 for his Sallary for this prefent year
and three pound fifteen Shillings to make
the money Good for the year paft — —   3-15-0

To Thomas Prentice for Being an afsefsor for yᵉ
year seventeen hundred and forty one —   0- 9-0

To Nathaniel Harwood for Ditto   0- 4-0
To Samvel Johnson for Ditto   0- 6-0
To Benj^a Goodridge for Ditto   0-14-6
To Edward Hartwell Esqr for Ditto   0-14-2½
To John Jenifon for taking care of ye meeting
  house   0- 8-9
To Nathanael Page for building ye pound in
  Lunenburg   0- 5-0
To Samvel Johnfon for repairing the meeting
  houfe   0- 8-0
To Benjamin Bellows J^r for a lock and key for
  ye pound   0- 1-8
To Samvel Davis for making two Jury Boxes   0- 0 4½
To Benj^a Goodridge and John Grout to pay to
  Capt Stevens   2-10-0

[58] At a legal Meeting of the freeholders and other Inhabitants of the town of Lunenburg Afsembled March ye Seventh A D 1742/3
Voted and Chofe Mr Thomas Prentice Moddr.

Edward Hartwell Esqr ⎫ Were
Benj^a Goodridge   ⎪ Chofen
Capt Jonathan Willard ⎬ Select
Mr John Grout   ⎪ men
Capt Jonathan Bradftreet ⎭

Benj^a Goodridge Chofen Town Clerk & Sworn
Mr Thomas Prentice Chofen Town Treafurer & Sworn
Mr Jonathan Page   ⎫
Mr Jonathan Hubburd jr ⎬ Chofen Conftables and Sworn

Mr Ezekeil Wyman   ⎫
Mr David Paree   ⎪
Mr John Martin   ⎪ Chofen Surveyers
Edward Hartwell Esqr ⎬ of High ways
Mr Eleazer Tarbal   ⎪ and Sworn
Mr Jonathan Smith   ⎪
Mr William Snow   ⎪
Mr Thomas Brown   ⎭

                              meafures Sworn
Mr Benj^a Bellows junr Chofen Sealer of waits &
Mr Solomon Stewart ⎫
Mr Samvel Comings ⎬ Chofen Tyding men
Mr John Grout   ⎫
Mr Samvel Davis   ⎬ Chofen fence veiwers & Sworn

Mr Joshua Goodridge \
Mr Jacob Gould ⎰ Chofen Deer rives & Sworn \
Mr Jofeph Fuller ⎱ \
Mr Thomas Brown ⎰ Chofen Hogg reves and Sworn \
Mr Nathan Heywood ⎱ \
Mr William Jones ⎰ Chofen to take of fire & Sworn

[59] Voted that Mr Thomas Prentice Mr William Jones and Mr Jeremiah Norcrofs be a Committe to provide a school mafter and to appoint and provide places to Keep the School in for y^e year Enfuing.

Voted and Granted the Sum of twenty five pound for the ufe of the school.

Voted and Granted the Sum of two pound ten shillings for Deacon Johnfon to repair the meeting houfe withall

Voted and Granted to Mr Benj^a Bellows for Service done for the town ten Shillings

Voted and Granted to Mr John Grout Six fhillings

Granted to Benj^a Goodridge Eleven fhillings

Granted Mr John Heywood Six Shillings

Granted to Capt. Jonathan Bradftreet three Shillings

Granted to Mr William Jones three fhillings

Granted to Mr Jonathan Page ten pence

Granted to Mr Thomas Prentice five pence half peny

Voted and Excepted of a town way Laid out by ye Selectmen Begining at Benjamin Goulds northwest corner on the South fide of north field Road and so runs about weft by John Fisks fence Being on ye South Side and then on Joseph Page^s fence till it comes to the corner of Bellows s meddow to a Black oak Stump then to a heap of Stones near ye meddow then to a great Stone about five rod South weft from the houfe where William Cannada lives then to a Black oak tree markt d then to another Black oak tree markt then to a white oak tree markt on or about ye head of houfe Lott No 6 in S^d town and then about weft till it comes over ye Stone Bridge into ye old way ye faid way to be four rod wide on ye north Side of S^d Marks

Voted and Excepted of a town way Laid out by acommitee appionted Begining about the Eaft Side of

Abraham Sanderfons Land at the Eaft end of ye Line Eaft of S^d Sanderfons houfe & So runing by S^d Sanderfons houfe & then to a heap of Stones then by y^e north fide of y^e Swamp to a white oak markt and then by other trees markt till it comes to Mulpus and then over Mulpus by markt trees till it comes to y^e other way at Abel Platts s Corner S^d way to be two rod wide the markt trees and other marks are on the north and weft sides

Recorded P$^)$
BENJ^A GOODRIDGE town Cler

[60] Att a Legual meeting of the freeholders and other Inhabitants of the town of Lunenburg afsembled auguft the 9th 1743

Voted and Chofe maj^r Jonathan Hubbard moderator for f^d meeting

Voted that a committe be chofen to mark out away to the weft Line of our town from the way already Excepted to the weft end of the wyman Land

Voted that Edward Hartwell Efq^r Mr Ephraim Wetherbe and Mr Jonathan Page be a Committe for the purpofe aforefaid

Voted that Mr Ephraim Wetherbe with a Eleven Hands with him go on Monday next to Clear faid way and that Mr Wetherbe overfee faid work

Voted that the hands abovefaid have two Shillings and Six pence P$^)$ Day each man

Voted and chofe Edward Hartwell Efq^r and Mr John Grout to make Reply to Coll$^{\underline{e}}$ Berry^s Complaint at Worcefter Court for our not having away to Dorchester Cannada or to the weft Line of our town

Recorded P$^)$ BENJ^A GOODRIDGE Cler

Att a legual meeting of the freeholders and other Inhabitants of the town of Lunenburg Afsembled September y^e 12th A D 1743

Voted and Chofe Maj^r Jonathan Hubbard modderartor

Voted that they will Chufe a Committe

Voted and Choofe Maj^r Jonathan Hubburd Mr Nathan Heywood and Capt Jonathan Bradftreet a committe to Lay out and mark away to the Weft Line of our town in order to anfwer the Requeft of the Honorable Thomas Berry Efq^r in Behalf of Ipswich Cannada and to accomodate Dorchefter Cannada and the new towns above us and make return to the town as foon as may Be where they have Laid it —— —— —— ——

[61] Voted and Granted the Sum of twenty pounds to be workt out at faid way at three Shillings ꝑ Day & if any man Dos not work when warned he Shall pay his money and if any over plus be to be workt out as other ways

Voted & Granted to the Revd Mr David Stearns fo much as will make his Sallary fifty pounds in Bills of the Last Emifsion for this prefent year

Voted and Granted ye Sum of ten pound to make Good any Deficiences in the Treafurey

Voted and Granted to Mr John Grout the Sum of four fhillings for Service Done for ye town

Recorded ꝑ BENJ^A GOODRIDGE *Clerk*

At a Legal Meeting of the freeholders and other Inhabitants of the town of Lunenburg Afsembled September ye twenty feventh A. D 1743

Voted and Choofe Mr Hilkiah Boynton Modderator

Voted that ye Report of ye Committee Be Excepted which is as follows

LUNENBURG September ye 17th 1743 We the Subscribers being appointed by faid town to Lay out a Highway from Some part or particular place of Some Road already Laid out in Said town to the weft Line thereof &c In purfuance whereof we have made Search and viewed the Land where we thought it moft probable faid Highway could be made and our opinions are that to Begin at the Road Laid out Between Ezekiel and John Wymans Land and fo to Mr David Pages and then in or near the Road where people now pafs to Dorchefter Cannada about a mile and a half then turn out of Said old Road to y^e

Right hand by a Black oak tree marked and going by or near trees marked till it comes to faid old Road again near Uptons Land there corfsing faid old Road and going over faid Uptons Land and
turn over

[62] And then by trees marked about three Quarters of a mile and coming into faid old Road again and Continuing in faid old Road to the Line of Lunenburg will be much the beft way much the Cheapeft made and much the eafieft to maintain and will beft accomodate the new towns which we are to have particular Regard to all thing Confidered

Voted that the faid   Jonathan Hubbard
way be two Rod wide   Nathan Heywood   *Com*^{tte}
                        Jonathan Bradftreet

Recorded $\bar{\text{p}}$ Benj^a Goodridge *Clerk*

At a meeting of the freeholders and other Inhabitants of the town of Lunenburg Afsembled March y^e fifth A D 1743/4

Voted and Chofe Maj^r Jonathan Hubbard Modderator

Voted and Chofe
Maj^r Jonathan Hubbard
Mr Jonathan Wood
Mr Joshua Goodridge   Selectmen
Mr Hilkiah Boynton
Mr John Grout

Benj^a Goodridge Chofen town Clerk and Sworn
Mr Thomas Prentice chosen Treafurer and Sworn
Mr David Parce
Mr William Page } Chofen Conftables   Voted that Mr Benjamin Bellows jun be Excepted Constable in the rome of faid Parce and Page

Mr John Bufs
Mr Benj^a Bellows jun } Surveyers of high ways
Mr Joseph Fuller

[63]   Mr Abraham Sanderfon
       Mr Jofiah Dodge
       Mr Jacob Gould   Chofen Surveyers of
       Mr Jonathan Page   high ways and Sworn
       Mr Nathanael Page

Mr Benjamin Bellows jun Sealer of weights and meaſures

Mr Eleazer Houghton Sealer of Leather
Mr Benjamin Bellows ⎫
Mr Jeremiah Norcrofs ⎭ fence viewers
Mr Solomon Stwart ⎫
Mr Jonathan Abbott ⎭ Deer reves and Sworn
Mr William Snow ⎫
Mr John Gibſon ⎭ tying men
Mr John Fisk ⎫
Mr Jacob Gould ⎭ Hogg reves
Mr William Jones ⎫
Mr John Fitch ⎭ Choſen to take care of fire

Voted that Edward Hartwell Eſq^r Capt Jonathan Bradſtreet and Mr Benjamin Bellows jun be a Com^tte to take care of the School and to provide a School Maſter for ye year enſuing

Voted that Mr Hilkiah Boynton Capt Jonathan Bradſtreet and Mr John Grout Be a Committee to agree with Major Jonathan Hubbard aboute Exchanging apeice of the miniſtreal Land with ſaid Hubbard for apeice of his Land and to Joyn with Mr Stearns in Giving a Deed of Exchange if they think proper and as they shall Judge Beſt

Voted that Mr John Jeniſon take care of ye meeting houſe ye year enſuing and granted to S^d Jeniſon for ſd service   0-10-0
Voted and Granted Maj^r Hubbard   0- 5-0
Voted & Granted to Mr Nathan Heywood   0- 5-0
Voted and Granted to Capt Bradſtreet   0 5-0

turn over

[64] Voted and Granted to Edward Hartwell Eſq^r   0- 2-6
Voted and Granted to Mr Ephraim Wetherbe   0- 2-6
Voted and Granted to Mr Jonathan Page   0- 2-6
Voted & Granted to Edward Hartwell Eſq^r   0- 9-0
Voted & Granted to Mr John Grout   0- 4-0
Voted & Granted to Capt Bradſtreet   0- 1-6
Voted & Granted to Capt Willard   0- 1-6
Voted & Granted to Benjn Goodridge   0-16-6
Voted & Granted to Mr Benj Bellows   0-12-6

Voted & Granted to Mr Thomas Prentice   0- 0-9

Voted that a town way be Excepted of from Mr Jofeph Fullers Land to ye Great Streem of ye north Branch as Laid out by the Committee appointed Begining at faid Fullers Land and Runing through Mr Jacob Stiles Land one hundred and twenty Rod two Rod wide and marked on ye north Side and then Runing Between Mr Samvel Cumingses & Mr John Martins Land twenty Rod and then through Said Cumingses Land half a mild two Rod wide & marked on the north Side and then on Land of Juftice Hartwell fourteen Rod and then on Land of Mr Prescut Eighty Seven Rod and then on Land of Mr Jacob Stiles forty Rod and then a few Rods on Common Land and then on Land of David Goodridge Eighty Rod all which way is two Rod wide and markt as aforefaid and Laid out by

                     Jofeph Fuller
                     John Martin
                     Jacob Stiles   Com^{ttee}
                     Samvel Cumings

Voted that ye way through Mr Jacob Stiles Land where it was formerly Laid out Be Discontinued from Being a way any Longer

Voted that a town way be Excepted Between Mr Ephraim Wetherbes and Mr Thomas Carters Land one rod on Each man's Land

Voted that ye town way as it was formerly Laid out on Mr Wetherbes Land Be Discontinued from Being away any Longer

[65] Voted that the way be Discontinued from Benjamin Bellows Land at ye Corner of ye meddow to John Fisks Corner all But two Rod wide next to fowlers Land to four rod upon faid Fisks Land and that ye way be Excepted as it Lyes by Jofeph Pages Barn provided Said Page make the way agood paffable way by Cafaring so that it may be Good pafsing for teams to the Exceptence of ye Selectmen By the firft of July next

               Recorded 𝔭

                     BENJ^A GOODRIDGE *Clerk*

At a meeting of the freeholders and other Inhabitants of the town of Lunenburg Aſsembled September the Seventeenth A D 1744

Voted and Granted to the Revd Mr David Stearns the Sum of fifty one pound five Shilling In Bills of the Last Emmiſtion for his Sallary this preſent year

Voted and Granted the Sum of twenty five pound for the uſe of the School

Voted that Maj^r Jonathan Hubbard Edward Hartwell Eſq^r and Mr Jonathan Page be a Committe to Reckon with the town treaſurer and to Give him a Diſcharge for So much as he has paid on the towns account

[66] At a meeting of the freeholders and other Inhabitants of the Town of Lunenburg Aſsembled March the fourth A D 1744/5

Voted and Choſe Mr Hilkiah Boynton Moddr of Said meeting

Edward Hartwell Eſq^r
Benj^a Goodridge
Mr John Grout } Choſen Selectmen
Capt Jonathan Willard and
Mr Eleazer Tarbal

Benj^a Goodridge Choſen town Clerk & Sworn

Thomas Prentice Eſq^r Choſen town treaſurer

Mr Samvel Cumings
Mr Jonathan Wood } Choſen Constables and Sworn

M^r Joſiah Dodge
Mr Joseph Fuller
Mr Samvel Davis   } Choſen Surveyers
Mr Jacob Gould   of Highways
Mr John Wyman   and Sworn
Mr Ezekiel Wyman
Mr Nathanael Harwood

Mr Thomas Brown
Mr Nathanael Harwood
Mr John Grout   } Choſen fence veiwers
Mr Samvel Davis   and Sworn

Mr Thomas Brown } Choſen Deer reives
Mr Joseph Fuller   and Sworn

Mr Ezekiel Wyman
Mr John Martin } Chosen tying men

[67] Mr John Grifin } choſen Hogg reives
Mr Stephen Boynton   and Sworn

Mr John Jenifon Chofen Sealer of Leather and Sworn
Mr Benjamin Bellows jr } Chofen Sealer of waits and meafures and Sworn
Mr Solomon Stewart }
Mr Benjamin Gary } Chofen to take care of fire
Maj^r Jonathan Hubburd Chofen Surveyer of Shingles and Sworn
Mr Nathanael Harwood }
Mr Samvel Larrabee } Chosen to take care of fire

Voted that Major Jonathan Hubburd Mr Nathan Heywood & Mr William Jones be a Committe to provide the town with a School Mafter for the year enfuing

Voted and Granted unto Mr Jacob Gould the Sum of Eleven pound Seventeen Shillings and nine pence for his Extraordinary Coft at the Courts with Andrew Flemin provided he Settle accounts with the town

Voted and Granted unto Mr John Grout y^e sum of	1 -	0 -	0
Voted & Granted unto Mr Hilkiah Boynton	0 -	3 -	6
Voted & Granted unto Mr Jofhua Goodridge	0 -	1 -	6
Voted and Granted to Mr Benj^a Bellows ju	0 -	7 -	0
Voted & Granted to Maj^r Hubburd y^e Sum of	0 -	7 -	6
Voted & Granted Jonathan Hubburd junr	0 =	11 =	3
Voted & Granted to Mr Samvel Johnfon	0 -	1 -	6

[68] An acount of way Excepted at S^d meeting Namly A two Rod way Begining at Dupees Land and Runing upon walkers and Carltons Land 53 Rod and then upon Walkers and Hazeltines Land 22 Rod and then Begining at Mr Stewarts Land and Runs Between Walkers and Woods Land to the faid Road 93 Rods & then Runing all on Hazeltines Land 44 rod and then all on Woods Land 66 Rods and Between Mr Stones and Mr Fullers Land 193 Rod unto the two Rod way and about ten Rod a crofs Mr Wetherbes Land and then Between Mr Wetherbes and Mr William Stearns Land 164 Rods and then through Mr Benjamin Forfters Land 55 Rods all markt on the North Side and then acrofs Mr Jenifons Land to the Road 124 Rods markt on ye South fide

Laid out by us   Hilkiah Boynton } *Select*
Jonathan Wood } *men of*
Jofhua Goodridge } *Lunenburg*

Alſo a two Rod way Laid out By us the Subſcribers Begining at the Road that comes from Hezekiah Wetherbes and Runs upon Mr Benj^a Bellows and Daniel Astins Land and Between the ſaid Auſtin and John Fifks Land and acroſs ſome common Land and acroſs the miniſtreal Land and acroſs Mr Preſcotts Land and acroſs Dunsmores Land and acroſs Mr Noah Dodges Land to Groton Line meeting with thier Road all markt on the north Side —

  Laid out by   Joſua Goodridge
           Hilkiah Boynton

Voted that this way be Eccepted provided the Land be Givin

[69] And alſo a two Rod way Being origainally Left for away by Mr Israel Reed and others purchaſers of Woborn farm Begining at or near John Divols Swamp Between Mr Dodges and Benj^a Goodridges Land & So on a ſtrait Line Between the firſt and ſecond Ranges of Lotts in ſaid farm till it comes John Hills Land alſo another two Rod way Left By ſaid Reed and others as aforeſaid Begining at Jonathan Pages Land Between William Holts and John Wymans Land and So Between the Second and third Ranges of Lotts till it comes to Unchechewalunk pond Between the Land of Thomas Carter and Joſeph Fuller

  Laid out by us   Joseph Fuller }
          Samvel Reed } Com^tte

And alſo away Laid out from the north River Begining at Said River by markes on the weſt ſide ſ^d way being two Rod wide and So runing through David Goodridges Land and then through Eleazer Houghtons Land and then through Sergants Land then though Juſtices Harrises Land & So Coming to the old path at the foot of a great hill and So runing in the old Path to Leominſter Line and So Continuing in the old path up to James Pools

     Laid out by   Jonathan Hubburd } Com^tte
           Hilkiah Boynton }

All which ways are Excepted as above Deſcribed and Recorded   Pr BENJ^A GOODRIDGE
                town Clerk

[70] Att a meeting of the freeholders and other Inhabitants of the Town of Lunenburg Afsembled Sept the ninth A D 1745

Voted and Choofe Maj^r Jonathan Hubburd Moderator of faid meeting

Voted and Granted the Sum of fifty two pounds ten Shillings to the Rev Mr David Stearns for his Sallary for the present year ——

Voted and Granted the Sum of twenty five pound for the ufe of the School in Said town

Voted that the men that Live within the Bounds of Major Hartwells Company Build the Bridge over the North Branch in way as it goes to David Goodridges and the Bridge over ye said north Branch in the way that goes to David Pages

And that the men that Live within the Bounds of Capt Willards Company Build the Bridge over Mullepus in the way by or neer Hezekiah Wetherbes and the Bridge over Said Mullepus in the way that goes to Townfhend Below the widdow Whites mill

Recorded p̄ BENJ GOODRIDGE Cler

At A meeting of the freeholders and other Inhabitants of the Town of Lunenburg Afsembled March the third A D 1745/6

Voted and Chofe Thomas Prentice Efq^r Modderator

Voted and Chofe

Edward Hartwell Efq^r \}
Capt Jonathan Willard
Benj Goodridge   } Selectmen
Mr Jacob Gould
Mr John Grout

[71] Benjn Goodridge Chofen town Clerk & Sworn

Thomas Prentice Chofen Town Treafurer

Mr Thomas Brown \}
Mr Eleazer Tarbal } Chofen Conftables & Sworn

Mr Samvel Johnson \}
Mr Arington Gibfon
Mr Joseph Fuller   } Chofen Surveyers of
Mr Jofiah Dodge   Highway & Sworn
Mr David Page   }

M{r} Ezekiel Wyman \
M{r} Thomas Carter } tyding men \
M{r} Jofiah Bayley \
M{r} John Jenifon } Chofen fence viewers & Sworn \
M{r} Thomas Carter Chofen Sealer of Leather \
Mr Benj Bellows jun Chofen Sealer of weights & meafures

M{r} Jonathan Abbot \
M{r} Benj Gary \
M{r} Thomas Little } Chofen Hogg reves \
M{r} Obediah Walker \
Mr Afael Hartwell

M{r} Philip Goodridge \
Mr Samvel Davis } Chofen Deer reves

M{r} David Goodridge \
Mr Jofeph Wood } Chofen to take care of fire

M{r} Jacob Gould \
M{r} Thomas Brown \
M{r} Ezekiel Wyman } Chofen Feild Drivers \
Mr Joseph Fuller

[72] Voted and Chofe \
Benj Goodridge \
Edward Hartwell Efq{r} } Afsefsors \
Capt Jonathan Willard

Voted and Granted the Sum of twenty five pound in Bills of the Laft Emifion for the ufe of the School

Voted & Granted to Capt Willard	0- 7-6
Voted & Granted to Capt Willard	0- 4-6
Voted & Granted Mr Jofiah Dodge	0-10-0
Voted & Granted to Mr John Grout	1- 0-0
Voted & Granted to Benj Goodridge	0- 9-0
Voted & Granted to Mr John Heywood	0- 1-6
Voted & Granted to Mr Eleazer Tarbal	0- 4-6
Voted & Granted to Juftice Prentice	0- 1-6

Voted that a town way Be Excepted as Laid out by the Selectmen and Reported to the town Begining at the Bridge over Pearl hill Brook and runs acrofs Collonel Downe Land near Hutchins Celler (so called) to a white oak markt then to a pitch pine markt then to another pitch pine tree markt then to a white oak tree markt then by two yellow oak trees markt then to a white oak tree markt Near Deacon Bancrofts Land then through faid Bancrofts Land by trees markt till it comes to the Line Between Benjamin Garys and Timothy Bancrofts Land Said way to Be two Rod wide on ye Southerly Side of Said marks then runs a rod on each Side of ye Line Between [73] Said Gary & Bancroft till it comes to the top of the Hill Between their Houfes and then turns northward to a white oak tree markt then to a Stub with a heap of Stones then to a Gray oak markt then to a Chefnut tree markt then to a yellow oak tree markt on faid Garys Land then to a maple tree markt on John Mansfeilds Land then to a Chefnut tree on the Line Between faid Mansfeilds and John Peirces Land faid way to be two Rod wide on the fouthwefterly fide of faid marks and faid Mansfeild Gary and Bancrofts Gives their Lands for faid way —— ——

Recorded p̄ BENJ GOODRIDGE *Clerk*

At ameeting of the freeholders and other Inhabitants of the town of Lunenburg Afsembled may ye twentieth A D 1746

Voted and Chofe Maj^r Jonathan Hubburd Modderator

Voted and Chofe Mr Nathan Heywood Mr Jonathan Wood Mr Jacob Stiles Major Jonathan Hubburd Mr Eleazer Tarbal a Committe to provide a fchool Mafter for the year Enfuing and to move the fchool as they think Beft

Voted that Mr John Grout Mr John Heywood and Benj Goodridge Be a committe to Reckon with the Treafurer or Treafurers of ye twon and to Report thereon to ye next town meeting

Voted that Hoggs go at Larege the prefent year

Recorded p̄ BENJ GOODRIDGE *Clerk*

[74] At a Legual Meeting of the freeholders and other Inhabitants of the town of Lunenburg Afsembled November the tenth A. D 1746

Voted and Chofe Mr John Heywood Modderator

Voted and Granted the Sum of three pound for the ufe of School in f^d town ———

Voted and Granted the Sum of fifty three pound Fifteen Shillings for the Rev Mr David Stearn-s- Sallary for the Prefent year

Voted that Town Meetings for the future be warned By the Conftables pofting up a Notification (under his hand) upon a poft to be fet up for that porpofe within two Rods of the meeting houfe faceing the Road Setting forth the articles of f^d meeting and to ftand Pofted as aforefaid fourteen Days at Leaft ———

Voted and Granted ye Sum of twelve Shillings and fix pence to Mr Benjamin Bellows ———

Voted and Granted ye Sum of two Shillings and Six pence to Mr Benjamin Bellows jun ——

Recorded ṕ BENJ GOODRIDGE Clerk

At a Legaul Meeting of the Town of Lunenburg Afsembled March ye 2nd A D 1746/7

Voted & Choofe Major Jonathan Hubburd Modderator

Benj Goodridge
Maj^r Jonathan Hubbard
Capt Jonathan Willard   } Selectmen
Thomas Prentice Esqr
Mr John Gibfon

Benj Goodridge town Clerk
Thomas Prentice Efq^r town Trerfurer

[75] Mr Solomon Stawart ⎫
    Mr Philip Goodridge ⎭ Constables

Mr Francies Buttrick ⎫
Mr James Leitch } Tyding men
Mr David Chaplin ⎭

Mr Jonathan Bradftreet jun ⎫
Mr Ezekiel Wyman
Mr Jonathan Wood } Surveyers of
Mr Samvel Reed } high ways
Mr Joliah Dodge
Mr Samvel Larrabee ⎭

Mr Joseph Fuller } fences veiwers
Mr Thomas Brown

Mr David Goodridge ⎫
Mr Benj Gary } Hogg reives
Mr John Darlin
Mr Jonathan Hartwell ⎭

Mr Benj Bellows jun Sealer of Weights & meafures
Mr Eleazer Houghton Sealer of Leather
Mr Amos Kimbal }
Mr Samvel Larrabe\} to take Care of fire
Mr Samvel Davis }
Capt Jonathan Hubburd\} Cullirs of Shingles
Mr Nathanel Harwood }
Mr Zechariah Whitney \} to take care of Deer

Voted & Granted to Edward Hartwell Efq^r — 0-2-3
Voted & Granted to Benj Goodridge ——— 1-2-6
Voted & Granted to Capt Jonathan Willard —— 0-2-3
Voted & Granted to Samvel Davis ——— 0-3-0

Voted that the town Discontinue the way from the way by Joseph Pages to Mulpus Brook and Except of the way Laid out from the way Petween the Houfe william Kannady Lives in and Jofeph Pages Houfe to Mulpus two Rods wide as Laid out By Mr Jacob Gould and Mr Hezekiah Wetherbe

turn over

[76] and Reported to the Towon Provided Mr Jofeph Page Give Leave to the widow Mary Lane and her heirs to pafs and Repafs with their Creatvers to faid way by the Bridge through Bars or Gates the which faid Joseph Page Confented

Voted that that part of the way which gos to John Mansfeilds Between Timothy Bancrofts and Benj^a Garys Land Be Difcontinued and the way through Benj^a Garys Land Be accepted in the Room therof Begining at a Black oak tree on the North fide of f.^{d} way and Runing through faid Garys Land two Rod wide till it comes to John Mansfeild Land as it is now fenced ———

Recored Pr BENJ GOODRIDGE Cler

At Meeting of the freeholders and other Inhabitants of the Town of Lunenburg Afsembled May the Ninteenth A. D. 1747

Voted that Major Jonathan Hubburd be Modderator of faid Meeting

Voted the prefent Committe for the School be a committe to provide a fchool Mafter for the town and to order where the School fhall be Kept the year Enfuing Saving that Nathanel Harwood be Joyned with faid Committee in the Room of Eleazer Tarball who is moved out of town

Voted that the Swine run at Large the prefent year

Recored p̃ Benj Goodridge.

At a Legual meeting of the freeholders and other Inhabitants of the town of Lunenburg afsembled March the 3rd 1745/6

Voted and Excepted of a two Rod town way through Mr William Jones Land on the Eaft fide of his houfe and Barn from Juftice Harrises Land till it comes to Mr John Scots Land where the way now is—this way by a Miftake is Recored in a wrong Place

p̃ Benj Goodridge.

[77] At a legual Meeting of the freeholders and other Inhabitants of the town of Lunenburg Afsembled September the 21th— 1747

Voted and Choofe Majr Jonathan Hubburd Moddr for Sd meeting

Voted & Granted the Sum of two Hundred and Eighty pound old tenour for the Rev. Mr David Stearns Sallary for the prefent year ———

Voted and Granted the Sum of one Hundred and forty pound old tenour for the Suport of the School in Said town ———

Voted and Granted the Sum of ten Shilling to Mr Jofiah Dodge for making the Stocks

Recorded p̃ Benj Goodridge Clerk

At a Legual Meeting of the freeholders and other Inhabitants of the town of Lunenburg Afsembled March the Seventh A D 1747/8

Voted and Choofe Majr Jonathan Hubburd Modderator ———

Voted that ye Report of ye Committe to Reckon with ye town Treasurer be Excepted so far as they have proceeded.

Voted and chofse
Mr John Grout
Benj: Goodridge
Capt Jonathan Bradftreet } Selectmen
Mr Benj: Forfter
Mr Jonathan Wood
Benj Goodridge Choofen town Clerk & Sworn
Mr Jofiah Dodge Chofen town Traefurer and Sworn
Mr Samvel Davis }
Mr Afhael Hartwell} Chofen Constables & Sworn
Mr John Heywood
Mr Abraham Sanderfon } were Chofen
Mr Solomon Stewart
Mr William Page } Surveyers of
Mr Philip Goodridge } High ways
Mr Amos Kimbal } &
Mr Nathanael Page } Sworn
Mr John Martin

Turn over

[78] March meeting march ye 7th 1747/8
Mr Joseph Fuller }
Mr Thomas Brown } Chosen fence viewers & sworn
Majr Jonathan Hubburd Chofen fealer of weights
& meafures & Sworn
Mr Eleazer Houghton Chofen Sealer of Leather
Mr James Leitch }
Mr Francis Buttrick } Chofen Tyingmen
Mr Isaac Gibfon }
Mr Ephraim Whitney } Chofen to take care of Deer
Mr David Goodridge
Mr James Colman
Mr Joseph Page } Chofen Hogg reives
Mr Edward Hartwell jun
Mr Jacob Gould } Chofen Surveyers of Shingles
Mr Philip Goodridge } Claborad ftaves &c & Sworn
Mr David Page } Chofon to take care of
Mr Timothy Bancroft } fire and Sworn
Voted and Choofe
Majr Jonathan Hubburd
Mr Mofes Mitchael } a committe to provide the
Mr John Gibfon } town with a School Mafter
Mr John Martin } and to provide places to
Mr William Snow } Keep the School in &c

Voted that the town ways for the future be mended by a Rate.

Voted that the wages from the firſt of may to the Last of September be four Shillings ℔ Day for a man and Two Shillings ℔ Day for a yoke of oxen and Six pence ℔ Day for a cart and two Shillings ℔ Day for a Great Plow and all other Materials to be found by the owners without pay and that from y͏ͤ firſt Day of october to the Laſt Day of April one half of y͏ͤ wages above mentioned for men oxen cart and plow ——

Voted that the Sum of one Hundred pound be Raiſed to mend the ways withall

[79] March meeting march y͏ͤ 7th 1747/8
Voted that the old Meeting Houſe Be Repaired and that
   Mr Samvell Johnson
   Mr John Grout
   Thomas Kimball Eſq^{r}
   Mr John Gibſon and
   Maj^{r} Hubburd
Be acommittee to Repair the old meeting Houſe

Voted the Rome in the meeting House Between Mr Clarks Pew and the Stairs be Granted to Mr Samvel Reed ——

Voted and Granted the Sum of twenty pound old tennor To Repair the old meeting Houſe with ——

Voted and Excepted of a town way Laid out by order of the Selectmen Begining at the South end of Appletree Hill at the old way Runing through a peice of Common Land and over the Bridge and through Amos Kimballs Land and Ephraim Kimballs Land ſaid way was Laid out by

              David Page   ⎫
              Amos Kimball ⎬ *Committee*
              Ephraim Kimball ⎭

and ſaid Kimballs gave the Land for ſaid way to the town ſaid way is two Rod wide ——

Voted and Excepted of a town way from James Pooles too the Line of Narraganſett No 2 Begining at ſaid Pooles where the way is Laid too and Excepted by the twon at a former meeting and is Defcribed by markt Trees on the Northerly fide of faid way till it comes to faid Narraganfett Line faid way was Laid out by

     Maj^r Jonathan Hubburd ⎫ *Selectmen*
     Capt Jonathan Willard   ⎬ *of*
     and Thomas Prentice Efq^r ⎭ *Lunenburg*

 Voted and Excepted of atown way Laid out through Mr Seeratary Willards Land Begining at the End of Northfield Road (so called) and is two Rod wide then through Mr Samvel Reeds Land on the Southerly Side of Reeds Houfe and than through more of f^d Willards Land and through Mr Crockers Land and Mr Samvel Johnfons Land   turn over

 [80] and through Mr Isaac Gibsons Land and through some part of Mr Reuben Gibsons to his Houfe and is Defcribed by markt trees and faid Road is partly throug The firft Land of faid Willard and Through faid Reeds near where the Road now is Traveled in Northerly on faid Willard Land northerly Through faid Crockers Land North-Easterly through faid Johnfons Land and northeasterly Throug Land of faid Isaac Gibsons and partly Eafterly through faid Reuben Gibfons Land under the Pearl Hills So called.

 the above way was Laid out and Defcribed by

     Mr John Gibson   ⎫ *Select*
     & Thomas Prentice Efq^r ⎭ *men*

   Recorded P̃ BENJ: GOODRIDGE *Town Cler*

 At A Legaul Meeting of the freeholders and other Inhabitants of the Town of Lunenburg Afsembled May the 23rd 1748

 Voted and Chofe Maj^r Jonathan Hubbard Modderator

 Voted that Swine go at Large the Prefent year

 Voted that Town Meetings for the future be warned by a notification Being pofted up Fourteen Days Before the time appointed for the meeting

 Voted and Granted ye Sum of Thirty pound for the ufe of the School.

    Recorded P̃ BENJ: GOODRIDGE *Cler*

[81] At a Legall Meeting of the freeholders and other Inhabitants of the Town of Lunenburg Afsembled Sept y[e] Sixth A D 1748

Voted Chofe M[r] John Heywood Modderator

Voted and Granted y[e] Sum of one Hundred pound for the Rev M[r] David Stearns Sallary for this Prefent year

Voted and Granted y[e] Sum of Twenty pound for y[e] ufe of the School

Voted and Granted to M[r] Bellows for Sweeping the Meeting Houfe two years ———	1-10-0-
Granted to M[r] John Heywood ———	0- 2-6
Granted to M[r] Afahel Hartwell ———	0- 2-6
Granted to M[r] Philip Goodridge ——	0- 4-0
Granted to Benj Goodridge ———	0-12-0
Granted to Thomas Prentice Efq[r] ——	0-10-0
Granted to Cap[t] Jonathan Willard —	0- 2-0
Granted to M[r] John Gibfon ———	0- 2-0
Granted Maj[r] Jonathan Hubburd —	0- 4-0

Voted and Granted y[e] Sum of one pound to pay the Committe for Reckening With the Treafurers. ———

Recorded P̃ BENJ: GOODRIDGE Town Cler

[82] At A Legall meeting of the freeholders and other Inhabitants of the Town of Lunenburg Afsembled March the Sixth A D 1748/9

Voted and Chofe M[r] Samvel Johnson Modderator

Voted and Chofe ———

Benj Goodridge ⎫
M[r] Samvel Johnson ⎪
M[r] John Grout ⎬ Selectmen
Cap[t] Jonathan Bradftreet ⎪
M[r] Jonathan Wood ⎭

Benj Goodridge Chofen Town Clerk

Thomas Prentice Efq[r] Chofen town Treafurer

M[r] Ezekiel Wyman ⎫
M[r] Samvel Reed ⎬ Chofen Conftables

Voted that M[r] Jonathan Willard jun be Excepted to Serve as Constable in the Room of M[r] Samvel Reed faid Reed having hired him ———

Mr Ephraim Whitney
Mr Stephen Boynton
Mr Mofes Mitchael   Chofen Surveyers
Mr Mofes Ritter   of
Mr Patrick White
Mr Thomas Brown   High ways
Mr Ephraim Parce
Mr William Jones
Mr Benj Fofter

Mr Jofiah Bayley
Mr Samvel Reed Chofen fence veiwers
Mr Thomas Carter Chofen Sealer of Leather
Mr William Jones
Mr Nathanael Page Chofen Tydingmen
Mr Jofeph Wood
Mr David Goodridge Chofen Deer Revees

[83] Mr Jeremiah Norcrofs
Mr Gabriel Ponchee Chofen Hogg reves
Mr Jacob Gould   Chofen Surveyers of
Mr Philip Goodridge ftaves and Shingles &c -

Mr Jofeph Fuller
Mr Thomas Brown
Mr William Jones   Chofen to take care
Mr Amos Kimball   of fire and to
Mr Isaac Gibfon   burn ye woods &c.
Mr Samvil Larrabee
Mr John Darlin

Edward Hartwell Efqr
Thomas Prentice Efqr   Chofen acommittee to
Mr John Martin   provide The Town with a
Mr John Bufs   School Mafter and to order
Mr Eleazer Tarbal   where the School fhall be
                       Kept for the ye year Infuing

Voted John Darlins Rates be forgiven him

Voted and Granted to Capt Jonathan Bradftreet - 0- 4-0
Granted to Mr Jonathan Wood   ———   0- 4-0
Granted to Mr Benj Fofter   ———   0- 6-0
Granted to Mr John Grout   ———   0- 8-0
Granted to Benj Goodridge   ———   1-15-0

Voted and Granted the Sum of fifteen fhillings for the taking care of the Meeting Houfe ye year Infuing Voted and Granted the Sum of one pound to mend the pound withall

Voted a Town way be Excepted off from y̆ᵉ way Between Obediah Walkers and David Woods Land to Solomon Stewards Houſe Between ſaid Stewards and ſaid Walkers Land ſaid way is two Rod wide and ſaid Steward gives the Land for ſaid way

      Recorded ṕ Benj Goodridge *town Clerk*

Voted and Granted at the above meeting one Hundred pound to mend the town ways withall

      Recorded ṕ Benj Goodridge *Town Clerk*

[84] At A Legal Meeting of the freeholders and other Inhabitants of the Town of Lunenburg Aſsembled May the 22ⁿᵈ A D 1749.

Voted and Choſe Mʳ Samvel Johnſon Modderator for ſaid meeting

Voted that they will Build A New Meeting Houſe in ſaid Town

Voted that ſaid new Meeting Houſe be Built as Neer the old Meeting houſe as may be with convenience Not to bee above five Rod from the old Meeting Houſe

Voted that Benjamin Goodridge Edward Hartwell Eſqʳ and Mʳ Joſiah Dodge Be aCommitte To agree with Mʳ Benjamin Bellows junʳ for apeice of Land to Build a new Meeting houſe upon and to Stake out the ſame and to conſider how Bigg ſaid Meeting Houſe ſhall be Built and in what form and Report the Same to the Town for their Acceptence

Voted that the Swine go at Large this preſent year

Voted that this Meeting Be ajorned to the Laſt Tueſday of June Next at two o Clock in the afternoon.

Tuesday June yᵉ 27ᵗʰ 1749 the freeholders & other Inhabitants of the Town of Lunenburg Being Met by ajournment Voted that the meeting be further ajourned to the firſt Tuesday of September Next at ten of the Clock in the forenoon

Tuesday September yᵉ 5ᵗʰ 1749 The freeholders and other Inhabitants of yᵉ Town of Lunenburg Being Met by a Journment Voted y^t the meeting be further a Journ-d till two o Clock in the afternoon and then met and Voted that the Meeting Houfe be Built Sixty feet Long and forty five feet wide and twenty five feet poſt Between Joynts

Voted that the Sum of three hundred pound new tennour Be Granted to Build a new Meeting Houfe withall and to be imediately Afsefed one half thereof to be paid in Six Months the other half to be paid in twelve Months

[85] Voted that Benjamin Goodridge Mr Samvel Johnſon and M^r Joſiah Dodge be a committe to manage the affair and then voted that the meeting be Still further ajournd till Monday Next at two o Clock in the afternoon

Monday Sept the Eleventh 1749 the freeholders and other Inhabitants of the town of Lunenburg Being Met again by a Journment

Voted that the Committe to manage the affair of Building a new Meeting Houfe Let out the work to fome one man that will Do it Cheapeſt and Beſt

Recorded p̄ BENJ GOODRIDGE *Town Cler*

At a Legual meeting of the freeholders and other Inhabitants of the Town of Lunenburg Afsembled & Met September the fifth A D 1749

Voted and Chofe Mr John Grout Modderator and then Voted that the Meeting be a Journ d till Monday Next at one of the Clock in the afternoon : Monday Sept the Eleventh 1749 the freeholders and other Inhabitants of the Town of Lunenburg Being met by a Journment —

Voted and Granted the Sum of Twenty five pound for the ufe of the School in faid Town —

Voted and Granted the Sum of one Hundred pound for the Rev Mr David Stearns Sallary This prefent year

            £ s d

Voted and Granted to Thomas Prentice Efq   0- 2-0
Voted and Granted to Mr Eleazer Tarball ——   0-14-9

Voted and Granted the Sum of ten pound to make good Deficences in the Town Treafury

Voted that fifty pound be Raised to Build two Bridges on the way To Narraganfet No 2. one over the River by David Goodridges and one over the River Between James Pooles and faid Narraganfet N⁰ 2 to be workt out at five Shillings ℔ Day

       Recorded ℔ BENJ GOODRIDGE *Cler*

[86] At a Legal Meeting of the Freeholders and other Inhabitants of the Town of Lunenburg Afsembled December the 21ᵗʰ A D 1749

Voted and Chofe Mʳ John Grout Modderator

Voted that the town will Shew Caufe why the prayer of the Petition (praying that the mile on the Eaſt fide of the Town may be Set off to Joyn with thofe on the weſt fide of Groton River) Should not be Granted

Voted that Benjamin Goodridge Mʳ Jofiah Dodge Mʳ John Grout Mʳ John Gibfon and Mʳ Mofes Mitchael be a Committe to Draw up Reafons to Shew why the prayer of the faid petetion Should not be Granted

Voted that two men be fent to Bofton to Make anfwer to faid petetion

Voted and Chofe Benjamin Goodridge and Mʳ Jofiah Dodge to Go to Bofton to make anfwer unto faid petetion ·

Voted that the Sum of ten pound in yᵉ Laſt Emifion Bills be Granted to Enable faid Goodridge and Dodge to go to Bofton and make anfwer to yᵉ faid petetion

       Recorded ℔ BENJ GOODRIDGE
          town Clerk

[87] At A Legal meeting of the Freeholders and other Inhabitants of the Town of Lunenburg Afsembled March the fifth A D 1749/50

Voted and Chofe Mʳ Samvel Johnson Modderrator for faid Meeting

 Benj Goodridge
 Mʳ Samvel Johnson
 Capᵗ Jonathan Bradstreet were Chofen Selectmen
 Mʳ Jofiah Dodge
 Mʳ Solomon Steward

Benj Goodridge was Chofen Town Clerk and Sworn

Thomas Prentice Esqr was Chosen Town Treasurer
Mr Thomas Cartter ⎫
Mr William Snow ⎭ were Chosen Constables

Voted that Mr Ezekiel Wyman be Excepted to serve as Constable in the Room of Mr Thomas Carter

Mr Josiah Dodge ⎫
Mr Thomas Brown ⎪
Mr John Griffin ⎪
Mr Arington Gibson ⎪ Were Chosen
Mr Philip Goodridge ⎬
Mr Josiah Bayley ⎪ Surveyers of Highways.
Mr Moses Mitchael ⎪
Mr George Kimbal ⎪
Mr David Wood ⎭

Mr Josiah Bayley ⎫
Mr Samvel Davis ⎭ were chosen fence veiwers

[88] Mr Nathanael Page ⎫
Mr Samvel Hunt ⎭ were Chosen Tyding men

Mr Joseph Wood ⎫ were Chosen to take Care
Mr Isaac Gibson ⎭ of Deer

Mr Josiah Dodge jun^r ⎫
Mr Ephraim Kimbal ⎬ were Chosen Hogreves
Mr David Carlile ⎭

Mr Samvel Davis ⎫ were Chosen Surveyers
Mr Josiah Bayley ⎭ of Shingles

Mr Eleazer Houghton was Chosen Sealer of Leather

Mr John Martin ⎫
Mr Nicholas Dike ⎭ were Chosen Surveyers of Staves

Mr William Jones ⎫
Mr John Scott ⎬ were Chosen to
Mr David Goodridge ⎭ take Care of fire

Voted that the School be Kept in four places in the town three mounths at aplace in the year for the future

Voted y^t Mr Benjamin Bellows jun^r Mr Nathan Heywood Mr Eleazer Tarbal Mr Solomon Steward and Mr William Snow be a committe to appoint the said four places and also to appoint places to Build four School Houses in and make Report of their Doings to the Town at Next May meeting

Voted that Mr Benjamin Bellows jun^r Mr Solomon Steward and Mr Eleazer Tarbal

be

[89] Be a committe to provide a School Marſter for the Town for the year Inſuing

Voted and Granted the Sum of Seventy five pound Laſt Emiſsion Bills for the Support of the School in ſaid Town

Voted that David Goodridge appoint a Day for thoſe that have not workt out their Rates at the High ways and that they work out their Rates under his Direction at the Bridge by his Houſe Between now and the Last of april next

Voted and Granted to Mr John Martin ——   2 = 5 = 0
Voted & Granted Thomas Prentice Eſq^r ——   1 = 4 = 0
Voted & Granted to Benj : Goodridge ———   1 - 5 - 0
Voted & Granted to Capt Jonathan Bradſtreet — 0-17 - 6
Voted & Granted to Mr Samvel Johnſon ——   1 - 5 - 0
Voted & Granted to Mr Jonathan Wood ——   0-12 - 6

Voted that Nathanael Harwoods Highway Rates be abated

Voted that it Be Left with the Selectmen to abate ſuch Rates as Shall appear to them to Be Reaſonable —— and then

Voted that the meeting be a Jorned to to morrow morning nine o Clock

Tueſday March ye Sixth nine o, clock A. M. A. D 1749/50 then the freeholders and other Inhabitants of the Town of Lunenburg Being met by ajornment

Voted that the new meeting Houſe that the Town of Lunenburg is about to Build be Built and Set up in the End of the Lane by the School Houſe the place already voted notwithstanding

                                           voted

[90] Voted that the Committe to manage the affair of Building a new Meeting Houſe agree with Mr Benjamin Bellows jun and with Juſtice prentice for a ſuitable Districk of Land for to Set the meeting Houſe upon and for Conveniences about the Same and Report the Same to the Town at Next may meeting for their acceptance

Voted that the Town Will Shew Cauſe why the prayer of the petetion Should not Be Granted and that the Committe appointed to anfwer the petetion of those praying to Joyn with thofe of Groton Shew Caufe why the prayer of the petetion of Edward Hartwell Efq[r] and Eight others praying to be annexed to the Town of Leominster as part of that Townfhip fhould not Be Granted

     Recorded p̃ BENJ GOODRIDGE *town Cler*

At a Legaul meeting of the freeholders and other Inhabitants of the town of Lunenburg Afsembled May the 21th 1750 Voted and chofe M[r] John Heywood Modderator for f[d] meeting.

Voted and Granted the Sum of fifty three pounds Six Shillings and eight pence to mend the town ways withall —— Voted that the wages for men be two Shillings & eight pence p̃ Day from May till the laft of auguft and a pair of oxen two fhillings and a cart eight pence p̃ Day from May till the Laft of auguft

Voted that the Selectmen Impower A a Surveyer to take a fuitable Number of hands and Cut the trees out of the way to Dorchefter Cannada

     Recorded p̃ BENJ GOODRIDGE *town Cler*

[91] At a Legall Meeting of the freeholders and other Inhabitants of the Town of Lunenburg Afsembled November the Ninteenth A D 1750

Voted and Chofe M[r] John Heywood Modderator

then Voted and Granted the Sum of Eleven pound Sixteen Shillings and Eight pence Lawfull Money to pay M[r] Benjamin Bellows and Thomas Prentice Efq[r] for the Land that the New Meeting Houfe Stands upon and for Conveniences about the Same

Voted and Granted the Sum of two pound fifteen Shillings to pay for the Rum ufed at the Raifing of the new meeting Houfe

Voted and Granted to M[r] Jofiah Dodge the Sum of Eighteen Shillings and Eight pence for the ufe of his Rope to Raife the new Meeting Houfe withall and then voted that the Meeting be ajournd to too Morrow Morning at ten O Clock tuesday November the 20th 1750 ten o Clock the freeholders and other Inhabitants of the Town of Lunenburg Being met by a Journment

Voted and Granted to Thomas Prentice Efq^r the Sum of ten Shillings and five pence for Rum and other articles ufed at the Raifing of the New Meeting Houfe

Voted and Granted the Sum of fifty three pound Six Shillings and eight pence to ye Rev Mr David Stearns for his Sallary for the prefent year

Voted and Granted to Mr John Grout the Sum of two pound

Voted and Granted to Mr Robert Speer the Sum of Eight Shilling

Voted and Chofe Mr Benjamin Bellows Mr John Grout and Mr Philip Goodridge a committe to Reckon with the Treafurer and to Give him a Difcharge for what he has payed by orders for the towns ufe

Voted that the Report of the committe for placing the School Houfes be Excepted

Recorded P̄ BENJ GOODRIDGE *town Cler*

[92] At a Legal Meeting of the freeholders and other Inhabitants of the town of Lunenbug Afsembled December the eighteenth A D 1750

Voted and Chofe Mr John Heywood Modderator for Said Meeting

Voted that thirty Eight pews be Built on the Lower floor of the new meeting Houfe

Voted that twenty one pews be Built on the Gallary floor of the new Meeting Houfe

Voted that Edward Hartwell Efq^r Mr Jofiah Dodge Benj Goodridge Mr Nathan Heywood and Mr Jonathan Wood be a committe to place the pews in the new meeting Houfe

Voted that the pew Ground in the New Meeting Houfe be fold

Voted that the pew Ground on the Lower floor be Sold to the Highesth Biders

Voted that the pew Ground in the Gallerys be fold to the Highest Bidders

Voted that Edward Hartwell Efq{r} Benj : Goodridge and Mr Samvel Johnfon be acommitte to Sell the pews to the Highest Bidders

Voted that the town Referve one pew for the ufe of the Town or aminiftreal pew

Voted that the Committe Sell but one pew to any one Man

Voted that the Committe take Money Down or notes on Demand of the perfons they Sell the the pews to

Voted that Major Edward Hartwell take Deeds of Mr Benjamin Bellows and of Thomas Prentice Efq{r} of the Land that the New meeting Houfe Stands upon and for Conveniences about the Same In behalf of the town

Voted and Granted to Mr Jofiah Dodge ——   0 = 16 = 0
Voted and Granted to Mr Jofiah Dodge ——   1 - 4 - 0
Voted and Granted to Mr Jofiah Dodge ——   0 - 18 - 8
Voted and Gran{t}:d to Benj Goodridge ——   2 - 8 - 9
Voted and Granted to Mr John Gibfon ——   0 - 7-10

Recorded p̃ BENJ GOODRIDGE town Cler

[93] At a Legaell Meeting of the freeholders and other Inhabitants of the town of Lunenburg afsembled Janvary the Eighth 1750/51 Voted and Chofe Mr John Heywood Modderator for f{d} meeting

Voted tha. they will come into anew Regulation concerning the Pews in the New Meeting Houfe notwithstanding any former vote.

Voted that two Hundred pound Lawfull money be Raifed on the pews Ground on Lower floor and the perfons that have them to take them for their Seats any former vote to the Contrary Notwithstanding

Voted that thirteen pound Six Shillings and Eight pence Lawfull money be Raifed on the pew Ground in the Gallarys and the perfons that have them to take them for their Seats any former Vote to the Contrary notwithstanding

Voted and Granted that one Hundred and Sixty pounds Lawfull money be Raifed to finish the New Meeting Houfe Withall

Voted that the Highest payers on Real Eftates Looking one year Back be perferred to have pews in the New Meeting Houfe

Voted that Edward Hartwell Efq^r Capt Jonathan Bradftreet Capt Jonathan Willard Mr John Heywood and Mr Jonathan Wood be a committe to Difpofe of the pews and to take Securety for the money in Behalf of the Town

Voted that the Committe Give three months payment to thofe that Do not pay money Down

Recorded $\tilde{p}$ BENJ GOODRIDGE town Cler

Whereas Wee the Subscribers on y^e 8th Day of Jan^r A. D. 1750 by a vote of the Town of Lunenburg at a Legal Town Meeting ware appointed a Committe to Difpose of the pew: Ground, On the Lower floor in the New Meeting house in S^d Town and to take Security for the same &c and also at a Legal meeting in S^d Town on the twenty Seventh of August A D : 1751 then the S^d Town voted that the Committe affore f^d profeed to Sell the Rest of the S^d pew Ground on the New meeting house on the floor of S^d house to the Next highest payers on Real Eftate in purfuance of S^d votes wee have Sold the third pew Ground on the Left hand Going in at the front Dore adjoining to Daniel Auftens : to Docter John Dunfmoor his Heirs & Afsigns & have taken Security for the Sum of four pounds fourteen Shillings & nine pence.

Dated Septm^r ye 30th 1751   Jonathan Bradftreet } Committe
John Heywood
Edward Hartwell

A True Record pr Jonathan Low
Town Clerk
Rec^d on Record November ye 21 : 1770

[94] LUNENBURG Janvary the 8th 1750

At a meeting of the freeholders and other Inhabitants of the Town of Lunenburg at the publick Meeting Houfe in faid town

Whereas it is propofed in Confequence of the firft Article of faid Meeting to Raife or Lay a a Certain Sum of

Money on the pews or on So much of the New Meeting houfe floors as they have voted to Build pews upon We hereby Decently Object againſt any Sum or Sums of Money Whatfoever Being in any ways or Manner Laid upon S^d pews or upon the S^d floors for Building S^d pews

    Benj^a Bellows
    John Gibfon
    John Grout

Alfo it is propofed in Confequence of the Second Article to vote who Shall be preffered to have the pews in the New Meeting Houfe we hereby Decently object againſt any other Rule or Method but only that the Highest payer towards Building the New Meeting houfe Draw the firſt pew & the Next Highest payer to Draw the next pew & So on in that Method through out the whole Diftribution of pews in S^d meeting Houfe

    Mofes Mitchael
    John Grout
    Samvel Reed
    Nathaniel Page
    Eleazer Houghton

[95] At A Legal meeting of the freeholders and other Inhabitants of the Town of Lunenburg Afsembled March the 4th 1750/1

    Voted and Chofe Mr Nathan Heywood Modderator

Mr Nathan Heywood ⎫
Mr Jonathan Wood ⎪
Mr John Gibfon   ⎬ Chofen Selectmen and
Mr Amos Kimbal   ⎪   Since Sworn
Mr Jofiah Bayley   ⎭

Benj Goodridge Chofen Town Clerk
                and Since Sworn

Thomas Prentice Efq^r Chofen Town Treafurer

Mr Nathanael Page   ⎱
Mr Zechariah Whitney ⎰ Chofen Conftables

Mr Jacob Gould   ⎱
Mr Mofes Ritter ⎰ Chofen Tydingmen

Mr James Leitch
Mr Mofes Mitchael
Mr Jonathan Taylor
Mr Obediah Walker   were chofen Surveyors
Mr John Bufs   of the
Mr Jofeph Fuller   Highways
Mr Samvel Hunt
Mr Jacob Gould
Mr Jofiah Dodge
Mr Noah Dodge

Mr Samvel Comings
Mr Jeremiah Norcrofs Chofen fence veiwers

Mr Ephraim Whitney
Mr Timothy Bancroft   Chofen to take Care of Deer

Mr Joseph Fuller
Mr Gabrial Pouchee
Mr Timothy Bancroft   Chofen Hogg reives
Mr Abraham Sanderfon

Mr Philip Goodridge
Mr Jacob Gould   Surveyors of Boards
                      and Shingles &c

[96] Mr John Martin
      Mr Nicholas Dike Chofen Surveyors of Staves

Mr Eleazer Houghton Chofen Sealer of Leather

Mr Noah Dodge
Mr Nathanael Calton   Chofen to take care
Mr David Goodridge   of fire

then Voted that the Meeting be ajorned to the Laft Wensday of this Inftant March at nine of the Clock in the morning

At ameeting of the freeholders and other Inhabitants of the town of Lunenburg Held by ajorment on the Laft wensday of March 1751

Voted that they will come in Some other Regulation concerning the pews in the new meeting Houfe

Voted that the twelve pews in the Body of Seats be flung up to Build Seats upon the Room

Voted that the pews in the Gallary be flung up

Voted that all the pews on the walls Except the Minustreal pew be Dismift for the prefent

Voted that the article of making the Highway Rate on the old Valluation be Dismift

Voted that Sixty pound be Granted to mend town Ways withall

Voted that the wages for a man from the firft of april to the Laft of august for working at the Highways be two Shilling ꝑ Day and one Shilling for apair of oxen and Sixpence for a cart

Voted that the Sum of four pound be Granted Mr Thomas Brown and others for mending the Bridge by David Goodridges to Be Subducted out of the Highway Rate this prefent year

Voted that the Laft article in the warrant be be Dismift

Voted that the meeting be further ajorn-d to to the third Tuesday of May next at three of ye clock in the afternoon

[97] May the twenty firft A D 1751

the freeholders and other Inhabitants of the Town of Lunenburg Being met by ajornment the Question was put whither the Town will proceed upon the article of the way Between the Lands of Thomas Prentice Efq^r Mr Benjamin Bellows and Mr Daniel Auftin and it pafed in the affirmative and after a Debate Voted that the article be Dismift

Recorded ꝑ Benj = Goodridge

town Cler

Voted that the Town way be altered which Runs through Eleazer Houghtons from where it now gos Begining at the Land of the Heirs of David Parce and Runs upon faid Houghtons Land two Rod wide as it is Defcribed by Markt trees on the wefterly fide of f^d way the faid way being three Rods wide against Darius Houghtons Houfe and it Runs part of the way on the Land of Epharium Parce Junr as it is Defcribed by markt trees on the wefterly fide of faid way

It was alfo voted at the firft ajornment of the above Meeting that a Bridle way be Excepted of by the town provided the perfons that own the Land Give the Land for the faid way which way is Defcribed as follows Begining ftanding in or neer the Line Between William Henerys and Capt Goulds Land and Run throng f^d Henerys

Land and and through afinal corner of David Parces Land in the old path and through Georges Ruffells Land in the old path to Mr James Leitches Land and through faid Leitches Land in or neer the old path and through the Land of the widdow Mary Ruffell then through the Land of Mr James Gordon and through acorner of the Land of Andrew Mitchael by the Bever Dam then on the fide of Francis Buttricks Land to the corner of Nathan Platts Land neer turkey Hill Brook then on f^d Buttrick by the fide faid Plattses Land then turning on f^d Buttricks Land on the foutherly fide of his Houfe then as the old path Gos to the Land of Nathan Platts and thro acorner of f^d platts Land to the Land of Mr Jofiah Dodge and through f^d Dodges Land to the Land of Capt Willard to the corner of the Buring Place and fo by the weft fide thereof into the Road

      Recorded Pr BENJ GOODRIDGE *town Cler*

[98] At A Legal meeting of the freeholders and other Inhabitants of the Town of Lunenburg Afsembled March the 27th 1751

Voted and Chofe Mr Nathan Heywood Modderator
Voted and Chofe

Mr Jofhua Goodridge ⎫ a committe to Hire
Mr John Grout   ⎪ a School Mafter
Mr William Snow   ⎬ and to order where
Thomas Prentice Efq^r⎪ the School fhall be
Mr John Martin   ⎭   Kept

Voted and Granted the Sum of Twenty Six pound thirteen Shillings and four pence for the Support of the School

                £ sh d
Voted and Granted to Jofeph Goodridge   0-8-0
Voted and Granted to Philip Goodridge   0-2-0
Voted and Granted to Jonathan Bradftreet Jun 0-2-0

Voted and Granted the Sum of two pound for the ufe of the poor

Voted that the former Committe Continue to be acommitte to profecute the affair of finifhing the new Meeting Houfe and Lay out the Money that is Afsefsed and Raifed for that porpofe

At A Legal Meeting of the freeholders and other Inhabitants of the town of Lunenburg Afsembled May the 27th 1751

Voted and Chofe Mr John Heywood Modderator

Voted and Granted the Sum of four pounds to Build a pound withall in f^d town

Voted that Edward Hartwell Efq^r and Benj : Goodridge Be added to the Committe to Reckon with the Town Trefurer

Voted and Granted to Mr Nathan Heywood — 0-5-4

[99] At a Legal meeting of the freeholders and other Inhabitants of the Town of Lunenburg Afsembled Auguft the the twenty Seventh A D 1751

Voted and Chofe Mr Samvel Johnfon Modderator

Voted and Chofe Mr William Stearns Town Treafurer

Voted and Granted the Sum of fifty three pound Six Shillings and Eight pence for the Rev Mr David Stearns Sallary for the prefent year

	£ Sh d
Voted and Granted to Mr Nathan Heywood —	0-4-0
Voted & Granted to Mr Jonathan Wood ——	0-4-0
Voted & Granted to Mr Jofiah Bayley ——	0-4-0
Voted & Granted to Benj : Goodridge ——	1-7-0
Voted & Granted to Edward Hartwell Efq^r —	0-2-0
Voted & Granted to Mr Philip Goodridge —	0-2-0

Voted that the Committe appointed to fell the pew Ground on the Lower floor in the New Meeting Houfe in faid Town be Directed forthwith to Call in the Money Due for the pew Ground and proceed to Sell the Reft to the Next Higheft payers on Real Eftates in cafe thofe that have the first offer Refufe to Give the money afsefst on them by the Committe

Voted that the Committe aforefaid be Directed to pay Decon Johnfon for the Nails Bought of Mr Blair forthwith and that the Remainder of the money be paid to the Committe appointed to manage the affair of Building the new meeting Houfe or their order to be by them applyed to finish the faid new meeting Houfe withall exclufive of Building the pews

Voted and Excepted of alift of Jury men to be put into the Box for the Superiour Court

Voted and Excepted of alift of Jury men to be put into the Box for the Inferiour Court

Voted that the Selectmen abate the Rates of fuch perfons as fhall appear Reafonable to them –

[100] At A Legal Meeting of the freeholders and other Inhabitants of the Town of Lunenburg Afsembled March the 2nd A D 1752

Voted and Chofe Mr John Heywood Modderator

Mr John Gibfon
Mr Jofiah Bayley
Mr Amos Kimball } Chofen Selectmen
Mr William Downe
Mr William Snow

Benj Goodridge Chofen Town Clerk

Mr William Stearns Chofen Town Treafurer

Mr James Leitch }
Mr John Griffin } Chofen Conftables

Voted that Mr Philip Goodridge be Excepted Conftable in the Room of Mr John Griffin

Mr Jofiah Dodge   Mr John Heywood
Mr Daniel Auftin   Mr William Gilchreft
Mr Caleb Taylor   Mr Samvel Reed
Mr Thomas Carter   Mr Abraham Ireland
Mr Thomas Dutton   Mr Hezekiah Wetherbe
Mr Ebenezer Going   were Chofen
Mr Mofes Mitchael
Mr Amos Hazeltine
       Surveyers of Highways

Mr Francis Buttrick }
Mr Samvel Davis } Chofen Tydingmen

Mr Nathanael Page }
Mr Jeremiah Norcrofs } Chofen fence veiwers

Mr Thomas Carter Chofen Sealer of Leather

Mr Samvel Davis Culer of Shingles & Clabords

Mr John Martin Culler of Staves

[101]   Mr John Fitch
       Mr Thomas Brown } Chofen Hogg reives
       Mr Joseph Fuller
       Mr Ephraim Whitney

Mr Isaac Gibson
Mr Samvel Hunt } Chofen to take care
Mr Thomas Dutton } of Deer

Mr Jofeph Fuller
Mr Ephraim Kimball
Mr Abraham Sanderfon } to take care of fire
Mr Mofes Mitchall
Mr Reuben Gibson

Voted and Granted to Mr Zechariah Whitney the sum of ——   £-s-d 0-4-0
Voted & Granted to Mr Nathaneal Page   0-1-0
Voted & Granted to Mr Nathan Heywood   0-8-0
Voted & Granted to Mr John Gibson ——   £-s-d 1-5-0
Voted & Granted to Mr Jofiah Bayley   0-4-0
Voted & Granted to Mr Amos Kimball   0-3-6
Voted & Granted to Mr Jonathan Wood   0-4-6
Voted & Granted to Mr Samvel Poole   0-2-8
Voted & Granted to Mr James Poole   0-2-8

Voted that the Third Article in the warrant be Difmift

Voted that any Perfon Being an Inhabitant that Shall Kill any Woffe within the Bounds of the Town Shall have twenty Shilling Reward out of the Town Treafury

[102] Voted and Excepted of A town way Laid out by order of the Selectmen Begining at Groton Road by Jacob Goulds Houfe on the Wefterly end of Thirfton Original Lot and Runing by Isaac Fofters Houfe till it comes to Land f^d Fofter Bought of william Moffatt Alfo another Peice of way Begining at the Northweft Corner of the Widow Randals Land at Groton Road and Runing on Benjamin Bellows Land by the widow Randals Land on the Wefterly fide of the f^d widow Randalls Land till it comes to Daniel Austins Land two Rod wide Being ten Rod and one Quarter on one fide and feven Rod and one Quarter on the other fide the above peice of way is excepted provided the Land be Given

the above ways were Laid out by
                        Daniel Austin }
                        Jacob Gould } *Committe*

Alfo an other town way Begining at the South Weft corner of the Land of Nathanael Harris Efq^r and Running about forty Rods on f^d Harris es Land and then turning unto Jofiah Bayleys Land and Runing Strait to the South weft Corner of Nathanael Carltons Land faid way to be two Rod wide and is Excepted away provided the Land be Given and was Laid o By the Selectmen

Voted that the meeting be ajorned to the fecond Monday of May Next at two of the Clock in the afternoon

Monday May the Eleventh 1752 the Town of Lunenburg Mett By Ajornment

[103] Voted that they will mend the Bridges on the way to Narragansett N^o two

Voted and Granted the Sum of fifteen pound to mend the Bridges and way to Narragansett N^o two withall

Voted that the Money be workt out at two fhilling and Eight pence $\bar{p}$ Day for aman

Voted that the wages for a pair of oxen be two fhillings and Eight pence $\bar{p}$ Day and Eight pence for acart

Voted that Lt Jofiah Dodge over fee the work

Voted that Lt Dodge Notifie the feveral Surveyors to Bring their proportion of men

Voted that the meeting Be further Ajornd to Monday the twenty fifth Day of this Inftant May at four a clock in the afternoon

May the the 25th 1752 the freeholders and other Inhabitants of the Town of Lunenburg Met by a further Ajornment and the Meeting was Difmift

Recorded $\bar{p}$ BENJ GOODRIDGE *town Cler*

At a Legal meeting of the freeholders and other Inhabitants of the Town of Lunenburg Afsembled May the 25th 1752

Voted and Chofe Mr Jofiah Bayley Modderator—

Voted that they will Choofe acommitte to Seat the New Meeting Houfe

Voted that they will Choofe five men for acommitte to Seat the New Meeting Houfe

Voted and Chofe
Mr Nathan Heywood
Mr William Snow   a committe to Seat
Mr Amos Kimbal   the New Meeting
Mr Jofiah Bayley   Houfe
Mr James Leitch

[104] Voted that the New Meeting Houfe Be Seated upon the Real Eftates that paid toward the Building of fd Houfe

Voted that after the perfons are Seated that Have Real Eftates thofe perfons that have no Real Eftates shall be Seated upon their perfonal Eftates according to their pay and that all polls that have been paid for towards Building the new Meeting Houfe fhall have afeat

Voted that they will meet in the New Meeting Houfe Next Sabbath Day come fortnight to attend the publick worfhip there

Voted and Chofe
Mr William Snow   A Committe to provide
Mr Jacob Gould   the town with a
Mr Afahel Hartwell   School Mafter

Voted and Granted the Sum of thirty five pound for the ufe of the School

Voted that the Selectmen Abate Such Rates as they think proper

Voted and Granted the fum of fifty pound to Mend
the Highways withall and that the wages be
for a man be ———   0 = 2 - 8
for a yoke of oxen ———   0 - 1 - 4
and for a cart ———   0 - 0 - 8

and that the money be workt out by the Laft of September Next

Voted that Hoggs Run at Large the prefent year

Recorded ṖBENJ GOODRIDGE Town_Cler

[105] At a legal Meeting of the freeholders and other Inhabitants of the Town of Lunenburg Afsembled Auguft ye 10th 1752

Voted and Chofe Benjamin Goodridge Modderator

Voted and Granted the Sum of fifty five pound for the Rev Mr David Stearns Sallary for the prefent year

Voted and Granted the Sum of two pound to Buy Weights & Meafures withall

Voted and Granted the Sum of fifteen pound to Mend the way withall from Mr Hunts to the weft Line of the Town the wages ye fame as on Narraganset Road

Voted & Granted to Mr William Snow ——   0-1-4
Voted & Granted to Mr Afahel Hartwell ——   0-1-4

Voted that they will Build Long pews Behind the Seats in the Gallarys in the New Meeting Houfe

Voted that they will Keep the old Meeting Houfe for town meetings &c and y^t Lt Jofiah Dodge take care of the old Meeting Houfe and Stop up the Windows &c

           Recorded p̃ Benj Goodridge *town Cler*

[106] At a Legal meeting of the Freeholders and other Inhabitants of the Town of Lunenburg Afsembled March 5th: A: D: 1753

Voted and chose Mr John Heywood Moderator

Mefs^rs John Gibson   ⎫
        Willm Downe ⎪
        John Grout   ⎬ Chosen Selectmen and sworn
        Jonathan Wood ⎪   ———— Afsefsors.
        Samuel Reed   ⎭

William Downe chosen Town Clerk and sworn
Deacon William Stearns chosen Town Treafurer

Mefs^rs Ephraim Peirce ⎱
        John Bufs   ⎰ chosen Constables

Voted that Mr Philip Goodridge be accepted Constable in the room of Mr John Bufs.

Voted that Mr Jonathan Page be accepted Constable in the Room of Mr Ephraim Pierce

Mefs^rs Josiah Dodge   ⎫
        Samuel Cummings ⎪
        William Stearns   ⎪
        Moses Ritter   ⎬ Surveyors of Highways
        Willm Jones   ⎪
        Moses Mitchell   ⎪
        Abraham Saunderfon ⎪
        Ephraim Kimball   ⎪
        Isaac Gibson   ⎭

Mefs.rs John Martin
       Arrington Gibson
       Patrick White   } Tything Men
       Jonathan Hartwell
Mefs.rs David Goodridge
       Timothy Parker
       Joseph Wood   } Hog reeves
       Reuben Gibson
Mefs.rs Ezekiel Wyman
       Abijah Stearns   } Fence Veiwers

[107] Mefs.rs Reuben Gibson
              Samuel Hunt   } Chosen Deer Reeves
M.r Thomas Carter chosen Sealer of Leather
Mefs.rs Jacob Gould   } chosen Surveyors of Boards
       Philip Goodridge   Shingles Clabboards and
                                Staves.
Mefs.rs Amos Kimball
       Samuel Pool   } chosen to take care of Fire

A Certificate signed by the Selectmen of the Town of Lunenburg informing f.d Town, that y.y had attended at Deacon W.m Stearns Town Treafur.r & examined his acco.ts find, that the Sum of $462\text{-}19\text{-}4\text{-}2^{qrs}_{sh\ d}$ had been ordered into his hands out of Sum he had rec.d from y.e Severall Con.stables $290\text{-}1\text{-}3\text{-}0$ and by orders from the Selectmen & Meeting houfe Com.te he had paid the Sum of $289\text{-}17\text{-}9\text{-}$ and that there still remains y.e following Sums in the hands of the Severall Conftables Viz.y Due from Ezekiel Wyman $28\text{-}4\text{-}3\text{-}3^{qr}$ From W.m Snow £6-5- from Jon.a Willard j.unr $15\text{-}15\text{-}7\text{-}3^{qr}_{sh\ d}$- From Zech.h Whitney $15\text{-}10\text{-}5\text{-}2^{qr}_{sh\ d}$ from Nath.? Page 5-17-11-3 and also from faid Page 17^{sh} and 4^{d} from James Leitch £53-7-8-1 from Philip Goodridge 46-19-8-1 the amount in Const.rs Hands 172-18-1-3

After reading The above certificate Voted y.e acceptance of it

A way two Rod wide from the Houfe of M.r Reuben Dodge where M.r John Fitch formerly lived, down by the Houfe of M.r W.m Jones in order to accomodate the said Dodge & others w.ch a convenient Road to come into the Town and w.ch was laid out at the Defire of the Selectmen — — Not accepted

The above Road is laid out from f'¹ Houfe of M'ʳ Dodge and is markt on the South Side of the Way and runs in and near the Old Troden path as Attested

The above Road not accepted by Reafon yᵗ Mʳ Benoni Wallis objected agⁿˢᵗ its going as proposed through his Land } by Willᵐ Jones
Reuben Dodge
John Fitch } The Committee to lay out Sᵈ Road

[108] A Road laid out two Rod wide and 107 Pole in length beginning at Narragansett Road by James Pooles Land and running thro Sᵈ Pools Land to Thoˢ Stearns Land, then turning and running between f'¹ Stearns & Pooles Land two Rod wide about Thirty Rod to yᵉ Town Line —
Voted not to be accepted.
—— By order — one other Road laid out beginning at the Foot of the hill below Samˡ Pooles Land and running near a Brook (called Monnsnut Brook) about fourscore Rod, then crofling the Brook and running about Thirty Rod to the Town Line through land of Esqʳ Harris —
Voted that the Sᵈ Road be accepted provided the land be given and that the old Road running thrô Sᵈ Harris Land be difcontinued
— The above Roads being laid out by
Amos Kimball
Samˡ Pool
James Pool } Comᵗᵗᵉ

Voted that there be a Bridle Road as laid out through part of Mʳ Samuel Hunts Land to Wᵐ Hendersons land, Beginning at a Stake by the Road about ten Rod North east of Mʳ Hunts Houfe & then runs North west about Twenty Rod to a Stake and Stones by the fence, then runs as the Fence now ftands to yᵉ said Hendersons Land and so along in a lane fenced out through said Hendersons Land between his houfe & Barn
Laid out by order of yᵉ Selectmen pʳ
Willᵐ Snow
Amos Kimball } Comᵗᵗᵉ

Voted that the above road be accepted — and the abovenamed Sam[l]. Hunt & W[m]. Henderfon have consented thereunto & given the land abovementioned — as given under their hands —

Voted and accepted of a Road lay'd out by order of the Selectmen : Beginning at the End of the Road that runs up to the Land of the Heirs of David Peirce & running on a ftrait Line with the Óld Road at the North : East End of the Houfe till it strikes the Stone Wall and then bounds on the Wall on the South Easterly side of the Road and so runs to a Chestnut Tree into the Old Road, the Road being two Rod wide accepted if ye land be given

Eleazer Houghton
Josiah Dodge
John Gibson
} being y[e] Comm[tte]

Voted that the Article in the Warrant respecting the Road laid out by the Selectmen between Lein[t] Bellows Land & Land of Thomas Prentice Esq[r] at y[e] Requeft of Jacob Gould & others — be dismifed

[109] Voted and accepted of a Road laid out by the Selectmen mark'd as follows. Beginning at a Stake at Groton line running on M[r] Goings Land to a white Oak Stump mark'd near his houfe then to a Rock in the Fence, then to white oak Tree these marks on the North side of said Way, then to a White Oak Tree mark't on the South side of s[d] Way on Robert Moffatts Land, then to a White Oak Tree mark'd, then to a Rock, then to a Stake and Stones between Going & Moses Gould, S[d] Way to be four Rod wide — —

Then the said meeting was adjourned to the Third monday of May next at one of the Clock afternoon

Recorded p[r] WILLIAM DOWNE *Town Clerk*

May 21th Anno Domini. 1753 The Freeholders and other Inhabitants of the Town of Lunenburg being mett by Adjournment

Voted and Granted to Tho[s] Prentice Esq[r]   0- 2-11-1$\frac{5}{12}$
Voted and Granted to M[r] James Leitch   — 0- 3- 0 —

Voted and Granted to Mr Ezekiel Wyman —   0- 1- 0
Voted and Granted to Mr Ezekiel Wyman —   0-16- 0- 0
Voted and Granted to Deacon Wm Stearns ⎫
  for his Service Two Years as Treafurer ⎭   2- 0- 0- 0

Voted that there be a Com^{tte} chose to treat wth & examine the acco^{ts} of Capt Benj^a Goodridge, Deacon Saml. Johnfon & Leiu^t Josiah Dodge the Meeting Houfe Committee

Voted that Major Hartwell Leiu^t Nathan Heywood — Willm Downe, John Grout, Jonathan Wood, be a Com^{ttee} for the purpose afore s^d

Voted that Jeremiah Norcrofs be one of the s^d Committee in the Room of Leiu^t Heywood who refuses ——

Voted that the Comm^{tte} be impowered to inquire of Capt Benj^a Goodridge, Deacon Saml Johnson Leiu^t Josiah Dodge the Meeting Houfe Com^{te} what Sums of Money they have received out of the Severall Sums granted and ordered for building and finifhing the New Meeting Houfe and how they have difpofed of the Same

—— verte.

[110] Voted that the s^d Committee make return to the Town Clerk of their Proceedings by the middle of June next.

Voted that the Sum of Sixty pounds be raised and that the Inhabitants of the Town of Lunenburg be afsefsed the s^d Sum to be workt out at the Highways, the Method as to raising the Money and the price of Labour to be the same as the last year — — — —

The Ninth Article in the Warrant being read, respecting the releiving & providing for M^r. Sam^{ll} Stow —— and Mr Stow being present and representing his Case & Circumftances before the Town ——— Voted — That the Selectmen deal with Mr Stow in the steps of the Law —

Voted & granted the Sum of Four pounds for the ufe of the Poor in s^d Town

Recorded p^r WILLIAM DOWNE *Town Clerk*

At a Legall meeting of the Freeholders and other Inhabitants of the Town of Lunenburg Afsembled July the 9th A. D. 1753

Voted and chose M.' John Gibson Moderator

The Report of a Comm.ᵗᵉᵉ chosen to treat with and examine the acco.ᵗˢ of Cap.ᵗ Benj.ᵃ Goodridge, Deacon Sam.ᵖ Johnſon & Leiu.ᵗ Josiah Dodge the Meeting Houſe Com.ᵗᵗᵉ was Read ——

It being put to vote whether the Town will choose a Comm.ᵗᵉᵉ to settle y.ᵉ acco.ᵗˢ of y.ᵉ Pew Committee ——— paſsed in the Negative

The Third Article in the Warrant being put to Vote to See whether the Town will chooſe Agents & instruct and impower them to bring an action in Common Law ag.ⁿˢᵗ Cap.ᵗ Goodridge & others y.ᵉ Meeting Houſe Committee

———————paſsed in the Negative

Voted and granted the Sum of Sixty Pounds lawſull money to the Rev.ᵈ M.ʳ David Stearns for his Salary this preſent year ——

[111] Voted and chose Meſs.ʳˢ Joshua Goodridge, Moses Mitchell Ephraim Whitney & Deacon W.ᵐ Stearns to be a Com.ᵗᵉᵉ to provide a School master ——

Voted and granted the Sum of Fifty Three pounds six shill.ˢ and eight pence Lawfull Money for the use of Schooling in said Town

Voted that the School be kept in the Quarters of the Town as it has already been till further orders ——

Voted that Notifications for Town Meetings for the future be posted up within Three foot of the South East Corner of Major Hartwells Horſe Stable

Recorded ṗ. : W.ᵐ DOWNE *Town Clerk*

Att a Legall Meeting of the Freeholders and other Inhabitants of the Town of Lunenburg Aſsembled October 22.ᵈ 1753.

Voted and chose M.ʳ Jonathan Wood Moderator

Voted that the Grammar School in S.ᵈ Town be kept in the four Quarters of the Town as formerly and that the Remainder of Money already voted for the uſe of Schooling be improved by the School Com.ᵗᵉᵉ in said uſe in such parts of the Town as S.ᵈ Committee ſhall judge most beneficial ——

The 2ᵈ Article in Warrant respecting granting Money to mend yᵉ Road beyond Mʳ Samˡˡ Hunts to the West Line of Sᵈ Town, being put to Vote — — — not Voted — Voted that Mʳ Amos Kimball be joyned to the Comᵗᵉᵉ for hiring a School master

The 4ᵗʰ Article in yᵉ Warrant being put to Vote. to see Whether yᵉ School Houſes Shall be built in the places already appointed for that purpoſe ——— No Vote.

and then the sᵈ meeting was dismiſsed ——

Recorded pʳ Wᴹ Downe *Town Clerk*

[112] At a Legall meeting of the Freeholders and other Inhabitants of the Town of Lunenburg aſsembled March 4ᵗʰ 1754

Voted and chose Deacon William Stearns Moderator

Capᵗ Benjamin Goodridge ⎫
Deacon John Heywood ⎬ Select men
Meſʳˢ Solomon Steward ⎬ Sworn Aſseſsors
     Moses Ritter
     John Bufs ⎭

William Downe   Town Clerk Sworn
Deacon Thoˢ Reddington   Town Treaſurer
Meſʳˢ David Chaplin ⎫
     John Hill ⎬ Constables

Upon a Motion made and seconded Voted that Mʳ John Hill be excused serving as Constable and Mʳ Arrington Gibson was chose in his Room & Sworn

Capᵗ John Gibson ⎫
Meſʳˢ William Jones
     Moses Ritter
     Charles White ⎬ chosen Surveyors
     Samuel Pool   of Highways
     Joseph Spafford
     Thoˢ Carter
     Moses Mitchell
     David Wood
     Abijah Hovey
     Samuel Larrabee ⎭

Meſʳˢ Benjamin Garey junʳ ⎫
     Eleazer Houghton
     Josiah Dodge junʳ ⎬ chosen Tything Men
     Patrick White
     Samuel Hammond ⎭

Mefs.rs Zebulon Dodge } Timothy Bancroft } chosen Hogreves
Mefs.rs Samuel Hunt } Isaac Gibson } chosen Deer. Reeves
Mefs.rs Timothy Parker } Samuel Hunt } chosen Fence Veiwers

[113] Mr. Thomas Carter chosen Sealer of Leather
Leiut Jacob Gould } chosen Surveyors of
Mr Josiah Dodge junr. } Boards shingles and Clabboards
Mefs.rs Jona. Wood junr } Paul Crocker } chosen Cullers of Staves
Mefs.rs Ephraim Kimball } Reuben Gibson } chosen to take of Fire

Voted and Granted Mr. Philip Goodridge one Shilling for his warning Mathew Davis out of Town —

Voted and Granted Mr Joshua Goodridge four shill.s for his going to procure a School Master

Voted and granted Mr. Moses Mitchell Two fhill.s for the ufe of his Horfe in the sd. Service —

Voted and accepted of Mr Patrick White to be a Conftable in the Room of Mr David Chaplin and he was Sworn to ye faith full Discharge of his office.

Voted to choose a Committee to reckon with the Town Treafurer

William Downe }
Mefs.rs Amos Kimball } Committee chosen for
John Grout } the Said Purpose —

The 4th 6th 8th 9th 10th 11th Articles in the Warrant being Read, and the Town Voted not to act upon any of the said Articles.

Voted that Swine run at large this Year ——and then said meeting was dismifsed —

Recorded pr. WILLIAM DOWNE *Town Clerk*

[114] At a Legall Meeting of the Freeholders and other Inhabitants of the Town of Lunenburg Afsembled April 16th A: D. 1754 —

Voted and chose Mr. John Heywood Moderator
Mefs.rs Josiah Bayley } a committee to
William Stearns } examine the accot.s
Chose Afahel Hartwell } of the Committee
appointed to manage the affairs

of building the New Meeting Houfe and make Report to the Town at their next Town meeting.

Voted that the Sum of Thirty pounds be granted and work't out between Mr Hunts and the West line of the Town ——

Voted that Ten pounds be raised and workt out from the South Side of the River to Narragansett Line — —

Voted and Granted the Sum of Sixty pounds to mend the Town Ways withal —— —— ——

Voted that the Wages from Mr Hunts to the West Line of the Town be 2-8 p^r Day and the same from the River to Narragansett Line and 0-1-6 p^r Day for a yoke of oxen and 0-0-8 for a Cart —— and 0-2-0 p^r Day for a man & 0-1-4 for a yoke of oxen & 0-0-8 for a Cart in Town —— and 0-1-4 p^r Day for a Plow, the whole of the Money to be workt out by the last of September next: . —

The above Attested by John Heywood Moderator and Recorded p^r WILLIAM DOWNE *Town Clerk*

At a Legall meeting of the Freeholders & other Inhabitants of the Town of Lunenburg Affembled May 20th A: D. 1754 —

Voted and chose Deacon Benj^a Foster Moderator

Voted and chose Mr Abijah Stearns Town Treafurer in the Room of Mr Thos Reddington who was chosen in March last and has refused to act in that Capacity ——

Report of the Committee appointed to reckon with Deacon William Stearns late Town Treafurer being read, Voted that the same be accepted.

as sett forth in S^d Report

Dated May 3^d 1754 – reference to ye same being had may appear

Report of the Committee chosen to reckon with the Com^{te} formerly appointed to manage the Affairs of building the New Meeting Houfe, being Read & put to Vote whether the Said Report be accepted, and y^t ye s^d Com^{tee} be discharged ye Sum of 521-19-5-1 & that ye said Committee be allowed the Sum of 1-19-5-1 as by s^d Report appears to be Due to said Committee to Ballance

—— —— NO Vote —

[115] The 4th Article in the Warrant being Read —
Voted that Capt Willard, Mr Auſtin & Mr Nathl Page be appointed to rectify the Fence round the burying Yard and clear up the Brush in sd burying place and bring in their accounts at the next Town Meeting —
Voted that Mr Bufs, Mr George Kimball & Mr Ireland be appointed to look out a place for a burying Yard and agree about the Price & report at ye next Town Meeting and then the said meeting was diſmiſsed ——

Recorded pr WILLIAM DOWNE *Town Clerk*—

At a Legall meeting of the Freeholders & other Inhabitants of the Town of Lunenburg Aſsembled Sepr 10th 1754
Voted and chose Willm Downe Esqr Moderator
Voted and granted the Sum of Sixty pounds Lawfull Money for the Revd Mr David Stearns's Salary for this present year ——
Voted and granted the Sum of Thirty pounds for the School.
Voted and chose Meſsrs Ezekiel Wyman & ⎫ a Comt
          David Wood   ⎪ to provide
       Capt John Gibson   ⎬ a School
       Lieut Jacob Gould & ⎪ Maſter or
       Mr   Benjn Garey junr ⎪ Maſters or
                 ⎭ Miſtreſses

Voted and granted the Sum of Eight pounds to repair the Bridge by Mr Paul Wetherbee's ——
Voted and granted the Sum of Six pounds to repair the Bridge between ye Great Bridge and Mr Amos Kimballs and also voted that the said Sums for repairing the said Bridges be work't out as usuall and the Work to be done by the middle of October next — — — —
Voted and granted the Sum of Four pounds for ye uſe of ye Poor.
Voted and granted to Lieut Josiah Dodge the Sum of one pound nineteen ſhill: and five pence one farthing being Due to him, for what he has done to ye New Meeting Houſe —
The 8th Article in the Warrant being put, paſsed in the Negative — — —

                Verte

[116] Voted That M.' John Heywood the Representative of the Town petition the Great & Generall Court in the behalf of the Town, that the unimproved Lands belonging to Perſons out of Town and who are now reſidents may be taxed to mend the High ways from M.' Sam: Hunts to Dorchester Canady and from David Goodridges to Narragansett N.º 2 at one half penny per Acre or such other Sum as y.ˢ shall think proper for the Term of Five Years — — —

Voted and granted the Sum of one pound Six ſhill.ˢ & 8 pence to Deacon Will.ᵐ Stearns for his Services as Treaſurer of the Town for the year 1753 — — — —

Voted and granted the Sum of one pound Six ſhill.ˢ & 8.ᵈ to M.' Ezekiel Wyman for his taking care of the New Meeting Houſe one year & one Quarter ——

Voted and granted the Sum of one pound Six ſhill.ˢ & 8.ᵈ to y.ᵉ Aſseſsors for y.ᵉ Year 1752 for y.ʳ Service in s.ᵈ Year

Voted and granted the Sum of one pound six ſhill.ˢ & 8.ᵈ to the Aſseſsors for y.ᵉ Year 1753 for their Service in s.ᵈ Year

The 11.ᵗʰ Article in y.ᵉ Warrant respecting the providing a Suitable place in the Westerly part of the Town for a burying place, with the report of a Committee thereon being read —— referred for further Consideration at the next Town Meeting — — — —

The 12.ᵗʰ Article, viz.! to hear an Extract of the exciſe Bill prepared by the Generall Court & now lying for the Governours Consent and to hear the Govern.ʳˢ Speech thereon & to shew their minds whether they would have said Bill paſs into a Law —— being read & putt to Vote —— paſsed in the Negative —— and then said Meeting was Diſmiſsed ——

Recorded p.ʳ W.ᴹ DOWNE *Town Clerk*

[117] Worcest.ʳ ſc: Anno Regni Regis Georgij secundi magno Brittaniæ Franciæ & Hiberniæ viceſsimo Octavo

Att a Court of Gen.ˡˡ Seſsions of Peaſe begun and held at Worcester within and for the County of Worcester the first Tuesday of November being the fifth Day of said Month A. D. 1754 — — —

Mefs.rs Jonathan White and Thomas Wilder both of Leominster in said County a Committee appointed in august last on the Petition of John Scott of Lunenburg in the County of Worcester Husbandman to lay out a Way or private Road agreable to the Report of the Committee of Lunenburg for laying out the Same as p.r s.d Committees Report to the Town of Lunenburg at their annual meeting in March last appears which way described as follows, beginning at the land of the S.d John Scott, and running North Eaft on John Bridges land described by mark'd Trees, then on land of M.r Mead then on land of Joseph Eaton, then on land of Joseph Spafford to the Road that comes from Isaac Gibsons said Road described by mark'd Trees, and the Road to be on the South Side of s.d mark'd Trees & to be two Rods wide

Reported that having veiwed the s.d Road have laid out the same to y.e great Satisfaction of M.r John Scott, and the owners of the land the Road goes through, who freely gave their Land for the Road and the Road to be on the South side of the mark'd Trees ——

Which Report was read and accepted by the Court & order that the Said Road for y.e future be deemed a private Road, Provided the said John Scott pay all the Charge relating to the affair, and upon his so doing order the same to be recorded ——

    Copy examined p.r TIMO.y PAINE *Clerk*

A True Copy of a Copy
    Attest W.m DOWNE *Town Clerk*

[118] At A Legal Meeting of the freeholders & other Inhabitants of the Town of Lunenburg Afsembled March y.e 3.d A D 1755

Voted and Chofe M.r John Heywood Moderator

Benj: Goodridge   ⎫
Cap.t Joshua Hutchins ⎟ Selectmen and
M.r Jonathan Wood   ⎬ Sworn Afsefsors
M.r Afahel Hartwell   ⎟
M.r Samvel Davis   ⎭

Benj: Goodridge Town Clerk and Sworn
M.r Abijah Stearns Town Treafurer & Sworn

Mr Mofes Mitchel
Mr Abraham Sanderfon } were chofen Conftables & Sworn

Mr Joseph Fuller
Mr Ezekiel Wyman
Mr Obediah Walker
Mr Daniel Auftin
Mr Amos Kimbal
Mr David Taylor
Mr Joseph Chaplin
Mr Thomas Brown
Mr Benj Stearns
Mr Jonathan Hartwell
Mr Samvel Poole
} were Chofen Surveyors of the Highways & Sworn

Mr David Wood
Mr John Griffin } were chofen fences viewers & fworn

Mr Thomas Carter Chofen Sealer of Leather

Mr David Wood
Mr Samvel Commings
Mr Ephraim Whitney
} were Chofen Tyding men

Mr James Poole
Mr Ephraim Whitney } were Chofen Dear Reives

Mr Samvel Johnfon jun
Mr Richard Fowler
Mr Reuben Dodge
Mr Jonathan Wood
Mr Benoni Wallis
} were Chofen Hogge Reives and Sworn

[119] Mr Thomas Leitch } were chofen Surveyors of
Mr Samvel Davis } Staves and Shingles &c and Sworn

Mr Ifaac Gibfon
Mr Amos Kimbal
Mr John Darlin
Mr James Poole
Mr John Fitch
} were chofen to take Care of fire

Voted that Mr John Bufs Mr Abraham Ireland and Mr George Kimbal be acommitte to agree with Mr John Wyman for a peice of Land for a Buriing place and to take a Deed for the Town

Voted & Granted the Sum of thirty pound for the ufe of the School

Voted and Granted the Sum of Six pound for the ufe of the poor

Voted and Granted the Sum of Sixty pound to mend the High ways withall to be workt out as it was the Laſt year

Voted that the Town Except of atown way two Rods wide Begining at the weſterly Side of John Fitchs Land and Runing in and Near the path as it is now Trood to Iſaac Gibſons and is Described by markt trees on the Northerly Side of ſaid way and was Laid out by

        John Buſs
        Iſaac Gibſon
        John Fitch

A Committee appointed By the Selectmen

Voted and Excepted of a Town way two Rods wide Begining at the way neer the Bottom of the Hill Weſt of James Pooles and Runs from thence to the Bridge over Wenoosnoock Brook and from the Brook by trees markt on the South weſterly ſide of S^d way Through Land of James Pooles to the Line Between S^d Pooles and Thomas Stearns Lands then on Said Stearns Land to the Town Line then Runs Southerly one Rod on S^d Stearns Land and one Rod on william Perkins Land about Seventy five Rod alſo a two Rod way from f^d Stearns Houſe to the way where it firſt came to his Land ſaid way was Laid out
      By the Selectmen.   turn over—

[120] Voted that part of the town way be Discontinued Between the Bridge by Paul Wetherbees and the Land of Edward Hartwell Eſq^r (viz) Begining at a pine tree neer ſ^d Wetherbes fence till it comes to ſaid Hartwells Land and that they Except of away in the Room thereof viz Begining at the aboveſaid pine tree and Runs acroſs ſaid Wetherbes Land till it comes into the way again By Samvel Commings Land and is Deſcribed by markt trees on the northerly ſide of ſaid way and was Laid out two rods wide by the Selectmen and ſaid wetherbe is to Clear ſaid way and make it fit to Travil in

Then voted that this meeting be Ajourned to the ſecond tuesday of May next at two of the Clock in the afternoon

LUNENBURG May the 13th 1755 the Freeholders and other Inhabitants of said Town Being Met again by ajornment

Voted and Excepted of a Town way Laid out by acommite appointed by the Selectmen Between the Lands of Capt Joshua Hutchins and Benjamin Bellows Esqr Begining at ye corner of said Hutchins House Lot and said Bellowses near the new meeting House two Rods wide upon said Bellowses Land and Runs North easterly upon said Bellowses Land 144 Rods upon a Strait Line to Where said Hutchins Corners upon said Bellows from thence set off two Rods wide upon said Hutchins Land & Runs a strait Line 144 Rods to the first mentioned Bounds near the new meeting House and from the said Hutchins North Easterly Corner two Rods wide upon Mr Daniel Austins Land 28 Rods in Length NorthEasterly then upon said Bellowes' Land two Rods wide by the widow Randalls Eleven Rods in Length till it Comes into the way that Leads to Shirley and Groton the Abovesaid way was Laid out by

     Capt Joshua Hutchins ⎫ A Comtte
     Mr Daniel Austin   ⎬ appointed
     Mr Jacob Gould   ⎪ by the
             ⎭ Selectmen

Voted and Excepted of a Town way Begining at Thomas Potters Land one Rod wide on Mr Secretary willards Land and one Rod wide on Caleb Taylors Land and on Land of sd Taylors Brothers then one Rod wide on David Taylors Land and one Rod wide on Arrinton Gibsons Land then one Rod [121] Wide on Josiah Bayleys Land and one Rod on Land that Mr Jones Reserved out of Benoni Wallises Deed then twenty feet wide on said Bayleys Land and Twelve feet wide on Benoni Wallis-es Land till it comes to the Brook then Tapering a Little till at the End of ten Rods it Comes to one Rod on said Bayleys And one Rod on said Wallis es Lands so continuing till it comes to said Bayleys Corner then continuing one Rod on said Wallis es Land and one Rod on Land of Nathanael Harris Esqr till it comes into the way that Gos

by Mr Jones Houfe faid way was Laid out and Deferibed by
     Mr Solomon Steward
     Mr John Bufs *Selectmen*
  Recorded Pr BENJ.. GOODRIDGE *town Cler*

At A Legal Meeting of the Freeholders & other Inhabitants of the Town of Lunenburg Afsembled May the 20th A D 1755

Voted and Chofe Mr John Heywood Modderator

Voted and Chofe Mr George Kimball Mr William Stearns and Mr Jofiah Bayley a committe to provide a Houfe to Set Idle perfons to work in

Voted and Granted the Sum of thirty pound to mend the ways from David Goodridge es to narraganfetts Line and from Samvel Hunts to Narraganfetts Line and from Reuben Gibfons to John Fitches the wages to be Same as Laft year

    Recorded Pr BENJ. GOODRIDGE *town Cler*

[122] At A Legal meeting of the freeholders and other Inhabitants of the Town of Lunenburg Afsembled September the ninth 1755

voted and Chofe Capt Jofhua Hutchins Modd^r

Voted and Granted the Sum of Sixty pound to the Rev Mr David Stearns for his Sallary for the prefent year

              £ s d

Voted and Granted to Capt John Gibfon ye Sum of 0- 4-4
Voted and Granted to Afael Hartwell   0- 1-0
Voted & Granted to Edward Hartwell jun   0- 1-0
Voted & Granted to Abijah Stearns the Sum of 0-12-0
Voted & Granted to Abraham Carlton   0- 1-0
Voted & Granted to ye Afsefsor for the year 1754 1- 6-8
  Voted and Chofe
    Mr Abraham Sanderfon } a Committe to
    Mr Edward Hartwell jun | provide the Town
    Mr Reuben Gibfon   { with School Marfters
    Mr Obediah Walker   (and mistrefses
    Mr Jacob Gould   &c
             } for ye year Infuing

  Voted and Granted the Sum of ten pound for the ufe of the School

Voted that the Selectmen be a committe to Reckon with with the Town Treafurer and to Give him a Difcharge for Such Sums as he has paid

Voted that the abatments of the Rates mentioned in the Sixth article be Refered to the Selectmen

     Recorded P̄ BENJ GOODRIDGE *Town Cler*

[123] At A Legal Meeting of the Freeholders and other Inhabitants of the Town of Lunenburg Afsembled March the firft A D 1756

Voted and Chofe Capt Jofhua Hutchins Modderator

Voted and Chofe

  Benj. Goodridge
Capᵗ Jofhua Hutchins   Chofen Selectmen
Mʳ Jonathan Wood   and
Mʳ Amos Kimball   Sworn as Afsefsors as the
Mʳ Afhael Hartwell   Law Directs

Benj. Goodridge Chofen Town Clerk & Sworn as the Directs

Capᵗ Jofhua Hutchins Chofen Town Treafurer & Sworn as the Law Directs.

Mʳ George Kimball   Chofen Conftables & Sworn
Mʳ Abijah Stearns   as the Law Directs

Mʳ Philip Goodridge
Mʳ David Wood
Mʳ John White
Mʳ Joseph Fuller   Chofen Surveyors of
Mʳ Nathanael Page
Mʳ Jonathan Parce   Highways
Mʳ Isaac Gibson   and
Mʳ Caleb Taylor   Sworn as the Law
Mʳ James Poole   Directs
Mʳ Timothy Parker

Mʳ Thomas Dutton   Chosen fence veiwers
Mʳ John Hereman   and Sworn as the Law Directs

Mʳ Ezekiel Goodridge   Chofen Tydingmen
Mʳ Ephraim Whitney   and Sworn as the
Mʳ Benj Gary Jun   Law Directs

Mʳ Jofeph Page
Mʳ Samvel Hammond   Chofen Hogg reives
Mʳ David Wood   and Sworn as the
Mʳ Thomas Brown   Law Directs

          Turn over

[124] Mr Isaac Gibson ⎱ cholen to take Care of Deer
Mr James Poole ⎰ and Sworn as the Law Directs
M^r Joſiah Dodge Jun ⎫ Choſen to take care of fire and
Mr Reuben Gibson ⎬ Burn the woods and Sworn
Mr David Goodridge ⎭ as the Law Directs
M^r Moſes Ritter   Choſen Sealer of Leather and Sworn
              as the Law Directs
Mr Jacob Gould   ⎱ choſen Surveyors of Staves and
Mr Philip Goodridge ⎰ ſhingles and to Meaſure Boards
          &c and Sworn as the Law Direct

Voted and Granted the Sum of Seventy pound to mend the High ways in the Town and that the Same be workt out at two Shillings p^r Day for aman and one ſhilling and four pence for a pair of oxen and eight pence for a cart Between the firſt of April and the Laſt of September

Voted and Granted the Sum of forty pound to Mend the ways from Capt Hunts to Narraganſett Line and from David Goodridges to Narragansett Line and from Reuben Gibſons to Dorcheſter Cannady to be workt at two Shillings and Eight pence pr Day for aman and one Shilling and four pence for a pair of oxen and Eight pence for a Cart the whole to be workt out Between the firſt of April and the Laſt of September

Voted and Excepted of a Town Way Laid out by order of the Selectmen Begining on the Eaſt of the Road that Leads from Lunenburg Meeting Houſe to Lancaſter Below Eſq^r Hartwells Barn through part of Eſq^r Hartwells Land and through Aſael Hartwells and Jonathan Hartwells Land to ſaid Jonathan Hartwells Eaſt Line one Rod and half Wide as it is Now fenced out ſaid way was Laid out and Deſcribed by

Said way was	M^r Aſael Hartwell and
excepted provided the	Mr Jonathan Hartwell
Land be Given	who were appointed by the Selectmen

[125] Voted and Excepted of a town way Laid out by order of the Selectmen Begining at the way by Ephraim Kimballs and So Ran through Phineas Stewards and Solomon Stewards jun Land to the Land of M^r Ed-

ward Robins and through S^d Robins Land to Naraganset road Discribed by marked trees on the North Side then Running from Naraganset road on f^d Robins and David Goodridges Land to the Land of James Richardfon juner and on S^d Richardfon Land to Lemenfter Line Discribed by markt trees on the North Side

Said way was Laid out and Deferibed by
         Mr David Goodridge
Said way was Excepted Mr Ephraim Kimbal
provided the Land   Mr Solomon Steward Jun
be Given

Voted and Excepted of a Town way Laid out by order of the Selectmen Begining at a Stake by Amos Kimbals Land between him & Land of Timothy Parker running one Rod upon S^d Kimbals Land to a heap of Stones till it comes to Mr Olivers Land then running Two Rod wide upon M^r olivers Land till it Comes to Land of Hezekiah Hodgkins & Ephraim Osbourn by mark'd Trees and runs between Ephraim Osbourns Land and Hezekiah Hodgkins Land two Rods wide till it comes to Land of Samuel Hodgkins & Silas Snow by mark-d Trees and then runs through S^d Samuel Hodgkins & sd Silas Snows Land two Rod wide by markd Trees till ^it goes throfi the westermost part of their Land which way was Laid out and Deferibed by

and was Excepted pro- Mr William Snow
vided the Land be Given Mr Abraham Ireland } Committe
          Mr Amos Kimbal } Appointed

[126] At A Legal Meeting of the freeholders and other Inhabitants of the Town of Lunenburg Afsembled May the 17th 1756

Voted and Chofe Mr Jonathan Wood Modderator
Voted that the firft Article in the Warrant be Dismift
Voted that Hoggs Run at Large the prefent year

At A Legal Meeting of the freeholders and other Inhabitants of the Town of Lunenburg Afsembled July the firft A D 1756

Voted and Chofe Mr Jonathan Wood Moddrator
Voted that they will chufe a committe to fhew Caufe why the prayer of the petetion fhould not be Granted
Voted that Edward Hartwell Esqr ⎫
 Benj Goodridge
 Capt John Gibfon
 Mr Nathan Heywood
 William Downe Efq^r ⎬ Bea Com^{tte}
 Mr Amos Kimbal
 Mr Jonathan Wood
 Mr Jacob Gould and
 Mr Jofiah Dodge ⎭
Fully Impowered to Shew Caufe why the prayer of the petetion of william Little and others Should not be Granted and to Anfwer and Reply thereto in behalf of the Town in all Respects as they think Belt and that any two of them go to Bofton and wait upon the General Court With their Anfwer

Recorded p̃ BENJ GOODRIDGE
Town Clerk

[127] At A Legal Meeting of the freeholders and other Inhabitants of the Town of Lunenburg Afsembled September the Sixth A D 1756
Voted and Chofe Mr Samvel Johnson Moddrator
Voted and Granted to the Rev Mr David Stearns for His Sallary for the prefent year the Sum of Sixty pound to be paid out of the Town Treafury
Voted and Chofe Benj. Goodridge Mr Jonathan Wood Capt John Gibfon Mr Samvel Johnfon and Mr Mofes Ritter a Committe to provide the Town with a School Mafter &c for the year Enfuing
Voted that ye Committe be Inftructed to place the Gramer School as near the places appointed for the four Quarters as they can and that they confider other parts of the town as Equally as may be
Voted that the Committe may Expend the Sum of fifty five pound for the Support of the Schools the year Enfuing
Voted and Granted the Sum of forty pound to be Afsefsed and paid into the Town Treafury

Voted that the Afsefsors for the year 1755 be paid
1-6-8 for their Service
Voted and Granted to Benj Goodridge —   0- 6-0
Voted and Granted to Afahel Hartwell   0- 4-0
Voted and Granted to Abijah Stearns   0-12-0
Voted and Granded Abraham Carlton   0-12-0
                    Recorded P̱ BENJ GOODRIDGE
                                    Town Clerk

[128] At a Legal Meeting of the freeholders and other Inhabitants of the Town of Lunenburg Afsembled March ye 7th A: D: 1757

Voted and Chose Mr Asael Hartwell Modderator

Benj Goodridge
Capt Joshua Hutchens | Chofen Selectmen and
Mr Asael Hartwell | Sworn Afsefsors
Mr Jonathan Wood | as the Law Directs
Mr George Kimball

Benj Goodridge Chofe Town Cleark and Sworn
                as the Law Directs

Mr Abijah Stearns Chofe Town Treafurer and
              Sworn as the Law Directs

Mr Stephen Boynton | Chofen Conftables and
Mr Partrick White | Sworn as the Law Directs

Mr Samuel Commings
Mr Josiah Dodge junr
Mr Stephen Stickney
Capt Samuel Hunt | Chofen Surveyers
Mr Isaac Bayley | of Highways
Mr Samuel Larrabee | and
Mr Reuben Gibson | Sworn
Mr Jacob Gould | as the Law Directs
Mr Richard Taylor
Mr Nathanel Page
Mr Ephraim Parce

Mr Nathanael Page
Mr Benj Reddington | Chofen fence viewers
Mr Abraham Ierland | and Sworn
Mr Samuel Johnfon jun | As the Law Directs

Mr Philip Goodridge | Surveyers of Boards and Shingles
Mr Timothy Parker | and Claboards
              and Sworn as the Law Directs

Mr Thomas Leitch } Chofen Surveyers of Staves and
Mr Paul Crocker } Sworn as the Law Directs
Mr Thomas Carter Chofe Sealer of Leather and
　　　　　　　　　Sworn as the Law Directs
Mr Abijah Stearns }
Mr Richard Taylor } Chofen Tydingmen and
Mr Stephen Stickney } Sworn as the Law
Mr Benj Stearns } Directs

[129] Capt Samuel Hunt } Chofen to take Care of
　　　Mr Isaac Gibson } Dear and Sworn as
　　　　　　　　　　　the Law Directs

Mr William Chadwick }
Mr Charles White }
Mr Jonathan Paree } Chofen Hoge reives and
Mr William Alexander } Sworn as the Law Directs
Mr David Goodridge }

Mr Samuel Pool }
Mr Noah Dodge } Chofen to take Care of fire
Mr Amos Kimball } and Sworn as the Law Directs
Mr Isaac Gibson }

The fourth article was Read and the Requeft of Samuel Hunt and others and after a debate Voted That Edward Hartwell Efq^r Mr Nathan Heywood Mr Amos Kimball Mr Thomas Stearns and Benj Goodridge be A committe to confider the Petetion of Samuel Hunt and others and Papers accompaning the fame and Report what they Judge proper for the Town to Do thereon on the third Tusday of May Next at one of the clock in the afternoon to which time This meeting is ajornd

Voted and Excepted of a Town way Laid out by order of the Selectmen Begining at the End of the way by Mr Jofiah Dodges Saw mill at a pitch pine Tree on the hill South of the Saw mill and Runs by markt trees markt on the Northerly fide of faid way to to David Parees and from thence by Trees Markt on the Eafterly Side of faid way To George Mcferlands said way was Laid out and Defcribed by
　　and Excepted provided the　　Jonathan Paree
　　Land be Given　　　　　　　George Mc ferlin
　　A Commite appointed　　　　David Paree

[130] Voted and Excepted of a town Way provided the Land be Given (viz) Begining at Ifaiah Witts and Runing Eafterly about 30 rod upon Jofhua Meads Land then upon Timothy Bancrofts Land about 40 Rod and then Runing upon Land of Mr Hobby and John Demary about 80 Rods then Runing about twenty Rods on f^d Hobbys Land into the County Road upon the Souther Side of markt trees the whole Length of way faid way Being two Rod wide and was Laid out and Defcribed by
John Demary
Ifaiah Witt

Voted that this meeting Be Ajorn d to the third Tuesday of May Next at one of the Clock in the afternoon
Recorded ṗ BENJ GOODRIDGE
Cler

May ye the 17th A: D: 1757
The free holders and other Inhabitants of the Town of Lunenburg being met on ajournment and after hearing the Report of the Committe on the Requeft of Samuel Hunt and others and a Debate thereon
Voted that the Report be Recommitted for amendment and that the Committe Report a gain att the Town Meeting in September next

At Legal Meeting of the freeholders and other Inhabitants of the Town of Lunenburg Afsembled May the 17 A: D: 1757
Voted and Chofe Capt John Gibfon Modderator
Voted that Swine Run at Large the prefent year
Voted and Granted the Sum of fifty pound to mend the Highways in Town withall
Voted & Granted the Sum of forty pounds to Mend High ways withall above the Town the wages the Same as Laft year   Recorded ṗ BENJ GOODRIDGE
Cler

[131] At a Legal Meeting of the Freeholders and other Inhabitants of the Town of Lunenburg Afsembled Sept ye 27th 1757

Voted and Chofe Mr John Heywood Modderator

Voted and Granted the Sum of Sixty pounds for the Rev Mr David Stearns es Sallery for the prefent year

Voted and Granted the Sum of forty pound for the ufe of the Schools the year Infueing

Voted that the Selectmen Support the poor out of the Town Treafury as prudently as they can the year Infueing and what is paft

Voted that the two Nurfses that attendded the families of the Simondses when Sick with the Small pox be Alow'd for every twenty four Hours the Sum of two Shillings and Eight pence each

Voted and Granted to Capt Joshua Hutchens   -0-12-0
Voted and Granted to Mr Daniel Austin   0- 2-0
Voted and Granted to Nathaniel Page   0- 2-0
Voted and Granted to the Heirs of Capt Willard   0- 2-0
Voted and Granted to Mr John Heywood   0- 2-0
Voted and Granted to Mr Asael Hartwell   0- 2-0
Voted and Granted to Mr Thomas Heywood   0- 2-0
Voted and Granted to Benj. Goodridge   0- 2-0
Voted and Granted to Benj Goodridge and Capt
  John Gibfon the sum seven pound   7- 0-0
  six Shilings and Eight pence for their time
  and Expences in Going to Bofton on the
  Towns Bufinefs

Voted and chofe Mr Jacob Gould Mr Josiah Bayley Mr Nathaniel Page Mr David Goodridge and Mr Edward Hartwell jun A Committe to provide the Town with Schools the year Infueing

Voted that the Committe be Inftructed to place the Grammer School as near the places appointed for the four Quarters as they can and that they Confider the other parts of the Town as Equally as may be

Voted that the Committe may Expend the Sum of fifty pounds for the ufe of the Schools

Voted and Granted to Abraham Carlton –   0-6-8
Voted and Granted to the Afsefsors for the year
  1756   1-6-8

      Recorded p^r BENJ GOODRIDGE *town Cler*

[132] At A Legal Meeting of the Freeholders and other Inhabitants of the Town of Lunenburg Assembled March yᵉ 6ᵗʰ 1758

Voted and Chofe Mʳ John Heywood Modderator for the Government of fᵈ Meeting

Mʳ Jonathan Wood
Mʳ Afael Hartwell
Mʳ William Stearns } Chofen Selectmen and Sworn Assefsors as the Law Directs
Mʳ Amos Kimball
Mʳ Thomas Carter

Benj Goodridge Chofen Town Clerk and Sworn as the Law Directs

Mʳ Abijah Stearns Chofen Town Treafurer and Sworn as the Law Directs

Mʳ John Wyman } Chofen Conftables and
Mʳ Ephraim Whitney Sworn as the Law Directs

Edward Hartwell Esqʳ
Mʳ William Jones
Mʳ Zecheriah Whitney
Mʳ Abraham Ireland } Chofen Surveyors of Highways
Mʳ William Gillghreaft
Mʳ Paul Wetherbee

Mʳ Philip Goodridge
Mʳ Samuel Hunt
Mʳ John Darling } and Collectors of Highway Rates and Sworn as the Law Directs
Mʳ Benjᵃ Reddington
Mʳ Thomas Leitch
Mʳ Nathaniel Burnam

Mʳ Jeremiah Norcrofs
Mʳ Samuel Davis
Mʳ Phinehas Whelock } Chofen Fence Veiwers and Sworn as the Law Directs
Mʳ Nathaniel Burnam jun

Mʳ Samuel Bradftreet
Mʳ Mofes Ritter
Mʳ Patrick White } Chofen Tyding men and Sworn as the Law Directs
Mʳ Jonathan Paree

[133] Mʳ Ephraim Kimball
Mʳ Phinehas Whelock
Mʳ William Chadwick } Chofen Hog reives and Sworn as the Law Directs
Mʳ Samuel Parker
Mʳ Benjamin Reddington

Mʳ Thomas Carter Chofen Sealer of Leather and Sworn as the Law Directs

Mʳ Thomas Leitch } Chofen Cullers of Staves and
Mʳ Paul Crocker Sworn as the Law Directs

Mr Philip Goodridge ⎫ Chofen Surveyors of clabbords
Mr Samuel Davis   ⎭ and Shingles and Sworn as
                 the Law Directs
Mr Isaac Gibfon ⎫ Chofen to take care of Dear
Mr James Poole ⎭ and Sworn as the Law Directs
Capt Samuel Hunt ⎫ Chofen to take care of Fire
Mr Perfon Eaton   ⎭ and burn the Woods and Sworn
                 as the Law Directs

Voted and Granted the Sum of forty pounds to Repair and mend the High ways in Town Withal

Voted and Granted the Sum of forty pounds to Repair and mend the High ways in the Woods above the Town withal

At A Legal Meeting of the Freeholders and other Inhabitants of the Town of Lunenburg Affembled May ye 25th A: D 1758

Voted and Chofe Mr Jonathan Wood Modderator

Voted that the affair of Repairing the old Meeting Houfe be left with the Selectmen

Voted that the Wages that Shall be Work'd out on the High ways the prefent year be the Same they were Laft year

Voted that they will Seat the Meeting Houfe

Voted that Swine Run at Large the prefent year

                 Recorded ῥ BENJ GOODRIDGE
                                  Town Clerk

[135] At A Legal Meeting of the Freeholders and other Inhabitants of the Town of Lunenburg Affembled September ye 18th A. D. 1758

Voted and Chofe Mr William Snow Modderrator

Voted and Granted the Sum of Sixty pounds for the Rev Mr David Stearnfes Sallerry the prefent year

Voted and Granted the Sum of Thirty pounds for the Support of Schools in the Town of Lunenburg

Voted and Chofe Mr Mofes Ritter Mr Jonathan Paree Mr Paul Wetherbee Mr Richard Taylor and Mr George Kimball A Committe to provide Schooling for the Town of Lunenburg the year Enfuing

Voted that the Committe be Inftructed to place the Grammer Schools as Near the places Appointed for the four Quarters as they can and that they Confider the other parts of the Town as Equally as may be

Voted that the Committe may Expend the Sum of fifty pounds for the ufe of the Schools

Voted and Granted to the Afsefsors for the
year 1757 the Sum of   1 = 6 = 8 = 0

Voted and Granted to Mr Abijah Stearns
Town Treafurer   0 = 12 - 0 - 0

Voted and Granted to Mr Afael Hartwell   0 - 2 - 8 - 0
Voted and Granted to Benj Goodridge   0 = 1 = 4 = 0
Voted and Granted to Mr Phinehas Hartwell 0 = 1 = 4 = 0
Voted and Granted to Capt Samuel Hunt   0 - 6 - 0 - 0

Recorded ??^{p} BENJ GOODRIDGE

town Cler

[136] At A Legal Meeting of the Freeholders and other Inhabitants of the Town of Lunenburg Affembled March y^e 5th A: D: 1759 At the Old Meeting Houfe

Voted and Chofe Mr Samuel Johnfon Modderrator and then Ajorn'd to the Houfe of Capt Jofhua Hutchens

Mr Jonathan Wood
Mr Afael Hartwell   Chofen Selectmen and
Mr Thomas Carter   Sworn Afsefors as the
Mr Amos Kimball   Law Directs
Mr Daniel Auftins

Benjamin Goodridge Chofen Town Clerk and
Sworn as the Law Directs

Mr Abijah Stearns Chofen Town Treafurer and
Sworn as the Law Directs

Samuel Hunt
Mr William Alexander   Chofen Conftables and
David Chaplin   William Alexander Sworn as
the Law Directs

Mr Benjamin Fofter
Mr Thomas Peobody
Mr Nehemiah Fuller
Mr Eleazer Houghton   Chofen Surveyors
Mr David Chaplin   of High ways
Mr Patrick White   and Collectors of
Mr William Shadwick   High way Rates
Mr David Goodridge   and all Sworn as
Mr Benjamin Steward   the Law Directs
Mr Nehemiah Lane   Except David Chaplin
Mr Daniel Holt

Mr Jereremiah Norcrofs ⎫ Chofen fence viewers
Mr Jofiah Bayley ⎬ and Sworn as the
Mr Ifaac Reddington ⎪ Law Directs
Mr John Fuller ⎭

[137] Mr Benjamin Reddington ⎫ Chofen Tyding men
Mr David Wood ⎬ and Sworn
Mr Jeremiah Norcrofs ⎭ as the Law Directs

Mr Thomas Carter   Chofen Sealer of Leather
          and Sworn as the Law Directs

Mr Paul Crocker   Chofen Culler of Staves

Jacob Gould ⎫ Chofen Surveyors of Shingles
Mr Philip Goodridge ⎭ and Sworn as the Law Directs

Mr Darius Houghton ⎫
Mr Zebulon Dodge ⎬ Chofen Hog reives and
Mr John Fuller ⎬ all Sworn as the Law
Mr Ephraim Kimball ⎬ Directs Except Ephraim
Mr Benjamin Fofter ⎭ Kimball

Mr James Pool ⎫ Chofen to take Care of
Mr Isaac Gibfon ⎭ Deer and James Pool
          Sworn as the Law Directs

Mr Jonathan Wood jun ⎫
Mr Phinehas Steward ⎬ Chofen to take Care
Mr Caleb Taylor ⎬ of fire and Jonathan Wood
Mr Nathaniel Carlton ⎭ jun and Nathaniel Carlton
          Sworn as the Law Directs

Voted and Granted the Sum of forty pounds to Mend the Highways in Town withal the wages to be the Same as Laft year viz two Shillings a Day for a Man one Shilling and four pence for A pair of Oxen and Eight pence for a Cart

Voted and Granted the Sum of forty pounds to mend the ways Above the Town withal the wages the Same as Laft year viz two Shillings and Eight pence per Day for A man one Shilling and four pence for a pair of oxen and Eight pence for A cart

[138] Voted and Excepted of A Town way Laid out by order of the Selectmem.

Begining at the Road on the Eaft Side of Ifaac Bayleys Land two Rods wide on Efqr Harris Land twenty five Rods then Coming into Isaac Bayleys Land and Running through his to Jofiah Bayleys jun and Through his to Mr Carltons Land and Runs one Rod on Mr Carltons and one Rod on Mr Goodhues Land to Townfhend Line on the Welterly Side of the Mark't Trees which way was Laid out and Defcribed by David Taylor and Ifaac Bayley

At A Legal Meeting of the Freeholders and other Inhabitans of the Town of Lunenburg Afsembled May ye 21st A: D: 1759

Voted and Chofe Mr John Heywood Moderator

Voted and Accepted of Mr John Wyman to Serve as Conftable in the Room of Capt Samuel Hunt he being Hired by Said Hunt and May ye 21st was Sworn as the Law Directs

Voted and Chofe Benj Goodridge Collector to gather the Half penny Acre Rate who has Since been Sworn as the Law Directs

Voted that the Town will make the Fence on the South Side of the way from the way Near the Meeting houfe between the way and Capt Hutchen's Land till it Comes to Mr Daniel Auftins Land

Voted and Granted to Mr Daniel Holt Eight Shillings old tenor pr Rod for building Said fence provided he makes it Good and finifhes it within four Months

Voted that the place for building a School Houfe Near Mr Stickneys be moved Near the Norweft Corner of Mr Isaac Reddington's Land

Voted that the Town will New build the Bridge over Mulpus Brook Near Mr Bellow's Mill

Voted and Granted Six pound to Rebuild Said Bridge withal and that Mr Thomas Peobody Take Care that f^d Bridge be built

Turn over

[139] Voted That Swine Run at Large the Prefent year

At A Legal Meeting of the Freeholders and other Inhabitants of the Town of Lunenburg Afsembled at the Old Meeting houfe in Said Town September ye 10th 1759

Voted and Chofe Mr Jonathan Wood Modderrator

Voted and Granted the Sum of Sixty pounds
for the Rev Mr David Stearns-s Sallery the
prefent year   £60 – 0 – 0

The Early Records of the Town of Lunenburg. 185

Voted and Granted to Mr Daniel Auftin   00 - 6 - 0
Voted and Granted to Mr Jonathan Page the
  Sum of   00 - 6 - 0
Voted and Granted to Mr Abijah Stearns for
  his Serving Town Treafurer for y^e year 1758   00 - 12 - 0
Voted and Granted to y^e Afsefsors for the year
  1758   01 = 6 = 8
Voted and Granted to Mr Ephraim Kimball   00 = 3 = 0

Voted and Chofe Mr Mofes Ritter Mr Jonathan Parce Mr Paul Wetherbee Mr Richard Taylor and Mr George Kimball A Committe to provide Schooling for the Town of Lunenburg the year Enfuing

Voted that the Committe be Inftructed to place the Grammar School as Near the places appointed for the four Quarters as they Can. and that they Confider the other parts of the Town as Eaqually as may bee

Voted that the Committe may Expend the Sum of fifty pounds for the Ufe of the Schools. And that the Committe Give Orders for the money that was Allowed by the laft years Committe to Any of ye Out fkirts of the Town when it Shall be School'd out

Voted and Granted to Benjamin Goodridge and Mr Jofiah Dodge the Sum of Nine pounds in full Difcharge of their Trouble in building the New Meeting houfe

[140] At A Legal Meeting of the Freeholders and Other Inhabitants of the Town of Lunenburg Afsembled March ye 3rd 1760

Voted and Chofe Mr William Snow Modderrator for the Goverment of Said Meeting

Benj. Goodridge
Mr John Heywood   were Chofen Selectmen
Capt Jofhua Hutchens   and Sworn Afsefsors
Mr Benj: Fofter   as the Law Directs
Capt Samuel Hunt

Benj: Goodridge   Chofen Town Clerk and Sworn
                  as the Law Directs

Mr George Kimball Chofen Town Treafurer and
                  Sworn as the Law Directs

Mr Jonathan Hartwell
Mr Mofes Ritter   Chofen Chofen Conftables

Voted and Excepted of Mr John Wyman to Serve as Conftable in the Room of Mr Jonathan Hartwell and Mr Mofes Ritter and Mr John Wyman were Took the Oaths of Conftables as the Law Directs

Mr Josiah Dodge jun
Mr Joseph Chaplin
Mr Richard Peobody
Mr Thomas Peobody
Leiut Josiah Dodge
Mr John Fuller
Mr Benj: Biglow
Mr Stephen Stickney
Mr Benj: Garey
Mr Mofes Mitchael
Mr Jonathan Mefsor
Mr Joseph Spaffard
} were Chofen Surveyors of High ways and Collectors of High way Rates

Mr Thomas Carter
Mr Zecheriah Whitney
Mr William Chadwick
Mr Phinehas Whelock
} were Chofen Fence Viewers and Sworn as the Law Directs

Mr Paul Wetherbee
Mr Amos Hazeltine
Mr Jeremiah Norcrofs
Mr Nathaniel Carlton
} were Chofen Tyding men

[141] Mr Thomas Carter—Chofen Sealer of Leather and Sworn as the Law Directs

Mr Josiah Bayley
Capt Jacob Gould
} chofen Surveyors of Shingles

Mr Jonathan Wood jun Chofen Cullor of Staves and Sworn as the Law Directs

Mr Joseph Wood
Mr Timothy Bancroft
Mr Darias Houghton
} Chofen Hog reives

Mr Ephraim Kimball
Mr William Chadwick
} Chofen to take Care of Deer and Sworn as the Law Directs

Mr Caleb Taylor
Mr Nehemiah Fuller
Mr James Poole
} Chofen to take care of fire and burn the Woods

Voted and Granted the Sum of fifty pounds to mend the High ways in Town withal

Voted and Granted the Sum of fifty pounds to mend the Highways on the Weft Side of the River and the way from Capt Hunts to Narragansett line towards Dorchester Canada and from Mr Reuben Gibsons to Mr John Fitches and So on to the Town line to Dorchester Canada

Voted that the Higway Rate be work'd by the Hour

Voted that the wages at the High ways be four pence an Hour for a man when they they are on the Spot at work and for Oxen and A Cart as it was the Laft year Viz one Shilling and four pence per day for a pair of Oxen and Eight pence for a cart

The Question was put upon the fourth Article in the Warrant and it pafsed in the Negative

Voted that Swine Run at Large the prefent year

Voted and Accepted of A town way Laid out by order of the Selectmen Beginning Near Mr Thomas Duttons Houfe and is Laid Through Said Duttons Land by Mark'd trees from thence Acrofs a peice of Common Land by mark'd trees from thence Round Mr Isaiah Witts North East corner from thence acrofs Mr Meeds Land by Mark'd Trees from thence upon the Ends of Mr Eaton's and Chadwick Land till it comes to Scotts Road then on that Road to Spaffords land and from thence Acrofs Spaffords land by mark'd Trees to the Road said way is two Rods wide on the Weft Side of said mark'd Trees said way was laid out and Described by Thomas Dutton and Isaac Gibfon and is Accepted as set forth provided the land be given

[142] Voted and Accepted of a Town way laid out by order of the Selectmen from Mr Samuel Pools to Mr Amos Kimballs beginning at the Road by Said Pools Runs by Trees Marked on the Wefterly Side of Said way Through part of Said Pools Land and Mr Olivers Land to said Kimballs and Through part of said Kimballs Land Said Way was Laid out and Defcribed by Mr James Poole and Mr Ephraim Kimball

Voted and Accepted of a Town way Beginning at a Stake Near Mr Samuel Larrabee's Corn Houfe and Runs Straight to the Corner of Jonathan Mefsurs Land then on the line of S^d Mefsurs Land which Devides his Land from Mr Noah Dodges Land to the Weft Side of the way and So to Run to way Leading from Groton Said way is one Rod wide and was Laid out and Defcribed by Mr Daniel Auftin Mr Samuel Larrabee and Mr Noah Dodge and Mr Noah Dodge appeared in the Town Meeting and Declared that he had Received full Satisfaction of Mr Samuel Larrabee for the land of this way and Said Larrabee Likewife Declared that he Gave the Land to the Town for a way and Defir'd it be So Recorded

At A Legal Meeting of the Freeholders and other Inhabitants of the Town of Lunenburg Afsembled May ye 26th 1760

Voted & Chofe Mr John Heywood Moderrator

Then the Town Voted and Accepted of A lift of Jurymen & put them into the Boxes

Voted that Capt Jacob Gould Mr Daniel Auftin and Mr Thomas Peobody be A Committe to take a deed of Capt Jofhua Hutchens and Benjamin Bellows Esqr in Behalf of the Town of the Land that is fenc'd out for A Town Way Between their Lands and to see that the fence be made Good

Voted that they will Repair the Old Meeting Houfe

Voted and Granted the Sum of thirteen pound six shillings & Eight pence to Repair the Old Meeting Houfe withal

Turn over

[143] Voted that Capt Jofhua Hutchens m^r Thomas Carter and m^r Benjamin Foster be a Committe to Repair the old Meeting Houfe

Voted that the Committe Chofen to Repair the Old Meeting Houfe take Care and Repair the Glafs and Doors of the New Meeting Houfe

At A Legal Meeting of the Freeholders & Other Inhabitants of the Town of Lunenburg Afsembled September ye 23rd 1760

Voted & Chofe m^r John Heywood Moderrator for the Government of Said Meeting

Voted and Granted the Sum of Sixty pounds for the Rev Mr David Stearnss Sallery the prefent year

Voted & Granted the Sum of one pound Six Shillings & Eight pence to the Aſseſsors for the year 1759

Voted & Granted to Mr Abijah Stearns the Sum of Twelve Shillings for his Service as Town Treaſurer for the year 1759

Voted & Granted for the Uſe of the Schools in Said Town the Sum of fifty pounds

Voted & Choſe m^r William Stearns Mr Philip Goodridge m^r William Snow Mr David Wood & m^r Joſeph Hartwell A Committe to provide Schooling for the Town of Lunenburg the year Enſuing

Voted that the Committe be Inſtructed to place the Grammar School as Near the places Appointed for the four Quarters as they Can. And that they Conſider the Other parts of the Town as Equally as may be

[144] At A Legal Meeting of the freeholders and other Inhabitants of the Town of Lunenburg Aſsembled March the ^nd2 — 1761 ——

Voted and Choſe m^r John Heywood Modderator

Voted and Choſe

Benj Goodridge
Capt Joſhua Hutchens
Mr John Heywood
Capt Samuel Hunt
Mr Benj Foster
} Selectmen and were Sworn Aſseſsors as the Law Directs

Mr Abraham Ireland
Mr Jonathan Hartwell
} were choofen wardens and Sworn as the Law Directs

Benj. Goodridge choofen Town Clerk and Sworn as the Law Directs

Mr George Kimball Chooſen Town Treaſurer and Sworn as the Law Directs

Mr David Wood and
Mr Samvel Johnſon jun
} Choſen Constables then voted that M^r Moſes Ritter be Excepted to Serve as conſtable in the Room of David Wood and Johnſon and Ritter were Sworn Conſtables as the Law Directs

Mʳ Benjamin Reddington
Mʳ Thomas Dutton
Mʳ Obediah Walker
Mʳ Zechariah Whitney   were Chofen
Mʳ Samuel Poole   Surveyors of
Mʳ Philip Goodridge   High ways and
Mʳ Thomas Wetherbe   were Sworn as
Mʳ Jofiah Dodge   the Law
Mʳ Benjamin Stearns   Directs
Mʳ David Taylor
Mʳ Mofes Mitchael

Mʳ Patrick White
Mʳ Caleb Taylor   were Chofen Tydingmen
Mʳ Samuel Davis   were chofen fence
Mʳ Richard Peabody   veiwers and Sworn as
         the Law Directs

Mʳ Thomas Carter Chofen Sealer of Leather
        & Sworn as the Law
        Directs
                      Turn over

[145] Mʳ Abraham Carlton Chofen Surveyor of Shingles and Sworn as the Law Directs

Mʳ Jonathan Wood Chofen Culler of Staves and Sworn as the Law Directs

Mʳ Ifaac Gibfon   Chofen to take care of fire
Mʳ James Poole   and Burn the Woods

Mʳ Amos Hazeltine
Mʳ Oliver Gould
Mʳ Phinehas Steward   were Chofen
Mʳ Silas Snow   Hogg reveis
Mʳ David Paree
Mʳ Elijah Grout

Mʳ Abraham Ireland   were Chofen a Committe
Mʳ Benj Fofter   to Buy a Buring place
Mʳ Jonathan Wood   in the wefterly part of
         the Town

Capᵗ Jacob Gould   were Chofen a Committe to
Capᵗ John Gibfon   Enquire into the Bounds of the
Mʳ Afahel Hartwell   Buring yard and Report what
         they Judge Beft to be Done
         to fence it

Voted and Granted the Sum of one Hundred pound to Repair and Mend the High ways withall fifty pound to be workt out in Town and fifty pound on the weft Side of the River and on the way from Capt Hunts to Weftminter Line and on the way from Reuben Gibfons to Dorchefter Line to be workt out as it was the Last year viz at four pence an Hour for aman on the Spot and one Shilling and four pence for a pair of Oxen pr Day and Eight for a Cart

Voted that Benjamin Goodridge buy a Burying Cloth

Voted & Accepted of A Higway Laid out by order of the Selectmen Begining at the Nor weft Corner of Isaiah Witts Houfe Lott & Runing Eafterly one Rod on Said Witts Land & one on Jofhua Meeds Land to the North eaft Corner of Said Witts Land thence Eafterly one Rod on Said Meeds Land & one Rod on Common Land as is Supposed to a Large Hemloct Tree at the Side of a Brook Mark'd on the South Side from thence About South eaft about Twenty Rods on Common Land as is Suppofed from thence the Same Courfe Acrofs Timothy Bancrofts Land Abot forty Rods from thence Eafterly [146] Acrofs Part of John Demarys Land to Dorchefter farm Line thence Running Southerly one Rod on Said Demary Land and one Rod on Mr Hobbys Land About Fourfcore Rods then Runing Eafterly Acrofs Mr Hobbys Land About Fifteen Rods to the County Rode Leading from Capt Hunts to the Meeting Houfe the Above way is Mark'd on the North & Eafterly Side with Spotts Cut in Trees & was Laid out & Defcribed by

      Benjn Fofter
      Samuel Hunt
      John Demary

At A Meeting of the Freholders & other Inhabitants of The Town of Lunenburg Afsembled March ye 10th — 1761

Voted & Chofe Mr John Heywood Modderator for the Government of Said Meeting

Voted that the Town will pay the Coft of the Late Rev'd Mr David Stearns Dec'd Funeral

Voted that they will Give the Late Revd Mr Stearns Brothers weed & Gloves & his Sifters Vails Handkerchiefs Gloves & Fans & his Sons in Law weeds & Gloves

Voted that the Selectmen Provide for the Funeral According to their Peſt Diſcreſsion & Lay the Account thereof before the Town at the Next Meeting

Voted & Granted the Sum of Sixty pounds to pay for Preaching for the Town

Voted that the Selectmen Provide preaching for the Town

At A Legal Meeting of the Freeholders & Other Inhabitants of the Town of Lunenburg Aſsembled May y^e 26 = 1761

Voted & Choſe Mr John Heywood Modderrator for the Government of Said Meeting

Voted & Granted the Sum of Thirty one pound Eight Shillings & three pence to pay the Coſt of the late Revnd Mr David Stearns's Funeral Withal

Voted & Choſe Edward Hartwell Esqr Mr Jonathan Wood and Mr William Stearns a Committe to provide preaching for the Town

Voted & Granted the Sum of Sixty pounds to pay for preaching that has been preached or Shall be preached out

Reſolved that the Sixty pound Granted the tenth of March laſt be not aſseſsed

Turn over

[147] The Fourth Article in the Warrant being Read Containing the Requeſt of Samuel Hunt & Others and the Town taking the Same into Conſideration

Voted that their Requeſt be So far Granted that one half of the land Within the Townſhip of Lunenburg & the Weſterly part thereof Running a parrelel Line with the Weſt Line of said Townſhip be & hereby is Set off a Separate Pariſh by it self Provided they Shall Place their Meeting Houſe as near the Centure of ſaid Pariſh as may be so as to accomodate the whole and that as Soon as they are Able and Do Maintain the Goſpel among themſelves that then they Shall be freed from all Coſts & Charges of Maintaining the Goſpel in the firſt Pariſh in Said Town Upon A Motion made & seconded by Some of the Requeſters Notwithſtanding the Above Vote the Queſtion was put wheither the Town would not Grant the Requeft in Full and it pafs'd in the Negative

Voted & Chofe Edward Hartwell Esqr Mr Nathan Heywood & Benjamin Goodridge A Committe to Lay out the School Lands in the Beft way & manner they can & See that they are put upon Record

Voted that Swine Run at Large the prefent year

At A Legal Meeting of the Freeholders & Other Inhabitans of the Town of Lunenburg Afsembled Auguft ye 4th 1761

Voted & Chofe Mr John Heywood Modderrator for the Government of Said Meeting

Voted that the Committe Appointed to Provide preaching for the Town forthwith wait upon the Revd Mr Jofiah Bridge to See if he will preach any more for the Town

Said Committe Return'd & Reported that he muft be away two Sabbaths after the Next Sabbath & then knew not but that he might preach for the Town again

Then the Town Taking into Confideration the Requeft of Amos Kimball & others & after a Debate theron the Queftion was put wheither the Town will Grant their Requeft and it pafsed in the Negative

[148] At A Legal Meeting of the Freeholders & Other Inhabitants of the Town of Lunenburg Afsembled September y^e 21th 1761

Voted & Chofe Mr John Heywood Modderrator for the Government of Said Meeting

Voted & Granted the Sum of Forty pounds to pay for preaching

Voted & Granted to Mr Abraham Ireland -   0 = 18 = 0
Voted & Granted to Mr Patrick White   0 - 18 - 0
Voted & Granted to Mr William Gillchreaft   0 - 18 - 0
Voted & Granted to Capt Jofhua Hutchens   0 = 7 = 2
Voted & Granted to Mr Jonathan Wood   1 = 19 = 4
Voted & Granted to James Defcomb   0 - 3 - 0
Voted & Granted to Benj Goodridge   0 - 18 - 0
Voted & Granted to Mr William Stearns   1 - 8 - 0
Voted & Granted to Madam Ruth Stearns for Boarding the Minifters   6 = 2 = 0

Voted & Granted to Mr George Kimball for
Serving as Treafurer for the year 1760   0 - 12 - 0
Voted & Granted to the Afsefsors for taking a
Valuation   6 - 14 - 0
Voted & Granted to Mr John Heywood   0 - 1 - 6
Voted & Granted to Benj Goodridge   0 - 1 - 6
Voted & Granted for the Ufe of the Schools the
Sum of   50 - 0 - 0

Voted that the Committe that Serv'd the Town the Laft year be the Committe to provide the Town with Schooling the year Enfuing and that their Inftructions be the Same as Laft year

Voted that the Laft Grant made to the Revd Mr David Stearns Dec^d be the whole of it paid to the widdow madam Ruth Stearns

Voted & Accepted of the Reconing made by the Selectmen with the Town Treafurer Mr George Kimball

[149] At A Legal Meeting of the Freeholders & other Inhabitants of the Town of Lunenburg Afsembled December ye 28th 1761

Voted & Chofe Mr Benjamin Fofter Modderrator

Then the Queftion was put wheither it was the minds of the Town to Hear m^r Samuel Payson any More than the Time they had Agred with him for and after a Debate

Voted that the Committe forthwith wait upon Mr Payson & Agree with him for four Sabbaths more if they Can & Report The Committe Returnd & Reported that they had waited upon Mr Payson & Agreed with him to Preach for the Town four Sabbaths more

Upon Reading the Accompts of Mr Thos Peobody Mr Daniel Auftins & Capt Jacob Gould the Queftion was put wheither they would Grant money to pay the Same & it pafs'd in the Negative

Then Voted that the Meeting be Adjourn'd to the Third Monday of January Next at one o Clock in the Afternoon

January ye 18th 1762 the Town being Met by Adjournment & then Voted that the Committe wait upon

Mr Samuel Payson & Agree with him to preach for the Town four Sabbaths more if they Can

Voted & Granted to Mr Thos Peobody the Sum of one pound Seven Shillings & the fencing Stuff which was left in Fencing out the Highway Between Capt Hutchens & Bellows s land

Voted & Granted to m^r Daniel Auſtin the Sum of Thirteen Shillings & Eight pence for what he Did towards fencing the Above Said way &c.

Voted & Granted to Capt Jacob Gould the Sum of Nine Shillings & Eight pence Two Farthings for what he Did toward fencing Said way &c.

Voted & Granted to Capt Jacob Gould Mr Daniel Auſtin & Mr Thos Peobody the Sum of Sixteen Shillings to pay Mr Nathaniel Haſtings for Setting up the fence of Said way

Voted & Granted to the aſseſsors for the year
1760—
£ s. d
1 = 6 = 8

[150] At a Legal Meeting of the Freeholders & Other Inhabitants of the Town of Lunenburg Aſsembled February y^e 15th — 1762

Voted & Choſe Mr Nathan Heywood Modderrator

Voted that the Town Concur with the Vote of the Church in the Choiſe of Mr Samuel Payſon for their Miniſter

Voted & Granted the Sum of Two Hundred pounds for the Incouragement of Mr Samuel Payſon and for & for his Comfortable Settlement in the work of the Miniſtry in the Town of Lunenburg provided he Shall Accept of the Town's Choiſe One half to be paid within one year after his Settlement and the Other half within Six months after the Time of the firſt payment

Voted that the Sum of Eighty pounds be Granted & Annually paid to Mr Samuel Payſon provided he Shall Accept of the Town's Choiſe & Settle in the work of the Miniſtry in Said Town So long as he Shall Continue their Miniſter Said Sum to be paid as his yearly Sallery

Voted that the Same Committe that waited upon Mr Payſon with the Church Vote wait upon him with the

Votes of the Town & Defire his Anfwer as Soon as may bee

The Fourth Article in the warrant was Read & the Queftion was put wheither they would Grant the Requeft & there was No Vote

1762. At a Legal Meeting of the Freeholders & other Inhabitants of the Town of Lunenburg Afsembled March ye 1st 1762

Voted and Chofe Capt Jofhua Hutchens Moderator

Mefs^{rs} William Snow }
Afael Hartwel } were chofen Wardens

Mefs^{rs} Jonathan Wood }
William Stearns }
David Wood } were chofen Selectmen &
Abijah Stearns } Sworn Afsefsors
Jonathan Low }

Thomas Sparhawk was Chofen Town Clerk and Sworn
Turn over

[151] Mr George Kimball } was Chofe Town Treafurer and Sworn

Mefs^{rs} Benjamin Redington } were chofen Constables
William Gilchrest } Gilchrest Sworn

Mefs^{rs} Samuel Cummings }
Abraham Sanderfon }
Ephraim Whitney }
Benoni Wallas }
Amos Hazeltine } were chofen Surveyors
Stephen Stickney } of High ways
James Pool } & Collectors of
John Litch } High way Rates
Thomas Peabody }
Mofes Mitchel }
Samuel Sanderfon }
Nehemiah Lane }

Mefs^{rs} Samuell Davis }
Elijah Grout } were chofen Tything Men
David Taylor }

Mefs^{rs} Samuel Davis } were chofen Fence Viewers
Ezekiel Wyman } and sworn as the Law directs

Mr Thomas Carter was chofen Sealer of Leather & sworn as the Law Directs

Mr Philip Goodridge, was chofen Surveyor of Shingles and sworn as the Law directs

Mr George Martin was chofen Culler of Staves

Mefs^{rs} Reuben Gibfon } were chofen to take
David Goodridge } care of Fires

Mefs^{rs} Edward Gary
William Chadwick
Solomon Steward } were chofen Hogreeves
John Fisk
Ephraim Pearce Junr

Mefs^{rs} Edward Scot } were chofen to take
Samuel Sanderfon } care of Deer

[152] Voted and granted the same Sum of Money to repair Highways as was granted Last year; and that it be work'd out in the same manner — —

Voted, that Swine go at Large this Year — —
Voted and Granted Capt Sam^{ll} Hunt   £1 - 2 - 0
Voted and Granted Dea^n Benjn Fofter   0 - 8 - —
Voted and Granted Mr James Dascomb   0 - 3 - —
Voted and Granted Leiut George Kimball the }
   Sum of one pound for his service as
   Town Treafurer for the Year 1761   } 1-0—

Voted y^t Mr David Goodridge's account against the Town for service done at at the Bridge near his Houfe be allowed out of next years High way Rate Viz ^{8}4-0

Voted y^t Mr Paul Weatherbee's acc^t for service done at s^d Bridge be alfo allowed out of next Years High- way Rate   Viz   £0—3-0

Voted and accepted of a Highway Laid out by order of the Seelectmen: Beginning at the Southerly Line of William Flaggs Land and runs to William Benjamins Land & through s^d Benjamins Land, then through the Secratary's Land (so called) then through a part of Browns Farm (so called) to where the Way was before laid out and accepted by the Town, the said Road to be two Rods wide & mark'd on the North westarly side beginning at s^d Flaggs South Line, a Red Oak Tree mark'd, and ending with a Hemlock Tree on the Northerly side of the Road already eftablifhed mark'd with two Spots and Three Notches

The above Road was discribed and laid out by
                       Mefs^{rs} Benjn Fofter
                       and John Fitch

      Recorded P^r Me Thos Sparhawk T. Clerk

[153] At a Legal Meeting of the Freeholders and other Inhabitants of the Town of Lunenburg Afsembled April 26th 1762

Voted & Chofe Capt: Jonathan Wood Moderator

Voted to Concur with the Churches Vote Refpecting the Time appointed for the Ordination of Mr Samuel Payson, Viz the Second Wenfday in September next —

Voted to choofe a Com^{tee} to agree with some Perfons to make provifion for the Venerable Council & other Gentlemen of Note and diftinction who shall attend the Ordination of Mr Sam^{ll} Payfon — — —

Voted to Choofe three Perfons as a Com^{tee} for s^d purpofe

Voted that Benjn Goodridge Efq^r } Be a Com^{tee} for
Leiut George Kimball } the purpofe
and Leiut Jonathan Low } aforef^d —

Voted that the Woman's Seats in the body of the Meeting Houfe be referved for the Church to Set in, on the Day Appointed for the Ordination

Voted that the Men's Seats be referved for the Venerable Council and such of the Church as cannot find Room in the Womans Seats

Voted and Choofe
Mefs^{rs} Richard Taylor } A Com^{tee} to keep the
Philip Goodridge } seats in the Meeting
Samuel Johnfon Junr } Houfe referved for the
Obediah Walker } Council and Church on
William Gilchrest } Ordination Day

Voted and choofe Mr Mofes Ritter a Com^{tee} man in the Room of Mr Philip Goodridge who refuf'd serving

Voted & Chofe Mefs^{rs} Jofiah Dodge } a Com^{tee} to
Abraham Carlton } Secure the
Meeting Houfe (upon Ordination Day) by Bracing the Galleries and what ever elfe they shall think proper relating thereto

The Second Article in the Warrant was Read, and the Question put to Vote whether they would Act upon it, & it pafsed in the Negative

Voted to accept of Mr Mofes Ritter to serve as Conftable in lieu of Mr Benjamin Redington who was Chofe at the anual meeting; He being hired by Mr Redington and was Sworn to the faithful discharge of his office as the Law directs

Voted to Erect a Monument over the Grave of the Late Rev.d Mr David Stearns ——

Voted and Chofe Mefs.rs Josiah Dodge ⎱ a Com.tee for the
Benj.n Foster ⎰ purpofe
Jon.a Low   afore f.d

[154] The Queftion was put to Vote whether the Town would Act upon the Fifth Article in the Warrant & it pafs'd in the affirmative

Voted that a Work Houfe be provided

Voted to accept of Mr Auftins offer Viz: of his most northerly old houfe; for a Work Houfe ——

Voted & Chofe Mefs.rs Daniel Auftin ⎱
Sam.ll Johnfon Jun.r ⎰ Overfeers of s.d
                     Houfe

And then the s.d Meeting was Difmif'd

Recorded Pr Me THO.S SPARHAWK *T. Clerk*

At a Legal meeting of the Freeholders & other Inhabitants of the Town of Lunenburg Afsembled Sept.r 27.th 1762

Voted and chofe Benj.n Goodridge Efq: Moderator

Voted that y.e Rev.d Mr Sam.ll Payson's Salery begin at y.e time of his ordination

The Second Article in the Warrant being read and y.e Question what instructions y.e town would give y.e Afsefsors refpecting Mr Payson's Salery? & it was thought convenient to conform to y.e vote of y.e Town in their call to Mr Payson

Voted and Granted Mr Thomas Carter for entertaining the Ordination Council   £-6-8

Voted and granted y.e Afsefsors for y.e Year 1761 - 1-6 8

Granted Joseph Bellows for keep:- Mr Payfons
 Horfe 16½ weeks   1-2.- —

Voted and Granted; (to defray y.e Charges of Erecting a Monument over the Grave of y.e Rev.d Mr Stearns Deceaf.d) the Sum of £8-

Voted and Granted for y.e ufe of y.e Schools —— 50. ——

Voted and Chofe Mefs.^rs^ Jofhua Goodridge ⎱
          Sam^ll^ Cummings   ⎟
          Thos Peabody   ⎬ School
          John Bufs   ⎟ Com^tee^
          Jofhua Hutchens   ⎠

Voted y^t^ ye School Com^tees^ Instructions be ye same as they were Last Year: & y.^t^ ye meeting be difmifsed

Recorded Pr Thos Sparhawk *Town Clerk*

[155] At a Legal meeting of the Freeholders & other Inhabitants of the Town of Lunenburg afsembled January the 21st 1763 ——

Voted & chofe Dea^n^ William Stearns Moderator

Voted to choofe some Perfon to serve the Town as Conftable for the Year 1762 in Lieu of Mr Mofes Ritter deceaf'd

Voted and Choofe Mr Abijah Hovey to serve as Conftable for the year 1762 in lieu of Mr Mofes Ritter deceaf'd who was accepted as Conftable at a Meeting in April 1762 inftead of Mr Benj.^a^ Redington who was chofe at the Annual Meeting 1762

Mr Hovey Being chofe Conftable (not being at the Meeting) the town thought proper to inform him of it immediately; whereupon Mr Wm Gilgrest Conftable was sent immediately, (being inftructed by the Town Clerk & Selectmen) to acquaint Mr Hovey with the Towns proceedings towards him, and to report to the Town whether Mr Hovey would serve the Town as Conftable for the year 1762 or not —— Then Voted that the meeting be adjournd for one Hour to the Houfe of Capt: Jofhua Hutchens

The Town being meet on adjournment

Voted y^t^ ye Settlement of all the Charges & accounts relating to the illnefs of Jonathan Whitney be refer'd to the Selectmen, and to be settled by them: Mr Wm Gilchrest being returned reported to the Town y.^t^ Mr Hovey would not serve the Town as Constable, would be glad if the Town would excufe him if they would not, he would pay His fine; unlefs they would accept of Jonathan Page to serve in his stead ——

Put to Vote whether the Town would accept of Jonathan Page to Serve as Constable instead of Abijah Hovey & it pas'd in the Negative

Voted and Chofe M[r] Jonathan Pearce to serve the Town as Conftable for the 1762

Voted to Adjourn the Meeting to Wensday the Twenty Sixth of this Inft: to this place (Viz) at one o'clock Capt: Joshua Hutchens Long Chamber

Recorded P[r] THO[s] SPARHAWK *Town Clerk*

[156] January y[e] 26th 1763 The Freeholders and other Inhabitants of the Town of Lunenburg being meet on Adjournment

M[r] Jonathan Pearce being prefent the Question was propofed to him whether he would serve the Town as a Conftable; he reply'd he did not choofe to serve unlefs he could be Sufficiently authorized to collect the Taxes ——

after a long Disputation and Debate; Mr Pearce was again defired to declare to the Town his acceptance or non-acceptance of the office of a Conftable; He defired Longer time for Confideration; & finally refufed to Serve as Constable then —

Voted and Chofe M[r] Jonathan Bradftreet to serve as Constable for the Year 1762

M[r] Bradftreet being immediately notified of the Town's Choice by M[r] Conftable Gilchreft, prefented himfelf to the Town, & Being ask'd by the Moderator, whether he would accept of the office of a Conftable for the Year 1762 M[r] Bradftreet reply'd he scrupled whether the Fine could be recovered of him; the Moderator infisting upon a peremptory anfwer, he reply'd again he Scrupled whether the fine could be recovered & finally refufed utterly to serve the Town as Constable then

Voted and chose M[r] Richard Taylor Conftable for the year 1762 —— who being notified thereof by the Conftable above-mentioned — made his appearance & declared he would not serve once & again —— Then by a motion, made and seconded, it was put to Vote whether the Town would excufe M[r] Richard Taylor from the service of a Conftable? and it pafs'd in y[e] affirmative

Voted and Chofe Mr Paul Weatherbee to serve the Town as Con Constable for the Year 1762 & then the meeting was Dismifsed

    Recorded Jan.y 26th 1763 Pr
      THOs. SPARHAWK *Town Clerk*

[157] At a meeting of the Free holders & other Inhabitants of the Town of Lunenburg Afsembled Feb.y 16th 1763

Voted and chofe Capt: Jonathan Wood Moderator

Voted to send for The Rev.d Mr Ebenezer Sparhawk to come and pray with the Town

Voted to send to the Rev.d Mr Timothy Harrington the Rev.d Mr John Mellen the Rev.d Mr: Samuel Dana the Rev.d Mr Jofeph Emerson the Rev.d Mr Francis Gardner the Rev.d Mr. Ebenezer Sparhawk the Rev.d Mr Samuel Dix and the Rev.d Mr Phinehas Whitney to attend the interment of the Rev.d Mr Samuel Payson deceaf'd

Voted to give the Father & Brethren of the deceaf'd Weeds, and Gloves, to the Mother of the deceaf'd & to the ½ Sister Vails Handkerchiefs and Gloves

Voted to give Mrs Elizabeth Stearns a Neat handfome Suit of Mourning

Voted that the Selectmen make provifion for thofe Gentlen who shall attend the Funeral of the Rev.d Mr Samuel Payson deceaf'd and their Horfes

    Recorded Pr THOs. SPARHAWK *Town Clerk*

At a Legal Meeting of the Freeholders and other Inhabitants of the Town of Lunenburg Afsembled March 7th 1763 ——

Voteded and chofe Dean. John HeyWood Moderator

Mefsrs. John Bufs   ⎱ were chofen Wardens and
 Darius Houghton ⎰ Sworn

Benj.n Goodridge Efq.r ⎫
Capt: Jofhua Hutchens ⎪
Dean. John Heywood ⎬ Were chofen Selectmen
Capt. James Reed   ⎪   and Sworn
Mr Thomas Carter   ⎭

Thomas Sparhawk was chofen Town Clerk & Sworn

Mr George Kimball was chosen Town Treasurer & Sworn

Mess.rs Abijah Hovey } were chosen Constables & Sworn
Richard Taylor }

Mr Isaac Gibson was chosen Constable before Mr Taylor, but he desiring a Dismission it was Voted — — —

[158] Mess.rs John Darling
Ezekiel Goodridge
George Martin
Sam.le Putnam
John White
Caleb Taylor
Jon.a Low
David Goodridge
Jon.a Holt
Joshua Goodridge
George Henry
Sam.ll Johnson Jun.r
Oliver Gould
Elijah Grout
} Were chosen Surveyors, Darling, E: Goodridge Putnam, Taylor, Low, D: Goodridge, Holt, Henry, Johnson and Gould were Sworn Martin Since Sworn

Mess.rs Jedediah Bailey } were chosen Tything-
Ezekiel Wyman } men & Sworn

Mess.rs Sam.le Davis } were chosen Fence viewers
Jeremiah Norcross } and Sworn

Mr Thomas Carter was chosen Sealer of Leather & Sworn

Mess.rs Philip Goodridge } were chosen Surveyors
Abraham Carlton } of Shingles &c: and Sworn

Mess.rs Thomas Litch & } were chosen Cullers of Staves
George Martin } Hoops &c: & Sworn

Mess.rs W.m Chadwick
Jon.a Wood
Edw.d Gary
W.m Henry
} were chosen Hog reeves
& Sworn

Mess.rs Eph.m Kimball } were chosen Deer reeves
Isaac Gibson } & Sworn

Mess.rs Reuben Gibson
Jon.a Pierce
Caleb Taylor
James Pool
} were chosen to take care of
Fires Gibson & Pierce Sworn

Voted and accepted of an Highway laid out by order of the Selectmen as follows, beginning at the End of the Road that runs from M.r Sam.le Cummingss to Daniel

Steward's Land runing Southwardly on the Eſtwardly Side of said stewards Land to Leominſter Line & lies wholly upon said Steward's Land who saith he
gives the

[159] gives the Land for said purpoſe, being mark'd upon the west side of said Road & being a Rod & Half wide

March 1ˢᵗ 1763 Laid out by David Wood ⎫
                            Paul Weatherbee ⎬ *Committe*
                            Daniel Steward ⎭

Voted to chooſe Three Perſons a Committee for to provide Preaching —— Voted to Chooſe yᵐ by written Votes

Meſsʳˢ Joſhua Hutchens ⎫
      James Reed   ⎬ were choſen a Committee
      John Heywood ⎭ for the Purpoſe aforeſᵈ

The 4ᵗʰ Article being read, after a long Debate thereon it was tho't proper not to act upon it ——

The 5ᵗʰ Being read it was put to vote whether the Town would act upon it? & it paſs'd in the Negative

The 6ᵗʰ alſo being read it was Voted not to have the Grammer School Kept in the Middle of the Town

Voted that the Conſideration of the 7ᵗʰ 8ᵗʰ & 9ᵗʰ Articles in the Warrant be adjournd to Wedneſday the Twenty Third of this Inſt. March to the New Meeting Houſe at 2 o'clock in the afternoon.

Recorded Pʳ Tʜᴏˢ Sᴘᴀʀʜᴀᴡᴋ *Town Clerk*

Upon the Petition of the Selectmen of Lunenburg the following Act paſsed Viz: ——

In the Houſe of Repreſentatives Febʸ: 4ᵗʰ 1763: Reſolved in Anſwer to the within Petition that the Town of Lunenburg be and Hereby is fully Authorized and impowred at a Meeting Legally warned to chooſe a Conſtable for said Town in the Room of Moſes Ritter deceaſ'd, who is hereby fully Impowred to gather and finish the Collection of the Taxes, that were comitted to said Ritter in his life time to collect, and remain unfiniſhed, any illegall proceedings of the Town of Lunenburg in the

choice and acceptance of said Ritter as Constable in the
Room of Benjᵃ Reddington notwithſtanding

    Sent up for Concurrence
        Timᵒ Rugby *Speaker*

In Council Febʸ 9ᵗʰ 1763 Read and Concurd
        Andʷ Oliver *Secᵗʸ*

Conſented to
    Francis Barnard

Copy Examined
    Tᴹ Jnᵒ Cotton *D Secʸ*

A true Copy of a Copy
  Attest: Thoˢ Sparhawk *Town Clerk*

BOOK B,
LUNENBURG TOWN RECORDS.

[1] Worcefter fs To William Gilchreft Conftable of the Town of Lunenburg Greeting: —

In His Majestys Name you are required to Notify and Warn the Freeholders and other Inhabitants of s^d Town qualifyed by Law to Vote in Town Meetings to afsemble & Meet at the New Meeting Houfe in said Lunenburg on Monday the Seventh Day of March next at Nine o'clock A. M. then and there being meet & duly form'd to act on the following Articles Viz. — — —

1st To choofe Selectmen & all other Town Officers for the prefents Year as the Law directs

2^{ly} To accept of any Roads or Town Ways that have been laid out by the Selectmen or their Order -

3^{ly} To choofe a Committee to provide Preaching & to Give y^m such Instructions as they shall think proper; or to proceed any other way to supply the Pulpit as they shall think best —

4ly To see if the Town will appropriate any Sum or Sums of Money (that is already afsefsed) towards the defraying the charges, y^t have arifen by the late Sicknefs & Funeral of ye Rev^d Mr Sam^{ll} Payfon late of Lunenburg deceaf'd —

5^{ly} To hear the Request of Benj^a Foster & Nine others: Viz: if the Town will Vote off from us the West:^{ly} part of the Town, into a distinct precinct by themfelves (Viz) all the Inhabitants on the Westwardly side of Pearl - Hill — Brook, & on the Weftwardly side of Dorchester Farm so called; with their Lands, or to Vote off any part of them & y^r Lands, & to releafe y^m from paying any further Taxes towards the Support of the

Minifter or to releafe them of any part of Taxes to the Minifter with us or to make any propofals, or to choofe any Com:tee or Com:tees if they think proper to accomodate and settle that Affair ——

6ly To See if the Town will Vote to have the Grammer - School kept in the middle of the Town at some convenient place during the Term of One Year

7ly To Grant a suitable Sum of Money to mend the highways & to repair or Build Bridges & to say in w.t manner y.e same shall be paid or Work'd out

8ly To make a Grant of Money suitable to y.e support of y.e Poor ——

9ly To Choofe a Committee to reckon with the Town Treafurer ——

Hereof fail not and make return of your doings on this Warrant to some one of us the Subfcribers, on or before the time of s.d meet.g

Given under our hands & Seals this Sixteenth Day of Feb.y A. D. 1763

and in the third year of his Majestys Reign

      Jon.o Wood
      W.m Stearns Select.n
      Jon.a Low   of
      David Wood Lunenburg
      Abijah Stearns

A true Copy
  Attest: Tho.s Sparhawk *Town Clerk*

N. B. a Return was made by s.d W.m Gilchrest y.t he had fulfild obey.d y.e orders of this Warrant
           Tho.s Sparhawk

[2] At a Legal Meeting of the Freeholders and other Inhabitants of the Town of Lunenburg afsembled March 7th 1763

Voted and chofe Dea.n John Heywood Moderator

Mefs.rs John Bufs } were chofen Wardens &
   Darius Houghton Sworn

Benj.n Goodridge Efq.r
Capt: Jofhua Hutchins were chofen Selectmen
Dea.n John Heywood and Sworn Afsefsors by
Capt: James Reed   the 1st Day of April
M.r Tho.s Carter

Thomas Sparhawk was chofen Town Clerk & Sworn
Mʳ George Kimball was chofen Town Treafurer & Sworn

Mefsʳˢ Abijah Hovey ⎱ were chofen Conftables and
Richard Taylor ⎰ Sworn as yᵉ Law Directs

Mefsʳˢ John Darling
Ezekiel Goodridge
George Martin
Samᵘ Putnam   ⎫ Were chofen Sur-
John White   ⎪ veyors, Darling,
Caleb Taylor   ⎪ Ezekiel Goodridge,
Jonᵒ Low   ⎪ Putnam, Taylor, Low,
David Goodridge   ⎬ David Goodridge, Holt
Jonᵃ Holt   ⎪ Henry, Johnfon, &
Joshua Goodridge   ⎪ Gould were Sworn
George Henry   ⎪ Martin since Sworn;
Samᵘ Johnfon Junʳ   ⎪ Jofhua Goodridge
Oliver Gould   ⎭ Sworn May 18ᵗʰ
Elijah Grout

Mefsʳˢ Jedediah Bailey ⎱ were chofe Tything men
Ezekiel Wyman ⎰ & Sworn

Mefsʳˢ Samᵘ Davis ⎱ were chofen Fence
Jeremiah Norcrofs ⎰ Viewers & Sworn

Mʳ Thomas Carter was chofe Sealer of Leather
& Sworn

Mefsʳˢ Philip Goodridge ⎱ were chofe Surveyors of
Abraham Carlton ⎰ Shingles Clapboards &c:
& Sworn

Mefsʳˢ Thomas Litch ⎱ were chofen Cullers of
George Martin ⎰ Staves Hoops &c & Sworn

Mefsʳˢ William Chadwick ⎱
Jonᵒ Wood   ⎬ were chofen Hog
Edwᵈ Gary   ⎰ reeves & Sworn
Wᵐ Henry

[3] Mefsʳˢ Ephraim Kimball ⎱ were chofen Dear
Isaac Gibfon ⎰ reeves and Sworn

Mefsʳˢ Reuben Gibfon ⎱
Jonᵒ Pierce   ⎬ Were chofe to take
Caleb Taylor   ⎰ care of Fires
James Pool   Gibfon & Pierce Sworn

Voted and accepted of an Highway laid out by order of the Selectmen as follows Viz: beginning at the End of the Road, yᵗ runs from Samᵘ Cummings's to Daniel Stewards Land running South wardly on the Eaftwardly side of said Stewards Land to Leominfter line & lies wholly upon said Stewards Land who saith he gives the Land for said purpofe, s.^{d} Road being mark'd on the weft side & is one Rod and an half wide Laid out by

David Wood
Paul Weatherbee } Com^{tee}
Daniel Steward

Voted to choofe by Written Votes a Committee of three Perfons to provide preaching

Voted & Chofe Capt: Joshua Hutchens } a Com^{tee} for
Capt: James Reed the purpofe
Dea^n John Heywood   afore f^d

The Fourth Article in the Warrant being read; after a long Debate, it was thought proper not to act upon it

The 5th Article being read; the Vote was put whether the Town would Act upon it? and it pafs'd in the Negative

The 6th Article was alfo read; & ye Vote was put whether the Grammer School should be kept in the Middle of the Town during the Term of One Year & it pafs'd in the Negative

Voted that the Confideration of the 7th 8th & 9th Articles in the Warrant be adjourned to Wednefday the Twenty Third Day of this Inftant March to the New Meeting Houfe at two o'clock in the afternoon

Recorded P^r

THO^s SPARHAWK *T Clerk*

[4] March 23 1763 the Freeholders and other Inhabitants of the Town being meet on Adjournment —

Voted to give the Com^{tee} choofe to provide preaching some Inftructions relative thereto —

Voted to hear Mr Ebenezer Champney 4 Sabbaths & then Mr. Fisk 4 Sabbaths if they may be procured —

Voted & Granted £100. to mend Highways & Bridges for the Year 1763; & that the said Sum shall be work'd out at the same price for Labour and in the same manner as it was last Year — —

The 8th Article being Read and a Vote propoſed, Whether the Town would Grant a Sum of Money for the Support of the Poor? and it paſs'd in the Negative —
Voted and Choſe a Comt ᵉᵉ to
Benjⁿ Goodridge Eſqʳ } reckon with
Capt: Joſhua Hutchens } yᵉ Town
Capt: James Reed } Treaſurer

Voted and choſe the Surveyors Collectors of their own particular Highway Rates

Then the following Warrant was Read Viz:

Worceſter ſs: To one of the Conſtables of the Town of Lunenburg Greeting — — —

In His Majestys name you are required forthwith to notify and warn the Freeholders & other Inhabitants of sᵈ Lunenburg to meet at this place (Viz the New Meeting Houſe) at four of the Clock this afternoon to agree and Vote whether the Swine shall go at large this preſent Year & to make return of this Warrant and your Doings therein at or before the Time of said Meeting unto us the Subſcribers Dated at Lunenburg March yᵉ 23ᵈ 1763

                                  BENJˢ GOODRIDGE } *Selectmen*
                                  JOHN HEYWOOD } *of*
A true Copy   JAMES REED } *Lunenburg*
   Atteſt   THOMAS SPARHAWK *Town Clerk*

Worceſter ſs: March 23ᵈ 1763 In Obedience to this Warrant I have warned all the Perſons within Named to meet at time & place.
                        RICHARD TAYLOR *Conſtable*

The Freeholders and Other Inhabitants being Meet & Legally formd March 23ᵈ 1763 at 4 o'clock P. M.

Voted that Swine go at large this Year —
   Recorded Pʳ
                   THOMAS SPARHAWK *T Clerk*

[5] A Copy of a Warrant for calling a Town Meeting

Worceſter ſs to the Conſtable or Conſtables of the Town of Lunenburg or either of them Greeting:

You are in His Majeſtys Name required to notify and warn the Freeholders and other Inhabitants of the Town of Lunenburg Qualifyed to vote in Town - Affairs to afsemble and meet at the New Meeting Houfe in said Town on Wednesday the Twenty Third of this Inftant March at One O, clock P. M. then and there being duly meet and form'd ———

1st And agreeable to an Act of the Great and General Court To choofe a Conftable in the Room of Mofes Ritter Deceaf'd to finish the Collection of the Rates and Taxes committed to said Ritter, that remain unfinifhed

2ly To hear the Accounts of the Charges of the Funeral & Sicknefs of the Revd Mr. Samuel Payfon deceaf'd, if they can be procured, & to agree on and vote any method shall be thought proper for the peaceable and quiet Settlement of the same

thereof fail not, & make return of your doings to some one of us the Subfcribers at or before the time of said Meeting

Sealed with our Seal Dated at Lunenburg this Seventh Day of March in the Third Year of His Majesty Reign Anno Domini 1763

A True Copy
Attest: Thos Sparhawk
        Town Clerk

Benjn Goodridge ⎫
Joshua Hutchens ⎬ Selectmen
James Reed ⎪ of
Thos Carter ⎭ Lunenburg

Worcefter fs:
Inobedience to this Warrant I have warned all the Perfons within named to meet at time & place
               Richd Taylor *Conftable*
A true copy
Attest
        Thos Sparhawk *T Clerk*

At a Legal Meeting of the Freeholders & other Inhabitants of the Town of Lunenburg Afsembled March 23d 1763

Voted and chofe Dean John Heywood Moderator

Voted and chofe Mr Jonathan Bradftreet Conftable in the Room of Mr Mofes Ritter Deceafed, and he was Sworn to the faithfull discharge of His Office ——

The Second Article in the warrant being read, Voted to hear the Will of the Revd Mr Saml Payfon

The Will being Read, after a long Debate the Meeting was difmifsed —

Recorded P^r T͟h͟o͟ˢ S͟p͟a͟r͟h͟a͟w͟k͟
Town Clerk

[6] Worcefter ff To the Conftable or Conftables of the Town of Lunenburg or to any or either of them Greeting —

In His Majestys Name you are required forthwith to notify and warn the Freeholders and other Inhabitants of said Town of Lunenburg Qualifyed by Law to vote in Town Meetings, to Afsemble and Meet at the Old Meeting - Houfe in said Town, on Thurfday the Nineteenth Day of this Inst: May, at Three O, clock P. M. then and there being duly meet and form'd to act on ye Following Articles Viz:

1ˢᵗ To give the Com^tee appointed to provide preach^g for the Town such further inftructions as they shall think proper

2^ly To hear any Accounts that shall be bro't by any Perfons to agree & act thereon as they shall think proper

3^ly To see, if the Town will agree with the Church in calling a Fast in said Town

4^ly To see, if the Town will Vote y^t ye Lands in s^d Lunenburg wh^ch lies West and Westwardly of the Line hereafter difcribed, should be set off from s^d Town y^t so, ye same Lands & Inhabitants thereon may be formed by the General Court into a Town or District if they think proper: wh^ch Line is difcribed as follows, viz, beginning at such place on Leominfter Line as y^t a strait Line therefrom may run between the Lands of Mr Paul Weatherbee & Mr Jonathan Wood to a Stake and Stones a small distance to the Westward of Mary Holts Houfe, then turning & running North 10 Degrees & a half East to Mr Ephraim Whitneys South-East Corner, then to keep the Eastwardly line of said Whitneys Farm, to the North-East Corner thereof, and from thence to continue to run Northwardly on the Eastwardly Line of John Whites Land, to the Northerly Corner of His Farm, and from y^t Corner to run North 4 Deg^r east to Townfhend Line.

Whereas the said Dividing Line will Divide the Lands of sundry Perſons, leaving part on the Eastwardly and part on the westwardly side thereof; to see if y.ͤ Town by a Vote will manifest it to be their deſire, y.ͭ whenſoever the aforeſ.ᵈ Lands West & Westwardly of said Line shall be formed into separate Town or District, that it may be done in such manner that all thoſe Perſons whoſe Lands by the said Line shall be Divided, and all Perſons for the future who shall own Improved Lands which Shall lie acroſs said Line, partly on one side & partly on the other side thereof, shall pay Rates & Taxes for the whole thereof, to that Town or District in which such Perſon or Perſons shall dwell, provided they shall dwell on any part of their Lands which may happen to be divided by said Line, that so the said propoſed Town or District may be formed under theſe Reſtrictions by the General Court if they think proper —— hereof fail not, and make return of this Warrant with your doings thereon, unto some one of us the Subſcribers at or before the Time of meeting Given under our Hands and Seals at Lunenburg afore ſ.ᵈ this Third Day of May in the Third Year of his Majestys Reign A. D. 1763.

      Benj.ᴺ Goodridge   *Select.ᵐ*
      Joshua Hutchins   *of*
      John Heywood   *Lunenburg*
      Tho.ˢ Carter

Worcester ſs. Lunenburg May 19ᵗʰ 1763

In Obedience to the within written I have notified and Warned all the Perſons within named to meet at time and place for the purpoſes within mentioned

            Constable
      Richard Taylor *of*
A true Copy   *Lunen͟g͟*
   Attest,   Tho.ˢ Sparhawk
        Town Clark

[7] At a Legal Meeting of the Freeholders and other Inhabitants of the Town of Lunenburg aſsembled May 19ᵗʰ 1763 —

Voted and Choſe M.ʳ Nathan Heywood Moderator

Voted y:t y:e spplying y:e Pulpit be left to the diferetion of the Committee chofen to provide preaching

Voted and Granted M:rs Ruth Stearns ⁶/₈ for boarding Minifters Three Sabbaths

Voted to concur with the Vote of the Church in calling a Fast in this Town on Tuefday come Fortnight

The 4:th Article in the Warrant was Read & the Question put whether the Town would comply with said Article as set forth in the Warrant? & it pafsed in the Negative ——

Then the Meeting was dismifsed ——

Recorded P:r THOMAS SPARHAWK
Town Clerk

At a Legal Meeting of the Freeholders & other Inhabitants of the Town of Lunenburg afsem:d Aug:t 22:d 1763

Voted and chofe Benj:a Goodridge Efq:r Moderator

Voted to hear Mr Nathan Davis preach a longer Time

Voted and Chofe D:r Benj:a Fofter, Mr Sam:ll Putnam & Edw:d Hartwell Efq:r a Com:tee to wait upon Mr Davis to see whether he would engage to preach a longer Term —— then voted that the said Com:tee agree with Mr Davis to preach four Sabbaths more

Voted y:t the Meeting be adjournd one hour — being meet on adjournment the afores:d Com:tee reported to the Town that M:r Davis would Supply the pulpit four Sabbaths, and y:t is was likely he should preach himfelf excepting One Day then the Meeting was dismifsd.

Recorded P:r THO:S SPARHAWK
Town Clerk

At a Legal Meeting of the Freeholders and other Inhabitants of the Town of Lunenburg Afsembled Sept:r 26:th 1763.

Voted and Choofe Capt: Jofhua Hutchens Moderator

Voted and Granted the Sum of Eighty Pounds to provide preaching the enfuing Year

Voted to accept the report of the Committee chofen to reckon with the Town Treafurer & y:t t:o see it recorded —

Verte.

[8] Voted and Granted the Sum of Fifty pounds for the ufe and support of the School the enfuing Year ——

Voted and choofe the same Committee to take Care of the School this year as was last and that their Inftructions be the Same alfo Viz: to place the Grammar School as Near the Center of each Quarter of the Town as may be; and that they Confider the other parts of the Town as equally as pofsibly they can

Voted that the Account exhibited to the Town by Mrs. Elizabeth Stearns Administratrix to the Eftate of the Rev^d Mr Samuel Payson late of Lunenburg deceaf'd (being Forty Nine pounds, Nineteen Shillings & Three pence one Farthing, bearing date this Twenty Sixth Day of September 1763) be allow'd, accepted and pay'd out of the One Hundred pounds already Afsefsed for Mr Payfons Settlement, and that she be discharg'd, in full, from the Legacy bequeath'd in s^d deceafed's Will to the Town, she giving the Town a difcharge in full as Adminiftratrix to said deceafeds Will —

Voted that the Selectmen be impowered to give Mrs Elizabeth Stearns Adminiftratrix to Mr Payfons Will a full discharge from the Legacy by him bequeathed to the Town of Lunenburg, and alfo to receive from s^d adminiftratrix a full difcharge as Adminiftratrix to s^d deceafeds Will —— ——

Voted and granted the afsefsors for the year 1762 the Sum of £1. 6. 8. for their Service ——

Voted and Granted Mr George Kimball £1-0-0-0 for serving as Treafurer for the Year 1762

Voted and granted Benjⁿ Goodridge Efq^r and Capt. Jofhua Hutchens $4/ for their Service and Trouble in reckoning with the Town Treafurer

Voted and Granted Mr George Kimball s2/Shillings for his Trouble and Service Reckong with y^e Com^{tee}

Voted and Granted Deaⁿ John Heywood 6 Shillings for going to Hire Mr. Davis to Come and Preach with us

Voted and Granted Mr Patrick White Three 3/Shilling for carrying Some of the Towns Money to Bofton to paying a Debt

Voted and Granted Thomas Sparhawk the Sum of 7/$\frac{d}{2}$ for providing a Book for the Town Records ——

Voted that the Town concur with the Vote of the Church in the Choice of Mr Nathan Davies for their Minifter

[9] Voted the Sum of Two Hundred pounds Lawful Money for the Settlement of Mr Nathan Davies provided he shall Settle in the Work of the Miniftry in the Town of Lunenburg ——

Voted and Granted the Sum of Seventy Five pounds to be paid annually to Mr Nathan Davies as his Sallery provided he shall accept the Towns propofals and Settle among us in the Work of the Miniftry and alfo the ufe of the Minifterial Lands in said Town

Voted and Choofe D^n Foster
                  D^n Heywood
                  D^n Kimball
                  D^n Putnam
                  Benjn Goodridge Efq^r

A Committee to wait upon Mr Nathan Davies with the propofals of the Town refpecting their Choice of him to the work of the Miniftry amongft them

            Recorded P^r Me
                THOMAS SPARHAWK *Town Clerk*

At a Legal Meeting of the Freeholders and other Inhabitants of the Town of Lunenburg Afsembled Novr ye 15th 1763

Voted and Chofe Benjn Goodridge Esqr Moderator

Voted that the Com^{tee} Chofen to provide Preaching Apply to Mr Adams first and engage him to preach four Sabbaths if pofsible; and if he is not at liefure Voted that they apply to Mr Williams and Engage him if at liefure if not that they ufe their Judgment in providing a Minifter for the Town ——

Voted to Choofe Agents to Meet and Confer with the Agents of the several Towns about to petition to the Court to be form'd into the County, and to make report of the several propofals that shall be made by said Towns respecting said affair

Voted and Chofe Benj⁚ Goodridge Efq⁚ⁿ } agents to transact
& Deacon John Heywood the aforefaid affair

Voted the the Article in the Warrant refpecting the old Meeting Houfe be defer'd to some future Meeting — and the the Meeting was dismifs'd

      Recorded P⁚ Thomas Sparhawk
           T Clerk

[10] At a Legal Meeting of the Freeholders and other Inhabitants of the Town of Lunenburg afsembled Jan⁚ʸ: 25ᵗʰ 1764

Voted and Choofe Dea⁚ⁿ John Heywood Moderator

Voted to adjourn the Meeting forthwith to the New-Meeting Houfe where being meet upon Adjournment

Voted that the first article in the Warrant be dismifsed

Voted to hear Mr Adams preach a Longer Term if he may be obtain'd

Voted to choofe a Com⁚ᵗᵉᵉ to wait upon Mr Adams forthwith to acquaint him with the Mind of the Town and to enquire something whether it would be worth while to proceed upon anything further refpecting him

Voted and Choofe Benj⁚ Goodridge Efq⁚ Leiut: Nathan Heywood & Dea⁚ⁿ Benjamin Foster a Com⁚ᵗᵉᵉ to wait upon Mr Adams for the purpofes aforesaid

Voted that the Request of Deacon Benj⁚ Foster, Dea⁚ⁿ Samuel Putnam and others (Viz: To see whether the Town will Vote that the Lands in said Lunenburg which ly West and westwardly of the Line hereafter difcribed should be set off from said Town that so the same Lands and Inhabitants thereon may be formed by the General Court into a Town or Diftrict if they shall think proper, which Line is difcribed as followeth Viz: beginning at such place on Leominfter Line as that a strait Line therefrom may run between the Lands of Mefs⁚ʳ Paul Weatherbee & Jonathan Wood to a Stake and Stones a Small Diftance to the Westward of Mary Holts Houfe then turning and running North 10½ degrees east to the South

East Corner of Mr Ephraim Whitney's Land then to keep the Eastwardly Line of said Whitneys Land to the North east Corner thereof, and from that Corner to run Northwardly on the Eastwardly Line of Mr John White's Land to the Northeastwardly Corner thereof and from that Corner to run North four Degrees East to Town-fhend Line) be granted as set forth in the Warrant provided the Inhabitants on said Lands shall pay their Minifters Tax as heretofore they have done untill they shall be formed Into a Town or District

Voted that the Meeting be adjourned till 5 o'clock to the Houfe of Capt: Joshua Hutchens

Being meet on Adjournment voted that the Meeting be adjourned to Monday 30th Inst : 11 o'clock A. M. to the New Meeting Houfe

Recorded Pr THOMAS SPARHAWK
Town Clerk

[11] The Freeholders and other Inhabitants of the Town of Lunenburg being met on Adjournment Jany 30th 1764 ——

Voted that the Confideration of the Article for supplying or providing for the pulpit be adjourned to ½ after Three in the afternoon — — —

At a Legal Meeting of the Freeholders and other Inhabitants of the Town of Lunenburg Afsembled Jan^y: 30th 1764

Voted and Choofe Deaⁿ John Heywood Moderator

Voted to Concur with the Church in the Choice of Mr Zabdiel Adams to the Work of the Gofpel Miniftry in this Town — —

Voted the Sum of Two Hundred pounds for the Encouragement of Mr Zabdiel Adams, and for his Comfortable Settlement in the Work of the Miniftry in the Town of Lunenburg, provided he shall accept of the Towns Choice one half to be paid in Twelve Months after his Ordination, the other in Eighteen Months after the time of his Ordination ——

Voted Mr Zabdiel Adams the Sum of Eighty pounds for his Yearly Sallery & Support, provided he shall settle in this Town in the Work of the Gofpel Miniftry, solong as he shall continue our Minifter —

Voted to choofe a Com:tee to prefer the propofals of the Church and Town to Mr Adams ——

Voted & Choofe

Benj:n Goodridge Efq:r
Dea:n Benj:n Foster
Dea:n Sam:ll Putnam
Leiut Nathan Heywood
Capt: Joshua Hutchens
Dea:n John Heywood
Capt James Reed

A Com:tee for the purpofes aforefd

Voted that the Supplying of the Pulpit untill such time as Mr Adams gives his Anfwer be referred to the standing Com:tee (to provide preaching) and Mr Adams

Recorded Pr

THO:S SPARHAWKE
T. Clerk

Isaac Farnsworth Town Clerk
1728 - 1736

Benj: Goodridge Town Cler
1737 - 1739   1741 - 1752
1755 - 1762

Benj^d Bellows Jr Town Clark
1740 - 1741

William Doune Town Clerk
1753 - 1754.

Thos Sparhawk T. Clerk
1762 - 1764.

David Hearns

Minister of the Town of Lunenburg.
1733 to 1760.

INTENTIONS OF MARRIAGE

INTENTIONS OF MARRIAGE

COPIED FROM THE

RECORDS OF THE TOWN OF LUNENBURG,

FROM 1732 TO 1764.

A.

B. S. L. T.

Purpose of marriage between William Alexander, and Elizabath Bradley enterd August ye 26th 1743.

Purpose of marriage enterd between William Adam of Dunstable and Mary Speer of Lunenburg, April ye 13th 1744.

Intentions of marriage between Daniel Austin Jun and Phebe Lovejoy both of Lunenburg was entered October 9th 1756.

Intentions of marriage betwen Amos Ardeway of Fitchburge and Lidya Thurla of Lunenburg, was entered December 27 1774.

B.

W. R. G. L. H. F.

Porpose of marriage between Jonathan Broadstreet of Lunenburg, and Olive Wheelock of Leominster entered May 16. 1741.

Purpose of marriage between Eliphelet Brown of Coventree and Elizabath Retter of Lunenburg entered August ye 18th 1744.

Pupose of marriage between Franice Buttrie and Hannah Gilson entred November ye 10th 1744.

Pupose of marriage entered between Nehemiah Bowers and Sarah Larrabee both of Lunenburg.*

Purpose of marriage entered between Jerahmeel Bowers of Lancaster, and Meriam Houghton of Lunenburg Sept. ye 27th 1745.

Purpose of marriage betwixt Capt Jonathan Bradstreet of Lunenburg and Mrs. Abigail Fleeher of Concord was entered September the 17th 1751.

---

*John R. Rollins, transcriber of Lunenburg records, states that the rest is lost, but that the date, no doubt, is 1744. [*W. A. D.*

B. (cont.)

G. L. L. F. L. B. C. W. G. D. H. G. B. J. A. R. W.

Purpose of marriage betwixt Benoni Boynton Jun, and Elizabeth Going both of Lunenburg was entered September the 28th 1751.

Purpose of marriage betwixt Isaac Bayley of Lunenburg and Mary Lovejoy of Andover was entered October ye 26th 1751.

Purpose of marriage betwixt William Baron of the Ashulot and Isabella Larrabee of Lunenburg was entered June the 4th 1752.

Purpose of marriage betwixt Joseph Brown of Cambridge and Abigail Foster of Lunenburg was entered December 11th 1752.

Purpose of marriage betwixt Stephen Boynton and Elizabeth Lovejoy both of Lunenburg was entered February 7th 1753.

Purpose of marriage between Nathaniel Burnam Junr of Lunenburg and Elizabeth Brown of Lunenburg was entered this (thirteenth) 13th day of July A. D. 1754.

Purpose of marriage between Benjamin Bigelow and Elisabeth Colman both of Lunenburg was entered this 30th day of September A. D. 1754.

Purpose of marriage between William Bemus of Narragansett No. 2 and Rezoma Wilder living on the counrtry land was entered May ye 14th 1755.

Purpose of marriage between Jonathan Bennet of Groton, and Mary Going of Lunenburg was entered June ye 12th 1755.

Purpose of marriage betwixt William Brabrook of Lancaster, and Thaukful Dutton of Lunenburg, was entered Febuary ye 16th 1757.

Intentions of marriage betwixt Timothy Bancroft & Mary Harriman both of Lunenburg were entered August ye 16th A. D. 1757.

Intentions of marriage betwixt Elisha Bigelo of Narragansett number two, so called, and Sarah Goodridge of Lunenburg was entered August ye 30th 1757.

Intentions of marriage betwixt Benoni Boynton Jun. of Lunenburg and Mary Buttrick of Leominster was entered December ye 24th A. D. 1757.

Intentions of marriage betwixt Benjamin Bellows Esq. of Wallpole and Mrs. Mary Jenison of Lunenburg was entred February ye 24th A. D. 1758.

Intentions of marriage between Unite Brown of a place called Dorchester Canada and Rebeckah Arno —— of Shrewsbury was entered June ye 30th 1759.

Intentions of marriage betwixt Josiah Bayley and Mary Reed both of Lunenburg was entered March ye 29th 1760.

Intentions of marriage betwixt Kendall Boutwell of Lunenburg & Mary Wilder of Leominster, was entered November ye 26th Annoq Domini 1761.

Intentions of Marriage.

B. (*cont.*)

F. C. W. H. W. W. M.

Intentions of marriage between James Bennet & Elizabeth Fuller both of Lunenburg was entred May 6th 1762.*

Intentions of marriage between Josiah Bailey Junr and Sarah Carter both of Lunenburg were entred Septr 11th 1762.

Intentions of marriage between Ebenezer Bridge & Mehitable Wood both of Lunenburg was entred April 16th 1763.

Intentions of marriage between Thomas Burns of Monson in the Provce of New Hampshire, and Elizabeth Harkness of Lunenburg were entred July 25th 1763.

Intentions of marriage between Joseph Bellows, and Lois Whitney both of Lunenburg was entred April 28th 1764.

Intentions of marriage between John Buss Junr of Fitchburgh and Mary Wood of Lunenburgh was entered May 28th 1766.

Intentions of marriage between Jonathan Boynton Jr of Fitchburg & Sally Martin of Lunenburg entred May 2^d 1796.

C.

F. B. A. H. G. F. H. S. F.

Porpose of marriage between Jacob Cory Junr of Tewksbury and Keziah Foster of Lunenburg entered Sept 5th 1741.

Purpose of marriage between James Colbourn Jur and Sarah Braodstreet, both of Lunenburg June ye 1st——.†

Purpose of marriage between Paul Crocker and Lydia Austin both of Lunenburg was entered April the 12th 1750.

Purpose of marriage between Benjamin Corey Junr of Lunenburg and Beulah Holden of Shirley was entered this nineteenth of October Anno Domini 1753.

Intentions of marriage betwixt William Chadwick of Lunenburg and Eunice Goss of Stow was entered September the 16th 1756.

Intentions of marriage between Nathanael Carlton and Olive Farwell both of —— was entered October ye 9th 1756.

Intentions of marriage betwixt William Cowdin of Worcester and Mary Henery of Lunenburg was entered Febuary ye 17th 1757.

Intentions of marriage betwixt Moses Childers and Sarah Stiles both of Lunenburg was entered Janavary ye 18th 1758.

Intentions of marriage betwixt Jesse Carlton of Lunenburg and Sarah Foster of Andover was entered October ye 27th 1759.

---

*J. R. Rollins, transcriber of the Lunenburg records, thinks this was a mistake for 1763. [W. A. D.

†John R. Rollins, transcriber, says this date is, no doubt, 1742. [W. A. D.

C. (cont.)

G. B. L. F. H. F. R. G. F.

Intentions of marriage betwixt James Carter and Sarah Gillson both of Lunenburg were entered October ye 30th 1761.

Intentions of marriage betwixt Asa Carlton & Ruth Bailey both of Lunenburg were entred July 29th 1762.

Intentions of marriage between Robert Crawford of Worcester and Elizabeth Litch of Lunenburg was entred Decr 11th 1762.

Intentious of marriage between William Cambell of Malborough & Catharine Fitch of Lunenburg was entred Decr 14th 1762.

Intentions of marriage between Joseph Chaplain and Lois Hastings both of Lunenburg was entred Decr 10th 1763.

Intentions of marriage between Jon^a Conant of Dorchester Canada and Eunice Farewell of Shirley District was entred Decr 24th 1763.

Intentions of marriage between Thos. Carter Junr & Priscilla Reed of Lunenburg was entred Decr 29th 1764.

Intentions of marriage between Elijah Carter of Fitchburg & Jane Goodridge of Lunenburg ware enterd September ye 7th 1769.

Intentions of marriage between Thomas Cowdin Junr of Fitchburgh and Mary Farrington of Lunenburg was entered August ye 10th 1774.

D.

B. W. L. F. S. H. P. B. B.

Purpose of marriage between John Darlin Jun and Ruth Boynton both of Lunenburg entered September ye 29th 1744.

Purpose of marriage between Arthur Darrah of Nottingham and Margaret Wallis of Lunenburg entered September the twenty first 1745.

Purpose of marriage entered between Samvel Davis of Lunenburg and Rebekah Lakin of Groton Janvary ye 13th 1746/7

Purpose of marriage entered between Dr John Dunsmore of Lunenburg and Ruth Fisher of Hatfield, Janvary ye 17th 1746/7.

Purpose of marriage entered between John Divol and Susannah Smith both of Lunenburg, February ye 28th 1746/7.

Purpose of marriage between Nicholas Dike and Mary Hastings both of Lunenburg entered June ye 10th 1748.

Purpose of marriage between Richard Day and Ruth Pouchee bouth of Lunenburg was entered November ye 18th 1748.

Purpose of marriage between Timothy Darlin of Lunenburg and Johanna Blood of Groton was entered June the 17th 1752.

Purpose of marriage between Timothy Dorman of Boxford and Eunice Burnam of Lunenburg was entered April the 6th A. D. 1754.

Intentions of Marriage. 227

D. (*cont.*)

S. F. F. S. F. C. W. W. S. S. W. K. W. B. W.

Purpose of marriage between William Dodge of Lunenburg and Elizabeth Salmon of Harvard was entered the 9th day of January A. D. 1755.

Intentions of marriage betwixt Thomas Dutton and Sarah Fitch both of Lunenburg was entered August ye 12th A. D. 1756.

Intentions of marriage betwixt Joseph Davis and Elizabeth Foster both of Lunenburg was entred October ye 22d 1757.

Intentions of marriage betwixt Seth Dodge of Lunenburg and Sarah Smith of Ipswich was entered March ye 18th A. D. 1758.

Intentions of marriage between James Dascomb of Lunenburg and Elizabeth Farrington of Andover was entered May ye 4th 1758.

Intentions of marriage betwixt Josiah Dodge jun now resident in Lunenburg & Hannah Conant of Leominster were entered October ye 24th 1761.

Intentions of marriage between Thomas Dodge & Keziah Willard both of Lunenburg were entred April 24th 1762.

Intentions of marriage between Silas Dutton and Sarah Whitney both of Lunenburg were entred Octor 22d 1762.

Intentions of marriage between Thomas Dodge of Lunenburg & Abigail Smith of Ipswich were entred Novr 19th 1762.

Intentions of marriage between Phinehas Divol and Abigail Stockwell both of Lunenburg was entred May 13th 1763.

Intentions of marriage between Noah Dodge junior and Sarah Wetherbee were entred May 21st 1763.

Intentions of marriage between John Dunsmoor Junr of Lunengh and Mary Kimball of Fitchburgh was entred Augt 6th 1766.

Intentions of marriage between Joseph Downe of Fitchburgh and Martha Wood of Lunenburgh was entered Augt 18th 1768.

Intentions of marriage betwen Oliver Davis of Fitchburg, and Anne Boynton of Lunenburg was entered June 25th 1776.

Intentions of marriage between Solomon Day of Fitchburg & Lucy Whitney of Lunenburg entred December 24th 1796.

E.

P.

Intentions of marriage between John Endecott of Danvers, and Martha Putnam of Lunenburg was enterd Febr 24th 1763.

F.

B. H. K. S. W. R. H. S. P. D. R. G. W. C. C. J. J. W.

Intentions of marriage betwixt Joseph French of Ipswich Canada & Sarah Burns of Concord, was entred March 31st 1732.

Porpose of marriage between Stephen Farnworth of number four, a new Town so called, and Eunice Hastings of Lunenburg entered December the 5th 1741.

Purpose of marriage between Richard Fowler and Ruth Kendel both of Lunenburg entered January 15th.*

Purpose of marriage between Michael Fuller of Upton, and Lois Sattle of Lunenburg, entered October ye 31th 1744.

Purpose of marriage between William Farmer of Lunenburg and Ruth Willard of Harvard, entered November ye 3rd 1744.

Purpose of marriage entered between Isaac Forster and Mary Rice both of Lunenburg, September ye 28th 1745.

Purpose of marriage entered between Robert Fletcher of Lancaster and Elizabeth Houghton of Lunenburg, January ye first 1747/8.

Purpose of marriage between Benjamin Foster jun, and Lucy Stiles both of Lunenburg, was entered, March ye 4th 1748/9.

Purpose of marriage betwixt John Fitch and Elizabeth Paree was entered December ye 18th 1750.

Purpose of marriage between Thomas Farnsworth of Lunenburg and Elizabeth Davis of Littleton was entered this twenty third day of Octor 1753.

Purpose of marriage between Stephen Foster of Lunenburg and Mary Rice of Stratford in the Colony of Connecticut was entered May 7th 1754.

Purpose of marriage between John Fuller and Prudence Gilson was entered September the 4th 1755.

Intentions of marriage betwixt John Farwell of Lunenburg and Susanah White of Townshend was entered November the 22d 1755.

Intentions of marriage between Nehemiah Fuller, and Mary Connant both of Lunenburg was entered, March ye 20th 1756.

Intentions of marriage between Jonas Fletcher of Groton and Johannah Crocker of Lunenburg was entered March ye 9th Annoq. Domini 1759.

Intentions of marriage betwixt Joseph Foster and Sarah Jones both of Lunenburg was entered July ye 20, 1759.

Intentions of marriage betwixt John Fosket jun of Bolton and Abigail Jones of Lunenburg was entered March ye 5th 1761.

Intentions of marriage betwixt Benjamin Foster of Lunenburg and Sarah Whitney of Littleton were entered, October ye 30th 1761.

---

*John R. Rollins says that the year is lost, but that it is, no doubt, 1742. [W. A. D.

Intentions of Marriage.

F. (cont.)

C. B. H. B. D. S.

Intentions of marriage between Tim⁰ Farley of Fitchburgh and Sarah Colburn of Lunenburgh was entred Septr 14th 1765.

Intentions of marriage between Ezekiel Fowler of Fitchburgh & Dorcas Bradstreet of Lunenburgh was entered Jany 30th 1768.

Intentions of marriage between John Farewell of Fitchburgh and Sarah Hovey were entered Feby 25th 1769.

Intention of marriage betwen Edmond Frost of Lunenburg and Lydia Boynton of Fitchburg was entered December ye 26, 1772

Intentions of marriage between Joseph Farnsworth Juner of Lunenburg & Hannah Danforth of Fitchburg was entred February 16th 1782.

Intentions of marriage between Eben Fullam of Fitchburg & Nabby Stiles of Lunenburg, entered September 3^d 1791.

G.

J. W. B. J. F. S. S. D. W. F. B.

Purpose of marriage between Thomas Gearfie —— of Weston and Rebekah Johnson of Lunenburg entered April the 7th 1742.

Purpose of marriage between William Gilchrest and Elizabath White both of Lunenburg, entered May ye 6. 174—*

Purpose of marriage enter^d between Philip Goodridge and Jane Boynton both of Lunenburg October ye 3rd 17——†

Purpose of marriage between Isaac Gibson and Keziah Johnson both of Lunenburg enter^d Janvary ye 5th 1744/5.

Purpose of marriage entered between Joseph Goodridge and Sarah Foster both of Lunenburg December ye 14th 1745.

Purpose of marriage entered between Reuben Gibson of this town and Lois Smith of Sudbury September ye 11th 1746.

Purpose of marriage betwixt John Grout Jun and Phebe Spafford both of Lunenburg were entered October ye 6th 1750.

Intentions of marriage betwixt Jonas Gilson and Sarah Divol both of Lunenburg was entered December the 6th 1755.

Intentions of marriage between Elijah Grout and Mary Willard both of Lunenburg were entered June ye 29th 1757.

Intentions of marriage betwixt Thomas Gary of Lunenburg and Elizabeth Farewell of Townshend, was entered July ye 20th 1759.

Intentions of marriage betwixt Jonathan Going of Lunenburg and Anne Bennet of Shirley District was entered February ye 22nd 1760.

---

*John R. Rollins states that this date is, no doubt, 1743. [W. A. D.

†John R. Rollins gives this date as probably 1743. [W. A. D.

G. (cont.)

H. W. G. S. F. G. P. B. B.

Intentions of marriage betwixt Silas Gates of Stow, and Anna Hammond of Lunenburg was entered Novr ye 13th 1760.

Intentions of marriage betwixt Ephraim Gibson & Lucy Wyman, both of Lunenburg was entered April ye 23. 1761.

Intentions of marriage between Mr. Francis Gardner of Stow and Mrs. Sarah Gibson of Lunenburg were entred Septr 18th 1762.

Intentions of marriage between Eliphalet Goodridge and Rebekah Snow both of Lunenburg was entred Octo 28th 1763.

Intentions of marriage between Benjamin Gould of Rowley Canada in the Province of New Hampshire and Sarah Foster of Lunenburg was entred Janr 14th 1764.

Intentions of marriage between Mr. Jacob Gates of Harvard and Mrs. Elizabeth Gibson of Lunenburg were entred April 5th 1764.

Intentions of marriage between Joseph Gilson of Lunenburgh & Esther Parce of Fitchburgh was entered Feby 20th 1768.

Intention of marriage betwen Silas Gibson of Lunenburg & Damaris Benit of Fitchburg was entered December ye 7th 1772.

Intentions of marrage between Abraham Gibson of Fitchburg & Mary Brown of Lunenburg was entred May ye 30th 1778.

H.

H. A. M. W. T. K. G. D. J.

Porpose of marriage between Jonathan Hammond of Lower Ashulott, and Abigail Hastings of Lunenburg, entered July 10th 1741.

Purpose of marriage enterd betwixt Joseph Holt of Lunenburg and Mary Abbott of Andover Septr ye 4th 1742.

Purpose of marriage enterd between William Holt and Mary Martin both of Lunenburg July 14 1744.

Purpose of marriage entered between Amos Hezeltine, and Susanna Willard both of Lunenburg, Janvary ye 6th 1745/6.

Purpose of marriage entered between Mr. Jonathan Hartwell and Mrs. Elizabeth Tarball both of Lunenburg, August ye 5th 1745.

Purpose of marriage entered between Goerge Henery and Elizabeth Kanady both of Lunenburg December ye 14th 1745.

Purpose of marriage entered between Amos Hazeltine and Eunice Gilson both of Lunenburg Janr ye 10th 1746/7.

Purpose of marriage entered between Joseph Hartwell and Tabatha Dodge both of Lunenburg July ye 30th 1747.

Purpose of marriage between John Hubbard and Hannah Johnson both of Lunenburg was entered February, the twenty first 1748/9.

Intentions of Marriage.

H. (*cont.*)

H. T. F. S. P. G. D. R. H. P. D. F. H. R. P. D. F. C.

Purpose of marriage entered between Daniel Holt of Lunenburg and Mehetable Holt of Andover June ye 11th 1748.

Purpose of marriage between John Henderson of Lancaster and Jane Turner of Lunenburg was entered May ye 4th 1749.

Purpose of marriage between Joseph Holt of Lunenburg and Dorcas Frost of Dunstable was entered May ye 20th 1749.

P. of m b. Darius Houghton and Jerusha Stearns both of Lunenburg was entered December ye 8th 1749.

Purpose of marriage between Thomas Henderson, late of Lunenburg and Bethsheba Preist of Stow was entered February the 16th 1750/1.

Purpose of marriage between Joseph Hammond of Lower Ashulott and Esther Gould of Lunenburg was entered August ye 14th 1752.

Purpose of marriage betwixt Gershom Hubbard of Dunstable and Lipha Dodge of Lunenburg was entered December ye 20th 1752.

Purpose of marriage between Thomas Heywood of Lunenburg and Elizabeth Richardson of Lancaster, was entered this 23^d day of March A. D. 1753.

Purpose of marriage between William Henery Junr and Mary Harper both of Lunenburg was entered this second day of October Anno Domini 1753.

Purpose of marriage between Phinehas Hartwell and Mary Peirce both of Lunenburg was entered this eighth day of November A. D. 1754.

Purpose of marriage between Henry Hogskins & Mary Dutton both of Lunenburg was entered April 19th 1755.

Purpose of marriage between Zimri Heywood of Dorchester Cannada (was entered) and Jane Foster of s^d Dorchester Cannada was entered Sept ye 6th 1755.

Intentions of marriage betwixt Joseph Hartwell of Lunenburg and Phebe Hart of Readen was entered Janavary ye 14 A. D. 1757.

Intentions of marriage betwixt Samuel Hogskins and Rebeckah Rice both of Lunenburg were entred July ye 16th A. D. 1757.

Intentions of marriage betwixt Ebenezer Hart and Sarah Poole both of Lunenburg was entered Janavary ye 6th A. D. 1758.

Intentions of marriage betwixt Thaddeus Harrington of Shirley and Thankful Dodge of Lunenburg was entered March ye 18th 1758.

Intentions of marriage betwixt Samuel Hart and Mary Fuller both of Lunenburg was entered April ye 1st 1758.

Intentions of marriage between Daniel Harper and Rachael Colman both of Dorchester Canada so called was entered August ye 4th A. D. 1758.

H. (cont.)

H. W. I. B. R. S. H. B. L. H. S. F.

Intentions of marriage betwixt George Huet of Rowley Canada so called and Triphene Hodgskins of Lunenburg was entered April 26th 1760.

Intentions of marriage betwixt John Heywood of Lunenburg and Silence White of Lancaster was entered December ye 12th 1760.

Intentions of marriage betwixt Abijah Hovey of Lunenburg & Lydia Inggols of Andover was entered Octr ye 9th 1761.

Intentions of marriage between Henry Hodgskins of Ipswich Canada and Jemima Ball of Princetown were entred Octr 9th 1762.

Intentions of marriage between Phinehas Hutchens & Abigail Reed both of Lunenburg was entred Oct^o 22^d 1763.

Intentions of marriage between Samuel Hilton and Rebekah Stickney both of Lunenburg was entred Oct^o 22^d 1763.

Intentions of marriage betwixt Eleazar Houghton Ju^r and Susannah Holman both of Lunenburg was entred Oct^o 28th 1763.

Intentions of marriage between Aaron Hodgskins and Eunice Bigsbee both of Ipswich Canada was entred Decr 18th 1763.

Intentions of marriage between Saml Hazen jun^r of Stow & Elizabeth Little of Shirley was entred Augt 26th 1764.

Intentions of marriage between William Holt of Fitchburg & Betty Hutchinson of Lunenburg was entred April 22^d 1782.

Intentions of marriage between Samuel Hutchinson of Fitchburg & Charlotte Stiles of Lunenburg was entred June 30th 1783.

Intentions of marriage between John Hartwell of Lunenburg & Polly Farwell of Fitchburg was entred April 24th 1792.

I.

B.

Intentions of marriage betwixt Abraham Ireland & Marabah Boynton both of Lunenburg was entered Febr ye 13th 1761.

J.

W. B. P.

Purpose of marriage between James Johnson of Lunenburg and Susannah Willard of Harvard entered May ye 30th 1747.

Intentions of marriage betwixt Abner Jackman and Elizabeth Bayley both of Lunenburg was entered October ye 2nd 1756.

Intentions of marriage between Ezekiel Jewet and ——— Plats both of a place called Rowley Canada May ye ——— [Probably 1759.— J. R. Rollins.]

Intentions of Marriage.

J. (cont.)

G. S.

Intentions of marriage between William Judevine and Patience Grout both of Lunenburg was entered June —— 1759.

Intentions of marriage betwixt William Jones of Lunen'g and Sarah Stone of Groton were entred July 29th 1762.

K.

W. P. M. P. S. F. H. M.

Purpose of marriage entered between Ephraim Kimball and Mary Wetherbe both of Lunenburg July the 18th 1746.

Purpose of marriage entered between Uzziah Kendel of Leominster and Elizabeth Parce jun. of Lunenburg April ye second 1748.

———— between George Kimball of Lunenburg and Sarah Mullickin of Bradford was entered Oct ye 1th 1748.

———— Samuel Kennedy and Sarah Page both of Lunenburg —— June ye 29th 1749.

Purpose of marriage betwixt Richard Kimball jun of Boxford and Elizabeth Seetown of Lunenburg was entered December ye 28th 1750.

Intentions of marriage betwixt William Kimball and Jane Farewell both of Lunenburg was entered February ye 23d 1760.

Intentions of marriage betwixt Benjamin Kidder of Billrica & Ruth Heywood of Lunenburg was entred January ye 6th 1761.

Intentions of marriage between William Kilburn Junr of Lunenburg & Polly Mace of Fitchburg was entred Novr 14th 1795.

L.

W. W. P. K. W. C.

Pupose of marriage entered between Samvel Larrabee of Lunenburg and Anne Williams of Groton March ye 3rd 1745/6.

Purpose of marriage between William Little of Lunenburg and Elizabeth Wallis of Worcester was entered November ye 4th 1748.

———— John Lovejoy and Sarah Parce both of Lunenburg —— December ye 8th 1749.

Purpose of marriage between Thomas Leitch & Jane Kannady both of Lunenburg were entered August ye 20, 1750.

Purpose of marriage betwixt Benjamin Larrabee of Lunenburg and Margarett Williams of Groton was entered August ye 15th 1752.

Intentions of marriage betwixt Samuel Larrabee and Johannah Crocker both of Lunenburg was entered September ye 18th 1758.

L. (cont.)

S. S. F. E. P.

Intentions of marriage between Samuel Larribee of Lunenburg and Mary Simonds of Shirley was entered November annoq Domini 1758.

Intentions of marriage between Nehemiah Lane of Lunenburg and Sarah Shaddock of Pepperell was entered February ye 6th Anno Domini 1759.

Intentions of marriage betwixt Nehemiah Lane of Lunenburg and Sarah Fletcher of Groton was entered March ye 3^d 1760.

Intentions of marriage betwixt John Larrabee of Lunenburg & Abiah Erven of Shurley was entered May ye 12th 1760.

Intentions of marriage betwixt William Larkin of Lunenburg and Hannah Parce of Groton was entered March ye 21th 1761.

M.

H. S. H. F. T. P. K. W. P. H.

Purpose of marriage entered between Robert Mitcheal of Lunenburg and Alice Harice of Lancaster March ye 10th 1743/4.

Pupose of marriage entered between Hugh Moors, and*

Purpose of marriage entered between John Marsh of Notthingham and Martha Seaverans of Lunenburg April ye 20th 1748.

Purpose of marriage between Thomas Matthews and Elizabeth Heborn both of Lunenburg was entered December ye 21th 1748.

Purpose of marriage betwixt William Moors of Lunenburg and Elizabeth Foster of Dorchester Cannada so called was entered December ye 10th 1751.

Purpose of marriage betwixt George Mc ferlin of Lunenburg and Margarett Terrance of Lancaster was entered March ye 7th 1752.

Purpose of marriage between Joseph Moffett of Ipswich Canady so called, and Dorithy Priest of Stow was entered this 23^d day of June A. D. 1753.

Purpose of marriage between William Machan jun^r of Worcester and Mary Kennedy of Lunenburg was entered this seventeenth day of September A. D. 1753.

Intention of marriage betwixt John Moors jun of Bolton and Unity Willard of Lunenburg were entered July ye 13th A. D. 1757.

Intentions of marriage betwixt Jonathan Messer of Lunenburg and Abigail Parker of Groton was entered October ye 13th 1759.

Intentions of marriage betwixt John Moffat of a place called Ipswich Canada, and Hannah Hodgskins of Lunenburg was entered January ye 5th 1760.

---

*John R. Rollins says the remainder is lost. [W. A. D.

Intentions of Marriage.

M. (cont.)

C. C.

Intentions of marriage betwixt John Martin and Betty Chaplin both of Lunenburg was entered Febry ye 14th 1761.

Intention of marriage between Sam¹ McCraken of Worcester & Lettice Carlifle of Lunenburg was entred Octor 29th 1762.

N.

B. W.

Intentions of marriage between Page Norcross and Elizabeth Bailey both of Lunenburg ware entred Septr 11th 1762.

Intentions of marriage between Hananiah Newton of Lunenburg & Chloe Wood of Fitchburg was entred July 8th 1785

O.

F. T. F.

Intentions of marriage between Ephraim Osbourn and Sarah Fisk both of Lunenburg was entered July ye 20th 1759

Intentions of marriage betwen Amos Ardeway of Fitchburge and Lydya Thurla of Lunenburg was entered December 27 1774.*

Intentions of marriage between Jacob Osburn of Lunenburg & Sibel Farwel of Fitchburg, entred September 14th 1786.

P.

H. D. D. N. R. P.

Purpose of marriage between Daniel Page of Lunenburg, and Ruth Haskell of Harvard entered October the 13th 1744.

Purpose of marriage entered between Jonathan Parce, and Sarah Dodge both of Lunenburg Janvary ye 19th 1745/6.

Purpose of marriage entered, between Amos Phillips of Dunstable and Abigail Dodge of Lunenburg February ye 8th 1745/6.

Purpose of marriage entered between William Porter and Mary Nickalls both of Lunenburg March ye 7th 1745/6.

Purpose of marriage entered between David Parce jun and Anne Retter both of Lunenburg April ye 5th 1746.

Purpose of marriage between Mr. Samvel Page of Lunenburg and Mrs. Sarah Peirce of Leominster June ye 20th 1747

---

*John R. Rollins says this was probably intended for Ordway. See letter A. [W. A. D.

P. (cont.)

G. J. P. W. B. H. P. P. W. N. B. S. S. M. R. F. H. H.

Purpose of marriage entered between Timothy Parker and Johannah Grout both of Lunenburg May ye 21st 1748.

Purpose of marriage betwixt Thomas Prentice Esq of Lunenburg and Madam Borredell Jackson of Newton was entered May the 25th 1751.

Purpose of marriage betwixt Joseph Platts of Rowley Canada and Deborah Page of Lunenburg was entered, September ye 30th 1752.

Purpose of marriage between Thomas Putnam of Charlestown in the Province of New Hampshire & Rachel Wetherbee of Lunenburg was entered January 5th A. D. 1754.

Purpose of marriage Jonathan Parker of Boston and Martha Brown of Lunenburg was entered this 8th day of Aug^st A. D. 1754.

Purpose of marriage between Thomas Page of Lunenburg and Dorothy Houghton of Leominister, was entered September ye 18th 1755.

Intentions of marriage betwixt Samuel Poole and Sarah Potter both of Lunenburg was entered November ye 19th 1756.

Porpose of marriage betwixt Nathan Ponchee of Ipswich Canada so called and Elizabeth Preist of Stow, was entered December ye 18th 1756.

Intentions of marriage between Abel Plats jun of a place called Rowley Canada, and Phebe Wetherbee of Lunenburg was entered March ye 7th A. D. 1759.

Intentions of marriage betwixt Ephraim Paree and Sarah Norcross both of Lunenburg was entered August ye 11th 1759.

Intentions of marriage betwixt Joseph Platts of Rowley Canada, and Sarah Bowers of Lunenburg, was entered September ye 12th 1760.

Intentions of marriage betwixt Samuel Paree and Mary Steward both of Lunenburg was entered November the 27th 1760.

Intentions of marriage betwixt Ebenezer Prat of Lunenburg and Lydia Stone of Groton were entered Sept ye 1th 1761.

Intentions of marriage betwixt David Poor of Ipswich Canada and Jane Martin of Lunenburg wer entered October ye 30th 1761.

Intentions of marriage between Bertholomew Pearson of Ipswich Canada and Lydia Randal of Lanenburg was enterd Septr 24th 1763.

Intentions of marriage between Joshua Pearce of Lunenburg and Molley Foss of Fitchburg ware enter^d October ye 14th 1769.

Intentions of marriage between James Paterson of Fitchburg & Miriam Hovey of Lunenburg was entered May ye 1. 1778.

Intentions of marriage between Amos Putnam of Fitchburg & Lydia Hovey of Lunenburg was entred May 2^d 1781.

Intentions of Marriage. 237

R.

S. W. H. M. H. S. M. M. B. M.

Porpose of marriage between Benjamin Randal and Lydia Stevens both of Lunenburg, entered Octo' 31th 1741.

Purpose of marriage entered between Amos Robbinson of Lunenburg and Lydia Wintworth of Topsfield, October ye 29 1743.

Purpose of marriage entered between John Russel of Lunenburg, and Thankfull Harris of Lancaster, March ye 4th 1744/5.

Purpose of marriage entered between George Russell, and Jane Mitchel both of Lunenburg March ye 29th 1746.

Intentions of marriage between Daniel Rugg of Lancaster, and Sarah Hastings of Lunenburg was entered April the 6th 1756.

Intentions of marriage betwixt Benjamin Reddington, and Ruth Stearns both of Lunenburg was entered November ye 17th 1756.

Intentions of marriage betwixt John Richards and Elizabeth Mitchael both of Lunenburg was entred Janvary 1th (A. D.) 1757.

Intentions of marriage betwixt Samuel Rufsel and Susannah Mitchael both of Lunenburg was entred April ye 30th A. D. 1757

Intentions of marriage betwixt Isaac Redington of Lunenburg, and Ruth Bodwell of Methuen, was entered November ye 30th Anno Domini 1759.

Intentions of marriage betwixt Mitchael Richards of Shirley and Esther Mitchael of Lunenburg was entered February ye 24th 1761.

S.

L. J. D. W. T. H. P.

Purpose of marriage entered betwixt John Sharer of Kingstown so called and Jane Little of Lunenburg December ye 15 174——*

Purpose of marriage entered between William Stearns and Elizabeth Johnson both of Lunenburg December ye 21th 1745.

Purpose of marriage entered between Hezekiah Sattle of Groton and Margaret Dodge of Lunenburg, Janvary ye 30th 1746/7

Purpose of marriage entered between Gustavus Swan of Lunenburg and Isabella Will of Townfhend October ye 2nd 1747.

Purpose of marriage betwixt Benjamin Steward and Rebeekah Taylor both of Lunenburg was entered September ye (13th) thirteenth 1751.

Purpose of marriage betwixt Abijah Stearns, and Sarah Heywood both of Lunenburg was entered Sept the 28th 1751.

Purpose of marriage betwixt Bradstreet Spafford of No. 4 and Mary Page of Lunenburg was entered September ye 30 1752.

―――――――――――――――――
*John R. Rollins says this date is, no doubt, 1742. [W. A. D.

S. (cont.)

L. H. T. H. F. T. P. I. S. F. B. I. M. D. I. S. P. H.

Purpose of marriage betwixt David Steel of Londondery and Jenet Little of Lunenburg was entered December ye 22^d 1752.

Purpose of marriage between John Smith of Petersborough and Mary Harknefs of Lunenburg was entered this 11th day of August A. D. 1753.

Purpose of marriage between Benjamin Stearns and Anna Taylor both of Lunenburg was entered this twentieth day of October, Anno Domini 1753.

Purpose of marriage between Moses Stearns of Narragansett No. 2. and Ruth Houghton of Lunenburg was entered February 4th A. D. 1754.

Purpose of marriage between Jonas Spafford and Dorcas Frost both of Lunenburg was entered this 19th day of October A. D. 1754.

Purpose of marriage between Solomon Steward Junr and Elizabeth Taylor both of Lunenburg was entered this third day of Febry Anno Domini 1755.

Purpose of marriage between John Simonds & Mercy Page both of Lunenburg was entered Febry 19th 1755.

Purpose of marriage between Phinehas Steward and Anne Ireland, both of Lunenburg, was entered July the 25th 1755.

Intentions of marriage betwixt Levi Stiles and Patience Smith both of Lunenburg was entered October the 25 1755.

Intentions of marriage betwixt Alexander Swan, and Lucy Foster both of Lunenburg was entered Feburary ye 11th 1756.

Intentions of marriage betwixt Benjamin Shed of Lunenburg and Elizabeth Blower of Lancaster was entered June ye 15th 1756.

Intentions of marriage betwixt Daniel Steward and Mary Ireland was entered October ye 16th 1756.

Intentions of marriage betwixt Joseph Spafford of Lunenburg and Mary Marble of Stow was entered Febuary ye 11th 1757.

Intentions of marriage betwixt Jonas Stearns and Submit Davis both of Lunenburg was entered April ye 15th 1758.

Intentions of marriage betwixt William Steward and Abigail Ireland both of Lunenburg was entered May ye 16th 1758.

Intentions of marriage between Thomas Sparhawk and Rebeckah Stearns both of Lunenburg, was entered June ye 24th Annoque Domini 1758.

Intentions of marriage betwixt Jonathan Stevens of Lunenburg and Elizabeth Parker of Pepperel was entered March ye 2nd 1761.

Intentions of marriage betwixt Jonathan Stedman of Westminster District, and Tabatha Hart of Lunenburg, was entered July ye 25th 1761.

S. (cont.)

P. P. B. A. L. S. P. M. W. B. A.

Intentions of marriage between Reuben Smith and Prudence Paree both of Lunenburg were entred Augt 20th 1762.

Intentions of marriage between Thomas Sweetland & Abigail Pushee both of Ipswich Canada were entred Novr 1st 1762.

Intentions of marriage between Solomon Shed of Lunenburg and Elizabeth Boynton of s^d Town ware entred March 11th 1763.

Intentions of marriage between Abraham Smith of Lunenburg & Lucy Allen of Weston was entred June 29th 1763.

Intentions of marriage between David Stearns and Mary Low both of Lunenburg was entred July 10th 1763.

Intentions of marriage between the Rev^d Mr. Ebenezer Sparhawk of Templetown & Mrs. Abigail Stearns of Lunenburg was entred July 19th 1763.

Intentions of marriage between Jacob Steward of Fitchburgh and Elizabth Paree of Lunenburg was entred May 29th 1766

Intentions of marriage between Joseph Symonds of Fitchburgh & Mary Martin of Lunenburgh was entered Octo^r 17th 1767.

Intentions of marriage between Edmond Stone of Fitchburg and Susanna Whitney of Lunenburgh was enter^d April 8th 1768.

Intentions of marriage by William Small of Fitchburg & Mary Bigelow of Lunenburg was entred Janu^y ye 23^d 1777.

Intentions of marriage between Doct. Peter Snow of Fitchburg and Mrs. Betsey Adams of Lunenburg was entred October 2^d 1789.

T.

H. S. G. G.

Purpose of marriage between David Taylor of Lunenburg and Bette Houghton of Lancaster were entred September ye 8th 1750.

Purpose of marriage between Caleb Taylor of Lunenburg and Susannah Shadock of Littleton was entered October ye 6th 1750.

Purpose of marriage betwixt Aaron Taylor and Mercy Gould both of Lunenburg was entered May the 30th 1752.

Purpose of marriage betwixt Zechariah Tarball and Mary Gould both of Lunenburg was entered February ye 22^d 1753.

U.

S.

Intentions of marriage between Oliver Upton of Fitchburg & Susanna Stiles of Lunenburg was entred November ye 8th 1777.

W.

W. W. B. H. G. B. P. B. P. R. M. P. S. W. H. H. W. B. M.

Porpose of marriage between Joseph Wood and Ruth Wetherbee, entered July 4th 1741. both of Lunenburg.

Purpose of marriage between Patrick White of Lunenburg and Jane White of Chesher entered December the 24th 1741.

Purpose of marriage enter^d between Jonathan Willard jun of Lunenburg and Phebe Ballard of Concord, September ye 17th 1743.

Purpose of marriage entered between David Wood of Lunenburg, and Mary Hovey of Boxford Janvary ye 3rd 1745/6.

Purpose of marriage entred between Obediah Walker of Lunenburg and Abbigaill Gary of Lynn August the 16th 1745.

Purpose of marriage entered, between Daniel Willard of Lancaster, and Lucy Butler of Lunenburg, September the 10th 1745.

Purpose of marriage entered between Michael Wood and Mary Platts both of this town November ye first A. D. 1745.

Purpose of marriage entered between Ephraim Whitney, and Jane Bancroft both of Lunenburg December ye 27th 1745.

Purpose of marriage entered between Paul Wetherbee and Hannah Parce both of Lunenburg May ye 10th 1746.

Purpose of marriage entered between Jacob Waren of Lunenburg and Melther Russell of Littleton June ye 21th 1746.

Purpose of marriage betwixt Archebald White of the place called New-Ipswich, and Margaret Mc'Clary of Lunenburg was entered November the third 1750.

Purpose of marriage betwixt Joseph Wheelock jun of Lancaster and Allice Page of Lunenburg was entered September ye 14th 1751.

Purpose of marriage betwixt Joseph Wood of Lunenburg and Ruth Simons of Littleton was entered September ye 16th 1752.

Purpose of marriage betwixt John White and Mary Whitney both of Lunenburg was entered November ye 10th 1752.

Purpose of marriage betwixt Abner Whitney of Shirley, and Sarah Hilton of Lunenburg was entered this 23d day of March A. D. 1753.

Purpose of marriage between Josh Wilder Tertius of Lancaster and Elizabeth Heywood of Lunenburg was entered this 18th day of May A. D. 1754.

Purpose of marriage between Jonathan Wood jun^r of Lunenburg, and Rachel Wood of Uxbridge was entered this 10th of September A. D. 1754.

Purpose of marriage between Benoni Wallis of Lunenburg and Rebecah Brown of Lyn was entered Febry 19th 1755.

Purpose of marriage between Benjamin Wetherbee of Lunenburg and Keziah Munroe of Carlile was entered September the 24th 1755.

W. (cont.)

F. M. G. R. F. B. B. W. T. S. H. H. W. L.

Intentions of marriage between Thomas Wheeler, and Abigail Foster, both of Dorchester Canada was entered January 29th 1756.

Intentions of marriage betwixt Thomas Wetherbe of Lunenburg and Hannah Munroe of Carlile was entered April ye 22d 1756.

Intentions of marriage betwixt Jonathan Wood and Sarah Gary both of Lunenburg were entered March ye 30th 1757.

Intentions of marriage betwixt Berzillai Willard and Hepsibeth Reddington both of Lunenburg, was entered September ye 10th 1757.

Intentions of marriage betwixt Winkeal Right of Dunstable, and Sibel Farewell of Lunenburg was entered February ye 25th A. D. 1758.*

Intentions of marriage betwixt Abner Whelock of Leominster and Mary Brown of Lunenburg, was entered March ye 11th 1758.

Intentions of marriage betwixt Reuben Wyman & Elizabeth Bancroft both of Lunenburg was entered January ye 15th 1761.

Intentions of marriage between Michal Wood of Lunenburgh & Lois Wilson of Leominster was entred July 28th 1764.

Intentions of marriage between John Wood of Lunenburgh & Sarah Thurston of Fitchburg was entered July 27th 1767.

Intentions of marriage between Israel Wyman of Lunenburg & Mary Stratton of Fitchburg ware enterd Ocber ye 7th 1769.

Intentions of marriage between Paul Wetherbee of Fitchburg, and Dorcas Hovey of Lunenburg was entered October ye 14th 17——.†

Intentions of marriage between Joseph Wyman of Lunenburg and Hannah Hilton of Fitchburg was entered December ye 28th 1776.

Intentions of marriage between James Wood of Fitchburg & Sarah Walker of Lunenburg was entred May 13th 1780.

Intentions of marriage between Seth Wyman of Lunenburg & Sarah Littlefield of Fitchburg was entred February 16th 1782.

NOTE.

"Dorchester Canada" is what is now known as Ashburnham.
"Narragansett No. 2" is what is now known as Westminster.
"Upper Ashuelott" is what is now known as Keene, N. H.

*J. R. Rollins says this name was probably intended for Wright. [W. A. D.
†John R. Rollins gives this date as, no doubt, 1774. [W. A. D.

MARRIAGES

MARRIAGES

COPIED FROM THE

RECORDS OF THE TOWN OF LUNENBURG,

FROM 1727 TO 1764.

A.

S.

William Adams of Dunstable and Mary Speer of Lunenburg were married May 31th 1744 by the Rev'd Mr. David Stearns minister of Lunenburg.

B.

S. J. W. G. L. R. H.

Benjamin Bellows jun^r and Abigail Stearns both of Lunenburg were married by ye Rev. Mr. David Stearns, minister of Lunenburg October ye 7th 1735.

Stephen Boynton and Sarah Johnson both of Lunenburg ware married November ye 14th 1737 by the Revnd Mr. David Stearns.

Jonathan Broadstreet of Lunenburg and Olive Wheellock of Leominster were married July the second 1741 by Mr. David Stearns minister of Lunenburg.

Francis Buttrick of Lancaster, and Hannah Gilson of Lunenburg were married by ye Rev Mr. David Stearns minister of Lunenburg December ye 4th 1744.

Nehemiah Bowers and Sarah Larrabee both of Lunenburg were married March ye 18th 1744/5 by ye Rev. Mr David Stearns minister of Lunenburg.

Eliphelet Brown of Coventree and Elizabeth Retter of Lunenburg were married June ye 13th 1745 by ye Rev Mr David Stearns, minister of Lunenburg.

Jerahmeel Bowers of Lancaster, and Miriam Houghton of Lunenburg were married March ye 19th 1745/6 by the Rev Mr David Stearns, minister of Lunenburg.

B. (cont.)

G. L. F. L. B. C. K. G. D. H. G. J. J. R. C. F.

Benoni Boynton Jun and Elizabeth Going both of Lunenburg were married March ye 24th 1752 by ye Rev Mr David Stearns, minister of Lunenburg.

William Barron of Upper Ashuelot ("so called,,) and Isabella Larrabee of Lunenburg were married September 28th 1752 by the Rev Mr. David Stearns minister of Lunenburg.

Joseph Brown of Cambridge and Abigail Foster of Lunenburg were married January 18th 1753 by the Rev Mr David Stearns minister of Lunenburg.

Stephen Boynton and Elizabeth Lovejoy both of Lunenburg were married March 6th 1753, by the Rev^d Mr David Stearns minister of Lunenburg.

Nathaniel Burnam Junr & Elizabeth Brown, both of Lunenburg were married July 29th 1754 by the Rev Mr David Stearns minister of Lunenburg

Benjamin Bigelow and Elizabeth Colman both of Lunenburg were married Octo^r 31st 1754 by Rev. Mr Stearns.

Joseph Beman and Hannah Knight both of Lancaster were married July the 23rd 1755 by Edward Hartwell Justice of the Peace.

Jonathan Bennett of Groton and Mary Going of Lunenburg were married October ye 15th 1755 by the Rev Mr David Stearns minister of Lunenburg.

William Barbrook of Lancaster and Thankful Dutton of Lunenburg were married together March ye 24 1757 by William Downe Justice of the pence.

Timothy Bancroft & Mary Harriman both of Lunenburg were married Nov^m ye 1st A. D. 1757 by William Downe Justice of pacis.

Elisha Bigelow of Narragansett No 2. and Sarah Goodridge of Lunenburg were married Dec^m ye 1st 1757 by the Rev Mr. David Stearns minister of Lunenburg.

Benjamin Bellows Esqr of Wallpole in the Province of New Hampshire and Mrs Mary Jenisson of Lunenburg were married April ye 21st 1758 by the Rev Mr David Stearns minister of Lunenburg.

Caleb Ball and Elizabeth Joyner both of a place called Narragansett No 2 were married December ye 4th 1758, by Edward Hartwell Justice of the peace.

Josiah Bailey & Mary Reed both of Lunenburg were married April 15th 1760 by ye Rev Mr. David Stearns minister of Lunenburg.

Josiah Bailey Junr & Sarah Carter both of Lunenburg were married by Edward Hartwell Justice of the peace Octo^r 7th 1762.

James Bennet and Elizabeth Fuller both of Lunenburg were married by Edward Hartwell Esqr Septr 6th 1763.

Marriages.

B. (cont.)
W. W.

Ebenezer Bridge and Mehetable Wood both of Lunenburg were married by Edward Hartwell Esqr Novr 3^d 1763.

Joseph Bellows & Lowis Whitney both of Lunenburg were married by the Rev^d Mr Adams Octo^r 3^d 1764.

C.
R. B. A. H. F. H. F. S. W. G. B. H.

Mr. Robart Clark and Mrs. Mary Reed both of Lunenburg ware married by ye Rev^d Mr. David Stearns minister of Lunenburg July the 31th 1738.

James Colburn and Sarah Bradstreet were married August ye 12th 1742 by the Rev Mr David Stearns minister of Lunenburg.

Paul Crocker and Lydia Austin both of Lunenburg, were married June the 4th 1750 by Thomas Prentice Justice of the peace.

Benj^a Corey Junr of Lunenburg & Beulah Holden of Shirley were married Decr 26th 1753 by the Rev^d Mr David Stearns, minister of Lunenburg.

Nathaniel Carlton jun and Olive Farewell both of Lunenburg were married November ye 1 1756 by the Rev^d Mr David Stearns minister of Lunenburg.

William Cowdin of Worcester and Mary Henry of Lunenburg were married September ye 7th 1757 by Edward Hartwell Justice of the peace.

James Clark and Anne Freeman both of Lancaster were married January ye 5th 1758 by Edward Hartwell Justice of pea——

Moses Child and Sarah Stiles both of Lunenburg were married March ye 28th 1758 by the Rev Mr David Stearns minister of Lunenburg.

Elias Carter & Deborah White both of Leominster were married March ye 12th 1761 by Edward Hartwell Justice of ye peace.

James Carter and Sarah Gilson both of Lunenburg were married by Edward Hartwell Justice of ye peace, December 3^d 1761.

Asa Carlton & Ruth Bailey both of Lunenburg were, married Feby 8th 1763 by the Rev^d Mr Samuel Payson.

Joseph Chaplain & Lois Hastings both of Lunenburg, were married by Edward Hartwell Esqr April 5th 1764.

D.

B. B. W. S. H. P. B. B. S. F. F. C. W. S.

Jacob Davis of Concord and Anne Boynton of Lunenburg were married by ye Rev^d Mr. David Stearns minister of Lunenburg on ye 19 day of April 1733.

John Darlin & Ruth Boynton both of Lunenburg were married October the 13th 1744 by the Rev Mr. David Stearns minister of Lunenburg.

Authur Darrah of Nothingham and Margaret Wallis of Lunenburg were married December ye 11th 1745 by ye Rev Mr David Stearns minister of Lunenburg.

John Divol and Susannah Smith both of Lunenburg were married March the 31th 1747 by the Rev Mr David Stearns minister of Lunenburg.

Nicholas Dike and Mary Hastings both of Lunenburg were married July ye 20th 1748 by Thomas Prentice, Justice of ye peace.

Richard Day and Ruth Pouchee both of Lunenburg were married by the Rev Mr. David Stearns minister of Lunenburg December ye 8th 1748.

Timothy Darling of Lunenburg and Joanna Blood of Groton were married Febr^y 8th 1753 by the Rev^d Mr. David Stearns, minister of Lunenburg.

Timothy Dorman of Boxford, and Eunice Burnam of Lunenburg were married May 27th 1754 by the Rev^d Mr. David Stearns minister of Lunenburg.

William Dodge of Lunenburg and Elizabeth Salmon of Harvard were married January ye 28th 1755 by the Rev Mr David Stearns minister of Lunenburg.

Thomas Dutton and Sarah Fitch both of Lunenburg were married together September ye 9th 1756 by the Rev Mr David Stearns minister of Lunenburg.

Joseph Davis & Elizabeth Foster both of Lunenburg were married Nov^m ye 8th A. D. 1757 by William Downe Justice of peace.

Josiah Dodge Junr resident in Lunenburg & Hannah Conant of Leominster were married by Edward Hartwell Justice of the peace November 8th 1761.

Silas Dutton and Sarah Whitney both of Lunenburg were married by Benjⁿ Goodridge Esqr March 3^d 1763.

Phinehas Divol & Abigail Stockwell both of Lunenburg were married by Benjⁿ Goodridge Esq June 6th 1763.

F.

H.

David Farnsworth and Hannah Hastings both of Lunenburg were married by ye Rev^d Mr. David Stearns, minister of Lunenburg August ye 15th 1735.

F. (cont.)

E. B. F. H. H. K. S. R. S. P. G. C. J.

Andrew Fleming of Lunenburg and Ann Ellit of Dunstable were married by ye Rev^d Mr David Stearns, minister of Lunenburg November ye 5th 1735.

Thomas Frost of Billerica and Dorcas Boynton of Lunenburg were married by the Rev^d Mr. Stearns June ye 6th 1737.

Jonathan Fisk and Jemima Foster both of Lunenburg ware married July the 28th 1738 by the Rev^d Mr. David Stearns.

Oliver Farewell of Dunstable and Abigail Hubbard of Lunenburg ware married by ye Rev^d Mr. David Stearns minister of Lunenburg December the 25th 1738.

Stephen Farnworth of (number four, so called) and Eunice Hastings of Lunenburg were married by Mr David Stearns, minister of Lunenburg December the 22^d 1741.

Richard Fowler and Ruth Kendell both of Lunenburg were married March the 17th 1741/2 by Mr. David Stearns minister of Lunenburg.

Micah Fuller of Upton and Lois Sattle of Lunenburg were married November ye 21th 1744 by ye Rev Mr. David Stearns minister of Lunenburg.

Isaac Foster & Mary Rice both of Lunenburg were married December ye 2nd 1745 by ye Rev Mr David Stearns minister of Lunenburg.

Benjamin Foster Jun and Lucy Stiles both of Lunenburg were married March ye 24th 1748/9 by the Rev Mr David Stearns minister of Lunenburg.

John Fitch and Elizabeth Parce both of Lunenburg, February the fourteenth 1750/1 by Thomas Prentice Justice of the peace.

John Fuller and Prudence Gilson both of Lunenburg were married December the 18th 1755 by the Rev Mr David Stearns minister of Lunenburg.

Nehemiah Fuller and Mary Connant both of Lunenburg were married May ye 4th 1756 by the Rev Mr. David Stearns minister of Lunenburg.

Joseph Foster & Sarah Jones both of Lunenburg were married January ye 17th 1760 by the Rev. Mr David Stearns minister of Lunenburg.

G.

B. B.

Mr. John Grout and Johannah Boynton married November ye 23th 1727.

Moses Gould and Mary Bellows married Novr 7th 1728.

G. (cont.)

G. H. S. P. W. J. W. B. J. F. S. D. W. S. F.

Mr. Jacob Gould of Lunenburg were married to Mrs. Dorothy Goodridge of Lunenburg by ye Revnd Mr. Andrew Gardner minister of Lunenburg Febr 4 1730/1.

John Gibson and Elizabeth Hartwell both of Lunenburg were married by Edward Hartwell Esqr on ye 9th of November 1737.

Joshua Goodridge and Lydia Stearns both of Lunenburg ware married by the Rev^d Mr. David Stearns minister of Lunenburg June the 25th 1739.

Benjamin Gould and Esther Pearce both of Lunenburg was married by the Revnd Mr David Stearns minister of Lunenburg October the 17th 1739.

William Grimes of Winchester and Mary White of Lunenburg were married by the Revnd Mr. David Stearns minister of Lunenburg September the 9th 1740.

Thomas Gearfield of Weston and Rebekah Johnson of Lunenburg were married October ye 21th 1742 by the Rev Mr David Stearns minister of Lunenburg.

William Gillchrest and Elizabeth White both of Lunenburg were married June ye 21th 1743 by the Rev. Mr David Stearns minister of Lunenburg.

Philip Goodridge and Jane Boynton both of Lunenburg were married November ye 3th 1743 by the Rev^d Mr. David Stearns minister of Lunenburg.

Isaac Gibson and Keziah Johnson both of Lunenburg were married Febry ye 4th 1744/5 by the Rev Mr. David Stearns minister of Lunenburg.

Joseph Goodridge and Sarah Forster both of Lunenburg were married January ye 30th 1745/6 by ye Rev Mr. David Stearns minister of Lunenburg.

John Grout Jun and Phebe Spafford both of Lunenburg were married October ye 22nd 1750 by ye Rev Mr. David Stearns minister of Lunenburg.

Jonas Gilson and Sarah Divol both of Lunenburg were married January ye 29th 1756 by the Rev. Mr David Stearns minister of Lunenburg.

Elijah Grout and Mary Willard both of Lunenburg were married July 17th A. D. 1757 by William Downe, Justice of the peace.

Elisha Gibs and Abigail Stevens both of the district of Westminster were married by Edward Hartwell Justice of the peace December ye 18th 1759

Thomas Gary of Lunenburg & Elizabeth Farewell of Townshend were married February ye 21st 1760 by the Rev Mr David Stearns minister of Lunenburg.

Marriages.

G. (cont.)

B. H. G. S. G. F.

Jonathan Going of Lunenburg & Anne Bennet of Shirley District were married April ye 15th 1760 by the Rev Mr David Stean minister of Lunenburg.

Silas Gates of Stow & Anna Hammond of Lunenburg were married December ye 1st 1760 by ye Rev. Mr. David Stearns minister of Lunenburg.

Mr. Francis Gardner of Stow & Mrs Sarah Gibson of Lunenburg were married by Edward Hartwell Justice of the peace Octo^r 5th 1762.

Eliphelet Goodridge & Rebekah Snow both of Lunenburg were married by Benjn Goodridge Esqr Decr 29th 1763.

Mr. Jacob Gates of Harvard & Miss Elizabeth Gibson of Lunenburg were married by Ed^d Hartwell Esqr May 9th 1764.

Benjn Gould of Rowley Canada in the Prov^ce of New-Hampshire, and Sarah Foster of Lunenburg were married by Benjn Goodridge Esqr May 14th 1764.

H.

K. G. W. H. H. M. K. T.

Edward Hartwell Junr and Elizabeth Kneeland both of Lunenburg ware married by the Rev^d Mr. David Stearns minister of Lunenburg August ye 7th 1739.

Jonathan Hubbard Junr of Lunenburg and Abigail Genison of Watertown was married by the Rev^nd Mr. David Stearns minister of Lunenburg September ye 24th 1739.

John Hill and Jane Walles both of Lunenburg was married by the Rev^nd Mr. David Stearns minister of Lunenburg March ye 19th 1739/40.

Nathaniel Hastings and Lois Houghton both of Lunenburg were married May the 21th 1741 by Edward Hartwell Justice of the peace.

Jonathan Hammond of Lower Ashnlott so called, and Abigail Hastings of Lunenburg were marryed July the 29th 1741 by Mr. David Stearns minister of Lunenburg.

William Holt and Mary Martin both of Lunenburg were married July 30th 1744 by the Rev^d Mr David Stearns minister of Lunenburg.

George Henry and Elizabeth Kenedy both of Lunenburg were married Febry ye 13th 1745/6 by the Rev. Mr. David Stearns minister of Lunenburg.

Jonathan Hartwell and Elizabeth Tarbal both of Lunenburg were married December ye 3rd 1745 by ye Rev. Mr. David Stearns minister of Lunenburg.

H. (cont.)

G. D. J. S. T. P. G. D. H. P. D. F. R. W. D. F.

Amos Hazeltine and Eunice Gilson both of Lunenburg were married March the 5th 1746/7 by ye Revd Mr. David Stearns minister of Lunenburg.

Joseph Hartwell and Tabitha Dodge both of Lunenburg were married September ye 22nd 1747 by Edward Hartwell Justice of ye peace.

John Hubbard and Hannah Johnson both of Lunenburg were married March ye 20th 1748/9 by the Rev. Mr. David Stearns minister of Lunenburg.

Darius Houghton and Jerusha Stearns both of Lunenburg were married by ye Revd Mr. David Stearns, minister of Lunenburg, January ye 24th 1749.

John Henderson of Lancaster and Jane Turner of Lunenburg were married August ye 4th 1749 by Thomas Prentice Justice of peace.

Thomas Henderson late of Lunenburg and Bethsheba Prist of Stow were married April the third 1751 by Thomas Prentice Justice of the peace.

Joseph Hammond of Lower Ashuelot so called, and Esther Gould of Lunenburg were married Novr 2d 1752 by the Revd Mr. David Stearns minister of Lunenburg.

Gershom Hubbard of Dunstable and Lipha Dodge of Lunenburg were married January 18th 1753 by the Revd Mr. David Stearns minister of Lunenburg.

William Henry Junr and Mary Harper both of Lunenburg were married December the sixth 1753; by Edward Hartwell Esqr Justice of the peace.

Phinehas Hartwell and Mary Peirce both of Lunenburg were married November 28th 1754 by Edward Hartwell Esqr Just⁓ Pacis.

Henery Hodgskins and Mary Dutton both of Lunenburg were married May the 8th 1755 by the Rev. Mr. David Stearns minister of Lunenburg.

Zimri Heywood and Jane Foster both of Dorchester Canada so called were married June ye 5th 1756 by Edward Hartwell Justice of the peace.

Samuel Hodgskins and Rebeckah Rice both of Lunenburg were married August ye 8th A. D. 1757 by William Downe Justice of peace.

Joseph Houghton and Mary Willson both of Leominster were married January ye 31st 1758 by Edward Hartwell, Justice of the peace.

Thaddeus Harrington of Shirley and Thankful Dodge of Lunenburg were married April 6th 1758 by the Rev. Mr. David Stearns minister of Lunenburg.

Samuel Hart and Mary Fuller both of Lunenburg were married April ye 20th 1758 by the Rev. Mr David Stearns minister of Lunenburg.

Marriages.

H. (cont.)

P. C. H. B. S. R. H.

Ebenezer Hart and Sarah Poole both of Lunenburg were married May ye 4th 1758 by the Rev. Mr. David Stearns, mininster of Lunenburg.

Daniel Harper and Rachel Colman both of Dorchester Canada so called were married November ye 23rd 1758 by ye Rev. Mr. David Stearns minister of Lunenburg.

George Hewett of Rowley Canada & Triphena Hodgskins of Lunenburg were married October ye 2nd 1760 by the Revd Mr. David Stearns minister of Lunenburg.

Henry Hodgskin of Ipswich Canada & Jemima Ball of Princetown were married by Benjn Goodridge Jusee Peace Novr 17th 1762.

Samll Hilton and Rebekah Stickney both of Lunenburg were married by Benjn Goodridge Esqr Nov.r 17th 1763.

Phinehas Hutchens and Abigail Reed both of Lunenburg were married by Benjn Goodridge Esqr Novr 24th 1763.

Eleazar Houghton Junr and Susannah Holman both of Lunenburg were married by Edwd Hartwell Esqr March 8th 1764.

J.

H. W. B. G.

John Jenison and Mary Hubburd were married by the Revd Mr. David Stearns July 21st 1740

James Johnson of Lunenburg and Susanna Willard of Harvard were married June ye 15th 1747 by Thomas Prentice Justice of the peace.

Abner Jackman and Elizabeth Bayley both of Lunenburg were married February ye 10th 1757. by the Rev Mr. David Stearns minister of Lunenburg.

William Judevine and Patience Grout both of Lunenburg were married June ye 26th 1759 by the Rev. Mr. David Stearns minister of Lunenburg.

K.

M. P. P.

John Kelsey of Groton and Martha Mc farlen of Lunenburg was married by the Revnd Mr. David Stearns minister of Lunenburg Jenevary the 10th 1739/40.

Uzziah Kendel of Leominister and Elizabeth Parce of Lunenburg ware married July the 6th 1747. by the Rev. Mr. David Stearns minister of Lunenburg.

Samuel Kennedy and Sarah Page both of Lunenburg, were married July 24th 1749 by Thomas Prentice Justice of ye peace.

K. (cont.)

S. F. H.

Richard Kimbal of Boxford and Elizabeth Seetown [Seaton?] of Lunenburg were married Janvary ye 23rd 1750/1 by ye Rev. Mr. David Stearns minister of Lunenburg.

William Kimball & Jane Farewell, both of Lunenburg were married March ye 13th 1760 by ye Rev. Mr. David Stearns minister of Lunenburg.

Benjamin Kidder of Billrica & Ruth Heywood of Lunenburg were married February ye 12th 1761 by the Rev^d Mr David Stearns minister of Lunenburg.

L.

W. P. K. W. S. F. A. P.

Samuel Larrabee jun^r of Lunenburg and Anne Williams of Groton were married April ye 23rd 1746 by ye Rev^d Mr. David Stearns minister of Lunenburg.

John Lovejoy and Sarah Paree both of Lunenburg, were married Janvary ye 25th 1749 by the Rev. Mr. David Stearns minister of Lunenburg.

Thomas Lietch and Jane Kennedy both of Lunenburg, were married September the 19th 1750 by Edward Hartwell Justice of the peace.

Benj^a Larrabee of Lunenburg and Margaret Williams of Groton were married December 7th 1752 by the Rev^d Mr David Stearns minister of Lunenburg.

Mr. Samuel Larrabee of Luneburg and wid^w Mary Simonds of Shirley District were married December ye 19th 1758 by the Rev. Mr. David Stearns minister of Lunenburg.

Nehemiah Lane of Lunenburg, & Sarah Fletcher of Groton were married April 17th 1760 by the Rev^d Mr. David Stearns minister of Lunenburg.

John Larrabee of Lunenburg & Abiel Arven of Groton, were married June ye 19th 1760 by the Mr. David Stearns, minister of Lunenburg.

William Larken of Lunenburg & Hannah Paree of Groton were married May ye 7th 1761 by Edward Hartwell Justice of ye peace.

M.

S. M.

Thomas Morrison of Londonderry and Mary Smith of Lunenburg was married by the Revnd Mr. David Stearns, minister of Lunenburg, October ye 2th 1739.

Hugh Moors and Ruth Mitchael both of Lunenburg, were married December ye 28th 1743 by the Rev^d Mr. David Stearns of Lunenburg.

Marriages.

M. (cont.)

H. K. W. C. C.

Thomas Matthews and Elizabeth Heborn both of Lunenburg were married Janvary ye 4th 1748/9 by Edward Hartwell Justice of ye peace.

Willm Machane Junr of Worcester & Mary Kennedy of Lunenburg, were married Decr 4th 1753 by the Rev^d Mr. David Stearns minister of Lunenburg.

John Moors jun of Bolton & Unity Willard of Lunenburg were married August ye 30th A. D. 1757 by William Downe Just pac.

John Martin and Betty Chaplin both of Lunenburg were married March ye 3rd A. D. 1761 by Edward Hartwell Justice of the peace.

Sam^ll Mc'Craken of Worcester & Lettice Carlisle of Lunenburg were married by Edwd Hartwell Justice of the peace Decr 8th 1762.

N.

B.

Page Norcross & Elizabeth Bailey both of Lunenburg, were married by Edwd Hartwell Esqr Feby 15th 1763.

O.

F.

Ephraim Osbourn and Sarah Fisk both of Lunenburg were married November ye 26th 1759 by the Rev^d Mr. David Stearns minister of Lunenburg.

P.

L. G. B. W. P.

Mr. John Prescott of Concord married to Mrs. Anne Lynde of Lunenburg by ye Rev^nd Mr. Andrew Gardner, minister of Lunenburg, November ye 25 1730.

Nathaniel Page and Marcy Gould both of Lunenburg were married by ye Rev^nd Mr. David Stearns minister of Lunenburg on ye 25 day of December A. D. 1733.

David Page and Priscilla Boynton both of Lunenburg were married by ye Reverand Mr. David Stearns minister of Lunenburg on ye 22 day of January A. D. 1734/5.

Thomas Prentice of Lancaster and Abigail Willard of Lunenburg were married by ye Rev^d Mr Stearns, August ye 2^d 1737.

Josiah Parker and Elizabeth Page, both of Lunenburg, were married October 31th 1737 by the Rev^nd Mr. David Stearns.

256   *The Early Records of the Town of Lunenburg.*

P. (cont.)

W. D. R. N. P. G. P. W. B. F. P. P. W. N. B.

Asael Phelps and Elizabeth Wilder both of Lancaster, were married February y⁶ 15th 1743/4 by Edward Hartwell Justice of y⁶ peace.

Jonathan Paree and Sarah Dodge both of Lunenburg, were married Febry y⁶ 4th 1745/6 by y⁶ Rev Mr. David Stearns minister of Lunenburg.

David Paree Jun and Anne Retter both of Lunenburg were married April y⁶ 20th 1746 by y⁶ Rev. Mr. David Stearns minister of Lunenburg.

William Porter and Mary Nichols both of Lunenburg, were married May the first 1746 by the Rev. Mr. David Stearns minister of Lunenburg.

Mr. Samvel Page of Lunenburg and Sarah Paree of Leominster were married July y⁶ 9th 1747 by the Revᵈ Mr. David Stearns minister of Lunenburg.

Timothy Parker and Johannah Grout both of Lunenburg were married September the 6th 1748 by the Rev. Mr. David Stearns minister of Lunenburg.

Joseph Platts of Rowley Canady (so called, and Deborah Page of Lunenburg were married Novʳ 16th 1752 by the Revᵈ Mr. David Stearns minister of Lunenburg.

Thomas Putnam of Charlestown in the Province of New-Hampshire & Rachel Wetherbee of Lunenburg were married Janry 24th 1754 by the Revᵈ Mr. David Stearns minister of Lunenburg.

Jonathan Parker of Boston and Martha Brown of Lunenburg were married Novʳ 8th 1754 by y⁶ Revᵈ Mʳ David Stearns.

Jacob Peabody and Dorothy Foster both of Leominster, were married March the 4th 1756 by William Downe, Justice of the peace.

Samuel Pool and Sarah Potter both of Lunenburg were married together December y⁶ 14th 1756 by William Downe Justice of the peace.

Nathan Pushee of Ipswich Canada and Elizabeth Priest of Stow were married together Janavary y⁶ 13th 1757 by William Downe Justice of the peace.

Abel Plats of Rowley Canada so called, and Phebe Wetherbee of Lunenburg were married April 26th 1759 by the Rev. Mr. David Stearns minister of Lunenburg.

Ephraim Paree & Sarah Norcross both of Lunenburg, were married January y⁶ 3rd 1760 by the Rev. Mr. David Stearns minister of Lunenburg.

Joseph Platts of Rowley Canada, and Sarah Bowers of Lunenburg were married October y⁶ 2nd 1760 by the Revᵈ Mr. David Stearns minister of Lunenburg.

Marriages. 257

P. (cont.)
S. S. M.

Samuel Parce & Mary Steward both of Lunenburg, were married March ye 19th 1761 by Edward Hartwell, Justice of the peace.

Ebenezer Pratt of Lunenburg & Lydia Stone of Groton were married by Edward Hartwell Justice of ye peace September ye 22^d 1761.

David Poor of Ipswich Canada so called & Jane Martin of Lunenburg were married by Edward Hartwell, Justice of the peace December 2^d 1761.

R.
B. W. S. S. M. M.

Samuel Reed and Mary Ballard both of Lunenburg ware married by the Rev^d Mr. David Stearns, minister of Lunenburg, October ye 26th 1738.

John Russel and Elizabeth Wallis both of Lunenburg were married by ye Rev Mr. David Stearns, minister of Lunenburg Novr the 13th 1740.

Benjamin Randal and Lydia Stevens, both of Lunenburg, were married December the 2nd 1741, by Mr. David Stearns minister of Lunenburg.

Benjamin Reddington and Ruth Stearns, both of Lunenburg were married March ye 24th 1757 by the Rev. Mr David Stearns, minister of Lunenburg.

John Richards and Elizabeth Mitchael, both of Lunenburg were married October ye 17th 1757 by David Stearns minister of Lunenburg.

Samuel Russel and Susannah Mitchael both of Lunenburg, were married November ye 28th 1757 by the Rev. Mr. David Stearns minister of Lunenburg.

S.
H. S. L. J.

April 7th 1736 The Rev^d Mr. David Stearns and Mrs. Ruth Hubbard were married by the Rev^d Mr. John Prentice of Lancaster.

William Steward and Margaret Sanderson of Lunenburg were married by the Rev^nd Mr. Stearns November 10th 1736.

John Sharer of Kingstown (so called) and Jane Little of Lunenburg were married Janvary ye 4th 1742/3 by the Rev. Mr. David Stearns minister of Lunenburg.

William Stearns and Elizabeth Johnson both of Lunenburg were married Janvary ye 22nd 1745/6 by ye Rev. Mr. David Stearns minister of Lunenburg.

S. (cont.)

W. R. T. H. P. L. H. T. H. F. P. T. S. F. I. L.

Gustavus Swan of Lunenburg and Isabella Willson of Townshend were married Novr ye 4th 1747 by Thomas Prentice Justice of ye peace.

William Swan of Petersbouroh so called and Mary Russell of Lunenburg were married February the twenty sixth 1750/1 by Thomas Prentice Justice of the peace.

Benjamin Steward and Rebecca Taylor, both of Lunenburg were married Janvary ye 9th 1751/2 by the Rev. Mr. David Stearns minister of Lunenburg.

Abijah Stearns and Sarah Heywood both of Lunenburg were married November ye 12th 1751 by the Rev. Mr. David Stearns minister of Lunenburg.

Bradstreet Spafford of N° 4 so called and Mary Page of Lunenburg were married October 16th 1752 by the Rev^d Mr. David Stearns, minister of Lunenburg.

David Steel of Loudonderry and Jennet Little of Lunenburg were married Febry 8th 1753 by the Rev^d Mr. David Stearns minister of Lunenburg.

John Smith of Petersborough & Mary Harkness of Lunenburg were married October 2^d 1753 by the Rev^d Mr. David Stearns minister of Lunenburg.

Benj^a Stearns & Anna Taylor both of Lunenburg were married Janry 15th 1754 by the Rev^d Mr. David Stearns minister of Lunenburg.

Moses Stearns of Narragansett No 2 and Ruth Houghton of Lunenburg were married June 13th 1754 by the Rev^d Mr David Stearns minister of Lunenburg.

Jonathan Spafford and Dorcas Frost both of Lunenburg were married Novr 13th 1754 by the Rev^d Mr. David Stearns.

John Simonds and Mercy Page both of Lunenburg were married March ye 13th 1755 by the Rev. Mr. David Stearns minister of Lunenburg.

Solomon Steward Jun. and Elizabeth Taylor, both of Lunenburg were married May ye 28th 1755 by the Rev. Mr. David Stearns, minister of Lunenburg.

Levi Stiles and Patience Smith both of Lunenburg, were married December ye 16th 1755 by the Rev. Mr. David Stearns minister of Lunenburg.

Alexander Swan and Lucy Foster both of Lunenburg were married March the 7th 1756 by William Downe Justice of the peace.

Phinehas Steward and Anne Ireland both of Lunenburg were married April 22^d 1756 by the Rev. Mr. David Stearns minister of Lunenburg.

Daniel Steward and Mary Ierland both of Lunenburg were married March ye 14th 1757 by ye Rev. Mr. David Stearns minister of Lunenburg.

Marriages.

S. (cont.)

G. D. S. I. G. L. F. H. P. S. L.

Ephraim Stockwell & Sarah Grout both of Petersham, were married Nov^m 21st A. D. 1757 by William Downe, Justice of pacis.

Jonas Stearns and Submit Davis, both of Lunenburg were married May ye 4th 1758 by the Rev. Mr. David Stearns minister of Lunenburg.

Mr. Thomas Sparhawk and Mrs. Rebecca Stearns both of Lunenburg were married July ye 10th 1758 by ye Rev. Mr. David Stearns minister of Lunenburg.

William Steward and Abigail Ireland both of Lunenburg were married July ye 25th 1758 by the Rev. Mr. David Stearns minister of Lunenburg.

Samuel Sanderson and Sarah Gould both of Lunenburg were married December ye 27th 1759 by the Rev. Mr. David Stearns minister of Lunenburg.

William Symonds of Shirley District & Abigail Larrabee of Lunenburg were married March ye 11th 1760 by ye Rev. Mr. David Stearns, minister of Lunenburg.

Silas Snow of Lunenburg & Anna Farwell of Groton were married November ye 20th 1760 by the Rev^nd Mr. David Stearns, minister of Lunenburg.

Jonathan Stedman of Westminster and Tabitha Hart of Lunenburg were married by Edward Hartwell, Justice of the peace, Septr ye 8th 1761.

Reuben Smith & Prudence Pearce both of Lunenburg were married by Edward Hartwell Justice of the peace Septr 6th 1762.

The Reverend Mr. Ebenezer Sparhawk of Templetown, and Mrs. Abigail Stearns of Lunenburg were married by the Rev^d Mr. Timothy Harrington of Lancaster, September the first, seventeen hundred and sixty-three.

Mr. David Stearns and Mrs. Mary Low both of Lunenburg were married by the Rev^d Mr. Timothy Harrington of Lancaster Octo^r ye 20th 1763.

T.

G. G.

Aaron Taylor and Mercy Gould both of Lunenburg were married December 21th 1752 by the Rev^d Mr. David Stearns minister of Lunenburg.

Zechariah Tarboll & Mary Gould both of Lunenburg, were married March 27th 1753, by the Rev^d Mr. David Stearns minister of Lunenburg.

W.

B. B. W. B. B. P. B. P. W. M. P. W. H. B. G.

Mr. Ephraim Wetherbe & Mrs. Johannah Bellows both of Lunenburg were married by ye Revnd Andrew Gardner, minister of Lunenburg (as he saith) Septr ye 18th 1732.

Zachariah Whitney and Sarah Boynton both of Lunenburg ware married by the Rev^d Mr. David Stearns minister of Lunenburg the 11th of April 1739.

Joseph Wood and Ruth Wetherbe both of Lunenburg were married July 30th 1741 by Mr. David Stearns minister of Lunenburg.

Jonathan Willard Junr & Phebe Ballard both of Lunenburg were married October ye 24th 1743 by the Rev^d Mr. David Stearns minister of Lunenburg.

Daniel Willard of Lancaster and Lucy Butler of Lunenburg were married November the 19th 1745 by the Rev. Mr. David Stearns minister of Lunenburg.

Michel Wood and Mary Platts both of Lunenburg were married December ye 2nd 1745 by ye Rev. Mr. David Stearns minister of Lunenburg.

Ephraim Whitney and Jane Bancroft both of Lunenburg were married January ye 16th 1745/6 by ye Rev. Mr. David Stearns minister of Lunenburg.

Paul Wetherbe and Hannah Paree both of Lunenburg were married June ye 11th 1746 by ye Rev. Mr. David Stearns minister of Lunenburg.

John White and Mary Wallis both of Lunenburg were married December ye 9th 1747 by Thomas Prentice, Justice of the peace.

Archibald White of Townshend & Margarett McClary of Lunenburg were married December ye 12th 1750 by ye Rev. Mr. David Stearns minister of Lunenburg.

Joseph Wheelock Jun of Lancaster and Alice Page of Lunenburg were married November ye 14th 1751 by ye Rev. Mr. David Stearns minister of Lunenburg.

John White and Mary Whitney both of Lunenburg were married Febry 22^d 1753 by the Rev^d Mr. David Stearns minister of Lunenburg.

Abner Whitney of District Shirley & Sarah Hilton of Lunenburg were married June 21st 1753 by the Rev^d Mr. David Stearns minister of Lunenburg.

Benoni Wallis of Lunenburg and Rebecca Brown of Lynn were married July the 2nd 1755 by the Rev. Mr. David Stearns minister of Lunenburg.

Jonathan Wood and Sarahrah Gary both of Lunenburg, were married April ye 19th 1757 by the Rev. Mr. David Stearns minister of Lunenburg.

W. (cont.)

R. F. B. M. P. B. F. W.

Barzillai Willard & Hepsabath Reddington both of Lunenburg were married Nov^m ye 18th A. D. 1757 by William Downe Justice pea.

Wineal Wright of Dunstable and Sibil Farewell of Lunenburg were married April ye 7th 1758 by the Rev. Mr. David Stearns minister of Lunenburg.

Abner Wheelock of Leominster and Mary Brown of Lunenburg were married April ye 12th 1758 by Edward Hartwell Justice of the peace.

Jesher Wyman of Lancaster and Dorrothy Moffat of Stow were married November ye 28th 1758 by Edward Hartwell Justice of the peace.

Joseph Wyman of Lunenburg and Keziah Parker of Lexington were married June 21th 1759 by Nathaniel Russel Justice of the peace for the County of Middlesex.

Reuben Wyman & Elizabeth Bancroft both of Lunenburg were married February ye 5th 1761 by the Rev^d Mr. David Stearns minister of Lunenburg.

Jacob Wilson & Margaret Freeman both of Leominster were married by Edwd Hartwell Justice of the peace Decr 6th 1762.

Michal Wood of Lunenburg & Lois Wilson of Leominster were married by Benjn Goodridge Esqr August 21st 1764.

LUNENBURG, 1857.

The following is a Copy of Certificates of Marriages Received and Recorded in compliance with the provisions of Chapter 84, Section 4, of the Acts of 1857.

CITY CLERK'S OFFICE WORCESTER Sept 14, 1857

To the Clerk of the Town of Lunenburg,

In compliance with the provisions of Chapter 84 Section 4 of the Acts of 1857, I herewith transmit to you a certified copy of the record of all Marriages recorded in the books of this City, where either or both of the parties married were resident of your Town at the time of said Marriages, to wit:

Date of Marriage. Names and Residence of Parties Married. By whom Married

"Decr 1st 1748. William Little of Lunenburg and } Elizabeth Wallis of Worcester by } Thad Maccarty,,

A copy of the Record,

Attest. SAMUEL SMITH, *City Clerk.*

A true copy, Attest. JAMES PUTNAM *Town Clerk.*

The Early Records of the Town of Lunenburg.

Samuel Johnson of Lunenburg & Mary Cooledge of Weston ware Married in Weston April the 12th 1732 per William Williams, Ministr of sd Town.
                    A true copy from the Records of Weston.
See Acts of 1857 Chap 84, Sec 4. Attest, NATHAN HAGAR *Town Clerk*
                    Oct. 6 1857.
    A true copy attest.   JAMES PUTNAM *Town Clerk*

                TOWN CLERK'S OFFICE BOLTON Oct 15, 1857
To the Clerk of the Town of Lunenburg —
    In compliance with the provisions of Chapter 84 Section 4 of the Acts of 1857, I herewith transmit to you a certified copy of the record of all Marriages recorded in the books of this town where either or both of the parties married were resident of your town at the time of said Marriage, to wit,
John Fosket of Bolton, Abigail Jones of Lunenburg, by whom Married Rev. Thomas Goss. Date May 28, 1761.
    A true copy of record.
                  Attest RICHARD S. EDES, *Town Clerk*
    A true copy.
                  Attest. JAMES PUTNAM *Town Clerk*.

                TOWN CLERK'S OFFICE LANCASTER Oct 2, 1857.
To the Clerk of the Town of Lunenburg.
    In compliance with the provisions of Chapter 84 Section 4 of the Acts of 1857, I herewith transmit to you a certified copy of the record of all Marriages recorded in the books of this Town, where either or both of the parties Married were resident of your Town at the time of said Marriage, to wit:

Date of Marriage.   Names & Residence of Parties Married.   By whom Married
May 23. 1733.   Benjamin Corey. Lunenburg.
                Judith Beaman Lancaster   Rev. John Prentice
Apr. 7 1736.
                Rev. David Stearns
                Ruth Hubbart Lunenburg   Rev. John Prentice
Nov. 29. 1750.
                David Taylor Lunenburg
                Betty Houghton Lancaster. Rev. Timo Harrington.
Apr. 16, 1752.
                George McFarling. Lunenburg
                Margaret Torrence Lancaster Joseph Wilder Jr. J. P.
July 19. 1756
                Benjamin Shed Lunenburg
                Elizabeth Bowers Lancaster Rev. Tim. Harrington.

Marriages.

Date of Marriage.	Names and Residence of Parties Married.	By whom Married.
July 2. 1761.	Mitchel Richards. Shirley. Ester Mitchel Lunenburg	Joseph Wilder J. P.
Apr. 1. 1762.	Kendall Boutel Lunenburg. Mary Wilder. Leominster.	Joseph Wilder J. P.
Jan 13. 1763.	Robert Crawford Worcester Elisebeth Leitch Lunenburg	Abijah Willard J. P.
May 24. 1763.	Solomon Shead Lunenburg Elisa Bornton Lunenburg.	Joseph Wilder J. P.

A true copy of Record.
    Attest, J. L. S. THOMPSON *Town Clerk.*
A true copy.
    Attest JAMES PUTNAM *Town Clerk.*

To the Clerk of the Town of Luningburg.

Pursuant to a law of the Commonwealth of Massachusetts passed by the Legislature of 1857, (see Chapter 84, Section 4 of the General Laws.)

I herewith transmit to you a certified list of all Marriages recorded in the Records of the Town of Woburn where one or both of the parties were at the time of said Marriage resident in the town of Luningburg.

William Jones of Luningburg and Sarah Locke of Woburn were Married December 25 1733.
(From the present ch. Recd)
William Henderson of Luningburg and Sarah Smith were married Mar. 13 1740.
Woburn Oct. 13. 1857.
  Attest   N. WYMAN *Town Clerk.*
A true copy. Attest.
           JAMES PUTNAM. *Town Clerk.*

Stephen Holden of Groton and Sarah Wheeler of Lunenburg were joined in Marriage in Boxford Before David Wood Esq. March 21. 1739.
A true copy of Record.
    Attest, WM H. WOOD, *Town Clerk of Boxford.*
BOXFORD October 28. 1857. See Act of /57 Chap. 84. Sec. 4.
Married February ye 19th 1745.
David Wood of Lunenburg and Mary Hovey of Boxford before Mr. John Cushing as recorded in Boxford WM H. WOOD. *Town Clerk*
 A true copy, Attest,
         JAMES PUTNAM *Town Clerk.*

Married by Rev. Caleb Trowbridge Nov. 2d 1732
Daniel Farmer of Luningburg to Elizebeth Woods of Groton.
Nov. 23d 1732.   Josiah Willard of Luningburg to
                 Hannah Hubburd of Groton.
June 21st 1733. John Gridridge of Lunenburg to
                 Eunice Scripture of Groton.
May 1st 1759.   Jonas Fletcher of Groton &
                 Wid. Johanna Crocker of Lunenburg.
Feb. 15, 1763.   By Rev. Samuel Dana,
                 William Jones of Lunenburg to
                 Sarah Stone of Groton.
    A true copy from the Records of Groton.
                    Attest.   GEO. D. BRIGHAM, *Town Clerk*.
Chap. 84. Sec. 4 of the Acts of 1857
To the Town Clerk of Lunenburg.
          A true copy. Attest. JAMES PUTNAM *Town Clerk*

Oliver Gould of Lunenburg and Mary Stockwell of Petersham were Married May ye 3rd 1759. By Aaron Whitney a Minister of the Gospel.
    A copy of the Record.
             Attest, LEWIS WHITNEY, *Town Clerk of Petersham*
    A true copy.
                    Attest JAMES PUTNAM *Town Clerk—*

1755. Dec 25.   Thomas Page of Lunenburg and
                  Dorothy Houghton of Leominster.
1758. Feb. 2d   Benoni Boynton of Lunenburg &
                  Mary Butrick of Leominster.
                            LEOMINSTER, Nov. 2, 1857.
    I certify the foregoing to be true copies from the Church Record of Marriages by Rev. John Rogers first pastor of the Church in Leominster.
                              J. C. ALLEN. *Town Clerk*
         A true copy. Attest.
                    JAMES PUTNAM *Town Clerk*

            TOWN CLERK'S OFFICE, IPSWICH, November 16, 1857.
To the Clerk of the town of Lunenburg,
    In compliance with the provisions of Chapter 84 Section 4 of the Acts of 1857, I herewith transmit to you a certified copy of the record of all Marriages which I find recorded in the books of this town prior to the year 1800, where either or both of the parties married were resident in Lunenburg at the time of the marriage. viz,—
1740. March 19th David Goodridge of Lunenburg & Eliza Martin of
      Ipswich, were joined in Marriage, By Theophilus Pickering. V. D. M.

Marriages.

The foregoing are true copies from the records of the town of Ipswich.
        Attest. ALFRED KIMBALL, *Town Clerk.*
 A true copy. Attest.   JAMES PUTNAM, *Town Clerk.*

"Reuben Gibson of Lunenburg, and Lois Smith of Sudbury were Married at Sudbury by Israel Loring Nov. 13, 1746."
A true copy from Records of Sudbury.
Sudbury Nov. 1857.   Attest I. S. HUNT, *Town Clerk* –
    A true copy. Attest JAMES PUTNAM *Town Clerk.*

To the Town Clerk of Lunenburg.
I herewith transmit to you the following Marriages in Conformity with Chapt. 84, Sec. 4 of Laws of 1857. The orthography is given as it appears on the Records.
October ye 10. 1754. Then were Married Jonathan Wood of Luninbourg & Rachel Wood of Uxbridge by Yr Mr N. Webb
 A copy of record. Attest.   H. CAPRON *Town Clerk.*
 A true copy.   Attest.   JAMES PUTNAM *Town Clerk.*

"Mr Bartholemew Pearson of Ipswich Cannada and Mrs. Lydia Randal of Lunenburg *houth* in the County of Worcester were Married November ye 3d 1763 by the Revd Mr. Daniel Stimson."
A Copy from the Town Records of Winchendon.
    Attest
        WEBSTER WHITNEY *Town Clerk.*
In compliance with Chap. 84 Sec. 4 of the Acts of 1857.
To the Town Clerk of Lunenburg.
  A true copy. Attest JAMES PUTNAM *Town Clerk.*

MARRIAGES.

1759 Mar 26. Nehemiah Lane of Lunenburg &
     Sarah Shattuck of Pepperell by Rev.
     Joseph Emerson.
1761. June 25. Jonathan Stevens of Lunenburg &
     Elizabeth Parker of Pepperell by Rev.
     Joseph Emerson.
A true copy from the Record of Marriages.
        Attest, CHAS. CROSBY. *T. Clerk*
 See Acts 1857. Ch. 84.
 Pepperell Jan 12, 1858.
   A true copy. Attest. JAMES PUTNAM *Town Clerk*

1733. July 11. William Page of Lunenburg &
Sarah Stevens of Andover were married
by Rev. John Barnard.

1739. Oct 8. Jonathan Abbott Junr of Lunenburg &
Martha Lovejoy of Andover ware Married
by Rev. Samuel Phillips.

1742. Oct. 14. Joseph Holt of Lunenburg and
Mary Abbott of Andover ware Married
by Rev. Samuel Phillips—

1748. Oct 13. Daniel Holt of Lunenburg &
Mehetibel Holt of Andover married
by Rev. Samuel Phillips.

1758 Nov. 23. James Descomb of Lunenburg &
Eliz'th Farrington of Andover Married
by Rev. William Symmes.

1759. Nov. 29. Jesse Carlton of Lunenburg and
Sarah Foster of Andover married
by Rev. Samuel Phillips.

1761 Dec. 3. Abijah Hovey of Lunenburg &
Lydia Ingalls of Andover Married
by Rev. William Symmes.

From the Marriage Records of the Town of Andover.
Andover Dec. 17, 1857. See General Laws 1857 Chap 84.

A true copy.   Attest   JAMES PUTNAM *Town Clerk*.

Isaac Redington of Lunenburg and Ruth Bodwell of Methuen Married Dec. 27, 1759, By Rev. Christopher Sargent.

Copy from the Marriage Records of the Town of Methuen Methuen, Jany 4. 1857.

Attest, CHAS. SHED *Town Clerk of Methuen*

A true copy.   Attest,   JAMES PUTNAM, *Town Clerk*.

HARVARD Jany 4. 1858.

Dear Sir:

Below please find a copy of record which I transmit to you in compliance with the requirements of Chap. 84 Sec. 4 of the Acts of 1857.

Names & Residence.	By Whom.	Date of.
Daniel Page of Lunenburg	Rev Mr	Nov. 22nd
Ruth Haskell	John Seccomb	1744

A true Copy   TRUMBULL BULL *Town Clerk*.

A true Copy. Attest, JAMES PUTNAM *Town Clerk*.

Marriages. 267

Joseph Wood of Lunenburg and Ruth Symonds of Littleton were married Oct 5th 1752.

Benjn Foster of Lunenburg & Sarah Witney of Littleton were Married Dec. 31. 1761.

Dea Benjn Foster of Lunenburg and Mrs. Sarah Whitney of Littleton were joined in Marriage by Rev. Daniel Rogers of Littleton Dec 3^d 1761.

From the Records of Littleton
Littleton Jan. 27/58   B. EDWARDS *Town Clerk.*

A true copy.   Attest   JAMES PUTNAM, *Town Clerk.*

            TOWN CLERK'S OFFICE, NEWTON, Jan 22^d 1858.
To the Clerk of the Town of Lunenburgh.

In compliance with the provisions of Chapter 84 Section 4 of the Acts of 1857, I herewith transmit to you a certified copy of the record of all Marriages recorded in the books of this town, where either or both of the parties married were residents of your Town at the time of said Marriage, to wit:

"Thomas Prentice Esqr of Lunenburgh & Mrs Borridel Jackson of Newton were Marryed June 27—1751 by the Rev. Mr. John Cotton."

" Middlesex S. S. Newtown July 26th A. D. 1763

Abraham Smith of Luningburg & Lucie Allen of Weston were Joyned in Marriage by Thos. Greenwood Justice of Peace."

    Attest.   MARSHALL S. RICE — *Town Clerk of Newton*

A true copy.   Attest.   JAMES PUTNAM *Town Clerk.*

Extracts from Marriage records of the town of Topsfield Massachusetts.

"December 3rd 1730 Joseph Page of Lunenburg & Deborah Gould of Topsfield were married."

"Amos Robinson of Lunenburgh & Priscilla Lake of Topsfield were married on ye 3rd day of Sept. 1733."

"Amos Robinson of Lunenburgh and Lydia Wentworth of Topsfield were married on y^e 24th of November 1743—"

From Marriage records of the town of Topsfield
Topsfield, Feb. 1858.   Attest   I. P. TOWNE *Town Clerk*

A true copy   Attest.   JAMES PUTNAM *Town Clerk*

BIRTHS

BIRTHS

COPIED FROM THE

RECORDS OF THE TOWN OF LUNENBURG,

FROM 1707 TO 1764.

A.

AUSTEN. AUSTIN.

Priscilla y^e daughter of Daniel Austen and Priscilla his wife born at Andover February ye 11 1725/6

Daniel ye son of Daniel Austen and Priscilla his wife born at Lunenburg Apriel ye 13 1727

Lydia ye daughter of Daniel Austen and Priscilla his wife, born at Lunenburg June ye 3, 1729.

Timothy ye son of Daniel Austen and Priscilla his wife, born at Lunenburg March ye 2, 1731

Ruth ye daughter of Daniel Austen, and of Priscilla his wife, born at Lunenburg April ye 1th 1733.

Hannah Austen ye daughter of Daniel Austen and of Priscilla his wife, born at Lunenburg February ye 1th 1734/5.

Phebe Austen ye daughter of Daniel Austen, and of Priscilla his wife, born at Lunenburg October ye 24th 1736.

Phebe Austin the daughter of Daniel Austin and of Phebe his wife, was born at Lunenburg April ye 15th 1758.

Timothy Austin the son of Daniel Austin and of Phebe his wife, was born at Lunenburg June ye 2nd 1759.

Daniel Austin son of Daniel Austin Jr. & Phebe, his wife was born January 6th 1761.

Samuel Austin son of Daniel Austin Jr. & Phebe, his wife was born February 12th 1762

Hannah Austin daughter of Daniel Austin Jr. & Phebe his wife was born January 2^d 1765

AUSTIN. ABBOTT. ALEXANDER.

John Austin son of Daniel Austin Jr. & Phebe his wife was born November 7th 1766.

Ruth Austin daughter of Daniel Austin Jr. & Phebe his (wife) was born October 2d 1768.

Jonathan Abbott the son of Jonathan Abbott and of Matha his wife was born at Lunenburg, August the twenty-ninth 1740.

Nathan Abbott the son of Jonathan Abbott, and of Mattha his wife, was born at Lunenburg, Janvary ye 22nd 1743/.4.

William Abbott the son of Jonathan Abbott, and of Mattha his wife, was born at Lunenburg, November the 24th 1745.

John Alexander, the son of William Alexander, and of Elizabeth his wife born at Lunenburg August ye 14th 1744.

Franice Alexander, the son of William Alexander and of Elizabeth his wife, born at Lunenburg March ye 18th 1745/6.

William Allexander, the son of William Allexander and of Elizabeth his wife, was born at Lunenburg November ye first A. D. 1749.

B.

BOYNTON.

Sarah Boynton ye davghter of Benoni Boynton and of Anne his wife born at Rowley March ye 9th 1707.

Sarah Boynton (a surviving) daughter of Benoni Boynton and of Anne his wife born at Rowley Jnne ye 17th 1708

Stephen Boynton ye son of Benoni Boynton and of Anne his wife, born at Rowley April 9th 1710.

Anne Boynton ye davghter of Benoni Boynton and of Anne his wife, born at Rowley November ye 21th 1713.

Dorcas Boynton ye davghter of Benoni Boynton and of Anne his wife, born at Groton December ye 21th 1715.

Jane Boynton ye davghter of Benoni Boynton & of Anne his wife born at Groton Angust ye 3th 1717.

Mary Boynton ye davghter of Benoni Boynton & of Anne his wife born at Groton November 27th 1718.

Elezebeth Boynton ye davghter of Benoni Boynton & of Anne his wife born at Groton July ye 10th 1720.

Mehittibel Boynton ye davghter of Benoni Boynton & of Anne his wife born at Groton November ye 1th 1721.

Mary Boynton ye davghter of Benoni Boynton & of Anne his wife born at Groton February ye 20th 1722/3.

BOYNTON.

Benoni Boynton ye son of Benoni Boynton & of Anne his wife born at Lunenburg June ye 1th 1726.

Joseph Boynton ye son of Benoni Boynton & of Anne his wife born at Lunenburg May ye 28th 1727.

The birth of ye Children of Hilkiah Boynton and of Priscilla his wife
(1.) Sarah born January ye 1th 1718/19
(2.) Jane born March ye 4th 1722/3
(3.) Ruth born March ye 31th 1727.
(4.) Jewet Boynton ye son of Hilkiah Boynton and of Priscilla his wife, born Feb^r ye 14th 1735/6

Sarah Boynton the daughter of Stephen Boynton and of Sarah his wife born at Lunenburg October ye 13th 1738

Joseph Boynton ye son of Stephen Boynton and of Sarah his wife born at Lunenburg January ye 30th 1740/1.

Stephen Boynton the son of Stephen Boynton, and of Sarah his wife, born at Lunenburg February the fifth 1743/4.

Susanna Boynton the daughter of Stephen Boynton and of Sarah his wife born at Lunenburg, September ye 1th 1746.

Elizabeth Boynton the daughter of Stephen Boynton (&) Sarah his wife was born at Lunenburg March the 26th 1749.

Sarah Boynton ye daughter of Stephen Boynton & Sarah his wife was born at Lunenburg February ye 19th 1751/2.

Joseph Boynton the son of Stephen and of Elizabeth his wife was born at Lunenburg April ye 30th 1755.

Samuel Boynton the son of Stephen Boynton and of Elizabeth his wife was born at Lunenburg August ye 28th A. D. 1757.

William Boynton ye son of Stephen Boynton & of Elizabeth his wife was born at Lunenburg March the 29th 1761.

Susannah Boynton daughter of Stephen Boynton & Elizabeth his wife was born at Lunenburg July 13th 1765.

Elizabeth Boynton, the daughter of Benoni Boynton Junr and Elizabeth his wife was born at Lunenburg the 21st day of Novr A: D: 1752.

Mary Boynton the daughter of Benoni Boynton Jn^a and Elizabeth his wife was born at Lunenburg December ye 20th A. D. 1754.

David Boynton the son of Jonathan Boynton and of Elizabeth his wife was born at Lunenburg February ye 25th 1759.

Mary Boynton the daughter of Jonathan Boynton and of Elizabeth his wife was born at Lunenburg October the 19th 1761.

BOYNTON. BIGELOW. BOWERS. BUTTRICK. BANCROFT.

Jonathan Boynton son of Jonathan Boynton Jur and of Elizabeth his wife was born at Lunenburg, October ye 12th 1771.

Solomon Learnard Boynton son of Solomon Boynton & Abigail his wife was born at Lunenburg October 18th 1778 with an uncommon mark on one of his ears.

Hannah Bigelow, daughter of Benjamin Bigelow and Love his wife was born at Lunenburg March the 5th A. D. 1754.

Benjamin Bigelow ye son of Benjamin Bigelow, and of Elisebeth his wife was born at Lunenburg, October ye 4, 1755.

Nehemiah Bowers the son of Nehemiah Bowers, and of Sarah his wife was born at Lunenburg, February the 26th 1752.

Esther Bowers the daughter of Nehemiah Bowers, and of Sarah his wife was born at Lunenburg 28th of May 1754.

Elizabeth Bowers the daughter of Nehemiah Bowers & of Sarah his wife, was born at Lunenburg August ye 29th 1756.

Susannah Bowers the daughter of Jerahmeel Bowers and of Meriam his wife, born at Lunenburg, February ye 4th 1746/7.

Francis Buttrick the son of Francis Buttrick, and of Hannah his wife, was born at Lunenburg April the 7th 1748.

Jonathan Buttrick the son of Francis Buttrick and of Hannah his wife was born at Lunenburg May ye 6th 1750.

Hannah Buttrick the daughter of Francis Buttrick and of Hannah his wife was born Lancaster Janvary 14th 1746.

Lucy Buttrick the daughter of John Buttrick & Mary his wife, was born at Lunenburg, Decr 18th 1752.

Timothy Bancroft ye son of Timothy Bancroft and of Elizabeth his wife, was born at Lunenburg, November ye 18th 1746.

John Bancroft ye son of Timothy Bancroft and of Elizabeth his wife, was born at Lunenburg November ye 14th 1753.

Timothy Bancrofft ye son of Timothy Bancrofft and of Elizabeth his wife was born at Lunenburg, August the 14th 1755.

Molley Bancroft the daughter of Timothy Bancroft & of Mary his wife was born at Lunenburg June ye 5th 1761.

BAYLEY. BAILEY.

Isaac Bayle ye son of Josiah Bayle and of Elezabath Bayle his wife born August 8th 1729

Elezabath Bayle ye davghter of Josiah Bayle, and of Elezabath his wife, born March ye 4th 1730/31

Josiah Bayle ye son of Josiah Bayle and of Elezabath Bayle his wife born July ye 14 1734

Ruth Bayley ye daughter of Josiah Bayley and of Elizabeth his wife, was born at Lunenburg Janvary the seventh 1740/1.

Molly Bayley ye daughter of Isaac Bayley & of Mary his wife was born at Lunenburg February ye 14th 1753 new style.

Isaac Bayley the son of Isaac Bayley and of Mary his wife was born at Lunenburg February ye 27 A. D. 1757.

John Bayley the son of Isaac Bayley & of Mary his wife was born at Lunenburg March ye 7th 1760.

Betty Bailey ye daughter of Isaac & Mary Bailey was born at Lunenburg June 2^d 1762.

Hannah Bailey daughter of Isaac Bailey and Mary his wife was born at Lunenburg June ye 30th 1764.

Samuel Bailey son of Isaac Bailey and Mary his wife was born at Lunenburg October ye 12th 1771.

Ruth Bailey daughter of Isaac Bailey & Mary his wife was born at Lunenburg August 23, 1775.

Molley Bailey daughter of John Bailey Junr and of Mary his wife was born at Lunenburg August 25th 1762.

John Bailey son of John Bailey Junr and of Mary his wife, was born at Lunenburg Octo^{r} 9th 1763.

Joseph Bailey son of Josiah Bailey Junr and of Sarah his wife was born at Lunenburgh June 20th 1763.

Benjn Bailey son of Josiah Bailey Junr and of Sarah his wife was born at Lunenburgh March 6th 1765.

Sarah Bailey daughter of Josiah Bailey Junr and of Sarah his wife was born at Lunenburg Decr 6th 1766

Josiah Bailey Tertius son of Josiah Bailey Junr and of Sarah his wife was born at Lunenburgh Jany 27th 1768.

Sarah Bailey daughter of Josiah Bailey Junr and Sarah his wife, was born at Lunenburg March ye 31st 1770.

Molly Bailey daughter of Josiah Bailey Junr & Sarah his wife, was born at Lunenburg April 1st 1772.

BAILEY. BURNAM. BELLOWS. BUTLER. BRADSTREET.

Joseph Bailey son of Josiah Bailey Junr & Sarah his wife was born at Lunenburg Septr ye 12th 1774.
Ruth Bailey daughter of Josiah Bailey Junr & Sarah his wife was born at Lunenburg May 15th 1777.
Thaddeus Bailey son of Josiah Bailey juner & Sarah his wife born at Lunenburg April 30th 1779.

Ruth Burnam daughter of Nathanael Burnam Jun and of Elizabeth his wife, was born at Lunenburg, December the 17th 1754.
Thomas Burnam the son of Nathanael Burnam Jun and of Elizabeth his wife was born at Littleton September the 9th 1756.

John Burnam the son of Nehemiah Burnam & of Elisabeth born at Lunenburg June the 25th 1745.

Abegail Bellows daughter of Benj^a Bellows Junr and of Abigail his wife born December ye 10th 1736.
Peter Bellows son of Benj^a Bellows Junr and of Abigail his wife born December ye 26th 1738.
Benjamin Bellows the son of Benjamin Bellows Jr and of Abigail was born September ye 25th 1740.
John Bellows the son of Benjamin Bellows and of Abigail his wife born October 22^d 1742.
Joseph Bellows the son of Benjamin Bellows and of Abigail his wife born May ye 26th 1744
Jonathan Bellows ye son of Benjamin Bellows and of Abigail his wife was born at Lunenburg March ye 29th 1746.
Abijah Bellows ye son of Benjamin Bellows & of Abigail his wife was born at Lunenburg March ye 20th 1748/9.

Lucy Butler the daughter of William Butler and of Lucy his wife, born at Lunenburg June the 25th 1738.
Rachel Butler the daughter of William Butler and of Lucy his wife, born at Lunenburg October ye 23th 1739.
Abigail Butler the daughter of the widow Lucy Butler born at Lunenburg November the 25th 1741; one and twenty day after her Father's decease.

John Bradstreet ye son of Samvel Bradstreet and Dorcas his wife was born at Rowley September ye 12th 1737.
Sarah Bradstreet the daughter of Samvel Bradstreet and Dorcas his wife, was born at Lunenburg July ye 24th 1740.

Births.

BRADSTREET. BUSS. BROWN.

Dorcas Bradstreet the daughter of Samvel Bradstreet and of Dorcas his wife, born at Lunenburg April ye 7th A. D. 1743.

Abigail Bradstreet ye daughter of Samvel Bradstreet and Dorcas his wife was born at Lunenburg May ye 19th 1745.

Olive Bradstreet ye daughter of Samvel Bradstreet and Dorcas his wife was born at Lunenburg May ye 19th 1748.

Phebe Bradstreet ye daughter of Samvel Bradstreet and of Dorcas his wife, was born at Lunenburg September ye 10th 1750.

Mary Bradstreet ye daughter of Samuel Bradstreet and Dorcas his wife, was born at Lunenburg Augst ye 1st 1752.

Releif Bradstreet the daughter of Samuel Bradstreet and of Dorcas his wife, was born at Lunenburg, June ye 2nd 1754.

Samuel Bradstreet the son of Samuel Bradstreet and of Dorcas his wife was born at Lunenburg June ye 17th 1757.

Abigail Bradstreet ye daughter of Samuel Bradstreet and of Dorcas his wife, was born at Lunenburg January ye 2nd 1759.

Vashtai Bradstreet the daughter of Samuel Bradstreet & of Dorcas his wife, was born at Lunenburg July ye 2nd 1761 after her Father's death.

Stephen Buss the son of John Buss and of Eunice his wife born at Lunenburg March ye 8th 1743/4.

Silas Buss the son of John Buss and of Eunice his wife was born at Lunenburg May ye 27th 1746.

Eunice Buss ye daughter of John Buss and of Eunice his wife was born at Lunenburg, September ye 7th 1748.

Aaron Buss the son of John Buss and of Eunice his wife was born at Lunenburg March ye 27th 1751.

Mellicent Buss the daughter of John Buss and Eunice his wife, was born at Lunenburg August 22^d 1753.

Jonathan Buss, the son of John Buss, and of Eunice his wife, was born at Lunenburg December ye 30th A. D. 1756.

Aaron Brown the son of Aaron Brown and of Abigail his wife, born at Lunenburg, Janvray the 31st 1744/5.

David Brown the son of Aaron Brown and of Abigail his wife, was born at Lunenburg, February ye 17th 1746/7.

Jonathan Brown ye son of Aaron Brown and of Abigail his wife, was born at Lunenburg, December the 13th 1754.

Hepsibeth Brown, the daughter of Aaron Brown and of Abigail his wife, was born at Lunenburg February ye 2nd 1757.

Jonathan Brown the son of Aaron Brown and of Abigail his wife, was born at Lunenburg October ye 1st 1759.

C.

CHADWICK. CARLTON. CORCKER. CARLILE. CARLTON.

Bette Chadwick the daughter of William Chadwick and of Eunice his wife, was born at Lunenburg, January ye 30th 1758.

Unice Chadwick the daughter of William Chadwick and of Unice his wife, was born at Lunenburg August ye 19th 1759.

The births of ye children of Asa Carlton and of Ruth his wife.
Asa Carlton born at Lunenburg Feby 14th 1764
Betty Carlton born at Lunenburg June 14th 1766.
Ruth Carlton daughter of Asa Carlton and Ruth his wife, was born at Lunenburg July ye 24th 1768.
Calven Carlton son of Asa Carlton and Ruth his wife, was born at Lunenburg June ye 26th 1770.
Luther Carlton son of Asa Carlton and Ruth his wife, was born at Lunenburg August ye 26th 1772.

Timothy Carlton the son of Abraham Calton and Mary his wife was born at Lunenburg May the 1st 1753.

Abigail Carlton daughter of Abraham Carlton and of Mary, his wife, was born at Lunenburg August ye 23d 1756.

Mary Carlton ye daughter of Abraham Carlton, and of Mary his wife, was born at Lunenburg January ye 7th Annoque Domini 1759.

Nathaniel Carlton son of Abraham and Mary Carlton was born at Lunenburg March 27th 1763.

Abigail Carlton daughter of Abraham & Mary Carton was born at Lunenburg June 5th 1765.

Mary Corcker the daughter of Paul Corcker and of Lydia his wife was born at Lunenburg March ye 19th 1750/1.

Daniel Carlile ye son of David Carlile and of Leatis his wife, was born at Harvard October ye 30th 1738.

David Carlile ye son of David Carlile and of Leatis his wife was born at Lunenburg Feburary ye 20th 1740/1.

Leatis Carlile ye daughter of David Carlile and of Leatis his wife was born at Lunenburg September ye 6th 1742.

John Carlile ye son of David Carlile and of Leatis his wife, was born at Lunenburg January ye 24th 1745/6.

Bette Chaplin the daughter of David Chaplin and of Mary his wife, born at Lunenburg June ye 9th 1740.

Joseph Chaplin, the son of David Chaplin and Mary his wife, born at Lunenburg January ye 23rd A. D. 1741/2.

CHAPLIN. CORY. COREY. CUMMINGS.

Mary Chaplin ye daughter of David Chaplin, and of Mary his wife born April ye 8th 1744.
Sarah Chaplin the daughter of David Chaplin and of Mary his wife, born at Lunenburg Janvary ye 9th 1746/7.
David Chaplin ye son of David Chaplin and of Mary his wife, was born at Lunenburg March ye 5th 1748/9.

Merey Chaplin the daughter of Joseph Chaplin and of Sarah his wife, was born at Lunenburg August the 27th 1748.
Anna Chaplin the daughter of Joseph Chaplin and of Sarah his wife, was born at Lunenburg May 14th 1753.
Sarah Chaplin daughter of Joseph Chaplin & Sarah his wife, was born at Lunenburg September ye 10th 1758.
Joseph Chaplin, son of Joseph Chaplin & Sarah his wife was born at Lunenburg October ye 17th 1760.

Rebekah Cory ye davghter of Benja Cory and of Rebekah his wife, born Janewary 17th 1718/19
Mary Cory ye daughter of Benja Cory and of Rebekah his wife, born February 10th 1725/6.
Sarah Cory ye daughter of Benja Cory and of Rebekah his wife, born April 1, 1728.
Benja Cory ye son of Benja Cory and of Rebekah his wife, born June 15th 1731.

Eunice Corey the daughter of Benjamin Corey junr and Beulah his wife was born at Lunenburg April 26th A. D. 1754.

Children of Samll Commings and of Sarah his wife.
Miriam born at Lunenburg October 1, 1728.
Thomas born in Lunenburg Septr 23. 1731.
Thaddeus Cummings ye son of Samll Commings and of Sarah his wife born December 30th 1734.
Samvel Cummings ye son of Samvel Cummings, and of Sarah his wife born at Lunenburg, febbr 13th 1736/7.
Sarah Comings ye daufter of Samvel Comings & Sarah his wife, was born June ye 30, 1740.
Thomas Commings the son of Samvel Commings and of Sarah his wife, born at Lunenburg February ye 23th 1742/3.
Thaddeus Cmmmings ye son of Samvel and of Sarah his wife, was born at Lunenburg June ye 16th 1746.
Jonathan Commings born November ye 20th 1748.

COFFEN. COLBURN. CLARK. CARTER.

Eliezer Coffeen ye son of Michael Coffen and Lydia his wife, born at Lunenburg September ye 14 1731.

Lydia Coffen ye davghter of Michael Coffen and of Lydia his wife, born in Lunenburg September 8th 1733.

Amme Coffen ye davghter of Michael Coffen, and of his wife, born December ye 1th 1735.

Henery Coffen the son of Michael Coffen and of Lydia his wife, was born at Lunenburg April ye 6th 1738.

Daniel Coffen the son of Mical Coffen and Lydia his wife was born April ye 26th 1740.

Abigail Coffen ye daughter of Michael Coffen and Lydia his wife, born April the 7th 1741.

Priscilla Coffen ye daughter of Michael Coffen, and of Lydai his wife born at Lunenburg, September ye 2nd 1742.

Thomas ye son of James Colburn and of Ruth his wife born in Lunenburg December 1th 1729.

Ruth ye davghter of James Colburn and of Ruth his wife, born in Lunenburg July 16th 1732.

Sarah Colburn ye daughter of James Colburn and of Ruth his wife, was born April ye 24th 1737.

Sarah Colburn the daughter of James Colburn, and of Sarah his wife, born August ye 24th 1743.

James Colburn, the son of James Colburn and of Sarah his wife, born at Lunenburg July the 27th 1745.

Sarah Clark the daughter of Mr. Robert Clark and of Mary his wife born at Lunenburg August ye 9th 1739.

Mary Clark the daughter of Mr. Robert Clark and of Mary his wife born at Lunenburg February the eleventh A. D. 1741/2.

William Clark the son of Mr. Robert Clark and of Mary Clark born at Lunenburg November the 30th 1743.

Thomas Carter Junr the son of Thomas Carter & of Bette Carter was born at Lunenburg May ye 4th 1741.

Elijah Carter the son of Thomas Carter and of Bette Carter was born at Lunenburg February the 26 1742/3.

David Carter the son of Thomas Carter and of Bette his wife, was born at Lunenburg April the twenty-sixth 1745.

Prudence Carter ye daughter of Thomas Carter and of Bette his wife, was born at Lunenburg June ye 15th 1746.

Births. 281

CARTER.

John Carter ye son of Thomas Carter and of Bette his wife, was born at Lunenburg September ye 13th 1748.

Phinehas Carter son of Thomas Carter and of Betty his wife, was born at Lunenburg April 30th 1751

Beatrix Carter daughter of Thos Carter & of Betty his wife, was born at Lunenburg November ye 18th 1753.

Ruth Carter daughter of Thomas Carter & of Betty his wife, was born at Lunenburg December ye 21st A. D. 1756.

Vashti Carter ye daughter of Thomas Carter and of Betty his wife, was born at Lunenburg May ye 17th 1758.

Jonas Carter son of James and Sarah Carter, was born at Lunenburg August 5th 1762.

Keziah, born Jany 25th 1765 daughter of James & Sarah Carter.

Jerusha born April 2nd 1767 daughter of James & Sarah Carter.

D.

DEMARY. DODGE.

John Demary the son of John Demary and of Rebeckah his wife, was born at Lunenburg, August the 27th 1751.

Rebecah Demerry the daughter of John Demerry and of Rebecah his wife, was born at Lunenburg Febry 24th 1754.

Hannah Demary the daughter of John Demary and of Rebecah his wife, was born at Lunenburg Feburay ye 13th A. D. 1756.

Anne Demary the daughter of John Demary and of Rebeckah his wife, was born at Lunenburg April ye 15th 1758.

Sarah Demary ye daughter of John Demary & of Rebecah his wife, was born at Lunenburg June ye 1th 1760.

Thomas Demary ye son of John Demary & of Rebekah his wife, was born at Lunenburg July 15th 1762.

Margaret Dodge ye daughter of Noah Dodge and of Margaret his wife, born October ye 21th 1729.

Miriam Dodge ye davghter of Noah Dodge and of Margaret his wife, born March ye 23th 1732

Lipha Dodge ye daughter of Noah Dodge and of Margaret his wife, born June ye 2th 1734

Thankfull Dodge ye daughter of Noah Dodge & of Margaret his wife, born July 6th 1736.

Rhoda Dodge the daughter of Josiah Dodge and of Susanah his wife, born at Lunenburg August ye 25 A. D. 1744.

DODGE.

Sarah Dodge ye daughter of Josiah Dodge Jun and of Susanna his wife, was born at Lunenburg May the 24th 1749.

Asahel Dodge the son of Josiah Dodge Jun and of Susanna his wife, was born at Lunenburg August the 26th 1752.

Benjamin Dodge son of Josiah Dodge Junr and of Susanna his wife, was born at Lunenburg May 1st 1754.

Phebe Dodge the daughter of Josiah Dodge Jun and of Susana his wife was born at Lunenburg, September ye 23rd 1759.

Elizabeth Dodge the daughter of Zebulon Dodge and of Martha his wife, was born at Lunenburg Novr 14th 1749.

Jemima Dodge the daughter of Zebulon Dodge and of Martha his wife, was born at Lunenburg March 13th 1750/1.

Sewall Dodge the son of Zebulon Dodge and of Martha his wife, was born at Lunenburg July 21st 1752.

Barzillai Dodge the son of Zebulon Dodge and Martha his wife was born at Lunenburg Febry 8th 1753.

Barzilia Dodge son of Zebulon Dodge and Martha his wife was born February ye 8th 1754. This record was don by order of the Father, as their was a mistake in the above record of one year.

GEORGE KIMBALL, Town Clerk.

Martha Dodge the daughter of Zebulon Dodge and of Martha his wife, was born at Lunenburg November ye 3th 1755.

Keziah Dodge daughter of Zebulon Dodge and of Martha his wife, was born at Lunenburg December ye 8th 1757.

Kerenhappuch Dodge the daughter of Zebulon Dodge and of Martha his wife, was born at Lunenburg August ye 30th 1759.

Hepsibath Dodge the daughter of Zebulon Dodge & of Martha his wife, was born at Lunenburg October ye 30th 1761.

Jesse Dodge the son of Reuben Dodge and of Ruth his wife, was born at Lunenburg August the 28th A. D. 1744.

Mary Dodge the daughter of Reuben Dodge and of Ruth his wife, born at Lunenburg, May ye 6th A. D. 1746.

Tabatha Dodge the daughter of Reuben Dodge and of Ruth his wife, was born at Lunenburg April ye 8th 1748.

Brewer Dodge the son of Reuben Dodge, and of Ruth his wife, was born at Lunenburg, December ye 4th A. D. 1749.

Levi Dodge, the son of Reuben Dodge, and of Ruth his wife, was born at Lunenburg November ye 21th A. D. 1751.

Births.

DODGE. DUTTON.

Tabitha Dodge the daughter of Reuben Dodge and of Ruth his wife, was born at Lunenburg December ye 31 175—*
Zadok Dodge the son of Reuben Dodge and of Ruth his wife was born at Lunenburg April ye 19. A. D. 1756.
Ester Dodge daughter of Reuben and Ruth Dodge was born at Lunenburg April 19th 1758.
John Perkins, son of Reuben and Ruth Dodge, was born at Lunenburg, July 27th 1760.
Ruth Dodge daughter of Reuben & Ruth Dodge was born at Lunenburg June 10th 1762.

Eli Dodge the son of Eli Dodge and of Abigail his wife, was born at Lunenburg, September ye 7th 1743.
Rebakah Dodge the daughter of Eli Dodge, and of Abigail his wife, was born at Lunenburg June ye 2nd 1745.
Isaac Dodge ye son of Eli Dodge & of Abigail his wife, was born at Lunenburg March ye 17th 1747/8.
Abigail Dodge the daughter of Eli Dodge and of Abigail his wife, was born at Lunenburg, December ye 25th 1751.
Prudence Dodge the daughter of Eli Dodge and of Abigail his wife, was born at Lunenburg September ye 25th 1752.

The births of the children of Seth Dodge and of Sarah his wife,
John Smith Dodge born at Lunenburg April 22^d 1761.
Hannah Dodge born at Lunenburg Jany 30th 1763.
Sarah Dodge born at Lunenburg Augt 3^d 1765.
Sarah Dodge, daughter of Seth and Sarah Dodge was born August ye 8th 1765 at Lunenburg.
Eunice Dodge daughter of Seth & Sarah Dodge was born September ye 11th 1767 at Lunenburg.

Hannah Dutton ye daughter of Thomas Dutton and of Mary his wife, born at Lunenburg, January the 28th 1744/5.
Sibel Dutton the daughter of Thomas Dutton and of Mary his wife, was born at Lunenburg December ye 9th 1747.
Thomas Dutton the son of Thomas Dutton and of Mary his wife, was born at Lunenburg, March the 18th 1749/50.
Elizabeth the daughter of Thomas Dutton and of Mary his wife, was born at Lunenburg, on the 24th day of December 1752.
Elizabeth Dutton the daughter of Thomas Dutton and of Mary his wife, was born at Lunenburg December the 18th 1752.

---

*John R. Rollins states that the remainder of the date is nearly obliterated, but he should judge it to be 1753. [W. A. D]

DUTTON. DIVOL. DARLING.

Joseph Fitch Dutton the son of Thomas Dutton and Sarah his wife, was born at Lunenburg June ye 3rd 1757.

Susannah Dutton the daughter of Thomas Dutton and of Sarah his wife, was born at Lunenburg March ye 7th 1759.

John Dutton the son of Thomas Dutton & of Sarah his wife, was born at Lunenburg July ye 9th 1761.

Ephraim Dutton the son of Ephraim Dutton and of Thankfull his wife, was born at Lunenburg Aug^st the 30th A. D. 1753.

Jerusha Dutton ye daughter of Ephraim Dutton and of Thankfull his wife, was born at Lunenburg, February the 4th A. D. 1755.

Susanna Divol daughter of Manassah Divol & Sarah his wife, was born at Lunenburg January 25th 17—— [Lost.]

Josiah Divol ye son of John Divol and Sarah his wife, born at Lunenburg March the 7th 1736/7.

Levi Divol ye son of John Divol and of Sarah his wife born at Lunenburg April ye 19th 1742.

The births of the children of John Divol and of Phebe his wife
Keziah Divol born at Lunenburg Feby 28th 1748.
Elizabeth Divol born at Lunenburg Feby 22d 1750.
Phebe Divol born at Lunenburg Jany 14th 1752.
Manasseh Divol born at Lunenburg Novr 17th 1753
Susannah Divol born at Lunenburg Jany 16th 1758.

John Darling ye son of John Darling Jun and of Ruth his wife was born at Lunenburg December ye 11th 1744.

Ruth Darling ye daughter of John Darling jun and of Ruth his wife was born at Leominster December ye 21th 1746.

Lois Darling ye daughter of John Darlin jun and of Ruth his wife, was born at Lunenburg June ye 26th 1749.

John Darling the son of John Darlin jun and of Ruth his wife, was born at Lunenburg October ye 4th 1751.

Unity Darlin was born at Lunenburg July ye 12th 1755.*

Amity Darling daughter of John & Ruth Darling was born at Lunenburg Octr 28th 1757.

Juet Boynton Darling ye son of John Darling jun. and of Ruth his wife, was born at Lunenburg, February ye 23rd 1760.

*John R. Rollins says no doubt the daughter of John Jr. and Ruth. [W.' A. D.

Births.

DARLING. DAVIS. DESCOMB. DOWNE. DUNSMOOR.

Timothy Darling son of Timothy Darling and of Joanna his wife, was born at Lunenburg April 6th 1754.

James Darlin the son of Timothy Darlin and of Joanna his wife, was born at Lunenburg March ye 7th 1756.

David & Benjamin Darling sons of Timothy Darling and of Joanna his wife, were born at Lunenburg October ye 6th Annoq: Domini 1758.

John Darling son of Timothy Darlin and of Joanna his wife was born at Lunenburg August ye 13th 1759.

Daniel Darling son of Timothy Darling and Joanna his wife, was born at Winchindon July ye 19: 1761.

The birth of ye children of Sam^{ll} Davis and of Sarah his wife
Samuell born at Lunenburg March ye 20: 1730
Sarah ye davghter of Sam^{ll} Davis and of Sarah his wife born in Lunenburg December ye 7th 1732.
Samuell Davis ye son of Sam^{ll} Davis and of Sarah his wife born June ye 7th 1735.
Joseph Davis ye son of Samvel Davis and of Sarah his wife born May ye 20th 1738.

Jacob Descomb the son of James Descomb & of Elizabeth his wife, was born at Lunenburg September ye 15th 1760.

Sarah Dascombe daughter of James and Elizabeth Dascombe was born at Lunenburg July 14th 1762.

Samvel Downe the son of Mr. William Downe and of Margaret his wife, born at Cambridge Janvary ye 17th A. D. 1744/5.

Sarah Downe the daughter of Mr. William Downe and of Margaret his wife, born at Lunenburg December the 20th 1746.

Margaret Downe ye daughter of Mr. William Downe and of Margaret his wife was born at Lunenburg August the 19th 1749.

Elizabeth Downe ye daughter of William Downe and Margaret his wife, was born at Lunenburg December the 18th 1751.

John Dunsmoor the son of Dr. John Dunsmoor and of Ruth his wife, was born at Lunenburg Janvary ye 25th 1747.

Phinehas Dunsmoor ye son of Dr. John Dunsmoor and of Ruth his wife, was born at Lunenburg April ye 4th 1750.

Ruth Dunsmoor the daughter of Dr. John Dunsmoor and of Ruth his wife, was born at Lunenburg May the 25th 1752.

Rebekah Dunsmoor the daughter of Dr. John Dunsmoor and of Ruth his wife, was born at Lunenburg May ye 4th 1754.

DUNSMOOR.

Hannah Dunsmoor daughter of John Dunsmoor, and Ruth his wife was born at Lunenburg May 4th 1756.

Ebenezer Dunsmoor son of John and Ruth Dunsmoor was born at Lunenburg August 29th 1758.

E.

EATON.

Rebekah Eaton daughter of Peirson Eaton and of Anna his wife was born at Lunenburg April 17th 1753.

Peirson Eaton son of Peirson Eaton and of Anna his wife born at Lunenburg June 10th 1754.

Joseph Eaton son of Pearson Eaton and of Anna his wife was born at Lunenburg March ye 29th 1756.

Anne Eaton daughter of Peirson Eaton and of Anna his wife was born at Lunenburg February ye 24th Anno Domini 1758.

John Eaton son of Person Eaton and of Anna his wife was born at Lunenburg February ye 5th 1760.

Benjn Eaton son of Pearson & Anna Eaton was born at Lunenburg March 4th 1762.

William Eatton son of Person Eatton born at Lunenburg March ye 12 1767.

Sarah Eaton daughter of Pearson & Anna Eaton was born at Lunenburg January ye 3d 1770.

Ebeneazer Eaton son of Pearson Eaton and Anna, his wife, was born at Lunenburg October ye 17th 1772.

Calven Eaton son of Pearson Eaton and Anna his wife was born at Lunenburg Nov: 6th 1774.

F.

FARNSWORTH. FARMER.

The birth of ye children of Isaac Farnsworth and of Sarah his wife.
Isaac born at Groton November 30: 1723.
William born at Lunenburg Febr 26. 1725/6.
Sarah born at Lunenburg Novembr 27: 1727.
Lydia born at Lunenburg July 4: 1729 and dyed July 10: 1729
Lydia ye 3d daughter born at Lunenburg July 25: 1730.
Mary born at Lunenburg June ye 2th 1735.

Rebekah ye daughter of John Farmer & of Rebekah his wife, born at Lunenburg June ye 1th 1732.

FARMER. FITCH. FOSTER.

Rachel ye davghter of John Farmer & of Rebekah his wife born in Lunenburg, June ye 27th 1733.

Rebekah Farmer ye daughter of John Farmer & of Rebekah his wife, born April ye 8th 1735.

Catherine Fitch ye davghter of John Fitch and of Susannah his wife, born April ye 28th 1735.

John Fitch Junr son of John Fitch and Susannah his wife was born at Lunenburg May ye 16th 1737.

Paul Fitch the son of John Fitch and of Susanna his wife, was born at Lunenburg Janvary ye 4th 1741/2.

Jacob Fitch the son of John Fitch and of Susannah his wife, was born at Lunenburg June ye 29th 1744.

Susanna Fitch the daughter of John Fitch, and of Susanna his wife, was born at Lunenburg Februray the 18th 1746/7.

Molly Fitch daughter of John and Elizabeth Fitch, was born at Lunenburg Novr 23d 1752.

Sarah Fitch daughter of John and Elizabeth Fitch was born at Lunenburg June 11th 1755.

Benjamin Forster the son of Benjamin Forster and of Mehetabel his wife, was born on Munday Jannary the tweneth 1729.

Stephen Forster the son of Benjamin Forster and of Mehetable his wife was born January ye (21st) twenty-first, on Thursday, 1731.

Joseph Forster ye son of Benjamin Forster and of Mehetable his wife was born on Satterday, March the twenty fourth 1732/3.

Abbigal Foster ye daughter of Benjamin Forster and of Mehetable his wife, was born on Sabath day March ye thirtieth 1735.

Elizabath Foster the daughter of Benjamin Forster and of Mehetable his wife was born on Friday, Febr the twenty first 1736/7.

Dorothy Forster the daughter of Benjamin Foster and of Mehetable his wife, born May the fifth 1739.

Nathan Foster ye son of Benjamin Foster & of Mehetabel his wife was born June ye 7th 1741.

James Foster ye son of Benjamin Foster and of Mehetabel was born April ye 19th 1743.

Enoch Foster the son of Benjamin Foster and of Mehetabel his wife was born August the 16th 1745.

Mehetabel Foster ye daughter of Benjamin Foster, and of Mehetabel his wife, was born at Lunenburg March ye 15th 1747/8.

Sarah Foster ye daughter of Benjamin Foster and of Mehetabel his wife, was born at Lunenburg March ye 7th 1751/2.

FOSTER. FULLER.

Mary Foster daughter of Isaac Foster and Mary his wife was born at Lunenburg November ye 8 1746.

Benj^a Foster son of Isaac Foster and Mary his wife was born at Lunenburg May ye 26. 1748.

Isaac Foster son of Isaac Foster and Mary his wife was born at Lunenburg August ye 15th 1751.

Keziah Foster daughter of Isaac Foster and Mary his wife was born February ye 10th 1753. was born at Lunenburg.

Richard Foster son of Isaac Foster and Mary his wife was born at Luneburg July ye 31 1756.

Rebeckah Foster ye daughter of Joseph Foster and of Sarah his wife, was born at Lunenburg September ye 16th 1760.

Enoch Foster son of Joseph & Sarah Foster was born at Lunenburg August 21st 1762.

James Foster son of Joseph & Sarah Foster was born at Lunenburg April 24th 1764.

Mary Fuller daughter of Joseph Fuller & Abigail his wife was born August the 15 1736.

Abigail Fuller ye daughter of John Fuller and of Prudence his wife, was born at Lunenburg August ye 30th A. D. 1756.

John Fuller ye son of John Fuller and of Prudence, his wife, was born at Lunenburg April ye 26th 1758.

Prudence Fuller, the daughter of John Fuller, and of Prudence his wife, was born at Lunenburg October the 21th 1759.

Elizabeth Fuller daughter of John and Prudence Fuller was born at Lunenburg Octo^r 21st 1764.

John & James Fuller sons of John & Prudence Fuller were born at Lunenburgh March 28th 1768.

Stephen Fuller ye son of Nehemiah Fuller and of Mary his wife, was born at Lunenburg August ye 19, 1757.

Joseph Fuller ye son of Nehemiah Fuller and of Mary his wife, was born at Lunenburg July ye 22nd 1759.

Nehemiah Fuller ye son of Nehemiah Fuller and Mary his wife was born at Lunenburg Jany 23^d 1762.

Azeriah Fuller son of Nehemiah Fuller & Mary his wife was born at Lunenburg May 28th 1764.

Births.

FISK. FOWLER. FLOOD.

Jemima Fisk the daughter of Jonathan Fisk and of Jemima his wife, born at Lunenburg, February the 8th 1738/9.

Ezekiel Fowler the son of Richard Fowler and of Ruth his wife, born at Lunenburg March ye 18th 1742/3

Susanna Fowler ye daughter of Richard Fowler and of Ruth his wife, was born at Lunenburg May ye 31th 1746.

Ruth Fowler ye daughter of Richard Fowler and of Ruth his wife was born at Lunenburg August ye 18th 1748.

Richard Fowler ye son of Richard Fowler and of Ruth his wife was born at Groton September ye 21th 1750.

Elizabeth Fowler the daughter of Richard Fowler and of Ruth his wife was born at Lunenburg Novembr 15th 1752.

Joshua Chever Fowler & Sarah Chever Fowler the son and daughter of Richard Fowler & of Ruth his wife, were born at Lunenburg January ye 16th 1757.

Alice Flood the daughter of Benjamin Flood, and Elizabath his wife was born at Lunenburg, November the 22d; 1743.

G.

GOODRIDGE.

Sarah Goodridge ye daughter of Benjamin Goodridge and of Sarah his wife, born Janewary ye 1th 1730/31

Eliphalet Goodridge ye son of Benjamin Goodridge and of Sarah his wife born March ye 27th 1733.

Olive Goodridge ye davghter of Benja Goodridge and of Sarah his wife, born July 3d 1736.

Daniel Goodridge ye son of Benjamin Goodridge & of Sarah his wife, born at Lunenburg, August ye eleventh, on Fryday 1738.

Benjamin Goodridge Junr the son of Benjamin Goodridge and Sarah his wife, was born at Lunenburg July ye 7th 1740.

Sewall Goodridge the son of Benja Goodridge and of Sarah his wife, was born at Lunenburg July ye 7th 1743 about midnight.

Lois Goodridge the daughter of Benjamin Goodridge and of Sarah his wife, was born at Lunenburg March the 21th 1744/5.

Lucy Goodridge the daughter of Benjamin Goodridge, and of Sarah his wife, was born at Lunenburg, Janvary the 25th 1746/7.

Oliver Goodridge the son of Benjamin Goodridge, and of Sarah his wife, was born at Lunenburg October the 27th 1749.

GOODRIDGE.

Lydia Goodridge the daughter of Joshua Goodridge and of Lydia his wife, was born at Lunenburg, August the first, 1740.

Mehetabel Goodridge the daughter of Joshua Goodridge and of Lydia his wife was born at Lunenburg May ye 9th 1742.

Relief Goodridge the daughter of Joshua Goodridge and Lydia his wife, was born at Lunenburg March ye 25th 1744.

Joshua Goodridge the son of Joshua Goodridge and of Lydia his wife, born at Lunenburg August ye 10th 1746.

Kathrine Goodridge the daughter of Joshua and of Lydia his wife was born at Lunenburg August the 28th 1749.

Ruth Goodridge the daughter of Joshua Goodridge and of Lydia his wife, was born at Lunenburg September the 13th 1751.

Abijah Goodridge the son of Joshua Goodridge & of Lydia his wife was (born) at Lunenburg February the 21th 1754.

Abigal Goodridge the daughter of Joshua Goodridge and of Lydia his wife, was born at Lunenburg November ye 24th A. D. 1756.

Phinehas Goodridge son of Joshua and Lydia Goodridge was born at Lunenburg Octo^r 17th 1759.

Lois Goodridge daughter of Joshua & Lydia Goodridge was born at Lunenburg March 9th 1763.

David Goodridge the son of David Goodridge and of Elizabath his wife, born at Lunenburg March ye 19th 1741/2.

Elizabeth Goodridge the daughter of David Goodridge & of Elizabeth, born November ye 6th 1743.

Mehetabel Goodridge the daughter of David Goodridge, and of Elizabeth his wife, born at Lunenburg, August the sixth A. D. 1745.

David Goodridge the son of David Goodridge and of Elizabath his wife, was born at Lunenburg April ye 23rd 1747.

Ebenezer Goodridge the son of David Goodridge, and of Elizabeth his wife, was born at Lunenburg May the 1th 1749.

Asaph Goodridge the son of David Goodridge and of Elizabeth his wife, was born at Lunenberg June ye 28th 1751.

Hannah Goodridge the daughter of David Goodridge & Elizabeth his wife, was born at Lunenburg, April 7th 1753.

John Goodridge the son of David Goodridge & of Elizabeth his wife, was born at Lunenburg March ye 17th 1755.

Eunice Goodridge the daughter of David Goodridge and of Elizabeth his wife, was born at Lunenburg August ye 6th 1757.

GOODRIDGE.

Abigail Goodridge the daughter of Philip Goodridge and of Jane his wife, was born at Lunenburg July ye 31th A. D. 1745.

Jane Goodridge ye daughter of Philip Goodridge and of Jane his wife, was born at Lunenburg July the 7th A. D. 1747.

Priscila Goodridge ye daughter of Philip Goodridge and of Jane his wife was born at Lunenburg Janvary ye 15th 1748/9.

Philip Goodridge the son of Philip Goodridge, and of Jane his wife, born at Lunenburg October the 4th 1750.

Sibil Goodridge the daughter of Philip Goodridge & of Jane his wife, was born at Lunenburg June the 10th 1752.

Mary Goodridge the daughter of Philip Goodridge & of Jane his wife, was born at Lunenburg February the 16th 1754.

Joseph Goodridge the son of Philip Goodridge and of Jane his wife, was born at Lunenburg September ye 14th 1755.

William Goodridge the son of Philip Goodridge and of Jane his wife, was born at Lunenburg July ye 17th 1757.

Juet Goodridge the son of Philip Goodridge and of Jane Goodridge was born August ye 8th 1759.

Abel Goodridridge son of Phillip and Jane Goodridge was born at Lunenburgh Septr 19th 1761.

Simon Goodridge son of Philip and Jane Goodridge was born at Lunenburgh August 9th 1763.

Sarah Goodridge daughter of Philip & Jane Goodridge was born at Lunenburgh Feby 12th 1766.

Elizebath Goodridge daughter of Philip Goodridge and Jane his wife, was born at Lunenburg July ye 14th 1768.

Ezekiel Goodridge the son of Ezekiel Goodridge and of Rebacca his wife was born at Lunenburg May ye 5th 1755.

Sarah Goodridge, daughter of Eliphalet (Goodridge) & Rebecca his wife, born at Lunenburg Octo^r 15th 1764.

Rebekah Goodridge, daughter of Eliphalet & Rebekah Goodridge was born at Lunenburg March 17th 1766.

Samuel Payson Goodridge son of Eliphelet & Rebekah Goodridge, was born at Lunenburgh Jany 23^d 1768.

Rebekah Goodridge daughter of Eliphelet Goodridge & Rebekah his wife, was born at Lunenburg December ye 7th 1769.

Elizabeth Goodridge daughter of Eliphalet Goodridge & Rebeekah his wife, was born at Lunenburg February ye 17th 1772.

Eliphalet Goodridge son of Eliphalet Goodridge & Rebeekah his wife, was born at Lunenburg August ye 10th 1773.

GILLSON. GOULD.

The Birth of the children of Jonas Gillson and of Hannah his wife,
(1.) Jonas born at Lunenburg August 31 1728
(2.) Evnice born at Lunenburg March 18 1731
(3.) Prudence Gillson ye daughter of Jonas Gillson and of Hannah his wife born May 8th 1734.
(4.) Joseph Gillson ye son of Jonas Gilson and of Hannah his wife born at Lunenburg September ye 16th 1738.

Sarah Gillson ye daughter of Jonas Gillson and of Sarah his wife, was born at Lunenburg Febuary ye 11th 1757.
Unice Gilson daughter of Jonas and Sarah Gilson was born at Lunenburg May 11th 1759.

Children of David Gould and Abigall his wife.
Abigill born at Topsfield February ye 8th 1726/7.
Rebekah born at Lunenburg March 25 1728
Solomon born at Lunenburg Decemb^r 15 1730
Joseph born at Lunenburg Janewary ye 18th 1732.

Nemiah Gould ye son of Moses Gould and of Mary his wife, born Febrvary ye 19th 1729/30.
Moses Gould ye son of Moses Gould, and of Mary his wife born July ye 4th 1732.
Benj^a Gould ye son of Moses Gould & of Mary his wife born August ye 15th 1734.

Jonathan Gould ye son of Jonathan Gould, and Lydia, his wife, born July ye 24th 1731.
Lydia Gould ye davghter of Jonathan Gould and of Lydia his wife born December ye 21th 1732.
Mary Gould davghter of Jonat^h Gould & of Lydia his wife born Janvary 1th 1734/5.
Margarate Gould the daughter of Jonathan Gould & of Lydia his wife, was born April ye 16th 1737.

Marcy ye davghter of Jacob Gould, and of Dorotha his wife born in Lunenburg March ye 4th 1731/2.
Oliver Gould ye son of Jacob Gould and of Dorotha his wife, born in Lunenburg October ye 3th 1733.
Sarah Gould ye daughter of Jacob Gould and of Dorrothy his wife, born at Lunenburg April the 6th 1735
Jacob Gould the son of Jacob Gould and of Dorothy his wife, born at Lunenburg October the 16th 1737.

Births.

GOULD. GIBSON.

Dorrothy Gould ye daughter of Jacob Gould and of Dorrothy his wife, was born at Lunenburg August ye 27th 1740.

Elijah Gould ye son of Jacob Gould and Dorrothy his wife, born at Lunenburg August ye 8th 1743.

Thomas Gould ye son of Jacob Gould and of Dorrothy, his wife, born at Lunenburg October ye 20th 1745.

Benjamin Gould Junr ye son of Benjamin Gould and of Esther his wife, was born at Lunenburg Janvary the 31th 1740/41.

Amos Gould the son of Benjamin Gould and of Eshter his wife, born February ye 7th 1743/4.

Oliver Gould ye son of Oliver Gould and of Mary his wife was born at Lunenburg, March ye 31th 1760.

Sarah Gould, daughter of Oliver and Mary Gould, was born at Lunenburg August 16th 1762.

Lucy Gould, daughter of Oliver & Mary Gould, was born at Lunenburg Septr 9th 1764.

Mary Gould daughter of Oliver & Mary Gould, was born at Lunenburg Octo^r 16th 1766.

Samvel Gibson ye son of Arrington Gibson and of Mary his wife, was born at Lunenburg June ye 4th 1741.

Silas Gibson ye son of Arrington Gibson, and of Mary his wife, was born at Lunenburg September the 1th 1747.

Sarah Gibson the daughter of John Gibson and of Elizabath his wife, was born at Lunenburg June ye 8th 1743.

Isaac Gibson ye son (of) Isaac Gibson & of Keziah his wife, was born at Lunenburg November ye 28th A. D. 1745.

John Gibson the son of Isaac Gibson, and of Keziah his wife, was born at Lunenburg July ye 25th 1747.

Abraham Gibson the son of Isaac Gibson and of Keziah his wife, was born at Lunenburg June ye 13th 1749.

Jacob Gibson the son of Isaac Gibson and Keziah his wife, born March the 6th 1751 at Lunenburg.

Nathaniel Gibson the son of Isaac Gibson & Keziah his wife, was born at Lunenburg Febry 22^d A. D. 1753.

David Gibson the son of Isaac Gibson & Keziah his wife, was born at Lunenburg Janvary ye 22nd 1757.

Jonathan Gibson the son of Isaac Gibson & of Keziah his wife was born at Lunenburg December ye 22nd 1757

GIBSON. GARY. GARDNER. GROUT.

Solomon Gibson the son of Isaac Gibson and of Keziah his wife, was born at Lunenburg November ye 19th 1758.
Abraham Gibson son of Isaac Gibson & of Keziah his wife was born at Lunenburg June 13th 1760.
Keziah Gibson, daughter of Isaac Gibson & Keziah his wife was born at Lunenburg Febuy 10th 1762.

Edward Garey the son of Edward Garey & Phebe his wife was born at Wobourn Septr the 2^d 1752.
Phebe Gary the daughter of Edward Gary and of Phebe his wife, was born at Lunenburg September ye 30th 1755.
Mary Garey the daughter of Edward Garey and of Phebe his wife, was born at Lunenburg, February ye 7th 1759.
John Gary son of Edward & Phebe Gary was born at Lunenburg August 25th 1761.
Elizabeth Gary daughter of Edward and Phebe Gary was born at Lunenburg Feby 26th 1764.

Benjamin Gary the son of Thomas Gary & of Elizabeth his wife was born at Lunenburg September ye 19th 1760.

Andrew Gardner ye son of Mr. Andrew Gardner and of Mrs. Susanna Gardner his wife, born at Lunenburg, Nouember ye 2th 1729.
Susanna Gardner ye daughter of Mr. Andrew Gardner and of Mrs. Susanna Gardner his wife, born at Lunenburg September ye 2th 1732.

The Birth of ye children of John Grout and of Johannah his wife.
Hilkiah born July ye 23th 1728
Johannah born Janewary ye 8th 1729/30.
John born June ye 13th 1731
Elijah born October ye 29th 1732
Joel born March the 6th 1734/5.
Jonathan born July the 23, 1737.
Sarah born November the 28 1738
Patience born August 23th 1740.
Peter born October 9 1744.
Abigail born March the 23 1745
Josiah born November 18 1748
Solomon born June 27th 1751
Jehosaphat born August 2^d 1753

Phebe Grout the daughter of John Grout jun and of Phebe his wife, was born at Lunenburg March the 21th 1751.

Births.

GROUT. GOWEN.

Elijah Grout ye son of John Grout jun and of Phebe his wife, was born at Charlestown in the Province of New-Hampshire Janvary ye 26th 1753.

Susannah Grout the daughter of John Grout jun and of Phebe his wife, was born at Lunenburg December ye 12th 1754.

Endymia Grout the daughter of John Grout and of Phebe his wife, was born at Lunenburg Decem ye 23d A. D. 1756.

Theodore Grout son of John & Phebe Grout, was born at Lunenburg August 23d 1759.

Endymia Grout daughter of John & Phebe Grout, was born at Lunenburg August 5th 1761.

John Butler Grout son of John & Phebe Grout was born at Lunenburg April 28th 1763.

Jonathan Gowin son of Jon{a} and Anne Gowen was born at Lunenburg Septr 25th 1762

Thos Gowen son of Jon{a} and Anne Gowen, was born at Lunenburg April 19th 1764.

Anna Gowen daughter of Jon{a} & Anna Gowen, was born at Lunenburgh June 14th 1766

Eliab Gowen son of Jonathan & Anna Gowen, was born at Lunenburg Sept{m} ye 6th 1770

Asahel Gowen son of Jonathan & Anna Gowen was born at Lunenburg June ye 30th 1772

Benjamin Gowen son of Jonathan & Anna Gowen, was born at Lunenburg June ye 14th 1774.

John Kendel Gowen son of Jonathan & Hannah Gowen was born at Lunenburg February ye 25th 1777

Hannah Going daughter of Jonathan & Hannah Going was born at Lunenburg January 11th 1779.

James Going son of Jonathan & Hannah Going was born at Lunenburg December 24th 1780.

H.

HAMMOND.

Susannah Hammond ye daughter of Jonathan Hammond and of Abigail his wife, was born at Lunenburg Janvary ye first 1746/7.

Mary Hammond ye daughter of Jonathan Hammond, and of Abigail his wife, was born at Lunenburg September ye 26th 1749.

Avis Hammon the daughter of Samuel Hammon and of Anna his wife, was born at Lunenburg April ye 3rd 1753.

HAMMON. HOUGHTON.

Anna Hammon the daughter of Samuel Hammon and of Anna his wife, was born at Lunenburg September ye 28th 1754.

Samuel Hammon the son of Samuel Hammon and of Anna his wife was born at Lunenburg July ye 25th 1756.

Phinehas Hammon ye son of Samuel Hammon and of Anna his wife, was born at Lunenburg September ye 11th 1758.

Elizabath Houghton ye daughter of Eleazar Houghton & of Elizabath his wife, born at Lunenburg December ye 5th 1728.

Ruth, ye daughter of Eleazar Houghton, and of Elizabath his wife, born at Lunenburg June ye 30th 1732.

Esther Houghton ye daughter of Eleazer Houghton and of Elizabeth his wife, born January ye 17th 1734/5.

Eleazer Houghton ye son of Eleazer Houghton and of Elizabath his wife, born at Lunenburg August ye 26: 1737.

Susanna Houghton the daughter of Eleazer Houghton and of Elizabath his wife, born at Lunenburg May ye 10th 1743.

Darius Houghton, the son of Darius Houghton, and of Jerusha his wife, was born at Lunenburg October the 4th 1751.

Darius Houghton son of Darius Houghton, and of Jerusha his wife, was born at Lunenburg April 12. 1754.

David Houghton the son of Darius Houghton and of Jerusha his wife, was born at Lunenburg April the 8th 1756.

Adonijah Houghton the son of Darius Houghton and of Jerusha his wife, was born at Lunenburg May ye 28th 1758.

Asael Houghton, the son of Darius Houghton and of Jerusha his wife, was born at Lunenburg January ye 11th 1760.

Elizabeth Houghton, daughter of Darius Houghton and Jerusha his wife, was born at Lunenburg November 9th 1761.

John Houghton son of Darius & Jerusha Houghton, was born at Lunenburg, Novr 21st 1763.

Anna Houghton daughter of Darius & Jerusha Houghⁿ was born at Lunenburg Septr 22^d 1765.

Susannah Houghton daughter of Eleazar Houghton Junr and of Susannah his wife, was born at Lunenburg August 8th 1764.

Manasseh Houghton son of Eleazar Houghton Junr and of Susannah his wife, was born at Lunenburgh Septr 28th 1765.

Judith Houghton daughter of Eleazar Houghton Junr and of Susannah his wife, was born at Lunenburgh Decr 1st 1766.

Births.

HOUGHTON. HARTWELL.

Sarah Houghton, daughter of Eleazar Houghton jun[r] and of Susannah his wife, was born at Lunenburgh, March 10th 1768.

Stephen Houghton, son of Eleazer Houghton Jun[r] & of Susanna his wife, was born at Lunenburg October y[e] 27th 1769.

Eleazer Houghton y[e] 3[d], son of Eleazer Houghton Jun[r] & of Susannah his wife, was born at Lunenburg, March y[e] 26 1771.

Esther Houghton, daughter of Eleazer Houghton jun[r] & of Susannah his wife, was born at Lunenburg November y[e] 6th 1772.

Ruth Houghton, daughter of Eleazer Houghton & Susannah his wife, was born at Lunenburg December 13th 1776.

Lois Houghton, daughter of Eleazer Houghton & Susannah his wife, born at Lunenburg December 15th 1778.

———

Joseph Hartwell the son of Edward Hartwell, and of Sarah, his wife, born May 14th 1727.

Benj[a] Hartwell y[e] son of Edward Hartwell and of Sarah his wife, born October 17th 1729.

Phenihas Hartwell y[e] son of Edward Hartwell and of Sarah his wife, born Janewary 2th 1731/2.

———

Thomas Hartwell the son of Edward Hartwell jun[r] and Elesibath his wife, was born at Lunenburg, June y[e] 5th 1740.

Solomon Hartwell son of Edward Hartwell jun[r] and Elizabeth his wife, born at Lunenburg December y[e] 2nd 1741.

Elizabath Hartwell the daughter of Edward Hartwell Jun[r] and of Elizabath his wife, was born at Lunenburg December y[e] 5th 1742.

Mary Hartwell the daughter of Edward Hartwell and of Elizabeth his wife, was born at Lunenburg October the 22nd 1744.

Edward Hartwell the son of Edward Hartwell jun and of Elizabeth his wife was born at Lunenburg August y[e] 22nd 1747.

Asahel Hartwell the son of Edward Hartwell jun and of Elizabeth his wife was born at Lunenburg August the 24th 1749.

Solomon Hartwell the son of Edward Hartwell jun, and of Elizabeth his wife, was born at Lunenburg July y[e] 18 1751.

Mary Hartwell the daughter of Edward Hartwell jun, and Elizabeth his wife, was born at Lunenburg Sept[r] y[e] 1st 1753.

Martha Hartwell the daughter of Edward Hartwell and of Elizabeth his wife, was born at Lunenburg August the 14th 1755.

John Hartwell the son of Edward Hartwell jun. and of Elizabeth his wife, was born at Lunenburg April y[e] 2nd 1758.

Samuel Hartwell son of Edward Hartwell jun. and of Elizabeth his wife, was born at Lunenburg April y[e] 20th 1760.

HARTWELL.

Lydia Hartwell, daughter of Edward and Elizabeth Hartwell, was born at Lunenburg April 11th 1765.

Sarah Hartwell ye daughter of Jonathan Hartwell, and of Elizabeth his wife was born at Lunenburg November ye 23d 1746.

Jonathan Hartwell ye son of Jonathan and of Elizabeth his wife, was born at Lunenburg October ye 25th 1748.

Elisabeth Hartwell, daughter of Jonathan Hartwell and Elisabeth his wife, was born at Lunenburg April the 14th 1751.

Tamar Hartwell daughter of Jon^a and Elizabeth Hartwell was born at Lunenburg August 5th 1753.

Lucy Hartwell daughter of Jon^a & Elizabeth Hartwell, was born at Lunenburg August 24th 1758.

Eunice Hartwell daughter of Jon^a & Elizabeth Hartwell was born at Lunenburg May 20th 1761.

Susanna Hartwell daughter of Jon^a & Elizabeth Hartwell was born at Lunenburg Septr 22d 1763.

Josiah Hartwell the son of Joseph Hartwell and of Tabatha his wife, was born at Lunenburg August ye 7th 1748.

Prudence Hartwell the daughter of Joseph Hartwell and of Tabatha his wife, was born at Lunenburg February ye 19th 1750/1.

William Hartwell ye son of Joseph Hartwell and of Tabatha his wife, was born at Lunenburg, February ye 15th 1752.

Ruth Hartwell the daughter of Joseph Hartwell and of Tabatha his wife, was born at Lunenburg, April ye 11th 1754.

Ephraim Hartwell son of Phinehas Hartwell & of Mary his wife, was born at Lunenburg Octo^r ye 7th 1755.

Molly Hartwell, daughter of Phinehas Hartwell & Mary his wife, was born at Lunenburg February ye 7th 1757.

Esther Hartwell daughter of Phinehas Hartwell & of Mary his wife, was born at Lunenburg, January ye 15th 1759.

Abijah Hartwell son of Phinehas Hartwell & of Mary his wife, was born at Lunenburg July ye 28th 1761.

Joseph Hartwell son of Joseph and Phebe Hartwell, was born at Lunenburg, Decr 28th 1757.

Benjamin Hartwell, son of Joseph and Phebe Hartwel was born at Lunenburg July 18th 1759.

Reuben Hartwel, son of Joseph & Phebe Hartwel was born at Lunenburg July 4th 1762.

Births.

HARTWELL. HART. HUNT. HAZELTINE.

Jacob Hartwell son of Joseph & Phebe Hartwell, was born at Lunenburg June 1st 1765.

Tabitha Hartwell daughter of Joseph and Phebe Hartwell was born at Lunenburgh July 14th 1768,

John Heartwell, son of Joseph Hartwell and Phebe his wife, was born at Lunenburg September ye 4th 1770.

Katharine Hartwell daughter of Joseph Hartwell & of Phebe his wife, was born at Lunenburg August ye 27: 1772.

Samuel Hart jun the son of Samuel Hart and of Mary his wife, was born at Lunenburg January ye 26th 1759.

Abigail Hart the daughter of Samuel Hart & of Mary his wife, was born at Lunenburg August ye 27th 1760.

Ebenezer Hart son of Sam^ll & Mary Hart, was born at Lunenburg Decr 6th 1762.

Mary Hart daughter of Samuel Hart and Mary his wife, was born at Lunenburg, February ye 25th 1765.

Elizabath Hart daughter of Samuel Hart and Mary his wife, was born at Lunenburg December ye 17th 1766.

Nathaniel Hart, son of Samuel Hart and Mary his wife, was born at Lunenburg September ye 27th 1768.

Jonathan Hunt ye son of Samuel Hunt and of Hannah his wife, was born at Lunenburg July the 2nd 1750.

Hannah Hunt the daughter of Samuel Hunt and of Hannah his wife, was born at Lunenburg July 22d 1754.

Martha Hunt the daughter of Samuel Hunt, and of Hannah his wife, was born at Lunenburg April ye 2nd A. D. 1757.

Ebenezer Hunt the son of Samuel Hunt, and of Hannah his wife, was born at Lunenburg April ye 18th 1760.

Pearley Hunt son of Samuel & Hannah Hunt was born at Lunenburg Novr 22d 1762.

Amos Hazeltine the son of Amos Hazeltine and of Eunice his wife, was born Lunenburg June the 22nd 1748.

Thomas Hazeltine the son of Amos Hazeltine, and of Eunice his wife, was born at Lunenburg December the first 1750.

Jonas Hazeltine son of Amos Hazeltine, and Eunice his wife, born at Lunenburg Febry 7th 1753.

William Hazeltine, son of Amos Hazeltine, and of Eunice his wife, born at Lunenburg May ye 8th A. D. 1755.

HAZELTINE. HUCHINGS. HUTCHENS. HARRINGTON.

Richard Hazeltine son of Amos Hazeltine and of Eunice his wife, was born at Lunenburg April ye 28th 1757.

Joseph Hazeltine, son of Amos Hazeltine and of Eunice his wife, was born at Lunenburg, July ye 1st 1759.

John Hazeltine son of Amos Hazeltine and of Eunice his wife, was born at Lunenburg, March ye 26th 1762

Ebenezer Hazeltine, son of Amos Hazeltine and of Eunice his wife, was born at Lunenburg September ye 19th 1764.

David Hazeltine, son of Amos Hazeltine and of Eunice his wife, was born at Lunenburg February ye 7th 1767.

Eunice Hazeltine daughter of Amos Hazeltine and of Eunice his wife, was born at Lunenburg July ye 11 1769.

Ephraim Hazeltine son of Amos Hazeltine and of Eunice his wife, was born at Lunenburg March ye 29. 1772.

Abraham Heseltine son of Amos & Eunice Heseltine, was born October 15th 1775.

Loas Huchings the daughter of Joseph Huchings and Sarah his wife, was born at Tuxbury Jenevary ye 22th 1737.

John Huchings the son of Joseph Huchings and Sarah his wife, was born at Tuxbury November ye 27th 1739

Sarah Hutchens daughter of Phinehas Hutchens & Abigail his wife, was born at Lunenburg April ye 6. 1764.

Abigail Hutchens, daughter of Phinehas (Hutchens) and Abigail Hutchens was born at Lunenburgh March 14th 1766.

Joshua Hutchens son of Phinehas and Abigail Hutchens was born at Lunenburgh May 27th 1768.

James Reed Hutchens son of Phinehas and Abigail Hutchens, was born at Lunenburg July the 17th 1770.

Ama Hutchens daughter of Phineas and Abigal Hutchens was born at Lunenburg August ye 22d 1772.

Phinehas Hutchens son of Phinehas (Hutchens) and Abigail Hutchens, was born at Lunenburg July ye 6th 1774.

John Sullivan Hutchins son of Phinehas & Abigail Hutchins was born at Fitzwilliam August 15th 1776.

Prudy Hutchins daughter of Phinehas & Abigail Hutchins was born at Fitzwilliam January 16th 1779.

Ammi Harrington ye daughter of Thaddeus Harrington & of Thankful his wife, was born at Lunenburg October ye 28th Annq Domini 1758.

HENDERSON. HARWOOD. HUBBARD.

The births of the children of William Henderson & of Sarah his wife, viz.

William born Janry 8th 1744 at Lunenburg.
Henry born at Lunenburg October 22d 1746
John born at Lunenburg Janry 10th 1748
Sarah born at Lunenburg August 3d 1750.
James born at Lunenburg July 23d 1753
David born at Lunenburg August 22d 1757

Jane Henderson the daughter of John Henderson and of Jane his wife, was born at Lunenburg May the 1th 1753.
Thomas Henderson the son of John Henderson, and of Jane his wife, was born at Lunenburg May the 20th 1755.

Mary Harwood ye daughter of Nathaniel Harwood, and of Hannah his wife, born December ye 19th 1728.
James Harwood ye son of Nathaniel Harwood and of Hannah his wife, born October ye 4th 1730.
Hannah ye daughter of Nathaniel Harwood, and of Hannah his wife, born April ye 1th 1732/3.
Sarah Harwood ye daughter of Nathaniel Harwood and of Hannah his wife, born June ye 26th 1735.
Nathaniel Harwood ye son of Nathanil Harwood, and of Hannah his wife, born May ye 7th 1737.
Eliphelett born December the 12th 1739.*
Elizabeth Harwood the daughter of Nathanel Harwood and of Hannah his wife, born at Lunenburg March the 9th 1742/3.
Lucy Harwood the daughter of Nathanael Harwood and of Hannah his wife, was born at Lunenburg Janvary ye 16th 1745/6.

Grace Hubbard the daughter of Jonathan Hubbard Junr and Abigail his wife, was born August ye 22th 1740.
Abigail Hubbard the daughter of Jonathan Hubbard Jr. and of Abigail his wife, was born at Lunenburg Sept the 17th 1742.
Rebekah Hubbard the daughter of Jonathan Hubbard and of Abigail his wife, born at Lunenburg Sept. ye 27th 1744.

Dorcas Hovey the daughter of Abijah Hovey and Lydia Hovey his wife, was born at Lunenburg June the 24th 1751.
Lydia Hovey ye daughter of Abijah Hovey and Lydia Hovey his wife, was born at Lunenburg August ye 17th 1753.

---

*John R. Rollins thinks this is, no doubt, Harwood. [W. A. D.

HOVEY. HOLT.

Miriam Hovey the daughter of Abijah Hovey & of Lydia his wife was born at Lunenburg October ye 8th 1758.

Abijah Hovey ye son of Abijah Hovey & of Lydia his wife, was born at Lunenburg October ye 16th 1760.

Joseph Holt the son of Joseph Holt and Mary his wife born at Lunenburg April ye 8th 1744.

Mary Holt ye daughter of Joseph Holt and of Mary his wife, born at Lunenburg August ye 17th A. D. 1745.

Abiel Holt the son of Joseph Holt and of Mary his wife, was (born) at Lunenburg July ye 18th 1748.

Joseph Holt, son of Joseph Holt and Dorcas his wife was born at Lunenburg Decr ye 18th 1752.

William Holt ye son of William Holt, and of Mary his wife, born at Lunenburg February the 16th 1744/5.

David Holt the son of William Holt and of Mary his wife, born at Lunenburg September ye 26th 1746.

Jonathan Holt the son of William Holt, and of Mary his wife, born at Lunenburg Janvary ye 22nd 1748.

Humphry Holt, the son of William Holt, and of Mary his wife, born at Lunenburg, Janvary ye 1st 1750.

Mary Holt daughter of W^m & Mary Holt, was born at Ipswich Canada Novr 8th 1754.

Sarah Holt daughter of William Holt & of Mary his wife was born at Lunenburg May ye 30th 1756.

Elizabeth Holt the daughter of Daniel Holt and of Mehetabel his wife, was born at Lunenburg November ye 7th 1749.

Mehetable Holt ye daughter of Daniel Holt and of Mehetabel his wife, was born at Lunenburg September the 20th 1751.

Abigail Holt ye daughter of Daniel Holt and of Mehetabell his wife, was born at Lunenburg March the 9th 1753.

Daniel Holt the son of Daniel Holt and of Mehetabel his wife, was born at Lunenburg March ye 26th 1756.

Sibbil Holt daughter of Daniel Holt, and of Mehetabel his wife, was born at Lunenburg April ye 6th 1758.

Rachel Holt the daughter of Jonathan Holt, and of Rachel his wife, was born at Lunenburg April ye 20 : A. D. 1753.

Jonathan Holt the son of Jonathan Holt and of Susana his wife was born at Lunenburg May ye 16th 1756.

HOLT. HENERY. HILTON. HASTINGS.

Susannah Holt ye daughter of Jonathan Holt, and of Susannah his wife, was born at Lunenburg, May ye 29th A. D. 1758.
Elijah Holt son of Jonᵃ Holt and Susannah his wife was born at Lunenburg Octoʳ 23 1759.
William Holt son of Jonᵃ & Susannah Holt, was born at Lunenburg April 11th 1761.

Hannah Holt daughter of Daniel & Allice Holt, born at Lunenburg February ye 15th 1763.
Thomas Holt, son of Daniel & Allice Holt, born at Lunenburg November ye 25th 1765.
Lydia Holt daughter of Daniel & Alice Holt, born at Lunenburg August ye 29 1767.
Enoch Holt son of Daniel & Allice Holt born at Lunenburg August ye 15th 1770.
Louis Holt daughter of Daniel & Allice Holt, born at Lunenburg September ye 19 1772.

William Henery ye son of George Henery and of Elizabeth his wife, was born at Lunenburg Janvary the 22ⁿᵈ 1746/7.
Mary Henery ye daughter of George Henery and of Elizabeth his wife, was born at Lunenburg September the 1th 1748.

Thomas Hilton the son of Samuel Hilton and of   his wife, was born at Lunenburg June ye 14th 1752.
David Hilton the son of Samuel Hilton, and of   his wife, was born at Lunenburg April ye 12th 1752.

Mary ye daughter of John Hastings and of Sarah his wife born in Lunenburg July ye 6 : 1731.

John Hastings the son of Nathanael Hastings, and Lois his wife, born at Lunenburg October the 20th 1741.
Lois Hastings the daughter of Nathanael Hastings and of Lois his wife, born at Lunenburg May ye 17th A. D. 1743.
Nathaniel Hastings the son of Nathanael Hastings and of Lois his wife, was born at Lunenburg May ye 28th 1745.
Caleb Hastings the son of Nathanel Hastings and of Lois his wife, was born at Lunenburg, March the 31th 1749.
David Hastings the son of Nathanael Hastings and of Lois his wife, was born at Lunenburg, March ye 31th 1751.

HASTINGS. HEYWOOD.

Elizabeth Hastings ye daughter of Nathaniel Hastings and of Lois his wife, was born at Lunenburg April 14th 1753.

Nicholas Hastings the son of Nathanael Hastings and of Lois his wife, was born at Lunenburg, June ye 30th 1755.

Jonathan Hastings the son of Nathaneal Hastings, and of Lois his wife, was born at Lunenburg August ye 16th 1756.

Susannah Hastings the daughter of Nathaniel Hastings and of Loas his wife, was born at Lunenburg March ye 11th 1759.

Samuel Hastings the son of Nathanael Hastings and of Lois his wife, was born at Lunenburg May ye 19th 1761.

Esther Hastings daughter of Nath^{ll} & Lois Hastings was born at Lunenburgh July 21st 1765.

Eunice Hastings daughter of Nathaniel Hastings & Lois his wife, was born at Lunenburg June ye 6th 1769.

Relief Heywood daughter to Nathan and Esther Heywood was born July ye 19th 1724 on a Sabbath day morning about break of day.

Willis Heywood son to Nathan Heywood and to Esther Heywood his wife, was born May ye 21th 1726 on a Satterday morning about break of day.

Thomas Heywood son to Nathan and Esther Heywood was born August ye 20th 1728 on a Tuseday morning about one of ye clock.

Zimri Heywood son to Nathan and Esther Heywood was born September ye 5th 1731 on a Sabbath day. sun about half an hour high at night.

Esther Heywood davghter to Nathan and Esther Heywood was born April ye 20th 1734 on a Satterday morning, sun about two houers high in ye morning.

Elizebeth Heywood daughter of Nathan Heywood and Esther Heywood, was born at Lunenburg October ye 6th 1736.

Mary Heywood daughter of Nathan Heywood and Esther Heywood, was born at Lunenburg July the 28th 1739.

William Heywood the son of Nathan Heywood and of Esther Heywood, was born at Lunenburg on Thursday morning before sunrise January ye 17th 1744/5.

Silent Heywood ye son of John Heywood and of Ruth his wife, born August ye 25th 1728.

Ruth Heywood ye davghter of John Heywood and of Ruth his wife, born February ye 15th 1729/30.

Sarah Heywood ye davghter of John Heywood and of Ruth his wife, born December ye 13th 1732.

Births.

HEYWOOD. HILL. HUTCHINSON.

Abigil Heywood ye davghter of John Heywood and of Ruth his wife, born August ye 13th 1733.

Prudence Heywood daughter of John Heywood and of Ruth his wife, born at Lunenburg August ye 26th 1734/5

Lucy Heywood ye daughter of John Heywood and of Ruth his wife, born at Lunenburg February ye 4th 1739.

Ruth Heywood the daughter of John Heywood and of Ruth his wife, born at Lunenburg February ye 4th 1741/2.

Martha Hill ye daughter of John Hill and of Jane his wife born at Lunenburg December ye 24th 1740.

John Hill ye son of John Hill and of Jane his wife, born at Lunenburg March ye fourth 1742/3

William Hill ye son of John Hill and of Jane his wife, was born at Lunenburg June ye 5th 1747.

Thomas Hill the son of John Hill and of Jane his wife, was born at Lunenburg August the 14th 1751.

Robert Hill the son of John Hill and of Jane his wife, was born at Lunenburg, March the 18th 1755.

David Hill the son of John Hill and of Jane his wife was born at Lunenburg October ye 20th 1760.

Samuel Hutchinson son of Samuel Hutchinson and of Elizebath his wife, was born at Lexinton January ye 11th 1761.

Elizebath Hutchinson, daughter of Samuel Hutchinson and of Elizebath his wife was born at Lunenburg October ye 22^d 1763.

Thomas Hutchinson, son of Samuel Hutchinson and of Elizebath his wife, was born at Lunenburg October ye 27th 1765.

I.

IRELAND.

Ann Ireland the daughter of Abram Ireland Junior & Méribah his wife, was born at Lunenburg April 13th 1762.

Mary Ireland daughter of Abraham Ireland Junr & Meribah his wife, was born at Lunenburg April 11th 1763.

Abraham Ireland son of Abraham Ireland Jr. & Meribah his wife, was born at Lunenburg January ye 2. 1765.

Abigail Ireland daughter of Abraham Ireland Jun & Meribah his wife, was born at Lunenburg Sept ye 16. 1766.

IRELAND.

Susannah Ireland daughter of Abraham Ireland Junr and Meribah, was born at Lunenburgh Jany 4th 1768.

Jonathan Ireland son of Abraham Ireland Jun & Meribah his wife, was born at Lunenburg July ye 25. 1769.

Elener Ireland daughter of Abraham Ireland & Meribah his wife, was born at Lunenburg August ye 1 1771.

Meribah Ireland daughter of Abraham Ireland Junr and Meribah his wife was born at Lunenburg Apriel ye 12th 1773.

Betty Ireland daughter of Abraham Ireland Jun and Meribah his wife, was born at Lunenburg June 22th 1775.

David Ireland son of Abraham Ireland Jun. and Meribah his wife, was born at Lunenburg August ye 27th 1777.

J.

JOHNSON.

Rebakah Johnson the davghter of Samuell Johnson and of Rebakah his wife, born Nouember ye 2th 1719.

Elifebeth Johnson ye daughter of Samuell Johnson and of Rebakah his wife, born Janewary ye 2th 1721.

Samvell Johnson ye son of Samuell Johnson and of Rebakah his wife, born Janewary ye 2th 1723.

Kezia Johnson ye davghter of Samuell Johnson & of Rebakah his wife, born September ye 7th 1725.

Hannah Johnson ye davghter of Samuell Johnson and of Rebakah his wife, born October 8th 1727.

Nathan Johnson ye son of Samuell Johnson and of Rebakah his wife, born August ye 18th 1731.

Mary Johnson ye daughter of Samvel Johnson Junr, and of Hannah his wife, was born at Lunenburg September the eighth 1747.

Benjamin Johnson the son of Samvel Johnson Junr and of Hannah his wife, born at Lunenburg July ye 8th 1749.

Samuel Johnson son of Samuel Johnson Jr. and of Hannah his wife was born at Lunenburg, the 6th of September Anno Domini 1751.

Lucy Johnson, daughter of Samuel Johnson Jr and of Hannah his wife, was born at Lunenburg August the 5th Anno Domini 1753.

Nathan Johnson the son of Samvel Johnson & of Hannah his wife, was born at Lunenburg November the 6th 1755.

Silvanus Johnson ye son of James Johnson and of Susanna his wife, was born at Lunenburg Februay ye 25th 1747/8.

Births.

JEWETT. JONES.

Enoch Jewett the son of Thomas Jewett, and of Hannah his wife, was born at Lunenburg July ye 25th A. D. 1757.

Sarah Jones ye davghter of William Jones and of Sarah his wife, born March ye 25th 1735.

William Jones ye son of William Jones and of Sarah his wife, was born May 11th 1737 at Lunenburg.

Abigail Jones ye davghter of William Jones and of Sarah his wife, was born April ye 18th 1740 at Lunenburg.

Hannah Jones and Enos Jones the daughter and son of William Jones and of Sarah Jones, born at Lunenburg the 14th of July 1742.

Josiah Jones the son of William Jones and of Sarah Jones was born at Lunenburg October ye 23rd 1744.

Isaac Jones the son of William Jones and of Sarah his wife, was born at Lunenburg July ye 15th 1747.

Silence Jones daughter of Wm Jones & Sarah his wife, was born at Lunenburg August the 18th 1753.

John Jones, son of William & Sarhah Jones was born at Lunenburg May 22^d 1764.

William Jones son of William & Sarah Jones was born at Lunenburgh May 15th 1765.

Sarah Jones daughter of Wm Jones & Sarah his wife was born at Lunenburgh April 5th 1766.

David Jones son of William Jones and of Sarah his wife, was born at Lunenburg March ye 30th 1773.

Abigail Jones daughter of William & Sarah Jones, was born at Lunenburg June ye 22^d 1775.

Emme Jones daughter of William & Sarah Jones, was born at Lunenburg January ye 29th 1769.

Amos Jones son of Joseph Jones & Mary his wife, was born at Lunenburg February ye 11th 1761.

Mary Jones daughter of Joseph Jones & Mary his wife, was born at Lunenburg June ye 8th 1763.

Amasa Jones, son of Joseph Jones & Mary his wife, was born at Lunenburg June ye 19th 1765.

Ruth Jones, daughter of Joseph Jones & Mary his wife was born at Lunenburg March ye 3^d 1768.

Elizabeth Jones daughter of Joseph Jones & Mary his wife, was born at Lunenburg March ye 28th 1770.

Samuel Jones, son of Joseph and Mary Jones, was born at Lunenburg May ye 1st 1772.

JONES. JENISON.

Elnathan Jones son of Joseph & Mary Jones was born at Lunenburg August ye 12th 1774.

Mary Jenison the daughter of John Jenison and of Mary his wife, was born at Lunenburg March the 12th 1741/2.
John Jenison the son of John Jenison and of Mary his wife, born at Lunenburg June ye 15th 1744.

K.

KENNEDY. KIMBALL.

William Kennedy the son of Samvel Kennedy and of Sarah his wife, was born at Lunenburg April ye 4th 1750.
Sarah Kennedy the daughter of Samvel Kennedy and of Sarah his wife, was born at Lunenburg February the 14th 1752.
Mary Kennedy the daughter of Samuel Kennedy and of Sarah his wife, was born at Lunenburg March the 27th 1754.

Elisabeth Kimball ye daughter of Amos Kimbal, and of Dorothy his wife, was born at Bradford April ye 20th 1745.
Phinehas Kimball ye son of Amos Kimball, and of Dorothy his wife, was born at Lunenburg Janvary ye 6th 174—.
Dolley Kimball ye daughter of Amos Kimbal and of Dorothy his wife, was born at Lunenburg October ye 25th 1749.
Amos Kimball ye son of Amos Kimball and of Dorothy his wife, was born at Lunenburg September ye 25th 1752.
Thomas Kimball ye son of Amos Kimball and of Dorothy his wife, was born at Lunenburg September ye 5th 1754.
Ebenezer Kimball son of Amos Kimball & of Dorothy his wife, was born at Lunenburg June ye 14 1760.

Mary Kimball ye daughter of Ephraim Kimball and of Mary his wife, was born at Lunenburg, Janvary ye 14th 1747/8.
Anne Kimball ye daughter of Ephraim Kimball and of Mary his wife, was born at Lunenburg December ye 24th 1749.
Ephraim Kimball the son of Ephraim Kimball and Mary his wife, was born at Lunenburg Febry 15th 1752.
Hannah Kimball the daughter of Ephraim Kimball and of Mary his wife, was born at Lunenburg December ye 1st A. D. 1758.
Rachel Kimball the daughter of Ephraim Kimball and of Mary his wife, was born September ye 5th 1754.

Births.

KIMBALL. KENDALL. KENDEL.

Levi Kimball the son of Ephraim Kimball and of Mary his wife, was born at Lunenburg October 23rd 1756.

Betty Kimball the daughter of Ephraim Kimball and of Mary his wife, was born at Lunenburg March ye 31th 1761.

Abigail Kimball, daughter of Ephraim & Mary Kimball, was born at Lunenburg April 23d 1763.

Thomas Kimball the son of George Kimball and of Sarah his wife was born at Luenburg March the 7th 1749/50.

Benjamin Kimball the son of George Kimball & Sarah his wife, was born at Lunenburg April 2d 1752.

George Kimball son of George Kimball and of Sarah his wife, was born at Lunenburg August ye 6th 1754.

George Kimball the son of George Kimball and of Sarah his wife, was born at Lunenburg August ye 12th 1756.

Sarah, daughter of George & Sarah Kimball was born at Lunenburg May 3d 1763.

William Kendall the son of William Kendall and of Mary his wife, was born at Lunenburg March ye 8th 1758

Hannah Kendall ye daughter of William Kendall and of Mary his wife, was born at Lunenburg May ye 3rd 1759.

Saml Kendall & Mary Kendall son & daughter of Wm Kendall & Mary his wife, were born at Lunenburg Jany 6th 1762.

Eusebia Kendall, daughter of Wm & Mary Kendal, was born at Lunenburg, October 30th 1763.

Alovisa Kendal, daughter of William & Mary Kendall was born at Lunenburg Septr 28th 1765.

Bezaleel Kendel ye son of Uzziah Kendel, and of Elizabeth his wife, was born at Lunenburg April ye 4th 1749.

Abiathar Kendel ye son of Uzziah Kendel & of Elizabeth his wife, was born at Lunenburg November ye 11th 1750.

L.

LOVEJOY.

John Lovejoy the son of John Lovejoy and of Sarah his wife, was born at Lunenburg December the 22nd 1749.

Sarah Lovejoy, the daughter of John Lovejoy and Sarah his wife, was born at Lunenburg April 3d 1754.

Jonathan Lovjoy the son of John Lovejoy and of Sarah his wife, was born at Lunenburg, January ye 17th 1757.

LOVEJOY. LILLY. LARRABEE. LECH. LANE. LOW. L.

Susannah Lovejoy the daughter of John Lovejoy and of Sarah his wife, was born at Lunenburg August ye 17th 1759.
Prudence Lovejoy daughter of John Lovejoy & of Sarah his wife was born at Lunenburg April 22^d 1762.

Ebenezer Lilly the son of John Lilly and of Elizabeth his wife, was born at Lunenburg June ye 20th 1756.

Mary Larrabee the daughter of Timothy Larrabee and of Mary his wife, was born at Lunenburg October ye 19th 1748.
Abigail Larrabee the daughter of Timothy Larrabee and of Mary his wife, was born at Lunenburg Janvary the 21th 1755.

Manasses Lech ye son of James Lech and of Janat his wife, born July ye 25th 1734.

Eleazer Lane the son of Nehemiah Lane and of Sarah his wife, was born at Lunenburg Janvary ye 8th 1761.
Sarah Lain daughter of Nehemiah Lain & Sarah his wife, was born at Lunenburg October ye 15th 1762.
Nehemiah Lain, son of Nehemiah Lain & Sarah his wife, was born at Lunenburg November ye 28th 1764.
Mary Lain daughter of Nehemiah Lain & Sarah his wife, was born at Lunenburg February ye 1st 1767.
Phebe Lain daughter of Nehemiah Lain & Sarah his wife, was born at Lunenburg October ye 21 1769.

The births of the children of Jonathan Low & Sarh his wife, all which war born at Ipswich in the County of Essex.
Benoni Low was born August the 6th 1732.
Sarah Low was born October the 6th 1734.
Elizabeth Low was born April the 1st 1736
Mary Low was born January the 11th 1740.
Hannah Low was born July the 1st 1744.
Joanna Low was born June the 17th 1746
Jonathan Low was born August ye 13th 1748
William Low was born October ye 31st 1750
Abagail Low was born March ye 29th 1753.
Abraham Low was born February 11th 1755.
Francis Low was born January ye 23^d 1757.

————ney Little daughter of John Little and Mar [t] his wife [ ]

Births.

M.

MESSUR. MERRILL. MOWERS. MOFFET. MARTIN.

Jonathan Messur son of Jonathan & Abigail Messur was born at Lunenburg Septr 7th 1760.

Abigail Merrill the daughter of Daniel Merrill and of Abigail his wife, was born at Lunenburg Sept ye 24th 1756.
Hitte Merrill the daughter of Daniel Merrill and of Abigail his wife, was born at Lunenburg Sept. ye 15th 1758.

Elizabeth Mowers, daughter of William Mowers and Elizabeth his wife, was born at Dorchester Canady 27 Decr 1752.
Ruth Moors the daughter of Hugh Moors and of Ruth his wife, born at Lunenburg December the 22nd 1744.

Robert Moffet the son of Joseph Moffet, and of Dorothy his wife, was born at Lunenburg August the 16th 1754.

Jon^a Martin son of Jon^a & Mercy Martin, was born at Lunenburg March 18th 1762.

Samvel Martin the son of John Martin and of Elizabeth Martin was born at Ipswich April ye 8th 1738.
John Martin the son of John Martin and of Elizabeth his wife, was born at Lunenburg October ye 12th 1740.
Jane Martin the daughter of John Martin and of Elizabeth his wife, was born at Lunenburg Sept ye 20th 1742.
Elizabeth Martin the daughter of John Martin, and of Elizabeth was born at Lunenburg June ye 12th 1744.
Hannah Martin ye daughter of John Martin and of Elizabeth his wife, was born at Lunenburg October ye 1th 1746.
Martha and Mary Martin the daughters of John Martin and of Elizabeth his wife, were born at Lunenburg October the 26th 1748,
Susana Martin the daughter of John Martin and of Elizabeth his wife, was born at Lunenburg April the first 1751 Annoq: Domini.
Prudence and Patience Martin the daughters of John Martin and of Elizabeth his wife, were born at Lunenburg May ye 6 A. D. 1753.

The Births of the children of George Martin and of Eunice his wife,
Jonathan Martin born at Ipswich Octo^r 26th 1747.
John Martin born at Ipswich Jany 26th 1749
Lucy Martin born at Ipswich July 11th 1751
Joseph Martin born at Ipswich July 24th 1753

MARTIN. MITCHEL.

Eunice Martin born at Ipswich Decr 15th 1758
Mary Martin born at Lunenburgh July 28th 1762.

Children of Andrew Mitchel and of Martha his wife.
Jane born Febr ye 14th 1723/4
Ruth born July ye 19th 1726.
Martha born Janewary ye 19. 1727/8.
Elezabath born December ye 12. 1729.
Susannah born December ye 27 1731.
Hannah born September ye 15 1734
Esther born October ye 15th 1740.
Mary born July the 18th 1745.

N.

NORCROSS.

Jabez Norcross ye son Jeremiah Norcross and of Faith his wife born in Lunenburg March ye 10th 1731/2.
Mary Norcross ye davghter of Jeremiah Norcross and of Faith his wife, born Janewary 24th 1733/4.
Sarah Norcross the daughter of Jeremiah Norcross and of Faith his wife, born at Lunenburg February ye 25th 1735/6.
Page Norcross the son of Jeremiah Norcross and of Faith his wife, born at Lunenburg April ye 9th 1738.
Hanah Norcross ye daughter of Jeremiah Norcross and of Faith his wife, was born at Lunenburg November 10th 1741.
Jeremiah Norcross ye son of Jeremiah Norcross and of Faith his wife, was born at Lunenburg February ye 15th 1743/4.
Elijah Norcross ye son of Jeremiah Norcross, and of Faith his wife, was born at Lunenburg March ye 7th 1749/50.

O.

OSBURN.

John Osburn the son of Ephraim Ozburn and of Sarah his wife, was born at Lunenburg August ye 25th 1760.

P.

PARKER.

Johannah Parker the daughter of Timothy Parker and of Johannah his wife, was born at Lunenburg September the 14th 1749.
Sarah Parker the daughter of Timothy Parker and of Johannah his wife was born at Lunenburg March ye 26th 1752.

Births.

PARKER. PRATT. PEIRCE.

Elijah Parker the son of Timothy Parker and Joanna his wife, was born at Lunenburg Novr 18th 1753.

Elijah Parker ye son of Timothy Parker, and of Joanna his wife, was born at Lunenburg February the 1th 1756.

Abijah Parker ye son of Timothy Parker and of Johannah his wife, was born at Lunenburg September ye 24th 1758.

Joanna Parker ye daughter of Timothy & Joanna Parker was born at Lunenburg May 20th 1762.

Sibil Parker, daughter of Timothy & Joanna Parker, was born at Lunenburg Septr 1st 1764.

Abigail Parker daughter of Tim^o Parker & Joanna his wife was born at Lunenburgh Decr 29th 1767.

The births of ye children of Ebenezer & Charity Pratt,

Oliver Prat born at Lunenburg 29th June 1761.

Anna Pratt, daughter of Ebenezer and Lydia Prat was born at Lunenburg July 19th 1762.

Sally daughter of Eben^r & Lydia Pratt was born at Lunenburg August 23^d 1763.

Anna Prat daughter of Eben^r & Lydia Prat, was born at Lunenburg Septr 10th 1765.

Esther Peirce ye davghter of Ephraim Peirce and of Esther his wife, born May ye 29th 1722.

Jonathan Peirce ye son of Ephraim Peirce and of Esther his wife, born November ye 27th 1724.

Ephraim Peirce ye son of Ephraim Peirce and of Esther his wife, born March ye 13th 1726/7

Amos Peirce ye son of Ephraim Peirce and of Esther his wife born July 8th 1729.

Sarah Peirce ye davghter of Ephraim Peirce and of Esther his wife, born Nouember ye 27th 1731.

Mary Peirce ye davghter of Ephraim Peirce and of Esther his wife, born March ye 5th 1733/4.

Benj^a Pierce ye son of Ephraim Pierce & of Esther his wife, born June ye 3^d 1736.

Prudence Parce the daughter of Ephriam Parce and of Esther his wife, born at Lunenburg February the sixth, Anno Dom. 1738/9.

Oliver Parce the son of Ephriam Parce and Esther his wife, born at Lunenburg July the 17th 1741.

Keziah Parce the daughter of Ephraim Parce and of Esther his wife, born at Lunenburg December ye 4th 1743.

Elizabeth Parce ye daughter of Ephraim Parce and of Esther his wife, was born at Lunenburg March ye 25th 1748.

PEARCE. PEIRCE. PARCE.

Children of David Pearce and Elizabeth his wife,
David born at Groton July 19 1726.
Lydia born at Lunenburg July 21 1728.
Elizabath born at Lunenburg Apriel 7. 1730.
Hannah born at Lunenburg March ye 9 1731/2.
Solomon born at Lunenburg Janewary y^c 28th 1733/4
Samvel born at Lunenburg November ye 25th 1737
Joshua born at Lunenburg Janvary the 13th 1745/6

Sibel Peirce the daughter of John Peirce and of Hannah his wife, was born at Lunenburg Jan. y^c 28th 1746/7

Ephraim Parce the son of Ephraim Parce Jun. and of Sarah his wife, was born at Lunenburg October the 31th 1760.

Sarah Parce daughter of Ephraim Parce Junr & of Sarah his wife, was born at Lunenburg May 26th 1762.

Relief Parce daughter of Eph^m Parce Junr and of Sarah his wife, was born at Lunenburgh Augt 9th 1767.

Elijah Pearce son of Ephraim Pearce Junr & Sarah his wife, was born at Lunenburg September y^c 15th 1769.

Phinehas Parce son of Ephraim Parce Junr and of Sarah his wife, was born at Lunenburg March ye 22^d 1773.

Jonathan Parce the son of Jonathan Parce and of Sarah his wife, was born at Lunenburg October y^c 27th 1747.

Sarah Parce the daughter of Jonathan Parce and of Sarah his wife, was born at Lunenburg April ye 13th 1750.

Esther Parce the daughter of Jonathan Parce and of Sarah his wife, was born at Lunenburg February ye 5th 1752.

Prudence Peirce the daughter of Jonathan Peirce and of Sarah his wife, was born at Lunenburg November the 14th 1753.

Mary Pierce the daughter of Jonathan Pierce and of Sarah his wife, was born at Lunenburg May ye 21st 1756.

Tabatha Parce ye daughter of Jonathan Parce and of Sarah his wife, was born at Lunenburg March ye 28th 1758.

Benjamin Parce the son of Jonathan Parce and of Sarah his wife, was born at Lunenburg March ye 8th 1760.

Josiah Parce the son of Jonathan Parce, and of Sarah his wife, was born at Lunenburg October y^c 28 : 1761.

Susannah Parce daughter of Jon^a & Sarah Parce, was born at Lunenburg Decr 30th 1763.

Abraham Parce son of Jonathan & Sarah Parce was born at Lunenburg Decr 20th 1765.

Births.

PARCE. PLATTS. PAGE.

Lucy Parce daughter of Jon^a & Sarah Parce was born at Lunenburg August 31st 1767.
Nahum Pearce son of Jonathan Pearce & Sarah his wife, was born at Lunenburg May the 4th 1770

Sarah Parce ye daughter of Samuel Parce & Mary his wife was born at Lunenburg June 7th 1762.

Abel Platts the son of Abel Platts and of Mary Platts was born at Lunenburg March the 28th A. D. 1738.
Hannah Platts the daughter of Abel Platts and of Mary Platts, was born at Lunenburg January the 13th A. D. 1741.
Sarah Platts the daughter of Abel Plats and of Mary his wife, born September ye 4th 1744.

Edward Platts the son of Nathan Platts & of Elizabeth his wife, was born at Lunenburg September ye 3rd 1749.
Thomas Platts the son of Nathan Platts & of Elizabeth his wife, was born at Lunenburg November ye 27th 1754.
Jane Platts the daughter of Nathan Platts & of Elizabeth his wife, was born at Lunenburg August ye 3rd 1756.

Elizabeth Page ye davghter of Sam^{ll} Page and of Martha (Page) his wife, born March 23th 1719.
Zachariah Page ye son of Sam^{ll} Page and of Martha Page his wife, born April 10th 1721.
Daniel Page ye son of Sam^{ll} Page and of Martha Page his wife, born August 10th 1722.
Martha Page, ye davghter of Sam^{ll} Page, and of Martha his wife, born May 31th 1725.
Benj^a Page ye son of Sam^{ll} Page, and of Martha his wife born October 12th 1727
Thomas Page ye son of Sam^{ll} Page, and of Martha his wife, born September 6th 1730.

Children of Jonathan Page and of Mary his wife,
(1.) Sarah born at Lunenburg October ye 15 1728
(2.) Alles born at Lunenburg Decembr 28. 1730.
(3.) Mary born at Lunenburg September ye 1 1732
(4.) Jonathan born at Lunenburg March ye 13th 1734/5
(5.) Eunice born at Lunenburg August ye 26th 1737
(6.) Peter Page born at Lunenburg June ye 2nd 1739

PAGE.

(7.) Joshua Page son of Jonathan Page & of Mary his wife, born at Lunenburg July ye 10th 1743.
(8.) Prudence Page ye daughter of Jonathan Page & of Mary his wife was born at Lunenburg August ye 25th 1746.
(9.) Benjamin Page ye son of Jonathan Page and of Mary his wife, was born at Lunenburg September the 15th 1747.
Phinehas Page the son of Jonathan Page and of Mary his wife, was born at Lunenburg April the 28th 1751.

The birth of ye children of Joseph Page & of Deborah his wife,
Joseph born at Lunenburg August 10 1731
Deborah Page ye daughter of Joseph Page & of Deborah his wife, born in Lunenburg, April ye 11th 1733.
Marcy Page ye davghter of Joseph Page & of Deborah his wife, born March 2th 1734/5.
Joseph Page ye son of Joseph Page and of Deborah his wife, born at Lunenburg Febr ye 21th 1736/7.
Hannah Page ye daughter of Joseph Page, and of Deborah his wife, born March ye 22nd 1738/9.
Elizabeth Page daughter of Joseph Page and of Deborah his wife, born April 24th 1741.
Amos Page the son of Joseph Page and of Deborah Page born at Lunenburg June the 2nd 1743.
Joseph Page ye son of Joseph Page and of Deborah his wife born at Lunenburg June the 22nd 1745.
Susanna Page ye daughter of Joseph Page and of Deborah his wife, was born at Lunenburg April ye 24 A. D. 1747.

Sarah Page ye davghter of William Page and of Sarah his wife born May 14th 1734
William Page ye son of William Page and of Sarah his wife, born November ye 6th 1735.
Samvel Page the son of William Page & of Sarah his wife, born at Lunenburg Janvary ye 15th 1737/8.
Timothy Page the son of William Page and of Sarah born at Lunenburg April ye 5th 1739.
Hannah Page the daughter of William Page and Sarah his wife, born at Lunenburg December ye 17th 1741.
Ruth Page ye daughter of William Page and of Sarah his wife, born at Lunenburg December 25. 1743.
Phebe Page ye davghter of William Page and of Sarah his wife, born at Lunenburg December ye 4th 1745
Phebe Page ye daughter of William Page and of Sarah his wife, born December the 5th 1745. [Also entered in another place Decr ye 4th 1745.]

Births.

PAGE.

Priscilla Page davghter of David Page, and of Priscilla his wife, born October ye 22d 1735.
Solomon Page ye son of David Page, and of Priscilla his wife, born June ye 6th 1737.
David Page the son of David Page, and of Priscilla his wife, born at Lunenburg August ye 6th 1738.
Caleb Page ye son of David Page and of Priscilla his wife, born at Lunenburg Febuary ye 29 1739/40.
Matha Page ye daughter of David Page and of Priscilla his wife, born at Lunenburg April the 26th 1741.
Sarah Page the daughter of David Page and of Priscilla his wife was born at Lunenburg August ye 8th 1743.
Mehetabel Page the daughter of David Page and of Priscila his wife, born at Lunenburg March ye fifth 1743/4.
David Page the son of David Page and of Priscila his wife, born at Lunenburg June ye 5th 1745.
Ruth Page ye daughter of David Page, and of Priscila his wife, was born at Lunenburg October ye 26th 1747.
Johannah Page ye daughter of David Page and of Priscila his wife, was born at Nichawogg February the 17th 1748/9

Ruth Page the daughter of Daniel Page and of Ruth his wife, born at Groton August the 25th 1746.

Sibil Page daughter of Nathanael Page and of Mercy his wife, was born at Lunenburg April ye 19th 1749.
Rachel Page, the daughter of Nathanael Page and of Marcy, his wife, was born at Lunenburg Janvary the 21th 1750/1.
Prudence Page the davghter of Nathaniel Page and of Mercy his wife, was born at Lunenburg March ye 29th 1752.
Nathaniel Page ye son of Nathaniel Page and of Marcy his wife, born Febr 7th 1734/5.
Marcy Page ye daughter of Nathaniel Page & of Marcy his wife, born June 26th 1736.
Nathaniel Page ye son of Nathaneel Page and of Mercy his wife, born Sept. ye 15th 1738.
Abner Page ye son of Nathaniel Page and of Mercy his wife, born March ye 31th 1740.
John Page ye son of Nathaniel Page, and of Mercy his wife, born July ye 16th 1741.
Moses Page the son of Nathanael and of Marcy his wife, born at Lunenburg April ye (5th) fifth 1743,

PAGE. POOLE. PRIEST.

Aaron (Page) born May Janvary ye 13th 1745.
Samvel (Page) born July ye 26th 1747.
Reuben Page ye son of Nathanael Page and of Mercy his wife, was born at Lunenburg February the 3rd 1753.
Caleb Page the son of Nathanael Page, and of Mercy his wife, was born at Lunenburg May ye 11th 1756.

———

Sarah Poole the daughter of Samvel Poole and of Prudence his wife, born at Lunenburg April the fifteenth 1740.
Bette Poole the daughter of Samvel Poole and of Prudence his wife, born at Lunenburg March ye twenty-seventh 1742.
Samvel Poole the son of Samvel Poole and of Prudence his wife, born at Lunenburg, February the second 1743/4
Jacob Poole the son of Samvel Poole and of Prudence his wife, born at Lunenburg March ye 11 1745/6.
Bette Pooole ye daughter of Samvel Poole & of Prudence his wife, was born at Lunenburg, March ye 12th 1747/8.
Judith Poole ye daughter of Samvel Poole & of Prudence his wife, was born at Lunenburg March ye 16th 1749/50.
Susanna Poole the daughter of Samvel Poole and Prudence his wife, was born at Lunenburg Janvary the 30th 1752.

———

James Poole Junr ye son of James Poole and of Elizabath his wife, was born at Lunenburg April the 30th 1741.
Joshua Poole the son of James Poole and of Elizabeth his wife, born at Lunenburg Sept ye 12th 1744.
Elizabeth Poole ye daughter of James Poole and of Elizabeth his wife, was born at Lunenburg Janvary ye 6th 1746/7.
James Poole ye son of James Poole and of Elizabeth his wife, was born at Lunenburg July ye 4th 1749.
Ruth Poole ye daughter of James Poole and of Elizabeth his wife, was born at Lunenburg August the 14th 1751.
Ruth Poole the daughter of James Poole and of Elizabeth his wife, was born at Lunenburg May the 27th 1754.
Prudence Poole the daughter of James Poole and of Elizabeth his wife was born at Lunenburg August the 19th 1756.
Sarah and Susannah Poole, twins, the daughters of James Poole and of Elizabeth his wife, was born at Lunenburg May ye 30th 1759.

———

Joseph Priest the son of Joshua Priest and of Sarah his wife, was born at Lunenburg Dec^mr ye 4th 1752.

Births.

PRIEST. PUTNAM. POWERS. PATERSON.

Samuel Priest the son of Joshua Priest and of Sarah his wife, was born at Lunenburg Dec^m ye 12th 1754

Molley Priest the daughter of Joshua Priest, and of Sarah his wife, was born at Lunenburg September ye 22^d A. D. 1756.

Hephzibah Putnam the daughter of Thomas Putnam and of Rachel his wife, was born at Lunenburg February the 2^d 1755.

Susannah and Seth Putnam, the daughter and son of Thomas Putnam and of Rachel his wife, was born at Lunenburg September ye 16th A. D. 1756.

Thomas Putnam the son of Thomas Putnam and of Rachel his wife was born at Lunenburg February ye 27 A. D. 1758.

Mary, the daughter of Jonas & Lydia Powers, was born at Framingham Jany 3^d 1763.

Jonas son of Jonas & Lydia Powers, was born at Lunenburg July 30th 1764.

Lovisa Paterson, daughter of James Paterson & Miriam his wife, was born at Fitchburg July 4th 1779.

Lydia Paterson daughter of James Paterson & Miriam his wife, was born at Lunenburg February 6th 1781, and died March 19th 1781.

James Patterson son of James Paterson & Miriam his wife, was born at Lunenburg March 9th 1782.

R.

REED.

Samvel Reed Junr the son of Samvel Reed and Mary his wife, was born at Lunenburg July ye 13th 1740.

Mary Reed the daughter of Samvel Reed & of Mary his wife, was born at Lunenburg July the 30th 1742

Hannah Reed the davghter of Samvel Reed & of Mary his wife, was born at Lunenburg April the 12th 1745.

Sarah Reed the daughter of Samuel Reed & of Mary his wife, was born at Lunenburg 23^d of July 1747.

Priscilla Reed the daughter of Samuel Reed & of Mary his wife, was born at Lunenburg Augst 10th 1749.

Jesse Reed the son of Samuel Reed & of Mary his wife was born at Lunenburg July 23^d 1751.

REED. REDINGTON.

Rebecah Reed the daughter of Samuel Reed & of Mary his wife was born at Lunenburg June 5th 1753.

Joshua Reed the son of Samuel Reed and of Mary his wife was born at Lunenburg February the 18th 1757.

James Reed ye son of James Reed and of Abigail his wife, was born at Lunenburg August ye 25th 1746.

Priscilla Reed the daughter of James Reed, and of Abigail his wife, was born December ye 17th 1748.

Fredrick Reed ye son of James Reed and of Abigail his wife, was born at Lunenburg August ye 16th 1752:

Sylvanus Reed son of James Reed and Abigail his wife, born at Lunenburg January 7th 1755.

Barzillai Reed son of James Reed and of Abigail his wife was born at Lunenburg Janvary ye 23d 1756.

Hinds Reed the son of James Reed and of Abigail his wife was born at Lunenburg November the 29th 1757.

Joseph Reed son of James Reed and of Abigail his wife was born at Lunenburg Feby 17th 1763.

Shefomith Reed daughter of James Reed and of Abigail his wife, was born at Monadnock No. 4 May 23d 1766.

Lucy Redington the daughter of Benjamin Redington and of Ruth his wife, was born at Lunenburg February ye 8th 1758.

Mary Reddington daughter of Benjamin Reddington and of Ruth his wife was born at Lunenburg September ye 15th Annoq: Domini 1759.

David Reddington the son of Benjamin Reddington & of Ruth his wife was born at Lunenburg July ye 1st 1761.

Benjn Redington son of Benjn and Ruth Redington, born at Lunenburg April 7th 1763.

Ruth Redington daughter of Benjn Redington and Ruth his wife, was born at Lunenburg April ye 30th 1764.

Thomas Redington son of Benjn Redington and Ruth his wife, was born at Lunenburg March ye 29th 1766.

Rebecca Redington daughter of Benjn Redington and Ruth his wife was born at Lunenburg November ye 13th 1767.

Hannah Redington, daughter of Benjn Redington and Ruth his wife, was born at Lunenburg November ye 6th 1769.

Isaac Redington son of Benjn Redington and Ruth his wife, was born at Lunenburg October 10th 1771.

Births.

REDINGTON. ROBINSON. ROBBE. RICHARDS. RITTER.

John Redington son of Benj^a Redington & of Ruth his wife, was born at Lunenburg July ye 3^d 1774.

Elizabeth Redington ye daughter of Isaac Redington and of Ruth his wife, was born at Lunenburg. April 22^d 1762.

Susannah Redington daughter of Isaac and Ruth Reddington was born at Lunenburg 2^d March 1763.

Sophia Redington daughter of Isaac & Ruth Reddington was born at Lunenburg August 22^d 1765.

Amos Robinson ye son of Amos Robinson and of Priscilla his wife, born July ye 26th 1734.

Eliezer Robinson ye son of Amos Robinson and of Priscilla his wife, born March ye 17th 1735/6.

Daniel Robinson ye son of Amos Robinson and Priscilla his wife, born at Lunenburg April the 13th 1738.

John Robbinson the son of Amos Robbinson & Lydia his wife, born August ye 14th 1744.

Margaret Robbe ye daughter of William Robbe and of Elizebath his wife, born August ye 10th 1717 in ye kingdom of Ireland.

Elizibath Robbe ye davghter of William Robbe and of Anne his wife, born October ye 2th 1733.

Mitchael Richards the son of Charles Richards, and of Jane his wife, born at Wenham October the seventh 1737.

Edward Richards the son of Charles Richards and of Jane his wife, was born at Lunenburg August 25th 1740.

Hannah Ritter the daughter of Moses Ritter and Hannah his wife, was born at Lunenburg February ye 11th 1749.

Marcy Ritter the daughter of Moses Ritter and of Hannah his wife, was born at Lunenburg March ye 15th 1751.

Moley Ritter the daughter of Moses Ritter and of Hannah his wife, was born at Lunenburg Janavary ye 29th 1753.

Abner Ritter the son of Moses Ritter and of Hannah his wife, was born at Lunenburg February ye 8th 1755.

S.

SPAFFORD. STEWART. STEWARD.

John Spafford son of Joseph and Mary Spafford, was born at Lunenburg Feby 19th 1758.
Sarah Spafford daughter of Joseph and Mary Spafford was born at Lunenburg June 25th 1761.
Judah Spafford son of Joseph & Mary Spafford, was born at Lunenburg August 25th 1762.

Hannah Spafford the daughter of Jonah Spaffard, and of Dorcas his wife, was born at Lunenburg Janavary ye 11th A. D. 1756.

John Stewart ye son of William Stewart and of Margeret his wife, born at Lunenburg August ye 28th 1737.
William Stewart ye son of William Stewart and of Margeret his wife, was born November ye (5th) fifth 1740.
Thomas Stewart the son of William Stewart and Margeret his wife, born at Lunenburg May ye 3rd 1743.
Charles Stewart the son of William Stewart and of Margeret his wife, was born at Lunenburg October ye 8th 1745.
Elizabeth Stewart ye davghter of William Stewart, and of Margeret his wife, was born April ye 8th 1748.

Mary Stweert the daughter of Saloman Stwart and of Martha his wife, born September ye 7th 1740.
Jacob Stweart the son of Solomon Stweart and of Matha his wife born at Lunenburg April ye 22nd A. D. 1743.

Martha Steward, the daughter of Benjamin Steward and of Rebeekah his wife, was born at Lunenburg, March the 18th 1754.

Samuel Bird Steward the son of Phinehaz Steward and of Anne his wife, was born at Lunenburg March ye 18th 1757.
Anne Steward the daughter of Phinehaz Steward & of Anne his wife, was born at Lunenburg Novm ye 23rd 1758.
Phinehas Steward the son of Phinehas Steward & of Anne his wife, was born at Lunenburg October ye 27th 1760.
Abraham Steward the son of Phinehas Steward and Anne his wife, was born at Lunenburg October ye 15th 1762.
Martha Steward daughter of Phineas Steward and Anne his wife, was born at Lunenburg June ye 28th 1772.

Births.

STEWARD. SHED. SHEED.

Mary Steward ye davghter of Solomon Steward Jun and of Elizabeth his wife, was born at Lunenburg June ye 8th 1757.

Betty Steward the daughter of Solomon Steward and of Elizabeth his wife, was born at Lunenburg May ye 10th 1759.

Rebeckah Steward the daughter of Solomon Steward & of Elizabeth his wife, was born at Lunenburg March ye 4th 1761.

Daniel Steward the son of Daniel Steward and of Mary his wife was born at Lunenburg October ye 3rd 1758.

Benjamin Steward the son of Daniel Steward and of Mary his wife, was born at Lunenburg February ye 12th 1761.

Mary Steward daughter of Daniel & Mary Steward was born at Lunenburg May 10th 1763.

John Steward son of Daniel & Mary born at Lunenburgh Augt 18th 1765.

Amasa Steward son of Daniel and Mary Steward was born at Lunenburgh Decr 18th 1768.

Amherst Steward son of Daniel Steward & Mary his wife was born at Lunenburg February the 17th 1770.

Sarah Steward daughter of Daniel Steward & Mary his wife, was born at Lunenburg August ye 22d 1772.

Betty Steward daughter of Daniel Steward and Mary his wife, was born at Lunenburg, May ye 14th 1775.

Abigail Steward daughter of William Steward and Abigail his wife, was born at Lunenburg May 19th 1762.

Lemuel Shed son of Benjn Elizabeth Shed, was born at Lancaster Feby 2d 1762.

John Shed son of Benjn & Elizabeth Shed was born at Lunenburg June 9th 1764.

Person Shed the son of Benjamin Shed and of Elizabeth his wife, was born at Lunenburg June ye 22nd 1757.

Hannah Shed daughter of Benjn Shed, and of Elizabeth his wife, was born at Lunenburgh July 4th 1767.

Solomon Sheed son of Solomon & Elizabeth Sheed, born March ye 6: 1764.

James & Bettey Sheed son & daughter of Sollomon Sheed & Elizabeth his wife, born April ye 6th 1766.

SHEED. STEARNS.

Joseph Sheed son of Solomon & Elizabath Sheed, born February ye 19 1768.

Zackiah Sheed son of Sollomon & Elizabath Sheed, born November ye 28, 1769.

Abigal Sheed daughter of Sollomon & Elizabath Sheed, born December ye 1st 1771.

Patty Shed, daughter of Solomon & Elizebeth Shed, born at Lunenburg November ye 28, 1773.

Ebenezer Shed son of Solomon Shed & Elizabeth his wife was born at Lunenburg September ye 6, 1776.

Ruth Stearns the daughter of the Revnd Mr David, and Mrs Ruth Stearns, born at Lunenburg January ye 3rd 1736/7.

Rebekah Stearns the daughter of the Revnd Mr. David Stearns and Mrs. Ruth Stearns, was born at Lunenburg November ye 4th 1738.

Abigail Stearns the daughter of the Revnd Mr. David Stearns and of Ruth his wife, born at Lunenburg July ye 6th 1740.

Elizabeth Stearns ye daughter of ye Rev Mr. David Stearns and of Ruth his wife, was born April ye 20th 1742.

David Stearns ye son of the Rev Mr. David Stearns and of Ruth his wife, was born at Lunenburg January ye 8th 1743/4.

Lucy Stearns ye daughter of the Rev. Mr. David Stearns and of Ruth his wife, was born at Lunenburg November ye 16th 1745.

Jonathan Stearns ye son of ye Rev. Mr. David Stearns and of Ruth his wife, was born at November ye 2nd 1747.

Hannah Stearns ye daughter of ye Rev. Mr. David Stearns and of Ruth his wife, was born November 21th 1748.

Mary Stearns the daughter of ye Rev^d Mr. David Stearns, and of Ruth his wife, was born March 9th 1749 at Lunenburg.

Jonathan Stearns the son of the Rev^d Mr. David Stearns and of Ruth his wife, was born at Lunenburg April the 19th 1751.

John Stearns the son of the Rev^d Mr. David Stearns, and of Ruth his wife, was born at Lunenburg April 20th 1753.

Thomas Stearns the son of the Rev^d Mr. David Stearns and of Ruth his wife, was born at Lunenburg March the 8th 1756.

Sarah Stearns daughter of the Rev. Mr. David Stearns and Ruth his wife, was born at Lunenburg April 25th 1758.

Sarah Stearns the daughter of Thomas Stearns and of Lydia his wife, born at Lunenburg July ye 2nd 1745.

Thomas Stearns the son of Thomas Stearns and of Lydia his wife, was born at Lunenburg May ye 9th 1747.

STEARNS.

Daniel Stearns the son of Thomas Stearns and Lydia his wife, was born at Lunenburg July ye 31th 1749.

Lydia Stearns the daughter of Thomas Stearns and of Lydia his wife, was born at Lunenburg July the 24th 1751.

Charles Stearns son of Thomas Stearns & Lydia his wife was born at Lunenburg July 19th 1753

Sarah Stearns the daughter of Thomas Stearns and of Lydia his wife, was born at Lunenburg March the 12th 1755.

Rebeckah Stearns the daughter of Thomas Stearns and of Lydia his wife, was born att Lunenburg March ye 2 1757

William Stearns the son of William Stearns and of Elizabeth his wife, was born at Lunenburg April the twentieth A. D. 1749.

Mary Stearns ye daughter of William Stearns and of Elizabeth his wife, was born at Lunenburg May ye 7th 1751.

Joseph Stearns the son of William Stearns and of Elizabeth his wife, was born at Lunenburg August the 21th 1754.

James Stearns the son of William Stearns and of Elizabeth his wife, was born at Lunenburg September ye 1st 1758.

Benjamin Stearns the son of Benjamin Stearns and of Anna his wife, was born at Lunenburg December the 3rd 1754.

Joseph Stearns ye son of Benjamin Stearns and of Anna his wife, was born at Lunenburg August ye 22nd 1756.

Anna Stearns ye daughter of Benjamin Stearns and of Anna his wife, was born at Lunenburg Feburaary ye 7th Annoq : Domini 1759.

Sam^ll Stearns, son of Jonas & Submit Stearns, was born at Lunenburg Sept 8th 1759.

Jonas Stearns, son of Jonas & Submit Stearns was born at Shirley Septr 9th 1761.

David Stearns son of David & Mary Stearns was born April ye 14th

---

David Stearns ye 2^d son of David Stearns & Mary his wife was born Sept^r ——

Mary Stearns ye daughter of David Stearns & Mary his wife, was born May ye 9: ——

Thomas Stearns son of David Stearns & Mary his wife was born June ye 2 ——

STILES. SPEAR.

Lucy Stiles y⁰ davghter of Jacob Stiles and of Sarah his wife, born in Lunenburg May y⁰ 6th 1729.

Levi Stiles y⁰ son of Jacob Stiles and of Sarah his wife, born in Lunenburg February y⁰ 18th 1732/3.

Sarah Stiles y⁰ davghter of Jacob Stiles and of Sarah his wife, born in Lunenburg May y⁰ 24th 1735.

Jacob Stiles y⁰ son of Jacob Stiles and of Sarah born att Lunenburg September y⁰ 26th 1737.

Nahum Stiles y⁰ son of Jacob Stiles and of Sarah his wife, April y⁰ 21th 1740.

Hannah Stiles y⁰ daughter of Jacob Stiles and of Sarah his wife, was born at Lunenburg Janvary y⁰ 19th 1742.

Jeremiah Stiles y⁰ son of Jacob Stiles and of Sarah his wife, was born at Lunenburg Febuary y⁰ 23rd 1744/5.

Prudence Stiles y⁰ daughter of Jacob Stiles and of Sarah his wife, was born at Lunenburg April y⁰ 3rd 1747.

John Stiles the son of Jacob Stiles and of Sarah his wife, was born at Lunenburg July y⁰ 27th 1749.

Jonathan Stiles the son of Levi Stiles and of Patience his wife, was born at Lunenburg October y⁰ 5th A. D. 1756.

Susannah Stiles the daughter of Levi Stiles and of Patience his wife, was born att Lunenburg October y⁰ 4th A. D. 1758.

Nahum Stiles y⁰ son of Levi Stiles, and of Patience his wife, was born at Lunenburg May y⁰ 14th 1761.

Patience Stiles daughter of Levi & Patience Stiles born at Lunenburg September 16th 1763.

Peleg Stearns Stiles son of Levi & Patience Stiles was born at Lunenburg March 25th 1766.

Levi Stiles son of Levi & Patience Stiles, was born at Lunenburg March 14th 1768.

Lusa Stiles daughter of Levi & Patience Stiles, was born at Lunenburg September y⁰ 3 : 1770.

Jacob Stiles son of Levi & Patience Stiles, born at Lunenburg July y⁰ 9 : 1772.

Caleb Stiles son of Levi & Patience Stiles, born at Lunenburg August y⁰ 20th 1774.

Hannah Stiles daughter of Levi Stiles & Patience his wife, born at Lunenburg August 31. 1780.

Robert Spear son of Robert Speer and of Martha his wife, was born at Lunenburgh Octo⁰ʳ 12th 1747.

Births.

SNOW. SCOTT. SANDERSON. SMITH.

Silas Snow ye son of William Snow and of Elizabath his wife, born November ye 29th 1733.

Jemima Snow ye davghter of William Snow and Elizabath his wife, born November ye 27th 1735.

Rebaekah Snow the daughter of William Snow and of Elizabath his wife, born May ye 24th 1737.

Esther Snow ye daughter of William Snow and of Elizabath his wife, born March ye 8th 1738/9.

Joseph Snow the son of William Snow and of Elizabath his wife, was born at Lunenburg March ye 26th 1741.

Abigail Snow the daughter of William Snow and of Elizabath his wife, born at Lunenburg November the sixth 1742.

William Snow, the son of William Snow and of Elizabeath his wife born at Lunenburg June ye 20th 1744.

Bette Snow ye daughter of William Snow and of Elizabeth his wife, was born at Lunenburg, November the 9th 1746.

Lucy Snow ye daughter of William Snow and of Elizabeth his wife, was born at Lunenburg Nouember ye 8th 1748.

William Snow the son of William Snow and of Elizabeth his wife, was born at Lunenburg, December ye 28th 1752.

Edward Scott ye son of John Scott and of Lydia his wife born May 21th 1734.

Mary Scot ye daughter of John Scot & of Lydia his wife born March ye 23d 1735/6.

Benjamin Scott ye son of John Scott and of Lydia his wife born April ye 21. 1739.

David Scott the son of John Scott and of Lydia his wife, born at Lunenburg April the 1th 1742.

Jonathan Scott the son of John Scott & of Lydia his wife, born at Lunenburg October the 1th 1744.

Elizabeth Scott the daughter of John Scott, and of Lydia his wife, born at Lunenburg August ye third A. D. 1747.

Samuell Sanderson son of Abraham Sanderson, and of Patience his wife, born April 26th 1734.

Abraham Sanderson ye son of Abraham Sanderson, and of Patience his wife, born February ye 23d 1735/6.

Patience Smith the daughter of Jonathan Smith, and of Susannah his wife, was born at Lunenburg April the 28th 1737.

SMITH. SPARHAWK.

Reuben Smith the son of Jonathan Smith and of Susanna his wife, was born at Lunenburg July ye 15th 1739.

Simon Smith ye son of Jonathan Smith and of Susanna his wife, born at Lunenburg Sept ye 20th 1741.

Mary Smith the daughter of Jonathan Smith and of Susanna his wife, born at Lunenburg October ye 19th 1743.

Susannah Smith the daughter of the widow, Susannah Smith, born at Lunenburg March the 3rd 1745/6.

Prudence Smith daughter of Reuben & Prudence Smith was born at Lunenburgh Decr 28th 1762.

Jonathan Smith son of Reuben & Prudence Smith, was born at Lunenburgh March 5th 1764.

Sarah Smith daughter of Reuben & Prudence Smith was born at Lunenburgh Decr 7th 1765.

Reuben Smith son of Reuben & Prudence Smith, was born at Lunenburgh Octo^r 18th 1767.

Thomas Sparhawk the son of Mr. Thomas Sparhawk and of Rebecca his wife, was born at Lunenburg April ye 12th 1760.

Oliver Stearns Sparhawk son of Thos. & Rebekah Sparhawke was born at Lunenburg July 23^d 1764.

Rebecca Sparhawk daughter of Thos & Rebecca Sparhawk was born at Lunenburg July 17th 1768.

T.

TAYLOR.

Mary Taylor the daughter of Caleb Taylor and of Susanna his wife was born at Lunenburg November ye 26th 1751.

Caleb Taylor the son of Caleb Taylor and of Susanna his wife, was born at Lunenburg December the 1st 1754.

Arthur Taylor the son of Caleb Taylor and of Susanna his wife, was born at Lunenburg May ye 1st 1757.

Martha Taylor the daughter of Caleb Taylor and of Susanna his wife, was born at Lunenburg October the 10th 1760.

Susannah daughter of David Taylor and Betty Taylor his wife, was born at Lunenburg April 6th 1752.

Betty Taylor the   David Taylor and of Betty his wife was born at Lunenburg July ye 1th 1760.

Births.

TAYLOR. TARBALL. TRULL.

Jonathan Taylor the son of Aaron Taylor & Mercy his wife was born at Lunenburg July 22^d 1753.

Aaron Taylor son of Aaron Taylor & Mercy his wife, was born at Lunenburg Janr^y 16th 1755.

Sarah Taylor the daughter of Aaron Taylor and of Mercy his wife, was born at Lunenburg July ye 24th 1757.

Matha Taylor ye daughter of Aaron Taylor & of Mercy his wife, was born at Rowley Canada September ye 6th 1760.

Rebekah Taylor daughter of Aron & Mercy Taylor, was born at Rowley Canada June 11th 1763.

David Taylor son of Aaron and Mercy Tayor was born at Rowley Canada April 25th 1765.

Molly Tarbal the daughter of Zachariah Tarball and of Mary his wife, was born at Lunenburg May the first 1753.

Zechariah Tarbal the son of Zechariah Tarball and of Mary his wife, was born at Lunenburg November the 9th 1754.

Elizabeth Tarball the daughter of Zechariah Tarball, and of Mary his wife, was born at Lunenburg December ye 5th 1755.

Moley Tarball the daughter of Zechariah Tarball and of Mary his wife, was born at Lunenburg March the 19th 1757.

Sibel Tarball the daughter of Zechariah Tarball, and of Mary his wife, was born at Lunenburg March the 9th 1758.

Sarah Tarball ye daughter of Zechariah Tarball and of Mary his wife, was born at Lunenburg September ye 20th 1760.

Susannah Trull ye davghter of John Trull and of Sarah his wife, born April ye 25th 1734.

Phebe Trull ye daughter of John Trull and of Sarah his wife, born July 4th 1736.

W.

WALLES.

Jane Walles ye davghter of William Walles and of Elizabath his wife born December ye 16th 1719.

Elizabath Walles ye davghter of William Walles and of Elizabath his wife, born December ye 20th 1721.

Martha Walles ye davghter of William Walles and of Elizabath his wife, born September ye 18th 1722.

Mary Walles ye davghter of William Walles and of Elizabath his wife, born April 3dth 1724.

WALLES. WALLIS. WYMAN.

Margarit Walles y⁽ᵉ⁾ davghter of William Walles and of Elizabath his wife, born June y⁽ᵉ⁾ 16th 1727.
Anne Walles y⁽ᵉ⁾ davghter of William Walles and of Elizabath his wife, born February y⁽ᵉ⁾ 27th 1728/9.
Susannah Walles y⁽ᵉ⁾ davghter of William Walles and of Elizabath his wife, born March y⁽ᵉ⁾ 5th 1730/31.
Samuell Walles y⁽ᵉ⁾ son of William Walles and of Elizabath, born March y⁽ᵉ⁾ 27th 1732/3.
Hannah Walles y⁽ᵉ⁾ davghter of William Walles and of Elizabath his wife, born March 27th 1735.
William Walles and David Walles the sons of William Walles and of Elizabeth his wife, were born at Lunenburg March y⁽ᵉ⁾ 26th 1737.
Sarah Walles the daughter of William Walles & of Elizabeth (his wife) was born at Lunenburg August y⁽ᵉ⁾ 1th 1739.

The births of the children of Benoni Wallis and of R——kah his wife.
Benjⁿ Wallis born April 15th 1756.
Curwin Wallis born April 21st 1758.
David Wallis born Octoʳ 16th 1760.
Molly Wallis born May 31st 1763.
Ebenezer Wallis born April 11th 1765
Frederick Wallis born Octoʳ 15th 1768.

Silas Wyman y⁽ᵉ⁾ son of John Wyman and of Rebeckah his wife, born at Lunenburg December y⁽ᵉ⁾ 10th 1736.
Ruben Wymon y⁽ᵉ⁾ son of John Wymon and Rebeckah his wife, was born at Lunenburg April y⁽ᵉ⁾ 26th 1738.
John Wyman junʳ the son of John Wyman and Rebeckah his wife, was born at Lunenburg September y⁽ᵉ⁾ 28th 1739.
David Wyman the son of John Wyman and of Rebeckah his wife, born at Lunenburg April y⁽ᵉ⁾ 30th 1744.

Abigail Wyman the daughter of Ezekiel Wyman and Abigail his wife, was born June y⁽ᵉ⁾ 9th 1740
Lucy Wyman the daughter of Ezekiel Wyman and of Abigail Wyman born at Lunenburg December y⁽ᵉ⁾ 15th 1741.
Israel Wyman the son of Ezekiel Wyman and of Abigail Wyman born at Lunenburg February y⁽ᵉ⁾ 19th 1743.
Susanna Wyman y⁽ᵉ⁾ daughter of Ezekiel Wyman & of Abigail his wife, born at Lunenburg February the 25th 1744/5.
Ezekiel Wyman the son of Ezekiel Wyman and of Abigail his wife, born July y⁽ᵉ⁾ 26th 1746.

WYMAN. WHITE.

Stephen Wyman the son of Ezekiel Wyman, and of Abigail his wife, was born at Lunenburg August ye 4th 1748.

Francis Wyman the son of Ezekiel Wyman and of Abigail his wife, was born at Lunenburg December ye 20th 1750.

William Wyman son of Ezekiel Wyman and Abigail his wife, was born at Lunenburg Novr 30th 1752.

Seth Wyman son of Ezekiel Wyman and Abigail his wife, was born at Lunenburg December 1st 1754.

Ruth Wyman the daughter of Ezekiel Wyman, and of Abigal his wife, was born at Lunenburg Dec. ye 30 : 1756.

John Wymon son of Joseph Wymon and Keziah his wife, was born at Lunenburg October ye 14th 1760.

David Wyman son of Joseph Wyman & Keziah his wife, was born at Lunenburg April 29th 1762.

Joseph Wyman son of Joseph and Keziah Wyman was born at Lunenburg April 3^d 1764.

Oliver Wyman son of Joseph & Keziah Wyman, was born at Lunenburg 26th March 1766.

Thomas Wymon son of Joseph Wymon & Keziah his wife, was born at Lunenburg September ye 27th 1768.

Sarah Wymon daughter of Joseph Wymon & Keziah his wife, was born at Lunenburg Febuary ye 27th 1771.

Elizabeth Wyman daughter of Joseph Wyman and Keziah his wife, was born at Lunenburg Novr ye 10th 1773.

Silas Wyman son of Reuben Wyman & Elizabeth his wife, was born at Lunenburg Octo^r 6th 1761.

John White the son of John White and of Mary his wife, was born at Lunenburg December ye 3rd 1748.

Charles White the son of John White and of Mary his wife, was born at Lunenburg February ye 5 1749.

William White the son of John White and of Mary his wife, was born at Lunenburg November ye 2nd 1751.

David White the son of John White and of Mary his wife, was born at Lunenburg. October ye 22. 1753.

Elizabeth White the daughter of John White and of Mary his wife, was born at Lunenburg July ye 1st A. D. 1755.

Lydia White the daughter of John White jun and of Mary his wife, was born at Leominster March the 5th 1755.

WHITE. WOOD.

Betty White the daughter of John White jur and of Mary his wife was born at Leominster April ye 19^(th) 1757.
Salmon White the son of John White jun and of Mary his wife, was born at Lunenburg June ye 5^(th) 1759.
Salmon White the son of John White jun and of Mary his wife, was born at Lunenburg April ye 3^(rd) 1761.

———

Bezelial Wood ye son of Jonathan Wood and of Sarah his wife born April ye 4^(th) 1735.
Jonathan Wood ye son of Jonathan Wood and of Sarah his wife, born October ye 8^(th) 1738.
Mehetabel Wood ye daughter of Jonathan Wood and Sarah his born December ye 23. 1741
John Wood ye son of Jonathan Wood and of Sarah his wife, born at Lunenburg Feburary ye 2^(nd) 1743/4.
Barnabus Wood the son of Jonathan Wood and of Sarah his wife, was born at Lunenburg May the 21^(th) 1746.
Sarah Wood ye daughter of Jonathan Wood and of Sarah his wife, was born at Lunenburg November ye 29^(th) 1748.
Sarah Wood the daughter Jonathan Wood and of Sarah his wife, was born at Lunenburg September ye 26^(th) 1751.
Bezaleel Wood ye son of Jonathan Wood and of Sarah his wife, was born at Lunenburg Septr 10^(th) 1758.
Molly Wood ye daughter of Jon^a Wood & of Sarah his wife was born at Lunenburg August 24^(th) 1761.
Jonathan Wood son of Jonathan & Sarah Wood was born at Lune—— April ye 2. 1767.

———

Jerusha Wood the daughter of Joseph Wood and of Ruth his wife, born at Lunenburg July ye 24^(th) 1742.
Joseph Wood the son of Joseph Wood and of Ruth his wife, born at Lunenburg June ye 8^(th) 1744.
Elizabeth Wood the daughter of Joseph Wood and of Ruth his wife, was born at Lunenburg April the second 1747.
Bette Wood the daughter of Joseph Wood and Ruth his wife, was born at Lunenburg Novr ye 8^(th) 1749.
Joseph Wood the son of Joseph Wood and of Ruth his wife, was born at Lunenburg October 28^(th) 1753.
David Wood son of Joseph Wood & Ruth his wife, was born at Lunenb——g August ye 31 1760.

WOOD. WHITNEY.

Isaac Wood the son of Michael Wood and of Mary his wife, born at Lunenburg September ye 7th 1746.

Mary Wood the daughter of Michael Wood and of Mary his wife, was born at Lunenburg November ye 1th 1749.

Elizabeth Wood y^e   of Michael Wood and of Mary his wife, was born at Lunenburg April ye 20th 1751.

Hannah Wood the daughter of Michael Wood & of Mary his wife was born at Lunenburg Jan^ry 18th 1754.

Mary Wood ye daughter of David Wood, and of Mary his wife, was born at Lunenburg July ye 8th 1747.

Martha Wood ye daughter of David Wood, and of Mary his wife, was born at Lunenburg July ye 15th 1749.

Bette Wood ye daughter of David Wood and of Mary his wife, was born October ye 21th 1751.

Sarah Wood the daughter of David Wood & of Mary his wife, was born at Lunenburg June 10th 1754

David Wood the son of David Wood and of Mary his wife was born at Lunenburg December ye 6th 1756.

Zepheniah Wood the son of David Wood & of Mary his wife, was born at Lunenburg July ye 4th 1760.

James Wood ye son of Jonathan Wood and of Rachel his wife, was born at Lunenburg March the 24th 1756.

Esther Wood the daughter of Jonathan Wood jun and of Rachel his wife, was born at Lunenburg March ye 19th A. D. 1758.

Jonathan Wood the son of Jonathan Wood & of Rachel his wife, was born at Lunenburg March ye 25th 1760.

George Wood son of Jon^a & Rachel Wood, was born at Lunenburg June 3^d 1762.

Sarah Whitney ye daughter of Zeckariah Whitney and of Sarah his wife, born at Lunenburg February the 27th 1739/40.

Jane Whitney ye daughter of Zechariah Whitney and of Sarah his wife, born Sept ye 22nd 1742.

Abigail Whitney daughter of Zechariah Whitney and of Sarah his wife, was born at Lunenburg Jan^ry 17th 1746.

Zechariah Whitney son of Zechariah Whitney & Sarah his wife, was born at Lunenburg Jan^ry 11th 1747.

Mary Whitney daughter of Zechariah Whitney and Sarah his wife, was born at Lunenburg April 8th 1752.

John Whitney son of Zechariah Whitney and Sarah his wife, was born at Lunenburg April ye 16th 1756.

WHITNEY. WETHERBE.

Moses Whitney yᵉ son of Ephraim Whitney and of Jane his wife, was born at Lunenburg Janvary yᵉ 11ᵗʰ 1747.

Ephraim Whitney yᵉ son of Ephraim Whitney and of Jane his wife, was born August yᵉ 12ᵗʰ 1749.

Molley Whitney the daughter of Ephraim Whitney and of Jane his wife, was born at Lunenburg September yᵉ 25ᵗʰ 1755.

Ezra Whitney son of Ezra Whitney and Agness his wife, was born at Lunenburg November 29ᵗʰ 1760.

Rebekah Whitney daughter of Ezra Whitney and Agness his wife, was born at Lunenburg Janʸ 2ᵈ 1762.

The birth of yᵉ children of Hezekiah Wetherbe and of Huldah his wife.

Benjamin born at Malborough November 3ᵗʰ 1728.

Thomas born at Lunenburg Nouember 27ᵗʰ 1730.

Phebe born at Lunenburg February yᵉ 12ᵗʰ 1733/4

Phebe born at Lunenburg July 7ᵗʰ 1740.

Sarah Wetherbee yᵉ daughter of Hezekiah Wetherbe and of Huldah his wife born at Lunenburg Novmber seventeeenth 1742.

John born at Lunenburg Septʳ 14ᵗʰ 1746.

Abraham born at Lunenburg June 5ᵗʰ 1752.

Mary Wetherbe yᵉ davghter of Ephraim Wetherbe and of Elizabath Wetherbe his wife, born at Lunenburg Janewary yᵉ 6ᵗʰ 1729/30.

Bette Wetherbe yᵉ davghter of Ephraim Wetherbee and of Elizabeth Wetherbe his wife, born at Lunenburg May yᵉ 15ᵗʰ 1732.

Rachel Wetherbe yᵉ davghter of Ephraim Wetherbe, and of Johanah Wetherbe his wife, born at Lunenburg April yᵉ 3ᵗʰ 1733.

Jonathan Wetherbee yᵉ son of Ephraim Wetherbe and of Johannah his wife, born October yᵉ 14ᵗʰ 1734.

Abigail Wetherbe yᵉ davghter of Ephraim Wetherbe and of Joanna his wife, born Febʳ 13ᵗʰ 1735/6.

Susannah Wetherbee yᵉ daughter of Ephraim Wetherbe and of Johannah his wife, born March yᵉ 27ᵗʰ 1738.

Abijah Wetherbe the son of Ephraim Wetherbe and of Johannah his wife, born at Lunenburg April yᵉ 24ᵗʰ 1740.

Johannah Wetherbe the daughter of Ephraim Wetherbe and of Johannah his wife, born at Lunenburg September yᵉ 13ᵗʰ 1742.

Samvel Wetherbee the son of Ephraim Wetherbe and of Johannah his wife born at Lunenburg April yᵉ 3ʳᵈ 1745.

WETHERBEE. WALKER.

Ephraim Wetherbe the son of Paul Wetherbe and of Hannah his wife, was born at Lunenburg August ye 24th 1747.
Paul Wetherbe the son of Paul Wetherbe and of Hannah his wife, was born at Lunenburg August the 12th 1749.
Hannah Wetherbe ye daughter of Paul Wetherbe and of Hannah his wife, was born at Lunenburg July ye 19th 1751.
Betty Wetherbee the daughter of Paul Wetherbee and of Hannah his wife, was born at Lunenburg December 13th 1753.
David Wetherbee the son of Paul Wetherbee and of Hannah his wife, was born at Lunenburg February ye 16th 1757.
Joab Wetherbee the son of Paul Wetherbee and of Hannah his wife, was born at Lunenburg April ye 26th 1759.
Abijah Wetherbee the son of Paul Wetherbee & of Hannah his wife, was born at Lunenburg August ye 26th 1761.
Esther Weatherbee daughter of Paul & Hannah Weatherbee was born at Lunenburg Decr 3^d 1763.
Daniel Weatherbee son of Paul & Hannah Weatherbe was born at Lunenburg Feby 16th 1766.

The births of the children of Thos & Hannah Weatherbee.
Thomas born August 7th 1757
Daniel born Decr 16th 1758
Hephsibah born Feb^r 28th 1760
Isaac born Sept^m 2^d 1761
Sarah born March 30th 1763.
David born May 31st 1764
Hannah born Feby 16th 1766
Lucy born August 4th 1767
Josiah born March 17th 1769
Patty born October 16th 1771
Molley born Novr 14th 1773.

Rebeccah Walker the daughter of Obediah Walker and of Abigail his wife was born at Lunenburg August the 16th 1746.
Benjamin Walker the daughter of Obediah Walker and of Abigail his wife, was born at Lunenburg, February ye 20th 1749.
Abigail Walker the daughter of Obediah Walker and of Abigail his wife, was born at Lunenburg January ye 21th 1753.
Betty Walker the daughter of Obediah Walker and of Abigal his wife, was born at Lunenburg July the 6th A. D. 1754.
Sarah Walker daughter of Obediah Walker and of Abigail his wife, was born at Lunenburg Novr 12th 1758.

WALKER. WILLARD.

Obediah & Nathaniel Waker sons of Obediah & Abigal Walker were born at Lunenburg March 3d 1761.

Mary Walker daughter of Obediah Walker and of Abigail his wife, was born at Lunenburg November ye 9th 1770.

Josiah Willard Junr son of Josiah Willard and of Hannah his wife born on Wensday in ——— Janewary ye 21th 1715/16.

Abigall Willard davghter of Josiah Willard and of Hannah his wife, born on Fryday July ye 4th 1718.

Susannah Willard ye davghter of Josiah Willard and of Hannah his wife, born on Satterday July ye 9th 1720.

Lois Willard ye davghter of Josiah Willard and of Hannah his wife, born on Sabbath day December ye 16th 1722.

Nathan Willard ye son of Josiah Willard and of Hannah his wife, born on Tuesday May ye 28th 1726.

Prudance Willard ye davghter of Josiah Willard and of Hannah his wife, born on Satterday September ye 30th 1727.

Oliver Willard ye son of Josiah Willard and of Hannah his wife, born on Fryday March ye 6th 1730.

Sampson Willard ye son of Josiah Willard and of Hannah his wife, born on Tuesday June ye 27th 1732.

Josiah Willard Tersus son of Josiah Willard Junr and of Hannah his wife, born September ye 22th 1734.

Wilder Willard ye son of Josiah Willard and of Hannah his wife, born on Monday June ye 30th 1735.

Jemima Willard ye daughter of Moses Willard and of Susana his wife, born June ye 29th 1728.

Susana Willard ye daughter of Moses Willard and of Susana his wife, born February ye 20th 1729/30

Hulday Willard ye daughter of Moses Willard and of Susanna his wife, born May ye 27th 1732.

James Nutting Willard ye son of Moses Willard and of Susanna his wife, born ye 28th of May 1734.

Moses Willard ye son of Moses Willard and of Susanna his wife, born August ye 15th 1738.

Miriam Willard the daughter of Moses Willard, and Susanna his wife, was born September ye 25th 1740.

Mary Willard, daughter of Jonathan Willard and of Kezia his wife, born Febr 13th 1734/5.

Births.

WILLARD. WARRIN.

Unity Willard and Amity Willard the daughters of Jonathan Willard, and of Kezia his wife, born at Lunenburg October ye 31th 1737.

Keziah Willard the daughter of Jonathan Willard Ju^r and of Phebe his wife, was born at Lunenburg March ye 12th 1743/4.

Jonathan Willard ye son of Jonathan Willard Ju^r and of Phebe his wife, was born at Lunenburg September ye 21th 1745.

Jeremiah Willard the son of Jonathan Willard Junr and of Phebe his wife, was born at Lunenburg Augst the 3rd 1747.

Phebe Willard the daughter of Jonathan Willard Junr and of Phebe his wife, was born at Lunenburg Augst the 4th 1749.

Mary Willard the daughter of Jonathan Willard Jun and of Phebe his wife, was born at Lunenburg Janry 27th 1751/2.

Amity Willard the daughter of Jonathan Willard Junr and of Phebe his wife, was born at Lunenburg Decr 26th 1752.

Mary Willard the daughter of Jonathan Willard Junr and of Phebe his wife was born at Lunenburg Febuary ye 15th 1755.

Thulah Willard the daughter of Jonathan Willard and of Phebe his wife, was born at Lunenburg January ye 14th 1758.

Katharine Willard the daughter of Barzillai Willard and of Hepsibath his wife, was born at Lunenburg July ye 23rd 1759.

Lucy Willard the daughter of Barzillai Willard and of Hepsibah his wife, was born at Lunenburg March 20th 1762.

Sarah Willard daughter of Barzillai Willard & of Hephsibah his wife, was born at Lunenburg March 31st 1765.

Pascal Paoli Willard son of Berzillah Willard & Hapsabath his wife, was born at Lunenburg May ye 10. 1769.

Unity Willard daughter of Barzillia Willard and Hepzibah his wife, was born at Lunenburg May ye 27 1775.

Mary Willard daughter of Berzillia Willard & Hepzibah his wife, was born at Lunenburg April 27th 1778.

Arathusa Willard daughter of Jonathan Willard and Sarah Colburn was born at Lunenburg Decr the 1st 1762.

Jacob Warrin ye son of Jacob Warrin and of Mary his wife was born at Lunenburg December ye 16th 1745.

Isaac Warrin the son of Jacob Warrin and of Matha his second wife, was born at Lunenburg March ye 11th 1746/7.

Elizabeth Warrin the daughter of Jacob Warren and of Matha his wife, was born at Lunenburg December ye 2nd 1748.

WOOLSON.

The births of the children of Asa Woolson & Elizabeth his wife,
Elizabeth born at Weston February ye 22 : 1763.
Lois was born at Weston March ye 13 1765
Asa was born at Townshend February ye 4 1767.
Elijah was born at Lunenburg December ye 1 1769
Ebenezer was born at Lunenburg April ye 18 1773
Amos was born at Lunenburg October ye 11 : 1778
Joseph was born at Lunenburg October ye 23 1783.

DEATHS

DEATHS

COPIED FROM THE

RECORDS OF THE TOWN OF LUNENBURG,

FROM 1707 TO 1764.

B.

BOYNTON.

Sarah Boynton ye davghter of Benoni Boynton & of Anne his wife dyed April 8th 1707.

Mary Boynton ye davghter of Benoni Boynton & of Anne his wife dyed April 13th 1721

Joseph Boynton ye son of Benoni Boynton and of Anne his wife dyed July 1727.

Elizabeth Boynton the wife of Benoni Boynton jun dec^d September ye 26th 1756.

Sarah Boynton ye daughter of Stephen Boynton and of Sarah his wife dec^d November ye 21st A. D. 1749.

Joseph Boynton ye son of Stephen Boynton and of Sarah his wife, dec^d November ye 12th 1749.

Sarah Boynton ye wife of Stephen Boynton dec^d March ye 15th A. D. 1752.

Susannah Boynton daughter of Stephen Boynton and Sarah his wife deceas^d June 3^d 1764 in ye 18th year of her age.

Elizabeth Boynton daughter of Stephen Boynton and Sarah his wife deceas^d June 3^d 1766 in the 18th year of her age.

Susannah Boynton, daughter of Stephen Boynton and Elizabeth his wife, deceas^d June 5th 1766 in her eleventh month.

Elizebath Boynton wife of Stephen Boynton deceas^d April ye 18 1772 in the 52^d year of her age.

Benoni Boynton deceas^d Decr 30th 1758 in the 77th year of his age.

Anne Boynton wife of Benoni Boynton deceas^d May 31st 1764 78 years old.

BUTLER. BELLOWS. BOWERS. BIGELOW. BANCROFT.
BRADSTREET. BROWN. BUSS.

William Butler deceast November the 4th 1741.
Abigail Butler the daughter of the widow Lucy Butler deceast September the 20th 1744 in the third year of her age.

Jonathan Bellows ye son of Benjamin Bellows & of Abigail his wife, deceast April ye 26th 1746.
Abijah Bellows the son of Benjamin Bellows and of Abigail his wife, deceast November ye 17th 1749.
Mrs. Dorcas Bellows ye wife of Mr. Benjamin Bellows deceas'd September ye 8th 1747.

Susana Bowers ye daughter of Jerahmeel Bowers and of Miriam his wife, deceasd August ye 7th 1749.
Miriam Bowers wife of Jerahmeel Bowers and daughter of Eleazer Houghton decd July 25th 1752.

Love Bigelow, wife of Benja Bigelow deceased, June 18th A. D. 1754.

Elizabeth Bancroft the wife of Timothy Bancrofft deceast Janvary ye 28th 1756.

Abigal Bradstreet the daughter of Samuel Bradstreet and of Dorcas his wife, deceasd Dec ye 9th A. D. 1754.
John Bradstreet the son of Samuel Bradstreet and of Dorcas his wife, deceas'd August ye 30th 1756.
Capt. Jonathan Bradstreet deceas'd May ye 22nd 1757.

Jonathan Brown the son of Aaron Brown and of Abigail his wife, decd July ye 17th 1759 in the filth year of his age.

Jonathan Buss, son of John Buss and Eunice his wife, deceas'd Decr 5th 1757.
Zephaniah Buss, son of John Buss and Eunice his wife deceas'd Decr 5th 1759.

C.

COLBURN.

Thomas Colburn dyed February 15th 1728/9.

Deaths. 343

COREY. COMINGS. COFFEN. CARLILE. CARLTON. CARTER.

Rebekah Cory ye wife of Benjⁿ Cory dyed July 24th 1731.
Rebackah Corey ye daughter of Benjᵃ Corey dyed November the eleventh A. D. 1736.

Marriam Comings the davghter of Samvel & Sarah Comings dyed July ye 9th 1740.
Thaddeus Comings the son of Samvel & Sarah Comings dyed July ye 16th 1740.
Thomas Comings the son of Samvel & Sarah Coming dyed July ye 20th 17—0 [1740 probably].
Thomas Cummings the son of Samvel Cummings & of Sarah Cummings, deceast September the 23rd 1746.
Samuel Commings Jun dec'd May ye 10th 1760, in the twenty forth year of his age.

Daniel Coffen the son of Michael Coffen and of Lydia his wife deceast October ye 3rd 1740.
Abigail Coffen ye daughter of Michael Coffen and of Lydia his wife, deceast October ye 29th 1741.

Elizabeth Carlile ye daughter of David and Leatis Carlile, deceast April ye 21th 1740.
John Carlile ye son of David and Leatis Carlile, deceast May ye 7th 1740.
David Carlile ye son of David and Leatis Carlile, deceast May ye 12th 1740.
Margaret Carlile ye daughter of David and Leatis Carlile, deceast May ye 26th 1740.

Abigail Carlton ye daughter of Abraham Carlton and Mary his wife, deceas'd October ye 6th 1755.
Abigail Carlton daughter of Abraham Carlton and of Mary his wife deceas'd July 7th 1766.
Abram Carlton deceas'd in the Continental Army September 16 1775.
Mr. Abraham Carlton deceased October ye 1st 1779.

Vashtai Carter the daughter of Thomas Carter & of Betty his wife dece'd October ye 20th 1760.

D.

DAVIS. DODGE. DIVOL. DARLING. DOWNE.

Samuell Davis Jr. ye son of Sam^{ll} Davis died October 19th 1734.

Sarah Davis the daughter of Samvel Davis and of Sarah his wife, dyed February ye 10th 1737.

Meriam Dodge ye daughter of Noah Dodge & of Margarit his wife dyed June 28th 1736.

Reuben Dodge deceas'd June 15th 1762.

Esther Dodge daughter of Reuben and Ruth Dodge deceased June 15th 1763.

Sarah Divol the wife of John Divol, deceas^t at Lunenburg April ye 14th 1746.

John Darling ye son of John Darling jun and of Ruth his wife, deceast August ye 27th 1746 at Leominster.

Sarah Downe the daughter of William Downe Esqr and Margaret his wife, deceast March ye 24th 1755 aged, eight years and three months.

F.

FARMER. FITCH. FLOOD. FROST. FOSTER.

Rebekah, daughter of John Farmer died July ye 31th 1732.

Hannah Farmer ye wife of John Farmer died February 22th 1730 ; 31.

John Farmer of Lunenburg dyed August ye 15th 1735.

Rebekah Farmer, widdow dyed September ye 5th 1736.

Susanna Fitch ye wife of Mr. John Fitch, deceas^t December ye 24th 1748 at Providence in ye Collony of Rhod Island.

Elizabeth Flood the wife of Benjamin Flood, deceased, April the 1th 1752 in the 30th year of her age.

Hannah Frost deceased May 23^d 1753.

Enoch Foster the son of Benjamin Foster and of Mehetabel Foster, deceas't July the 15th 1749 in ye 7th year of his age.

Benjamin Foster Junr deceast Sept ye 8th 1755 in the 27th year of his age.

Deaths.

FOSTER. FULLER.

Nathan Foster ye son of Benjamin Foster and Mehetabel Foster, deceast November ye 10th 1755 in the 15 year of his age.

James Foster the son of Benjamin Foster and Mehetabel Foster deceast February ye 3rd 1757 in ye 14th year of his age.

Mehetabel Foster ye wife of Benjamin Foster dec^d February ye 1st 1761.

John Fuller the son of John Fuller and of Prudence his wife deceast June ye 12th 1758.

G.
GOODRIDGE. GOULD. GROUT.

Lt. Phillip Goodridge dyed Janewary ye 16th 1728/9.

David Goodridge the son and child of David Goodridge, and of Elizabeth his wife, deceast October the 4th 1744.

Relieff Goodridge, the daughter of Joshua Goodridge and of Lydia his wife, deceast October ye 8th 1746.

The widow, Mrs. Mehetabel Goodridge, deceased February the 24th 1755 in the seventy eight year of her age.

Sibil Goodridge the daughter of Philip Goodridge & of Jane Goodridge, deceased September ye 3rd 1754 in the third year of her age.

Amos Gould a son of the widow Esther Gould, deceast September the 10th 1746.

Edymia Grout, daughter of John and Phebe Grout died April 24th 1759.

H.
HARTWELL. HEYWOOD.

Joseph Hartwell son of Edward Hartwell died November 19th 1726.

Solomon Hartwell the son of Edward Hartwell Junr and of Elizebeth Hartwell, deceast January ye 1th 1741/2.

Mary Hartwell the daughter of Edward Hartwell Jun and of Elizabeth his wife, deceast September ye 22nd 1746.

Sarah Hartwell the wife of Edward Hartwell Esqr, deceas^d August 7th 1764.

Tabatha Hartwell the wife of Joseph Hartwell deceased April ye 25. 1756.

Esther Heywood daughter of Nathan Heywood and Esther Heywood, deceast December ye 28th 1739.

HEYWOOD. HOUGHTON. HOLT. HUNT. HENDERSON. HILTON.

Relieff Heywood daughter of Nathan Heywood and Esther Heywood, deceas^t February the 24th 1739/40.

Willis Heywood son of Nathan and Esther Heywood, deceast March the 6th 1739/40.

Mary Heywood daughter of Nathan Heywood and Esther Heywood deceas^t June ye 13th 1741.

Ruth Heywood the daughter of John Heywood and of Ruth his wife deceas^t May the 28th 1740.

Abigail Heywood the daughter of John Heywood and of Ruth his wife, deceas^t May the 28th 1740.

Prudence Heywood the daughter of John Heywood, and of Ruth his wife, deceas^t May ye 30th 1740.

Lucy Heywood ye daughter of John Heywood and of Ruth his wife, deceas^t May the 31th 1740.

Ester Heywood wife of Nathan Heywood deceas^d June 18th 1765.

Robert Houghton the son of Eleazer Houghton and of Elizabath his wife, deceast August the 7th 1740.

Susanah Houghton ye daughter of Eleazer Houghton and of Elizabeth, deceasted September ye 7th 1746.

Esther Houghton the daughter of Eleazer Houghton and of Elizabeth his wife, deceas^d May ye 5th 1759 in the twenty-fifth year of her age.

Darius Houghton son of Darius Houghton and Jerusha his wife, deceased Octo^r 3^d A. D. 1753.

Joseph Holt the son and child of Joseph Holt and Mary Holt, deceas^t July ye 26th 1744.

Mrs. Dorcas Holt, relict of Mr. Joseph Holt, deceased June ye 11th 1775 in ye sixtyeth year of her age.

Rachel Holt the wife of Jonathan Holt, deceased April 21, 1753.

William Holt deceased Novr 14th 1759.

Hannah Hunt the daughter of Samvel Hunt and of Hannah Hunt, deceast December ye 9th 1749.

John Henderson son of Willm Henderson and Sarah his wife, deceased April ye 9th 1747.

Samuel Hilton deceased March ye 21 1756.

Deaths.

HOVEY.

Lydia Hovey, the wife of Abijah Hovey dec'd November ye 28th 1760.
Abijah Hovey ye son of Abijah Hovey & of Lydia his wife dec'd December ye 1st 1760.

J.

JOHNSON. JEWET. JONES.

Rebakah Johnson ye wife of Sam^{ll} Johnson dyed August 29 : 1731.

David Jewet the son of Thomas and Hannah Jewet deceased December ye 1st 1757.
Thomas Jewet deceased February ye 20th 1758

William Jones dec'd January ye 26 1761.
Isaac Jones the son of William Jones and of Sarah his wife dec'd ———

K.

KIMBALL.

Thomas Kimball Esqr deceast September the eleventh 1748 at Lunenburg.
George Kimball the son of George Kimball and of Sarah his wife, deceased October ye 16th 1755.
Mrs. Elizabeth Kimball relict of Thos Kimball Esqr deceas'd Octo^r 1st 1765.

M.

MARTIN.

John Martin deceas'd April the 17th A. D 1753.

P.

PAGE.

Zachriah Page ye son of Sam^{ll} Page and of Martha Page his wife dyed September 2th 1721.
— Matha Page dyed April 1, 1728.
John Page the son of Mr. Samvel Page of Lunenburg dyed at Jamaica, being there on ye Spainish expedition, December the twenty-ninth A. D 1740 as they hear.
Mrs Martha Page ye wife of Mr. Samvel Page, deceast September ye 22nd 1746.
Mr. Samvel Page deceast September ye 7th A. D. 1747.

PAGE. PARCE.

Marcy Page ye daughter of Joseph Page & of Deborah his wife, dyed June ye 21th 1736.

Joseph Page Junr son of Joseph Page & of Deborah his wife, dyed July ye 1th 1736.

Nathaniel Page Junr ye son of Nathaniel Page and of Marcy his wife, dyed August ye 12th 1736.

Abner Page ye son of Nathanel Page and of Mercy his wife, deceast August the 4th 1740.

Nathaniel Page Jun the son of Nathaniel Page and of Mercy his wife dec'd November ye 24th 1759.

Aaron Page ye son of Nathanael Page deceast May ye 28th 1746.

Caleb Page the son of David Page and of Priscilla Page, deceas^t November the 4th 1741.

David Page the son of David Page and of Priscilla Page, deceast November the 12th 1741.

Solomon Page the son of David Page and of Priscilla Page, deceast November the 15th 1741.

Samuel Page ye son of William Page and of Sarah Page deceas^t April ye 5th 1746.

Submit Page the daughter of William Page and of Sarah his wife, deceast November the 21th 1748.

Benjamin Page deceast Sept ye 16, A. D 1746.

Prudence Page ye daughter of Jonathan Page, and of Mary his wife, deceast September ye 10th 1746.

Mary Page the wife of Jonathan Page, deceast July the ninteenth A. D. 1756 in the forty-ninth year of her age.

Unice Page the daughter of Jonathan Page and of Mary Page, deceas'd August the sixth A. D. 1756 and in the ninteenth year of her age.

Jonathan Page deceased February the 6th 1770.

Solomon Parce ye son of David Parce and Elizabath Parce, deceast June ye 20th 1740.

Lydai Parce the daughter of David Parce and of Elizabeth Parce, deceast September ye 3rd 1746.

David Parce of Lunenburg deceast September ye 19th 1746.

Amos Parce the son of Ephraim Parce and Esher Parce, deceast January (y^e) the 11th A. D. 1741/2.

Keziah Parce, the daughter of Ephraim Parce & of Esther his wife, deceast September the 18th 1746.

Benjamin Parce son of Ephraim Parce and of Esther his wife, deceased Decr 23^d 1757.

Ester Parce, wife of Deacon Ephraim Parce, deceased June 28th 1768.

Deaths.

POOLE. PEABODY. PAYSON.

Judith Pool the daughter of Samuel Pool & Prudence his wife, deceased August the 5th 1752.

Samvel Poole Jun the son of Samvel Poole, deceast May the 8th A. D. 1756, in the 13th year of his age.

Prudence Poole the wife of Mr. Samvel Poole, deceas'd April the sixth A. D. 1756 in 30 year of her age.

The widow. Dorrathy Peabody deceas'd at Lunenburg March ye 29th 1758.

Samuel Peabody son of Thomas Peabody & Ruth his wife, deceas'd Octor 1760.

Ruth Peabody the wife of Thomas Peabody, deceased June 15th 1766.

The Revd Mr. Samuel Payson deceased Feby 14th 1763.

R.
REED. RITTER. REDINGTON.

Rebecca Reed daughter of Samuel Reed and Mary his wife, deceased June ye 10th A. D. 1753.

Mary Ritter the daughter of Moses Ritter and of Hannah his wife, deceased May ye 3rd 1753.

Mr. Thomas Redington of Lunenburg, deceas'd August ye 10th A. D. 1755.

S.
STEARNS.

Sarah Stearns ye daughter of Thomas and Lydia Stearns, deceast August ye 31th 1746 in ye second year of her age.

Jonathan Stearns ye son and child of ye Rev. Mr. David Stearns, deceast November ye 12th 1747.

Mary Stearns the daughter of the Revd Mr. David Stearns and of Ruth his wife, deceased March 19th 1749.

Lucy Stearns the daughter of the Revd Mr. David Stearns and of Ruth his wife, deceas'd Febry 21th 1750.

The Revd Mr. David Stearns deceas'd March 9th 1761.

Mr. Benjamin Stearns deceas'd November 22d 1761.

Joseph Stearns the son of William Stearns and of Elizabeth his wife, deceased September the 25th 1754 aged one month and four days.

STEARNS. STILES. SPAFFORD. SMITH.

Mr. William Stearns son of Deacon William Stearns deceased October 28th 1783 at Worcester in the thirty-fifth year of his age.

Mrs. Elizabeth Stearns the wife of Deacon William Stearns, deceased February ye 25th 1784 in the sixty-third year of her age.

Mr. Jacob Stiles of Lunenburg, deceast April the twenty-first 1750.

Jonah Spaffard deceased November ye 17: A. D. 1755.

Sarah Smith deceased Novr 15th 1746.

W.
WETHERBEE. WYMAN. WARRIN. WOOD.

Elizabath Wetherbe wife of Ephraim Wetherbe dyed in Lunenburg June 17th 1732.

Capt. Ephraim Wetherbee died at Boston November ye 7th A. D. 1745.

Abigail Wyman the daughter of Ezekiel and of Abigail deceast May 30th 1741.

Ezekiel Wyman the son of Ezekiel Wyman & of Abigail his wife, dec'd December ye 6th 1761 & in ye 16th year of his age.

David Wyman ye son of John Wyman and of Rebekah his wife, deceast August ye 1th 1744.

John Wyman Jun dec'd in September 1759 in his Majesty's service up Mohawk River being about twenty years of age.

John Wyman deceas'd Septr 9th 1762.

Mary Warrin ye wife of Jacob Warrin of Lunenburg deceast, December ye 23rd 1745.

Sarah Wood the daughter of Jonathan Wood and of Sarah his wife, deceast July ye 23rd 1749.

Sarah Wood daughter of Jonathan Wood and Sarah his wife, deceas'd Septr 21st 1756.

Sarah Wood the wife of Jonathan Wood, deceas'd September 22d 1756.

Bezaleel Wood ye son of Jonathan Wood & of Sarah his wife, deceas'd July 9th 1758.

Jonathan Wood ye son of Jonathan & Sarah Wood, deceas'd October ye 9th 1758.

Joseph Wood Jun ye son of Joseph Wood and of Ruth his wife, deceas'd March ye 26th A. D. 1758.

INDEX

INDEX OF NAMES.

Abbit, see Abbott.
Abbott, 115.
——, Jonathan, Jr., 94, 100, 106, 122, 128, 266, 272.
——, Jonathan, 272.
——, Martha (J.), 266, 272.
——, Mary (Holt), 230, 266, 302, 346.
——, Nathan, 272.
——, William, 272.
Adam, see Adams.
Adams, Betsey, 239.
——, William, 223, 245.
——, Rev. Zabdiel, 216–219, 247.
Alexander, Elizabeth (W.), 272.
——, Franice, 272.
——, John, 272.
——, William, 177, 182, 223, 272; 272.
Allen, J. C., 264.
——, Jeremiah, 16, 20, 23, 56, 114.
——, Joseph, 15, 23, 56.
——, Lucie or Lucy (Smith), 239, 267.
Allien, see Allen.
Ames, John, 8, 9.
Amey, John, 15, 22.
——, Philip, 15.
Anger, 10.
——, Mrs., 33.
Ardeway, Amos, 223, 235.
Arno, Rebeckah (Brown), 224.
Arven, Abiah or Abiel (Larrabee), 234, 254.
Asten and Austen, see Austin.
Austin, Daniel, 36, 56, 66, 69, 72, 74, 79, 96, 106, 114, 126, 146, 149, 152, 153, 165, 168, 170, 179, 182, 184, 185, 188, 194, 195, 199, 271.
——, Daniel, Jr., 223, 271, 272.
——, Daniel, 271.
——, Hannah, 271.
——, John, 272.
——, Lydia (Crocker), 225, 271, 278.
——, Phebe (D. Jr.), 223, 271, 272.
——, Phebe [2], 271.
——, Priscilla (D.), and dau. do., 271.
——, Ruth, 271; 272.
——, Samuel, 56; 271.

Austin, Timothy [2], 271.
Austing, see Austin.

Bailey, Benjamin, 275.
——, Betty, 275.
——, Elezabath (Josiah), 275.
——, Elizabeth (Jackman), 232, 253, 275.
——, Elizabeth (Norcross), 235, 255.
——, Hannah, 275.
——, Isaac, 176, 183, 184, 224, 275; 275.
——, Jedediah, 203, 208.
——, John, 275.
——, John, Jr. [2], 275.
——, Joseph, 275, 276.
——, Josiah, 36, 56, 72, 80, 87, 88, 90, 91, 99, 103, 104, 107–109, 128, 137, 141, 147, 151–155, 163, 170, 171, 179, 183, 186, 224, 246, 275.
——, Josiah, Jr., 183, 225, 246, 275, 276.
——, Josiah, Tertius, 275.
——, Mary (I.), 275.
——, Mary (John, Jr.), 275.
——, Molly [3], 275.
——, Ruth (Carlton), 226, 247, 275, 278.
——, Ruth, 275; 276.
——, Samuel, 275.
——, Sarah (Josiah, Jr.), 225, 246, 275, 276.
——, Sarah, 275.
——, Thaddeus, 276.
Ball, 31.
——, Caleb, 246.
——, Jemima (Hodgskins), 232, 253.
——, Jonathan, 57.
——, Joseph, 15, 23, 56.
Ballard, Jeremiah, 92, 96, 99, 101, 102, 104.
——, Mary (Reed), 257, 319, 320, 349.
——, Phebe (Willard), 240, 260, 337.
Ballord, see Ballard.
Bancroft, Elizabeth (T.), 274, 342.
——, Elizabeth (Wyman), 241, 261, 331.

Bancroft, Jane (Whitney), 240, 260, 334.
——, John, 274.
——, Mary (Dea. T.), 224, 246, 274.
——, Molly, 274.
——, Dea. Timothy, 129, 131, 133, 148, 163, 178, 186, 191, 224, 246, 342.
——, Timothy [2], 274.
Barbrook, Thankful (W.) 224, 246.
——, William, 224, 246.
Barnard, Gov. Francis, 205.
——, Rev. John, 266.
Baron, see Barron.
Barron, Elias or Elles, 14, 22, 55, 57.
——, William, 224, 246.
Baylay, Bayle, Baylee, Bayley, see Bailey.
Beaman, Judith (Corey), 262.
——, see Beman.
Beeth, 67.
Bees, Walter, 15, 23, 29, 50, 56.
Bellows, 184.
——, Abegail, 276.
——, Abigail (Benj., Jr.), 245, 276, 342.
——, Abijah, 276, 342.
——, Benjamin, 87, 95, 342; 276.
——, Benjamin, Jr., 99, 103, 106-113, 116-118, 121-123, 125, 126, 128, 130, 131, 136, 138, 141-145, 147, 149, 153, 159, 170, 188, 195, 224, 245, 246, 276, 342.
——, Dorcas (B.), 342.
——, Johannah (Wetherbee), 260, 334.
——, John, 276.
——, Jonathan, 276, 342.
——, Joseph, 199, 225, 247, 276.
——, Lois, (Jos.), 225, 247.
——, Mary, (B., Esq.), 246.
——, Mary, (Gould), 249, 292.
——, Peter, 276.
Beman, Hannah (Jos.), 246.
——, Joseph, 246.
——, see Beaman.
Bemus, William, 224.
Benit, Damaris (Gibson), 230.
—— and Benith, see Bennett.
Benjamin, William, 197.
Bennett, Anne (Going), 229, 251.
——, Elizabeth (Jas.), 225, 246.
——, James, 225, 246.
——, Jonathan, 224, 246.
——, Mary (Jona.), 224, 246.
——, Samuel, 27, 29, 43, 44, 56.
Berry, Col. Thomas, 119, 120.
Bigelow, Benjamin, 186, 224, 246, 274, 342; 274.

Bigelow, Elisha, 224, 246.
——, Elizabeth (B.), 224, 246, 274.
——, Hannah, 274.
——, Love (B.), 274, 342.
——, Mary, 239.
——, Sarah (E.), 224, 246.
Biglow, see Bigelow.
Bignal, Mark, 29.
Bigsbee, Eunice, 232.
Blair, Mr., 151.
Blood, Johanna (Darlin), 226, 248, 285.
Blount, David, 15.
——, William, 15, 22, 55.
Blower, see Bowers.
Blunt, see Blount.
Bodwell, Ruth (Reddington), 237, 266.
Borman, 44, 46, 55.
Boutell, see Boutwell.
Boutwell, Kendall, 224, 263.
——, Mary (Kendall), 224, 263.
Bowers, Elizabeth (Shed), 238, 262, 323.
——, Elizabeth, 274.
——, Esther, 274.
——, Jerahmeel, 223, 245, 274, 342.
——, Miriam (J.), 223, 245, 274, 342.
——, Nehemiah, 223, 245, 274; 274.
——, Sarah (Platts), 236, 256.
——, Sarah (N.), 223, 245, 274.
——, Susannah, 274, 342.
Boyden, Lieut. Jonathan, 8, 9, 11, 15, 19, 23, 26, 56.
——, Josiah, 15.
Boynton, Abigail (Solomon), 274.
——, Anne (B.), 272, 273, 341.
——, Anne (Davis), 227, 248, 272.
——, Benoni, 37, 39, 40, 57, 341, 272, 273.
——, Benoni, Jr., 224, 246, 273, 264.
——, David, 273.
——, Dorcas (Frost, Holt), 231, 249, 272, 302, 346.
——, Eleazer, 67.
——, Elezebeth, 272.
——, Elizabeth (B., Jr.), 224, 246, 273, 341.
——, Elizabeth (Jona., Jr.), 273, 274.
——, Elizabeth (Shed), 239, 263, 323, 324.
——, Elizabeth (Stephen), 224, 246, 273, 341.
——, Elizabeth [2], 273, 341.
——, Hilkiah, 56, 64, 65, 72-75, 79, 81, 82, 84, 91, 106, 120-122, 124-126, 273.
——, Jane, 272; 273; (Goodridge), 229, 250, 291, 345.

Boynton, Jewet, 273.
—, Johannah (Grout), 249, 294.
—, Jonathan, 273, 274.
—, Jonathan, Jr., 225.
—, Joseph, 273, 341.
—, Lydia (Frost), 229.
—, Mary, 273; 272, 273, 341.
—, Mary (B.), 224, 264.
—, Mehittibel, 272.
—, Meribah, 232, 305, 306.
—, Priscilla (Page), 255, 317, 348.
—, Priscilla (Hilkiah), 273.
—, Ruth (Darlin), 226, 248, 273, 284, 344.
—, Samuel, 273.
—, Sarah (Stephen), 245, 273, 341.
—, Sarah (Whitney), 260, 273, 333.
—, Sarah, 272, 341.
—, Solomon, 274.
—, Solomon Learnard, 274.
—, Stephen, 94, 107, 124, 137, 176, 224, 245, 246, 272, 273, 341; 273.
—, Susannah, 273, 341.
—, William, 273.
Brabrook, see Barbrook.
Bradley, Elizabeth (Alexander), 223, 272.
Bradstreet, Abigail, 277; 277, 342.
—, Dorcas (Fowler), 229, 277.
—, Dorcas (S.), 276, 277, 342.
—, John, 276, 342.
—, Capt. Jonathan, 106, 110, 111, 113, 115, 117, 118, 120–122, 133, 136, 137, 140, 142, 146, 223, 342.
—, Jonathan, 223, 245.
—, Jonathan, Jr., 130, 150, 201, 211.
—, Mary, 277.
—, Olive, 277.
—, Phebe, 277.
—, Releif, 277.
—, Samuel, 180, 276, 277, 342; 277.
—, Sarah (Colburn), 225, 247, 280.
—, Sarah, 276.
—, Vashtai, 277.
Braudstreet, see Bradstreet.
Brewer, John, 56.
Bridge, Ebenezer, 225, 247.
—, John, 167.
—, Rev. Josiah, 193.
—, Mehitable (E.), 225, 247.
Brigham, George D., 264.
Broadstreet, see Bradstreet.
Brown, 197.
—, Aaron, 277, 342.
—, Abigail (Aaron), 277, 342.
—, Amos, 16, 23, 56.
—, David, 277.
—, Eliphelet, 223, 245.

Brown, Elizabeth (Burnam) 224, 246, 276.
—, Hepsibeth, 277.
—, Jonathan, 277, 342; 277.
—, Joseph, 224, 246.
—, Martha (Parker), 236, 256.
—, Mary (Gibson), 230.
—, Mary (Wheelock), 241, 261.
—, Rebeckah (Arno), 224.
—, Rebecca (Wallis), 240, 260.
—, Thomas, 113, 117, 118, 124, 127, 128, 130, 133, 137, 141, 149, 152, 168, 172.
—, Unite, 224.
Bull, Trumbull, 266.
Burbeen, James, 16, 24, 56, 67.
Burnam, Elisabeth (Nehemiah), 276.
—, Elizabeth (Nathaniel, Jr.), 224, 246, 276.
—, Eunice (Dorman), 226, 248.
—, John, 276.
—, Nathaniel, 180.
—, Nathaniel, Jr., 180, 224, 246, 276.
—, Nehemiah, 276.
—, Ruth, 276.
—, Thomas, 276.
Burnap, Joseph, 40.
Burnet, Gov. William, 63.
Burnham—see Burnam.
Burns, Sarah (French), 228.
—, Thomas, 225.
Burrill, John, 16, 23, 56.
Buss, Aaron, 277.
—, Eunice (John), 277, 342.
—, Eunice, 277.
—, John, 121, 137, 148, 156, 162, 165, 168, 169, 171, 200, 202, 207, 277, 342.
—, John, Jr., 225.
—, Jonathan, 277, 342.
—, Mellicent, 277.
—, Silas, 277.
—, Stephen, 277.
—, Zephaniah, 342.
Butler, Abigail, 276, 342.
—, Lucy (Willard), 240, 260.
—, Lucy (W.), 276, 342.
—, Lucy, 276.
—, Rachel, 276.
—, William, 276, 342.
Buttric, see Buttrick.
Buttrick, Francis or Franice, 130, 133, 150, 152, 223, 245, 274.
—, Francis, 274.
—, Hannah, 274.
—, John, 274.
—, Jonathan, 274.
—, Lucy, 274.
—, Mary (Boynton), 224, 264.

46

Buttrick, Mary (John), 274.

CALF or CALFE, John, 15, 22, 55, 57.
Calton—see Carleton.
Cambell, William, 226.
Cannada, William, 118; see Kennedy.
Capron, H., 265.
Carlile, Daniel, 278.
——, David, 104, 141, 278, 343; 278, 343.
——, Elizabeth, 343.
——, John, 278; 343.
——, Leatis (David), 278, 343.
——, Lettice (McCraken), 235, 255, 278.
Carlisle, see Carlile.
Carlton, 125, 183.
——, Abigail, 278, 243.
——, Abraham, 171, 176, 179, 190, 198, 203, 208, 278, 343.
——, Abram, 343.
——, Asa, 226, 247, 278; 278.
——, Betty, 278.
——, Calven, 278.
——, Jesse, 225, 266.
——, Luther, 278.
——, Mary (Abraham), 278, 343.
——, Mary, 278.
——, Nathaniel, Jr., 148, 154, 183, 186, 225, 247.
——, Nathaniel, 278.
——, Olive (Nathaniel, Jr.), 225, 247.
——, Ruth (Asa), 226, 247, 278.
——, Ruth, 278.
——, Sarah (J.), 225, 266.
——, Timothy, 278.
Carter, Beatrix, 281.
——, Betty (T.), 280, 281, 343.
——, David, 280.
——, Elias, 247.
——, Elijah, 226, 280.
——, James, 226, 247, 281.
——, Jerusha, 281.
——, John, 281.
——, Jonas, 281.
——, Keziah, 281.
——, Phinehas, 281.
——, Prudence, 280.
——, Ruth, 281.
——, Sarah (Bayley), 225, 246, 275, 276.
——, Sarah (Jas.), 226, 247, 281.
——, Thomas, 101, 114, 123, 126, 128, 137, 141, 152, 157, 162, 163, 168, 177, 180, 182, 183, 186, 188, 190, 196, 199, 202, 203, 207, 208, 211, 213, 280, 281, 343.
——, Thomas, Jr., 226, 280.
——, Vashti, 281, 343.
Cartter, see Carter.

Chadwick, 187.
——, Bette, 278.
——, Ebenezer, 15, 23, 56.
——, Eunice (W.), 225, 278.
——, Unice, 278.
——, William, 177, 180, 182, 186, 197, 203, 208, 225, 278.
Champney, Rev. Ebenezer, 209.
Chandler, Henry, Jr., 15, 22, 55, 56.
——, John, Jr., 71.
Chaplain, see Chaplin.
Chaplin, Anna, 279.
——, Betty (Martin), 235, 255, 278.
——, David, 130, 162, 163, 182, 278, 279; 279.
——, Joseph, 168, 186, 279; 226, 247, 278; 279.
——, Lois (J.), 226, 247, 303.
——, Mary (D.), 278, 279.
——, Mary, 279.
——, Mercy, 279.
——, Sarah (J.), 279.
——, Sarah, [2], 279.
Child, John, 22, 55, 57.
——, Jonathan, 14.
——, or Childers, Moses, 225, 247.
——, Sarah (M.), 225, 247.
Clark, 80.
——, Anne (J.), 247.
——, James, 247.
——, Mary (R.), 247, 280.
——, Mary, 280.
——, Robert, 247, 280.
——, Sarah, 280.
——, William, 16, 20, 23, 56, 114, 134; 280.
Coffen, Abigail, 280, 343.
——, Amme, 280.
——, Daniel, 280, 343.
——, Eliezer, 280.
——, Henery, 280.
——, Lydia (M.), 280, 343.
——, Lydia, 280.
——, Michael, 280, 343.
——, Priscilla, 280.
Colbern, Colbourn, see Colburn.
Colburn, Lt. James, 56, 64, 65, 68, 69, 72, 79, 80, 81, 83, 85, 87, 91, 93, 94, 96, 97, 99, 104, 107, 112, 280.
——, James, Jr., 225, 247, 280; 280.
——, Ruth (J.), 280.
——, Ruth, 280.
——, Sarah (Farley), 229, 280.
——, Sarah (J., Jr.), 225, 247, 280.
——, Sarah (Willard), 337.
——, Sarah, 280.
——, Thomas, 280, 342.
Colman, Elizabeth (Bigelow), 224, 246, 274.

Colman, James, 133.
—, Rachael (Harper), 231.
Commings, Jonathan, 279.
Coming, Comings, Commius, Commings, see Cummings.
Conant, Hannah (Dodge), 227, 248.
—, Jonathan, 226.
—, Mary (Fuller), 228, 249, 288.
Connant, see Conant.
Converse, Robert, 38.
Cooledge, Mary (Johnson), 262.
Coory, see Cory.
Corcker, see Crocker.
Corey or Cory, Benjamin, 56, 66, 67, 69, 73, 91, 262, 279, 343.
—, Benjamin, Jr., 225, 247, 279.
—, Beulah (B., Jr.), 225, 247, 279.
—, Eunice, 279.
—, Jacob, Jr., 225.
—, Judith (B.), 262.
—, Mary, 279.
—, Rebekah, 279, 343.
—, Rebekah (B.), 279, 343.
—, Sarah, 279.
Cotton, Rev. John, 267.
—, Tm. Jno., 205.
Cowdin, Mary (T., Jr.), 226.
—, Mary (W.), 225, 247.
—, Thomas, Jr., 226.
—, William, 225, 247.
Crawford, Elizabeth (R.), 226, 263.
—, Robert, 226, 263.
Crocker, 135.
—, Johannah (Fletcher), 228, 233, 264.
—, Lydia (P.), 225, 271, 278.
—, Mary, 278.
—, Paul, 163, 177, 180, 183, 225, 247.
Crosby, Charles, 265.
Cummings, Miriam, 279, 343.
—, Samuel, 84, 99, 101, 106, 117, 123, 124, 148, 156, 168, 176, 196, 200, 203, 208, 279, 343.
—, Samuel, Jr., 279, 343.
—, Sarah (S.), 279, 343.
—, Sarah, 279.
—, Thaddeus, 279, 343; 279.
—, Thomas, 279, 343.
Cushing, John, 263.

DANA, Rev. Samuel, 202, 264.
Danforth, Hannah (Farnsworth), 229.
Darlin, see Darling.
Darling, Amity, 284.
—, Benjamin, 285.
—, Daniel, 285.
—, David, 285.
—, Johanna (T.), 226, 248, 285.

Darling, John, Jr., 130, 137, 168, 189, 203, 208, 226, 248, 284, 344.
—, John, 285; 284, 344.
—, Juet Boynton, 284.
—, Lois, 284.
—, Ruth (John, Jr.), 226, 248, 273, 284, 344.
—, Ruth, 284.
—, Timothy, 226, 248, 285; 285.
—, Unity, 284.
Darrah, Arthur, 226, 248.
Dascomb or Dascombe, Elizabeth (Jas.), 227, 266, 285.
—, Jacob, 285.
—, James, 193, 197, 227, 266, 285.
—, Sarah, 285.
Davies, see Davis.
Davis, Anne (Jacob), 248, 272.
—, Anne (O.), 227.
—, Daniel, 14, 22, 55, 57.
—, Elizabeth (Farnsworth), 228.
—, Elizabeth (Joseph), 227, 248, 287.
—, Jacob, 248.
—, Joseph, 227, 248, 285.
—, Mathew, 163.
—, Rev. Nathan, 214–216.
—, Oliver, 227.
—, Rebekah (S.), 226.
—, Samuel, 72, 73, 84, 88, 92, 117, 124, 128, 131, 133, 141, 152, 167, 168, 180, 181, 190, 196, 203, 208, 226, 285, 344.
—, Samuel, Jr., 285, 344.
—, Sarah (S.), 285, 344.
—, Sarah, 285, 344.
—, Submit (Stearns), 238, 259, 325.
Day, Richard, 226, 248.
—, Ruth (R.), 226, 248.
—, Solomon, 227.
Demary, Anne, 281.
—, Hannah, 281.
—, John, 178, 191, 281; 281.
—, Rebecah, 281.
—, Rebekah (J.), 281.
—, Sarah, 281.
—, Thomas, 281.
Descomb, see Dascomb.
Dike, Mary (N.), 226, 248, 303.
—, Nicholas, 141, 148, 226, 248.
Divel, see Divol.
Divol, Abigail (P.), 227, 248.
—, Elizabeth, 284.
—, John, 90, 96, 99, 106, 109, 126, 226, 248, 284, 344.
—, Josiah, 284.
—, Keziah, 284.
—, Levi, 284.
—, Manassah, 284.
—, Manasseh, 284.

Divol, Phebe (John), 284.
——, Phebe, 284.
——, Phinehas, 227, 248.
——, Sarah (Gillson), 229, 250, 292.
——, Sarah (J.), 284, 344.
——, Sarah (M.), 284.
——, Susannah (John), 226, 248, 328.
——, Susanna, 284.
——, Susannah, 284.
Dix, Rev. Samuel, 202.
Dodge, Abigail (E.), 283.
——, Abigail (T.), 227.
——, Abigail, 235; 283.
——, Asahel, 282.
——, Barzillai, 282.
——, Brewer, 282.
——, Benjamin, 282.
——, Eli [2], 283.
——, Elizabeth (W.), 227, 248.
——, Elizabeth, 282.
——, Esther, 283, 344.
——, Eunice, 283.
——, Hannah (Josiah, Jr.), 227, 248.
——, Hannah, 283.
——, Hepsibath, 282.
——, Isaac, 283.
——, Jemima, 282.
——, Jesse, 282.
——, John Perkins, 283.
——, John Smith, 283.
——, Joseph, 84, 104.
——, Lt. Josiah, 121, 124, 127, 128, 130, 132, 133, 138-141, 143-145, 148, 150, 152, 154, 156, 159-161, 165, 175-177, 185, 186, 190, 198, 199, 281.
——, Josiah, Jr., 141, 162, 163, 173, 176, 186, 227, 248, 282.
——, Kerenhappuch, 282.
——, Keziah, 282.
——, Levi, 282.
——, Lipha (Hubbard), 231, 252, 281.
——, Margaret (N.), 281, 344.
——, Margaret, 237; 281.
——, Martha (Z.), and dau. do., 282.
——, Mary, 282.
——, Miriam, 281; 344.
——, Noah, 64-66, 96, 126, 148, 177, 187, 188, 281, 344.
——, Noah, Jr., 227.
——, Phebe, 282.
——, Prudence, 283.
——, Rebakah, 283.
——, Reuben, 157, 158, 168, 282, 283, 344.
——, Rhoda, 281.
——, Ruth (R.), 282, 283, 344.
——, Ruth, 283.
——, Sarah (Paree), 235, 314, 315, 256.

Dodge, Sarah (Seth), 227, 283.
——, Sarah, 282; [2] 283.
——, Seth, 227, 283.
——, Sewall, 282.
——, Susanah (Josiah), 281.
——, Susanna (Josiah, Jr.), 282.
——, Tabatha, 282.
——, Tabitha (Hartwell), 230, 252, 298, 345.
——, Tabitha, 283.
——, Thankful, 231, 252, 281.
——, Thomas, 227.
——, William, 227, 248.
——, Zadok, 283.
——, Zebulon, 163, 183, 282.
Dorman, Timothy, 226, 248.
Downe, Col., 128.
——, Elizabeth, 285.
——, Joseph, 227.
——, Margaret (W.), 285, 344.
——, Margaret, 285.
——, Martha (Joseph), 227, 333.
——, Samuel, 285.
——, Sarah, 285, 344.
——, William, 152, 156, 159-167, 175, 246, 248, 250, 252, 255, 256, 258, 259, 261, 285, 344.
Dows, Judge Jonathan, 16, 23, 56, 105.
Dudley, William, 63.
Dunsmore, 126; see Dunsmoor.
Dunsmoor, Ebenezer, 286.
——, Hannah, 286.
——, Dr. John, 146, 226, 285, 286.
——, John, Jr., 227, 285.
——, Mary (J., Jr), 227.
——, Phinehas, 285.
——, Rebekah, 285.
——, Ruth (Dr. J.), 226, 285, 286.
——, Ruth, 285.
Dupee, 125.
Dutton, Elizabeth, 283.
——, Ephraim [2], 284.
——, Hannah, 283.
——, Jerusha, 284.
——, John, 284.
——, Joseph Fitch, 284.
——, Mary (Hodgkins), 231, 252.
——, Sarah (S.), 227, 248, 333.
——, Sarah (T.), 227, 248, 284.
——, Sibel, 283.
——, Silas, 227, 248.
——, Susannah, 284.
——, Thankful (Barbrook), 224, 246.
——, Thankful (E.), 284.
——, Thomas, 152, 153, 172, 187, 190, 227, 248, 283, 284; 283.

EATON, 187.
——, Anna (P.), 286.

Eaton, Anne, 286.
——, Benjamin, 286.
——, Calven, 286.
——, Ebeneazer, 286.
——, John, 286.
——, Joseph, 167; 286.
——, Pearson, Peirson or Person, 181, 286; 286.
——, Rebekah, 286.
——, Sarah, 286.
——, William, 286.
Edes, Richard S., 262.
Edmunds, Mr., 41.
Edwards, B., 267.
Ellit, Ann (Fleming), 249.
Emerson, Edward, 14, 22, 55, 57.
——, Rev. Joseph, 202, 265.
Endecott, John, 227.
——, Martha (J.), 227.
Erven, see Arven.
Estey, Richard, 56.

FAIRBANK, Jabez, 23.
Farewell, see Farwell.
Farley, Sarah (T.), 229, 280.
——, Timothy, 229.
Farmer, Daniel, 264.
——, Elizabeth (D.), 264.
——, Hannah (J.), 344.
——, John, 84, 286, 287, 344.
——, Rachel, 287.
——, Rebekah (John), 286, 287, 344.
——, Rebekah, 286, 344; 287.
——, Ruth (W.), 228.
——, William, 228.
Farnworth, see Farnsworth.
Farnsworth, Elizabeth (T.), 228.
——, Hannah (Jos., Jr.), 229.
——, Eunice (Stephen), 228, 249.
——, Isaac, 37, 40, 57, 61–78, 80–91, 93–97, 286; 286.
——, Ensign John, 8–11.
——, Joseph, Jr., 229.
——, Lydia, 286.
——, Mary, 286.
——, Samuel, 27, 56, 57, 80.
——, Sarah (I.), 286.
——, Sarah, 286.
——, Stephen, 228, 249.
——, Thomas, 228.
——, William, 286.
Farrington, Elizabeth (Dascomb), 227, 266, 285.
——, Mary (Cowdin), 226.
Farwell, Abigail (O.), 249.
——, Anna (Snow), 259.
——, Elizabeth (Gary), 229, 250, 294.
——, Eunice (Conant), 226.
——, Jane (Kimball), 233, 254.
——, John, 228; 229.

Farwell, Olive (Carlton), 225, 247.
——, Oliver, 249.
——, Polly, 232.
——, Sarah (J.), 229.
——, Sibel, 235.
——, Sibil (Wright), 241, 261.
——, Susanah (J.), 228.
Fisher, Ruth (Dunsmoor), 226, 285, 286.
Fisk, Jemima (Jonathan), 249, 289.
——, Jemima, 289.
——, John, 52, 57, 64, 88, 118, 122, 123, 126, 197.
——, Jonathan, 249, 289.
——, Rev. Mr., 209.
——, Sarah (Osbourn), 235, 255, 312.
Fitch, Catherine (Cambell), 226, 287.
——, Elizabeth (John), 228, 249, 287, 314.
——, Jacob, 287.
——, John, 94, 99, 122, 152, 157, 158, 168, 169, 171, 187, 197, 228, 249, 287, 344.
——, John, Jr., 287.
——, Molly, 287.
——, Paul, 287.
——, Sarah (Dutton), 227, 248, 284.
——, Sarah, 287.
——, Susannah (John), 287, 344.
——, Susanna, 287.
Flagg, Maj. Eleazer, 16, 23, 56.
——, William, 197.
Flecher, Mrs. Abigail, 223.
Fleming, Andrew, 92, 95, 125, 249.
——, Ann (A.), 249.
Fletcher, Johannah (Jones), 228.
——, John, 14, 21, 55, 57.
——, Jonas, 228, 264.
——, Robert, 228.
——, Sarah (Lane), 234, 254.
——, see Flecher.
Flood, Alice, 289.
——, Benjamin, 289, 344.
——, Elizabeth, (B.), 289, 344.
Forster, Forstor, see Foster.
Fosket, Abigail (J., Jr.), 228, 262, 307.
——, John, Jr., 228, 262.
Foss, Molley, 236.
Foster, Abigail (Brown), 224, 246, 287.
——, Abigail, 241.
——, Dea. Benjamin, 73, 96, 99, 125, 133, 137, 164, 182, 183, 185, 188–191, 194, 197, 199, 206, 214, 216, 217, 219, 228, 267, 287, 344, 345.
——, Benj., Jr., 228, 249, 287, 344.
——, Benjamin, 288.
——, Dorothy (Peabody), 256, 287.
——, Elizabeth (Davis), 227, 248, 287.

Foster, Elizabeth (Moors), 234, 311.
—, Enoch, 288; 287, 344.
—, Isaac, 153, 228, 249, 288; 288.
—, James, 287, 345; 288.
—, Jane (Heywood), 231, 252.
—, Jemima (Fisk), 249, 289.
—, Joseph, 228, 249, 288, 287.
—, Keziah, 225; 288.
—, Lucy (B., Jr.), 228, 249, 326.
—, Lucy (Swan), 238, 258.
—, Mary (I.), 228, 249, 288.
—, Mary, 288.
—, Mehetabel (B.), 287, 344, 345.
—, Mehetabel, 287.
—, Nathan, 287, 345.
—, Rebeckah, 288.
—, Richard, 288.
—, Sarah (Dea. B.), 228, 267.
—, Sarah (Carlton), 225, 266.
—, Sarah (Goodridge), 229, 250.
—, Sarah (Gould), 230 251.
—, Sarah (Joseph), 228, 249, 288, 307.
—, Sarah, 287.
—, Stephen, 228, 287.
Fowler, 123.
—, Dorcas (E.), 229, 277.
—, Elizabeth, 289.
—, Ezekiel, 229, 289.
—, Joshua Chever, 289.
—, Richard, 168, 228, 249, 289; 289.
—, Ruth (R.), 228, 249, 289.
—, Ruth, 289.
—, Sarah Chever, 289.
—, Susanna, 289.
Freeman, Anne (Clark), 247.
—, Margaret (Wilson), 261.
French, Joseph, 228.
—, Sarah (J.), 228.
Frost, Dorcas (Spafford), 238, 258, 322.
—, Dorcas (Thos.), 231, 249, 272, 302, 346; see Holt, Dorcas.
—, Edmond, 229.
—, Hannah, 344.
—, Lydia (E.), 229.
—, Thomas, 249.
Fullam, Eben, 229.
—, Francis, 7, 9–12, 16–21, 24–39, 41–43, 57.
—, Jacob, 14, 22, 29, 55, 57.
—, Nabby (E.), 229.
Fuller, 125.
—, Abigail (Joseph), 288.
—, Abigail, 288.
—, Azeriah, 288.
—, Elizabeth (Bennett), 225, 246.
—, Elizabeth, 288.
—, James, 288.

Fuller, John, 183, 186, 228, 249, 288, 345; 288, 345; 288.
—, Joseph, 99, 101, 106, 110, 113–115, 118, 121, 123, 124, 126–128, 130, 133, 137, 148, 152, 153, 168, 172, 288; 288.
—, Lois (M.), 228, 249.
—, Mary (N.), 228, 249, 288.
—, Mary (Hart), 288, 231, 252, 299.
—, Micah or Michael, 228, 249.
—, Nehemiah, 182, 186, 228, 249, 288; 288.
—, Prudence (John), 228, 249, 288, 292, 345.
—, Prudence, 288.
—, Stephen, 288.

Gardner, Rev. Andrew, 57, 61, 62, 68–71, 75, 76, 78, 83, 250, 255, 260, 294.
—, Andrew, 294.
—, Rev. Francis, 202.
—, Francis, 230, 251.
—, Sarah (F.), 230, 251.
—, Susanna (Rev. A.), 294.
—, Susanna, 294.
Garey, see Gary.
Gary, Abigail (Walker), 240, 335, 336.
—, Benjamin, 125, 128–131, 162, 165, 172, 186; 294.
—, Edward, 197, 203, 208, 294; 294.
—, Elizabeth (T.), 229, 250, 294.
—, Elizabeth, 294.
—, John, 294.
—, Mary, 294.
—, Phebe (E.), 294.
—, Phebe, 294.
—, Sarah (Wood), 241, 260, 332, 350.
—, Thomas, 229, 250, 294.
Gates, Anna (S.), 230, 251.
—, Elizabeth (J.), 230, 251.
—, Jacob, 230, 251.
—, Silas, 230, 251.
Gearfield, Rebekah (T.), 229, 250, 306.
—, Thomas, 229, 250.
Genison, Abigail (Hubburd), 251, 301.
Gibs, Abigail (E.), 250.
—, Elisha, 250.
Gibson, Abraham, 230, 293; 294.
—, Arrington, 127, 141, 157, 162, 170, 293.
—, Damaris (Silas), 230.
—, David, 293.
—, Elizabeth (John), 250, 293.
—, Elizabeth (Gates), 230, 251.

Index. 363

Gibson, Ephraim, 230.
——, Isaac, 133, 135, 137, 141, 153, 156, 163, 167–169, 172, 173, 177, 181, 183, 187, 190, 203, 208, 229, 250, 293, 294; 293.
——, Jacob, 293.
——, Capt. John, 91, 104, 106, 109, 110, 113, 122, 130, 133–136, 140, 145, 147, 152, 153, 156, 159, 161, 162, 165, 171, 175, 178, 179, 190, 250, 293.
——, John, 293.
——, Jonathan, 293.
——, Keziah (Isaac), 229, 250, 293, 294, 306.
——, Keziah, 294.
——, Lois (R.), 229, 265.
——, Mary (Abraham), 230.
——, Mary (Arrington), 293.
——, Nathaniel, 293.
——, Reuben, 135, 153, 157, 163, 171, 173, 176, 187, 191, 197, 203, 208, 229, 265.
——, Samuel, 293.
——, Sarah (Gardner), 230, 251, 293.
——, Silas, 230, 293.
——, Solomon, 294.
——, Timothy, 27, 56, 57.
Gilchrest, Elizabeth (W.), 229, 250.
——, William, 152, 180, 193, 196, 198, 200, 201, 206, 229, 250.
Gillson, see Gilson.
Gilson, Esther (Joseph), 230.
——, Eunice (Hazeltine), 230, 252, 292, 299, 300.
——, Hannah (Buttrick), 223, 245, 274.
——, Hannah (Jonas), 292.
——, Jonas, 15, 29, 57, 66, 69, 84, 96, 103, 292; 229, 250, 292.
——, Ensign Joseph, 15, 23, 56, 79.
——, Joseph, 230, 292.
——, Prudence (Fuller), 228, 249, 288, 292, 345.
——, Sarah (Carter), 226, 247, 281.
——, Sarah (Jonas), 229, 250, 292.
——, Sarah, 292.
——, Unice, 292.
Gipson, 67; see Gibson.
Going, 159.
——, Anna, 295.
——, Anna or Anne (Jona.), 229, 251, 295.
——, Asahel, 295.
——, Benjamin, 295.
——, Ebenezer, 152.
——, Eliab, 295.
——, Elizabeth (Boynton), 224, 246, 273, 341.
——, Hannah (Jona.), 295.

Going, Hannah, 295.
——, James, 295.
——, John Kendel, 295.
——, Jonathan, 229, 251, 295; 295.
——, Mary (Bennet), 224, 246.
——, Thomas, 295.
Gold, see Gould.
Goodhue, 184.
Goodridge, 67.
——, Abel, 291.
——, Abigail, 291.
——, Abigal, 290.
——, Abijah, 290.
——, Asaph, 290.
——, Benjamin, 56, 68, 72, 77–79, 82–86, 88, 90, 91, 93, 95–124, 126–133, 135–140, 142–147, 149–152, 154–156, 160–162, 167, 171, 172, 175–182, 184, 185, 189, 191, 193, 194, 198, 199, 202, 207, 210, 211, 213–217, 219, 248, 251, 253, 261, 289.
——, Benjamin, Jr., 289.
——, Daniel, 289.
——, David, 113, 127, 128, 130, 133, 137, 140, 141, 142, 148, 149, 157, 166, 171, 173, 174, 177, 179, 182, 197, 203, 208, 264, 290, 345; 290? 290, 345.
——, Dorothy (Gould), 250, 292, 293.
——, Ebenezer, 290.
——, Eliphalet, 230, 251, 289, 291; 291.
——, Elizabeth (D.), 264, 290, 345.
——, Elizabeth, 290; 291.
——, Elizebath, 291.
——, Eunice, 290.
——, Ezekiel, 172, 203, 208, 291; 291.
——, Hannah, 290.
——, Jane (Carter), 226.
——, Jane (Philip), 229, 250, 272, 273, 291, 345.
——, Jane, 291.
——, John, 57; 290.
——, Joseph, 150, 229, 250; 291.
——, Joshua, 66, 80, 91, 99, 111, 113, 116, 118, 121, 125, 126, 150, 161, 163, 200, 203, 208, 250, 290, 345; 290.
——, Juet, 291.
——, Kathrine, 290.
——, Lois, 289; 290.
——, Lucy, 289.
——, Lydia (Joshua), 250, 290, 345.
——, Lydia, 290.
——, Mary, 291.
——, Widow Mehetabel, 345.
——, Mehetabel, [2], 290.
——, Olive, 289.

Goodridge, Oliver, 289.
—, Philip, 15, 22, 55, 128, 130, 133, 136, 137, 141, 144, 148, 150–152, 156, 157, 163, 172, 173, 176, 180, 181, 183, 189, 190, 196, 198, 203, 208, 229, 250, 291, 345; 291.
—, Lt. Phillip, 345.
—, Phinehas, 290.
—, Priscila, 291.
—, Rebacca (Ezekiel), 291.
—, Rebekah (Eliphalet), 230, 251, 291, 327.
—, Rebekah, 291.
—, Relief, 290, 345.
—, Ruth, 290.
—, Samuel Payson, 291.
—, Sarah (B.), 289.
—, Sarah (Bigelow), 224, 246, 289.
—, Sarah (Joseph), 229, 250.
—, Sarah [2], 291.
—, Sewall, 289.
—, Sibil, 291, 345.
—, Simon, 291.
—, William, 291.
Goold, see Gould.
Gordon, James, 150.
Goss, Eunice (Chadwick), 225, 278.
—, Rev. Thomas, 262.
Gould, Abigail (D.), 292.
—, Abigill, 292.
—, Amos, 293, 345.
—, Benjamin, 106, 118, 250, 293; 292.
—, Benjamin, Jr., 230, 251, 293.
—, David, 56, 66, 292.
—, Deborah (Page), 267, 316, 348.
—, Dorothy (Jacob), 250, 292, 293.
—, Dorrothy, 293.
—, Elijah, 293.
—, Esther (Benj.), 250, 293, 313, 345; (Hammond), 231, 252.
—, Lt., Capt. Jacob, 66, 82, 84, 96, 97, 102, 106, 110, 118, 121, 122, 124, 125, 127, 128, 131, 133, 137, 147–149, 153, 155, 157, 159, 163, 165, 170, 171, 173, 175, 176, 179, 183, 186, 188, 190, 194, 195, 250, 292, 293.
—, Jacob, 292.
—, James, 15, 23, 56.
—, Jonathan, 80, 292; 292.
—, Joseph, 292.
—, Lucy, 293.
—, Lydia (Jona.), 292.
—, Lydia, 292.
—, Margarate, 292.
—, Mary (M.), 249, 292.
—, Mary (O.), 264, 293.
—, Mary (Tarball), 239, 259, 292, 329.

Gould, Mary, 293.
—, Mercy (Page), 255, 317, 318, 348.
—, Mercy (Taylor), 239, 259, 292, 329.
—, Moses, 57, 159, 249, 292; 292.
—, Nemiah, 292.
—, Oliver, 190, 203, 208, 264, 292, 293; 293.
—, Rebekah, 292.
—, Sarah (Benj., Jr.), 230, 251.
—, Sarah (Sanderson), 259, 292.
—, Sarah, 293.
—, Solomon, 292.
—, Thomas, 293.
Gowen, Gowin, see Going.
Green, Eleazer, 12, 14, 22, 55, 57.
Greenwood, Thomas, 267.
Gridridge, Eunice (J.), 264.
—, John, 264.
Griffin, John, 124, 141, 152, 168.
Grimes, Mary (W.), 250.
—, William, 250.
Grout, Abigail, 294.
—, Elijah, 190, 196, 203, 208, 229, 250, 294; 295.
—, Endymia, 295, 345.
—, Hilkiah, 294.
—, Jehosaphat, 294.
—, Joel, 294.
—, Johannah (John), 249, 294.
—, Johannah (Parker), 236, 256, 294, 312, 313.
—, John, 57, 65, 66, 69, 79, 80, 83–85, 88, 95–97, 99, 102, 106, 111, 113, 116–122, 124, 125, 127–129, 133, 134, 136, 137, 139, 140, 144, 147, 150, 156, 160, 163, 249, 294.
—, John, Jr., 229, 250, 294, 295, 345.
—, John Butler, 295.
—, Jonathan, 294.
—, Josiah, 294.
—, Mary (Elijah), 229, 250, 336.
—, Patience (Judevine), 233, 253, 294.
—, Peter, 294.
—, Phebe (John, Jr.), 229, 250, 294, 295, 345.
—, Phebe, 294.
—, Sarah (Stockwell), 259, 294.
—, Solomon, 294.
—, Susannah, 295.
—, Theodore, 295.
Gutrog, Mr., 46.

HAGAR, Nathan, 262.
Hale, Joshua, 15.
—, Samuel, 20.
—, Thomas, 15, 22, 57,

Hall, Thomas, 55; see Hale.
Hammon, Anna (S.), 295, 296.
——, Anna, 296.
——, Avis, 295.
——, Phinehas, 296.
——, Samuel, 295, 296; 296.
Hammond, Abigail (Jona.), 230, 251, 295.
——, Anna (Gates), 230, 251.
——, Esther (Jos.), 231, 250, 252, 293, 313, 345.
——, Jonathan, 230, 251, 295.
——, Joseph, 231, 252.
——, Mary, 295.
——, Samuel, 162, 172.
——, Susannah, 295.
Harice, Alice, 234; see Harris.
Harkness, Elizabeth, 225.
——, Mary (Smith), 238, 258.
——, Thomas, 104.
Harper, Daniel, 231.
——, Mary (Henery), 231, 252.
——, Rachael (Daniel), 231.
Harres, see Harris.
Harriman, Mary (Bancroft), 224, 246, 274.
Harrington, Ammi, 300.
——, Thaddeus, 231, 252, 300.
——, Thankful (T.), 231, 252, 281, 300.
——, Rev. Timothy, 202, 259, 262.
Harris, 67.
——, Justice, 126, 132, 158, 183.
——, Nathaniel, 14, 21, 55, 57, 154, 170.
——, Roberd, 14, 22, 55, 57.
——, Thankfull, 237.
——, Timothy, 14, 20, 22, 55, 57.
——, see Harice.
Harriss, see Harris.
Hart, Abigail, 299.
——, Ebenezer, 231, 253; 299.
——, Elizabeth, 299.
——, Mary (Saml.), 231, 252, 288, 299.
——, Mary, 299.
——, Nathaniel, 299.
——, Phebe (Hartwell), 231, 298, 299.
——, Samuel, 231, 252, 299.
——, Samuel, Jr., 299.
——, Sarah (Ebenezer), 231, 253, 318.
——, Tabitha (Stedman), 238, 259.
Hartwell, 127.
——, Abijah, 298.
——, Asahel, 128, 133, 136, 155, 156, 163, 167, 171-173, 176, 179, 180, 182, 190, 196.
——, Asahel, 297.
——, Benjamin, 297; 298.

Hartwell, Edward, Lt., Capt., Maj., Justice, 16, 23, 34, 37-39, 56, 57, 62-70, 72, 73, 76, 77, 83-90, 94-99, 103, 104, 106, 108, 110, 111, 115, 117, 119, 122-124, 127, 128, 131, 137, 138, 143-146, 151, 160, 161, 169, 173, 175, 177, 180, 192, 193, 214, 246-248, 250-257, 259, 261, 297, 345.
——, Edward, Jr., 133, 171, 179, 251, 297, 298, 345.
——, Edward, 297.
——, Elisabeth, 298.
——, Elizabath, 297.
——, Elizabeth (E., Jr.), 251, 297, 298, 345.
——, Elizabeth (Gibson), 250, 293.
——, Elizabeth (Jona.), 230, 251, 298.
——, Ephraim, 298.
——, Esther, 298.
——, Eunice, 298.
——, Isaac, 15, 56.
——, Jacob, 299.
——, John, 232, 299.
——, John, 297.
——, Jonathan, 14, 22, 55, 57, 130, 157, 168, 173, 185, 186, 189, 230, 251, 298; 298.
——, Joseph, 189, 230, 231, 252, 297-299, 345; 298.
——, Josiah, 298.
——, Katharine, 299.
——, Lucy, 298.
——, Lydia, 298.
——, Martha, 297.
——, Mary (P.), 231, 252, 298, 313.
——, Mary, 297; 297, 345.
——, Molly, 298.
——, Phebe (Joseph), 231, 298, 299.
——, Phinehas, 182, 231, 252, 297, 298.
——, Prudence, 298.
——, Reuben, 298.
——, Ruth, 298.
——, Samuel, 15, 23, 56; 297.
——, Sarah (Edward), 297, 345.
——, Sarah, 298.
——, Solomon, 297, 345; 297.
——, Susanna, 298.
——, Tabitha (Joseph), 230, 252, 298, 345.
——, Tabitha, 299.
——, Tamar, 298.
——, Thomas, 297.
——, William, 298.
Harwood, Constable, 107.
——, Eliphelett, 301.
——, Elizabeth, 301.
——, Hannah (N.), 301.
——, Hannah, 301.

Harwood, James, 301.
—, Lucy, 301.
—, Mary, 301.
—, Nathaniel, 15, 23, 66, 73, 84, 91, 97, 110, 114, 115, 117, 124, 125, 131, 132, 142, 301; 301.
—, Peter, 15, 23, 56.
—, Sarah, 301.
Haskell, Ruth (Page), 235, 266, 317.
Hastings, Abigail (Hammond), 230, 251.
—, Caleb, 303.
—, David, 303.
—, Elizabeth, 304.
—, Esther, 304.
—, Eunice (Farnworth), 228, 249.
—, Eunice, 304.
—, John, 15, 23, 56, 303; 303.
—, John, Jr., 101.
—, Jonathan, 304.
—, Lois (Chaplain), 226, 247, 303.
—, Lois (N.), 251, 303, 304.
—, Mary (Dike), 226, 248, 303.
—, Nathaniel, 195, 251, 303, 304; 303.
—, Nicholas, 304.
—, Samuel, 304.
—, Sarah (John), 303.
—, Sarah, 237.
—, Susannah, 304.
Haward and Haywood, see Heywood.
Hazeltine, 125.
—, Abraham, 300.
—, Amos, 152, 186, 190, 196, 230, 252, 299, 300; 299.
—, David, 300.
—, Ebenezer, 300.
—, Ephraim, 300.
—, Eunice (Amos), 230, 252, 292, 299, 300.
—, Eunice, 300.
—, John, 300.
—, Jonas, 299.
—, Joseph, 300.
—, Richard, 300.
—, Thomas, 299.
—, William, 299.
Hazen, Samuel, 232.
Heartwell, see Hartwell.
Heborn, Elizabeth (Matthews), 234, 255.
Henderson, Bethsheba (Thos.), 231, 252.
—, David, 301.
—, Henry, 301.
—, James, 301.
—, Jane (John), 231, 252, 301.
—, Jane, 301.
—, John, 231, 252, 301; 301, 346.

Henderson, Sarah (Wm.), 263, 301, 346.
—, Sarah, 301.
—, Thomas, 231, 252; 301.
—, William, 158, 159, 263, 301, 346; 301.
Henery, see Henry.
Henry, Elizabeth (G.), 230, 251, 303.
—, George, 203, 208, 230, 251, 303.
—, Mary (Cowdin), 225, 247.
—, Mary (Wm., Jr.), 231, 252.
—, Mary, 303.
—, William, 149, 203, 208; 303.
—, William, Jr., 231, 252.
Hereman, John, 172.
Heseltine, see Hazeltine.
Hewett, George, 232, 253.
—, Triphena (G.), 232, 253.
Heywood, Abigail, 305, 346.
—, Elizabeth, 240, 304.
—, Esther (N.), 304, 345, 346.
—, Esther, 304, 345.
—, Jane (Z.), 231, 252.
—, Dea. John, 56, 62, 66, 67, 72, 76, 79, 87, 90, 91, 96, 97, 99, 102, 103, 105, 108, 113, 115, 116, 118, 128, 129, 133, 136, 143-146, 151, 152, 156, 162-164, 166, 167, 171, 179, 180, 184, 185, 188, 189, 191-194, 202, 204, 207, 209-211, 213, 215-219, 232, 304, 305, 346.
—, Lucy, 305, 346.
—, Mary, 304, 346.
—, Nathan, 14, 22, 55, 57, 64, 65, 67, 69, 74, 77, 79, 87, 89, 94, 96, 97, 105, 120-122, 125, 129, 141, 144, 147, 150, 151, 153, 155, 160, 175, 177, 193, 195, 219, 304, 345, 346.
—, Petter, see Harwood, Peter.
—, Prudence, 305, 346.
—, Relief, 304, 346.
—, Ruth (John), 304, 305, 346.
—, Ruth, 304, 346.
—, Ruth (Kidder), 233, 254, 305.
—, Sarah (Stearns), 237, 258, 304.
—, Silence (John), 232.
—, Silent, 304.
—, Thomas, 179, 231, 304.
—, William, 304.
—, Willis, 304, 346.
—, Zimri, 231, 252, 304.
Hill, David, 305.
—, Jane (J.), 251, 305, 329.
—, John, 57, 73, 126, 162, 251, 305; 305.
—, Martha, 305.
—, Robert, 305.
—, "Old Mr." Thomas, 48, 56.
—, Thomas, 305.

Hill, William, 305.
Hilton, David, 303.
——, Hannah, 241.
——, Rebekah (S.), 232, 253.
——, Samuel, 303, 346; 232, 253.
——, Sarah (Whitney), 240, 260.
——, Thomas, 303.
Hobbard, see Hubbard.
Hobby, Mr., 178, 191.
Hoberd, see Hubbard.
Hodgkins, see Hodgskins.
Hodgskins, Aaron, 232.
——, Henry, 231, 232, 252, 253.
——, Hezekiah, 174.
——, Hannah, 234.
——, Jemima (H.), 232, 253.
——, Mary (H.), 231, 252.
——, Rebeckah (S.), 231, 252.
——, Samuel, 174; 231, 252.
——, Triphena (Hewett), 232, 253.
Hogskins, see Hodgskins.
Holden, 26, 28.
——, Beulah (Cory), 225, 247, 279.
——, Nathaniel, 14, 22, 55, 57.
——, Sarah (S.), 263.
——, Stephen, 263.
Holdin, see Holden.
Holman, Susannah (Houghton), 232, 253.
Holt, 107.
——, Abiel, 302.
——, Abigail, 302.
——, Allice (Daniel), 303.
——, Daniel, 182, 184, 203, 266, 302, 303; 302.
——, David, 302.
——, Dorcas (Jos.), 231, 302, 346.
——, Elijah, 303.
——, Elizabeth, 302.
——, Enoch, 303.
——, Hannah, 303.
——, Humphry, 302.
——, Jonathan, 208, 302, 303; [2], 302.
——, Joseph, 230, 231, 266, 302, 346; 302, 346; 302.
——, Louis, 303.
——, Lydia, 303.
——, Mary (Joseph), 230, 266, 302, 346.
——, Mary (W.), 230, 251, 302.
——, Mary, 212, 217; [2], 302.
——, Mehetable, 302.
——, Mehetibel (Daniel), 266, 302.
——, Rachel (Jonathan), and dau. do., 302, 346.
——, Sarah, 302.
——, Sibbil, 302.
——, Susannah (Jona.), 302, 303.
——, Susannah, 303.

Holt, Thomas, 303.
——, William, 126, 230, 232, 251, 302, 346; 302; 303.
Houghton, Adonijah, 296.
——, Anna, 296.
——, Asael, 296.
——, Betty (Taylor), 239, 262, 328.
——, Darius, 149, 183, 186, 202, 207, 231, 252, 296, 346; 296, 346.
——, David, 296.
——, Dorothy (Page), 236, 264.
——, Eleazer, 64, 73, 80, 81, 91, 99, 103, 104, 106, 107, 111, 113, 122, 126, 131, 133, 141, 147–149, 159, 162, 182, 296, 346.
——, Eleazer, Jr., 232, 253, 296, 297.
——, Eleazer, 3d, 297.
——, Elizabeth (E.), 296, 346.
——, Elizabeth, 228, 296; 296.
——, Esther, 296, 346; 297.
——, Jerusha (Darius), 231, 252, 296, 346.
——, John, 296.
——, Jonathan, 71, 73.
——, Joseph, 252.
——, Judith, 296.
——, Lois (Hastings), 251, 303, 304.
——, Lois, 297.
——, Manasseh, 296.
——, Mary (Jos.), 252.
——, Miriam (Bowers), 223, 245, 274, 342.
——, Robert, 346.
——, Ruth (Stearns), 238, 258, 296.
——, Ruth, 297.
——, Sarah, 297.
——, Stephen, 297.
——, Susannah (E., Jr.), 232, 253, 296, 297.
——, Susannah, 296, 346; 296.
——, Thomas, 83.
Hovey, Abijah, 162, 200, 201, 203, 208, 232, 266, 301, 302, 347; 302, 347.
——, Dorcas, 241, 301.
——, Lydia (A.), 301, 302, 347.
——, Lydia [2d] (A.), 232, 266.
——, Lydia, 236, 301.
——, Mary (Wood), 240, 263, 333.
——, Miriam (Paterson), 236, 302, 319.
——, Sarah (Farewell), 229.
Hubard, see Hubbard.
Hubbard, Abigail (Farewell), 249.
——, Abigail (Jona., Jr.), 251, 301.
——, Abigail, 301.
——, Gershom, 231, 252.
——, Grace, 301.
——, Hannah (John), 230, 252, 306.
——, Hannah (Willard), 264, 336.

Hubbard, John, 230, 252.
—, Jonathan, Lt., Capt., Maj., 12, 14, 16, 22, 24, 26, 31, 32, 55, 57, 83, 85–88, 90, 92, 93, 95–97, 99, 102, 103, 105, 107–110, 112, 116, 119–122, 124–127, 129–136.
—, Jonathan, Jr., 115, 117, 125, 251, 301.
—, Joseph, 14, 22, 55, 57.
—, Lipha (Gershom), 231, 252, 281.
—, Mary (Jenison), 253, 308.
—, Rebekah, 301.
—, Ruth (Stearns), 193, 194, 214, 257, 262, 324, 349.
Hubbart, and Hubbird, and Hubburd, see Hubbard.
Huchings, John, 300.
—, Joseph, 300.
—, Loas, 300.
—, Sarah (Joseph), 300.
—, see Hutchins.
Huet, see Hewett.
Hunt, Ebenezer, 299.
—, Hannah (J.), 299, 346.
—, Hannah, 299; 346.
—, I. S., 265.
—, Jonathan, 299.
—, Martha, 299.
—, Pearley, 299.
—, Capt. Samuel, 141, 148, 153, 156–159, 162–164, 166, 171, 173, 176–178, 180–182, 184, 185, 187, 189, 191, 192, 197, 299, 346.
Hutchens, see Hutchins.
Hutchins, 128.
—, Abigail (P.), 232, 253, 300.
—, Abigail, 300.
—, Ama, 300.
—, James Reed, 300.
—, John Sullivan, 300.
—, Capt. Joshua, 36, 40, 56, 64, 65, 167, 170–172, 175, 179, 182, 184, 185, 188, 189, 193, 195, 196, 200–202, 204, 207, 209–211, 213–215, 218, 219.
—, Joshua, 300.
—, Phinehas, 232, 253, 300; 300.
—, Prudy, 300.
—, Sarah, 300.
—, see Huchings.
Hutchinson, Bettey, 232.
—, Elizebath (S.), and dau. do., 305.
—, Samuel, 232, 305; 305.
—, Thomas, 305.

INGALLS, Lydia (Hovey), 232, 266.
Ireland, Abigail (Steward), 238, 259.
—, Abigail, 305.
—, Abraham, 152, 165, 168, 174, 176, 180, 189, 190, 193, 232, 305, 306; 305.

Ireland, Ann, 305.
—, Anne (Steward), 238, 258, 322.
—, Betty, 306.
—, David, 306.
—, Elener, 306.
—, Jonathan, 306.
—, Mary (Steward), 238, 258, 323.
—, Mary, 305.
—, Meribah (Abraham), 232, 305, 306.
—, Meribah, 306.
—, Susannah, 306.

JACKMAN, Abner, 232, 253.
—, Elizabeth (A.), 232, 253, 275.
Jackson, Madam Borredell (Prentice), 236, 267.
Jenison, John, 105, 111, 116, 117, 122, 125, 128, 253, 308; 308.
—, Mary (J.), 253, 308.
—, Mary, 308.
Jenisson, Mrs. Mary (Bellows), 246.
—, see Genison.
Jewell, James, 64.
Jewett, David, 347.
—, Enoch, 307.
—, Ezekiel, 232.
—, Hannah (T.), 307, 347.
—, Thomas, 307, 347.
Johnson, Benjamin, 306.
—, Elizabeth (Stearns), 237, 257, 306, 325, 350.
—, Hannah (Hubbard), 230, 252, 306.
—, Hannah (Saml., Jr.), 306.
—, James, 232, 253, 306.
—, Keziah (Gibson), 229, 250, 293, 306.
—, Lucy, 306.
—, Mary (S.), 262.
—, Mary, 306.
—, Nathan [2], 306.
—, Rebakah (S.), 306, 347.
—, Rebekah (Gearfield), 229, 250, 306.
—, Dea. Samuel, 56, 64–66, 69, 72, 74, 76–78, 80, 83, 84, 87, 90, 96, 99, 100, 102–106, 110, 111, 113, 115–118, 125, 127, 134–136, 138–140, 142, 145, 151, 160, 161, 175, 182, 262, 306, 347.
—, Samuel, Jr., 168, 176, 189, 198, 199, 203, 208, 306; 306.
—, Sarah (Boynton), 245, 273, 341.
—, Silvanus, 306.
—, Susannah (J.), 232, 253, 306.
Jones, Abigail (Fosket), 228, 262, 307.
—, Abigail, 307.
—, Alnathan, 56.

Jones, Amasa, 307.
——, Amos, 307.
——, David, 307.
——, Elizabeth, 307.
——, Elnathan, 308.
——, Emme, 307.
——, Enos, 307.
——, Hannah, 307.
——, Isaac, 307, 347.
——, John, 307.
——, Joseph, 307, 308.
——, Lt. Josiah, 14, 22, 55, 57.
——, Josiah, 14; 307.
——, Mary (Joseph), 307, 308.
——, Mary, 307.
——, Ruth, 307.
——, Samuel, 9, 11, 17, 19, 21, 24-26, 28, 29, 33, 34, 36, 37; 307.
——, Sarah (Foster), 228, 249, 288, 307.
——, Sarah (W.), 263, 307, 347.
——, Sarah (W., Jr.), 233, 264, 307.
——, Sarah, 307.
——, Silence, 307.
——, William, 66, 73, 80, 83, 88, 93, 94, 96, 97, 105, 109, 110, 113, 118, 122, 125, 132, 137, 141, 156-158, 162, 170, 171, 180, 263, 307, 347.
——, William, Jr., 233, 264, 307; 307.
Jonson, see Johnson.
Joyner, Elizabeth, 246.
Judevine, Patience (W.), 233, 253, 294.
——, William, 233, 253.

Kannady, William, 131; see Kennedy.
Keen or Keene, William, 14, 22, 28, 55, 57.
Kelsey, John, 253.
——, Martha (John), 253.
Kembal, Kembel, see Kimball.
Kendal or Kendall, Alovisa, 309.
——, Eusebia, 309.
——, Hannah, 309.
——, Mary (William) and dau. do., 309.
——, Ruth (Fowler), 228, 249, 289.
——, Samuel, 20; 309.
——, William [2], 309.
Kendel, Abiathar, 309.
——, Bezaleel, 309.
——, Elizabeth (U.), 233, 253, 309, 314.
——, Uzziah, 233, 253, 309.
Kennedy, Elizabeth (Henry), 230, 251, 303.
——, Jane (Leitch), 233, 254.
——, Mary (Machane), 234, 255.
——, Mary, 308.
——, Samuel, 233, 253, 308.

Kennedy, Sarah (S.), 233, 253, 308, 315.
——, Sarah, 308.
——, William, 308; see Cannada and Kannady.
Kibby, James, 62, 70.
Kidder, Benjamin, 233, 254.
——, Ruth (B.), 233, 254, 305.
Kilburn, William, Jr., 233.
Kimball, Abigail, 309.
——, Alfred, 265.
——, Amos, 131, 133, 134, 137, 147, 152, 153, 155, 157, 158, 162, 163, 165, 168, 172, 174, 175, 177, 180, 182, 187, 193, 308; 308.
——, Anne, 308.
——, Benjamin, 309.
——, Betty, 309.
——, Dea., 216.
——, Dolley, 308.
——, Dorothy (Amos), 308.
——, Ebenezer, 308.
——, Elisabeth, 308.
——, Elizabeth (R., Jr.), 233, 254.
——, Elizabeth (T.), 347.
——, Ephraim, 134, 141, 153, 156, 163, 173, 174, 180, 183, 185-187, 203, 208, 233, 308, 309; 308.
——, Lt. George, 141, 165, 168, 171, 172, 176, 181, 185, 189, 194, 196-198, 203, 208, 215, 233, 282, 309, 347.
——, George, 309, 347; 309.
——, Hannah, 308.
——, Jane (W.), 233, 254.
——, Joseph, 16, 20, 24.
——, Levi, 309.
——, Mary (Dunsmoor), 227.
——, Mary (Ephraim), 233, 308, 309, 334.
——, Mary, 308.
——, Phinehas, 308.
——, Rachel, 308.
——, Capt. Richard, 16, 20, 24, 56.
——, Richard, Jr., 233, 254.
——, Sarah (Geo.), 233, 309, 347.
——, Sarah, 309.
——, Thomas, Jr., 16, 23, 55, 56, 134, 347.
——, Thomas, 308; 309.
——, William, 233, 254.
Kimbel, see Kimball.
Kneeland, Elizabeth (Hartwell), 251, 297, 298, 345.
Knight, Hannah, 246.

Lake, Priscilla (Robinson), 267, 321.
Lakin, Rebekah (Davis), 226.
Lain, see Lane.
Lane, Eleazer, 310.

Lane, Widow Mary, 131.
—, Mary, 310.
—, Nehemiah, 182, 196, 234, 254, 265, 310; 310.
—, Phebe, 310.
—, Sarah (N.), 234, 265.
—, Sarah [2d], (N.), 234, 254, 310.
—, Sarah, 310.
Larkin, Hannah (W.), 234, 254.
—, William, 234, 254.
Larrabee, Abiah or Abiel (J.), 234, 254.
—, Abigail (Symonds), 259.
—, Abigail, 310.
—, Anne (S.), 233, 254.
—, Benjamin, 233, 254.
—, Isabella (Barron), 224, 246.
—, John, 234, 254.
—, Margaret (B.), 233, 254.
—, Mary (S.), 234, 254.
—, Mary (T.), and dau. do., 310.
—, Samuel, 125, 130, 131, 137, 162, 176, 187, 188, 233, 234, 254.
—, Sarah (Bowers), 223, 245, 274.
—, Timothy, 310.
Laurance or Larrance, William, 11, 15, 17, 19, 21, 23, 56.
Lech, James, 310.
—, Janat (Jas.), 310.
—, Manasses, 310.
—, see Leitch and Litch.
Leitch, Elizabeth (Crawford), 226, 263.
—, James, 130, 133, 148, 150, 152, 155, 157, 159.
—, Jane (T.), 233, 254.
—, Thomas, 168, 177, 180, 233, 254.
—, see Lech and Litch.
Lilly, Ebenezer, 310.
—, Elizabeth (John), 310.
—, John, 310.
Litch, James, 103, 104.
—, John, 196.
—, Thomas, 203, 208.
—, see Lech and Leitch.
Little, Elizabeth (W.), 233, 261.
—, Elizabeth, 232.
—, Jane (Sharer), 237, 257.
—, Jennet (Steel), 238, 258.
—, John, 310.
—, Thomas, 114, 128.
—, William, 175, 233, 261.
Littlefield, Sarah, 241.
Locke, Sarah (Jones), 263, 307, 347.
Loring, Israel, 265.
Lovejoy, Elizabeth (Boynton), 224, 246, 341.
—, John, 233, 254, 309, 310; 309.
—, Jonathan, 309.

Lovejoy, Martha (Abbott), 266, 272.
—, Mary (Bayley), 224, 275.
—, Phebe (Austin), 223, 271, 272.
—, Prudence, 310.
—, Sarah (John), 233, 254, 309, 310, 313.
—, Sarah, 309.
—, Susannah, 310.
Low, Abagail, 310.
—, Abraham, 310.
—, Benoni, 310.
—, Elizabeth, 310.
—, Francis, 310.
—, Hannah, 310.
—, Joanna, 310.
—, Jonathan, 146, 196, 198, 199, 203, 207, 208; 310.
—, Mary (Stearns), 239, 259, 310, 325.
—, Sarah (Jona.), and dau. do., 310.
—, William, 310.
Lynde, Mrs. Anne (Prescott), 255.

MACCARTY, Thad, 261.
Mace, Polly, 233.
Machane, Mary (W., Jr.), 234, 255.
—, William, Jr., 234, 255.
Mackfeddres, Archa, 57.
Mackfatrich, Archibald, 67.
Mansfeild, John, 129, 131.
Marble, Mary (Spafford), 238, 322.
Marsh, John, 234.
Martin, Betty (John), 235, 255, 278.
—, Elizabeth (Goodridge), 264, 290, 345.
—, Elizabeth (John), and dau. do., 311.
—, Eunice (Geo.), and dau. do., 312.
—, George, 197, 203, 208, 311.
—, Hannah, 311.
—, Jane (Poor), 236, 257, 311.
—, John, 117, 123, 124, 133, 137, 141, 142, 148, 150, 152, 157, 311, 347; 235, 255, 311; 311.
—, Jonathan [3], 311.
—, Joseph, 311.
—, Lucy, 311.
—, Martha, 311.
—, Mary (Holt), 230, 251, 302.
—, Mary, 239, 311; 312.
—, Mercy (Jona.), 311.
—, Patience, 311.
—, Prudence, 311.
—, Sally (Boynton), 225.
—, Samuel, 311.
—, Susana, 311.
Matthews, Elizabeth (T.), 234, 255.
—, Thomas, 234, 255.
McClary, Margaret (White), 240, 260.

McCraken, Lettice (S.), 235, 255, 278.
——, Samuel, 235, 255.
McFarlen, Martha (Kelsey), 253.
McFarling, see McFerlin.
Meferland, George, 177.
McFerlin, George, 177, 234, 262.
——, Margaret (G.), 234, 262.
Mead or Meed, Joshua, 167, 178, 187, 191.
Mellen, Rev. John, 202.
Merrill, Abigail (D.), and dau. do., 311.
——, Daniel, 311.
——, Hitte, 311.
Messer, Messor, see Messur.
Messur, Abigail (Jona.), 234, 311.
——, Jonathan, 186, 187, 234, 311; 311.
Michael, Mitcheal, see Mitchel.
Mitchel, 80.
——, Andrew, 111, 150, 312.
——, Elizabeth (Richards), 237, 257, 312.
——, Esther (Richards), 237, 263, 312.
——, Hannah, 312.
——, Jane, 237, 312.
——, Martha (A.), and dau. do., 312.
——, Mary, 312.
——, Moses, 110, 133, 137, 140, 141, 147, 148, 152, 153, 156, 161, 162, 163, 168, 186, 190, 196.
——, Robert, 234.
——, Ruth (Moors), 254, 312.
——, Susannah (Russel), 237, 257, 312.
Moffat, Dorrothy (Wyman), 261.
——, John, 234.
——, Joseph, 234, 311.
——, Robert, 159, 311.
——, William, 114, 153.
Moffett, see Moffat.
Moors, Elizabeth (Wm.), and dau. do., 311.
——, Hugh, 234, 254, 311.
——, John, Jr., 234, 255.
——, Ruth (H.), 254, 311.
——, Ruth, 311.
——, Unity (J., Jr.), 234, 255, 337.
——, William, 234, 311.
Morrison, Mary (T.), 254.
——, Thomas, 254.
Mowers, see Moors.
Mullickin, Sarah (Kimball), 233, 309, 347.
Munroe, Hannah (Wetherbee), 241, 335.
——, Keziah, 240.

NEWTON, Hananiah, 235.

Nichols or Nickalls, Mary, 235, 256.
Norcross, Elijah, 312.
——, Elizabeth (P.), 235, 255.
——, Faith (Jere.), 312.
——, Hannah, 312.
——, Jabez, 312.
——, Jeremiah, 64, 66, 72–74, 78, 87, 88, 92, 103, 106, 109, 111, 113, 122, 137, 148, 152, 160, 180, 183, 186, 203, 208, 312; 312.
——, Mary, 312.
——, Page, 61, 235, 255, 312.
——, Sarah (Parce), 236, 256, 312, 314.

OLIVER, 174, 187.
——, Andrew, 205.
Ordway, see Ardeway.
Osbourn, Ephraim, 174, 235, 255, 312.
——, Jacob, 235.
——, John, 312.
——, Sarah (E.), 235, 255, 312.
Osburn, see Osbourn.
Osgood, Phinehas, 94.

PAGE, Aaron, 318, 348.
——, Abner, 317, 348.
——, Alice (Wheelock), 240, 260, 315.
——, Amos, 316.
——, Benjamin, 315, 348; 316.
——, Caleb, 317, 348; 318.
——, Daniel, 235, 266, 315, 317.
——, David, 94, 103, 120, 127, 133, 255, 317, 348; 317, 348; 317.
——, Deborah (Jos.), 267, 316, 348.
——, Deborah (Platts), 236, 256, 316.
——, Dorothy, 236, 264.
——, Elizabeth (Parker), 255, 315.
——, Elizabeth, 316.
——, Eunice, 315, 348.
——, Hannah [2], 316.
——, Johannah, 316.
——, John, 347; 317.
——, Jonathan, 69, 80, 113, 116–119, 121, 122, 124, 126, 156, 185, 200, 201, 315, 316, 348; 315.
——, Joseph, 15, 26, 29, 52, 56, 66, 114, 118, 123, 131, 133, 172, 267, 316, 348.
——, Joseph, Jr., 316, 348.
——, Joshua, 316.
——, Marcy, 316, 348.
——, Martha (Samuel), and dau. do., 315, 347.
——, Mary (Jonathan), 315, 316, 348.
——, Mary (Spafford), 237, 258, 315.
——, Matha, 317.
——, Mehetabel, 317.

Page, Mercy (N.), 255, 317, 318, 348.
——, Mercy (Simonds), 238, 258.
——, Mercy, 317.
——, Moses, 317.
——, Nathaniel, 73, 74, 80, 111, 113, 116, 117, 121, 133, 137, 141, 147, 152, 153, 157, 165, 172, 176, 179, 255, 317, 318, 348.
——, Nathaniel, Jr., 317, 348.
——, Peter, 315.
——, Phebe, 316.
——, Phinehas, 316.
——, Priscilla (David), 255, 317, 348.
——, Priscilla, 317.
——, Prudence, 316, 348; 317.
——, Rachel, 317.
——, Reuben, 318.
——, Ruth (Daniel), 235, 266, 317.
——, Ruth, 316; [2], 317.
——, Samuel, 12, 15, 19, 23, 28, 29, 37, 56, 64, 68, 69, 71-74, 78-80, 84, 97, 102, 103, 235, 256, 315, 347; 316, 348; 318.
——, Sarah (Kennedy), 233, 253, 308, 315.
——, Sarah (S.), 235, 256.
——, Sarah (W.), 266, 316, 348.
——, Sarah, 316; 317.
——, Sibil, 317.
——, Solomon, 317, 348.
——, Submit, 348.
——, Susanna, 316.
——, Thomas, 236, 264, 315.
——, Timothy, 316.
——, William, 121, 133, 266, 316, 348; 316.
——, Zachariah, 315, 347.
Paine, Timothy, 167.
Parce, see Pearce.
Parker, Abigail (Messur), 234, 311.
——, Abigail, 313.
——, Abijah, 313.
——, Elijah, 313.
——, Elizabeth (Josiah), 255, 315.
——, Elizabeth (Stevens), 238, 265.
——, Joanna, 313.
——, Johanna (T.), 236, 256, 294, 312, 313.
——, Johanah, 312.
——, Jonathan, 236, 256.
——, Josiah, 255.
——, Keziah (Wyman), 261, 331.
——, Martha (Jona.), 236, 256.
——, Phinehas, 9, 11, 15, 17, 19, 21, 23, 56.
——, Samuel, 180.
——, Sarah, 312.
——, Sibil, 313.
——, Timothy, 157, 163, 172, 174, 176, 236, 256, 312, 313.

Paterson, James, 236, 319; 319.
——, Lovisa, 319.
——, Lydia, 319.
——, Miriam (J.), 236, 302, 319.
Paul, Robert, 57.
Payson, Rev. Samuel, 194, 195, 198, 199, 202, 206, 211, 215, 247, 349.
Peabody, Dorothy (Jacob), 256.
——, Widow Dorrathy, 349.
——, Jacob, 256.
——, Richard, 186, 190.
——, Ruth (T.), 349.
——, Samuel, 349.
——, Thomas, 182, 184, 186, 188, 194-196, 200, 349.
Pearce, Abraham, 314.
——, Amos, 313, 348.
——, Anne (D., Jr.), 235, 256.
——, Benjamin, 313, 348; 314.
——, David, 57, 73, 81, 91, 97, 104, 106, 117, 121, 149, 159, 314, 348.
——, David, Jr., 150, 177, 190, 235, 256, 314.
——, Elijah, 314.
——, Elizabeth (D.), 314, 348.
——, Elizabeth (Fitch), 228, 249, 287, 314.
——, Elizabeth, 239, 313.
——, Elizabeth, Jr. (Kendel), 233, 253, 314.
——, Dea. Ephraim, 14, 22, 55, 57, 64, 65, 67, 69, 73, 76, 78, 80, 84, 87, 89, 90, 92, 96, 104, 105, 109, 110, 137, 156, 313, 348.
——, Ephraim, Jr., 149, 176, 197, 236, 256, 313, 314.
——, Ephraim, 14; 314.
——, Esther (Dea. E.), 313, 348.
——, Esther (Gilson), 230.
——, Esther (Gould), 250, 293, 313, 345.
——, Esther, 314.
——, Hannah (John), 314.
——, Hannah (Larkin), 234, 254.
——, Hannah (Wetherbee), 240, 260, 314, 335.
——, John, 129, 314.
——, Jonathan, 172, 177, 180, 181, 185, 201, 203, 208, 235, 256, 313, 314, 315; 314.
——, Joshua, 236, 314.
——, Josiah, 314.
——, Keziah, 313, 348.
——, Lucy, 315.
——, Lydia, 314, 348.
——, Mary (Hartwell) 231, 252, 298, 313.
——, Mary (Samuel), 236, 257, 315, 322.
——, Mary, 314.

Pearce, Nahum, 315.
—, Oliver, 313.
—, Phinehas, 314.
—, Prudence (Smith), 239, 259, 313, 328.
—, Prudence, 314; 328.
—, Relief, 314.
—, Samuel, 236, 257, 314, 315.
—, Sarah (Ephraim, Jr.), 236, 256, 312, 314.
—, Sarah (Jona.), 235, 256, 314, 315.
—, Sarah (Lovejoy), 233, 254, 309, 310, 313.
—, Sarah (Page), 235, 256.
—, Sarah [2], 314; 315.
—, Sibel, 314.
—, Solomon, 314, 348.
—, Susannah, 314.
—, Tabatha, 314.
Pearly, Thomas, 15.
Pearson, Bartholomew, 236, 265.
—, Lydia (B.), 236, 237, 257, 265; as Randal, 153, 170.
Peobody, see Peabody.
Perham, John, 24, 52, 53, 55, 56.
Perkins, William, 169.
Perlin, David, 28.
Perly or Perley, Jeremiah, 15, 22, 55, 56.
—, Lt. Thomas, 16, 22, 24, 48, 56.
—, Capt. Thomas, 55, 56.
Perram, see Perham.
Phelps, Asael, 256.
—, Elizabeth (A.), 256.
Phillips, Amos, 235.
—, Rev. Samuel, 266.
Pickering, Theophilus, 264.
Plats, 232.
Platts, Abel, 119, 315.
—, Abel, Jr., 236, 256, 315.
—, Deborah (J.), 236, 256, 316.
—, Edward, 315.
—, Elizabeth (Nathan), 315.
—, Hannah, 315.
—, Jane, 315.
—, Joseph, 236, 256.
—, Mary (A.), 315.
—, Mary (Wood), 240, 260, 333.
—, Nathan, 150, 315.
—, Phebe (A., Jr.), 236, 256, 334.
—, Sarah (J.), 236, 256.
—, Sarah, 315.
—, Thomas, 315.
Plympton, Joseph, 20.
Pouchee, see Pouchee.
Pool or Poole, 67.
—, Bette [2], 318.
—, Elizabeth (Jas.), and dau. do., 318.

Poole, Jacob, 318.
—, James, 126, 134, 140, 153, 158, 168, 169, 172, 173, 181, 183, 186, 187, 190, 196, 203, 208, 318; 318.
—, James, Jr., 318.
—, Jonathan, 72.
—, Joshua, 318.
—, Judith, 318, 349.
—, Prudence (S.), 318, 349.
—, Prudence, 318.
—, Ruth [2], 318.
—, Samuel, 153, 157, 158, 162, 168, 177, 187, 190, 236, 256, 318, 349.
—, Samuel, Jr., 318, 349.
—, Sarah (Hart), 231, 253, 318.
—, Sarah (S.), 236, 256.
—, Sarah, 318.
—, Susanna, 318.
—, Susannah, 318.
Poor, David, 236, 257.
—, Jane (D.), 236, 257, 311.
—, Jonathan, 15, 22, 55, 56.
Porter, William, 235, 256.
Potter, Sarah (Poole), 236, 256.
—, Thomas, 170.
Pouchee, Abigail, 299.
—, Gabriel, 137, 148.
—, Elizabeth (N.), 236, 256.
—, Nathan, 236, 256.
—, Ruth (Day), 226, 248.
Powers Jonas [2], 319.
—, Lydia (J.), 319.
—, Mary, 319.
Pratt, Anna, 313.
—, Charity (E.), 313.
—, Ebenezer, 236, 257, 313.
—, Lydia (E.), 236, 257, 313.
—, Oliver, 313.
—, Sally, 313.
Prentice, Abigail (T.), 255, 336.
—, Borridel (T.), 236, 267.
—, Rev. John, 257, 262.
—, Thomas, 110, 112, 113, 116-118, 121, 123, 124, 127, 128, 130, 135-137, 139, 141-145, 147, 149, 150, 159, 236, 247-249, 252, 253, 255, 258, 260.
Prescott, 126.
—, Anne (John), 255.
—, Lieut. Benjamin, 8, 9, 11, 15, 23, 56.
—, John, 255.
—, Capt. Jonas, 24.
—, Jonas, Jr., 8.
Prescut, 123.
Priest, Bethsheba (Henderson), 231, 252.
—, Dorothy (Moffett), 234, 311.
—, Elizabeth (Pouchee), 236, 256.
—, Joseph, 318.

Priest, Joshua, 318, 319.
—, Molley, 319.
—, Samuel, 319.
—, Sarah (Joshua), 318, 319.
Pushee, see Pouchee.
Putnam, Amos, 236.
—, Hephzibah, 319.
—, James, 261-267.
—, Martha (Endecott), 227.
—, Rachel (T.), 236, 256, 319, 334.
—, Dea. Samuel, 203, 208, 214, 216, 217, 219.
—, Seth, 319.
—, Susannah, 319.
—, Thomas, 236, 256, 319; 319.

RANDAL, Benjamin, 237, 257.
—, Lydia (Pearson), 153, 170, 236, 237, 257, 265.
Read, 28.
Reddington, Benj., 176, 180, 183, 190, 196, 198, 199, 200, 237, 257, 320, 321; 320.
—, David, 320.
—, Elizabeth, 321.
—, Hannah, 320.
—, Hepsibeth (Willard), 241, 261, 337.
—, Isaac, 183, 184, 237, 266, 321; 320.
—, John, 321.
—, Lucy, 320.
—, Mary, 320.
—, Rebecca, 320.
—, Ruth (B.), 237, 257, 320, 321, 324.
—, Ruth (I.), 237, 266, 321.
—, Ruth, 320.
—, Sophia, 321.
—, Susannah, 321.
—, Dea. Thomas, 162, 164, 349.
—, Thomas, 320.
Redington, see Reddington.
Reed, Abigail (Hutchens), 232, 253.
—, Abigail (Capt. Jas.), 320.
—, Barzillai, 320.
—, Fredrick, 320.
—, Hannah, 319.
—, Hinds, 320.
—, Israel, 126.
—, Capt. James, 202, 204, 207, 208, 210, 211, 219, 320.
—, James, 320.
—, Jesse, 319.
—, Joseph, 320.
—, Joshua, 320.
—, Mary (Bayley), 224, 246.
—, Mary (Clark), 247, 280.
—, Mary (Saml.), 257, 319, 320, 349.

Reed, Mary, 319.
—, Priscilla (Carter), 226.
—, Priscilla, 319; 320.
—, Rebecca, 320, 349.
—, Samuel, 94, 111, 126, 130, 134-137, 147, 152, 156, 257, 319, 320, 349.
—, Samuel, Jr., 319.
—, Sarah, 319.
—, Shefomith, 320.
—, Sylvanus, 320.
Retter, Anne (Parce), 235, 256.
—, Elizabath (Brown), 223, 245.
—, see Ritter.
Rice, Marshall S., 267.
—, Mary (I. Foster), 228, 249, 288.
—, Mary, 228.
—, Rebeckah (Hodgskins), 231, 252.
Richards, Charles, 321.
—, Edward, 321.
—, Elizabeth (J.), 237, 257, 312.
—, Esther (M.), 237, 263, 312.
—, Jane (C.), 321.
—, John, 237, 257.
—, Mitchael, 237, 263, 321.
Richardson, Ebenezer, 67.
—, Elizabeth, 231.
—, James, 27.
—, Capt. James, 15, 23, 56.
—, James, Jr., 174.
—, Phinehas, 16, 24, 27, 56.
—, Samuel, 38, 39, 40.
—, William, 15, 23, 27, 56.
Right, see Wright.
Ritter, Abner, 321.
—, Hannah (M.), 321, 349.
—, Hannah, 321.
—, Marcy, 321.
—, Mary, 349.
—, Moley, 321.
—, Moses, 137, 147, 156, 162, 173, 175, 180, 181, 185, 186, 189, 198, 200, 204, 205, 211, 321, 349.
—, see Retter.
Robbe, Anne (W.), 321.
—, Elizabath (W.), 321.
—, Elizibath, 321.
—, Margaret, 321.
—, William, 321.
Robins, Edward, 174.
Robbinson, Robbingson, see Robinson.
Robinson, Amos, 87-89, 91, 92, 99, 107, 110, 113, 237, 267, 321; 321.
—, Daniel, 321.
—, Eliezer, 321.
—, John, 321.
—, Lydia (A.), 237, 267, 321.
—, Priscilla (A.), 267, 321.
Rogers, Rev. Daniel, 267.

Rogers, Rev. John, 264.
Rugby, Timothy, 205.
Rugg, Daniel, 237.
Russel or Russell, Elizabeth (J.), 257.
——, George, 150, 237.
——, John, 237, 257.
——, Mary (Swan), 258.
——, Widow Mary, 150.
——, Matha or Meltha (Warrin), 240, 337.
——, Nathaniel, 261.
——, Robert, 104.
——, Samuel, 237, 257.
——, Susannah (S.), 237, 257, 312.

Salmon, Elizabeth (Dodge), 227, 248.
Sanderson, Abraham, 94, 111, 119, 121, 133, 148, 153, 156, 168, 171, 196, 327; 327.
——, Margaret (Stewart), 257, 322.
——, Patience (A.), 327.
——, Samuel, 196, 197, 259, 327.
——, Sarah (S.), 259, 292.
Sargent, Rev. Christopher, 266.
Sattle, Hezekiah, 237.
——, Lois (Fuller), 228, 249.
Sautle, David, 14.
——, Ephraim, 14, 22, 27, 36, 37, 55, 57.
——, Zachariah, 14, 22, 55, 57.
Scott, Benjamin, 327.
——, David, 327.
——, Edward, 197, 327.
——, Elizabeth, 327.
——, John, 57, 88, 96, 97, 106, 132, 141, 167, 327.
——, Jonathan, 327.
——, Lydia (John), 327.
——, Mary, 327.
Scripture, Eunice (Gridridge), 264.
Seaton, see Sectown.
Seaverans, Martha, 234.
Sectown, Elizabeth (Kimball), 233, 254.
Seecomb, Rev. John, 266.
Shaddock or Shattuck, Sarah, 234, 265.
Shadock, Susannah (Taylor), 239, 328.
Shadwick, see Chadwick.
Sharer, Jane (J.), 237, 257.
——, John, 237, 257.
Shed, Abigal, 324.
——, Benjamin, 238, 262, 323.
——, Bettey, 323.
——, Charles, 266.
——, Ebenezer, 324.
——, Elizabeth (B.), 238, 262, 323.
——, Elizabeth (S.), 239, 263, 323, 324.

Shed, Hannah, 323.
——, James, 323.
——, John, 323.
——, Joseph, 324.
——, Lemuel, 323.
——, Patty, 324.
——, Person, 323.
——, Solomon, 239, 263, 323, 324; 323.
——, Zackiah, 324.
Sheed, see Shed.
Sheple, Capt. John, 7, 9-12, 16-19, 21, 24-26, 28-42, 57.
Shiple, Shipley, see Sheple.
Shiply, John, Jr., 29.
——, Jonathan, 16, 23, 34.
——, see Sheple.
Shute, Samuel, 8.
Simonds, 179.
——, John, 238, 258.
——, Wid. Mary (Larrabee), 234, 254.
——, Mercy (J.), 238, 258.
——, see Symonds.
Small, William, 239.
Smith, Abigail (Dodge), 227.
——, Abraham, 239, 267.
——, Aron, 14, 22, 55, 57.
——, Elisha, 93.
——, John, 238, 258.
——, Jonathan, 99, 105, 106, 117, 327, 328; 328.
——, Lois (Gibson), 229, 265.
——, Lucie or Lucy, (Abraham), 239, 267.
——, Mary (John), 238, 258.
——, Mary (Morrison), 254.
——, Mary, 328.
——, Moses, 14, 21, 55, 57.
——, Patience (Stiles), 238, 258, 326, 327.
——, Sarah (Henderson), 263, 301, 346.
——, Reuben, 239, 259, 328; 328.
——, Samuel, 261.
——, Sarah (Dodge), 227, 283.
——, Sarah, 328; 350.
——, Simon, 328.
——, Susannah (Divol), 226, 248.
——, Susannah (Jonathan), 327, 328.
——, Susannah, 328.
Snow, Abigail, 327.
——, Anna (S.), 259.
——, Bette, 327.
——, Elizabeth (W.), 327.
——, Esther, 327.
——, Jemima, 327.
——, Joseph, 327.
——, Lucy, 327.
——, Dr. Peter, 239.

Snow, Rebekah (Goodridge), 230, 251, 291, 327.
——, Silas, 174, 190, 259, 327.
——, William, 99, 111, 117, 122, 133, 141, 150, 152, 155–158, 174, 181, 185, 189, 196, 327; [2], 327.
Spafford, 187.
——, Bradstreet, 237, 258.
——, Dorcas (Jonah), 238, 258, 322.
——, Hannah, 322.
——, John, 322.
——, Jonah, Jonas or Jonathan, 238, 258, 322, 350.
——, Joseph, 162, 167, 186, 238, 322.
——, Judah, 322.
——, Mary (B.), 237, 258, 315.
——, Mary (Jos.), 238, 322.
——, Phebe (Grout), 229, 250, 294, 295, 345.
——, Sarah, 322.
Sparhawk, Abigail (Rev. E.), 239, 259, 324.
——, Rev. Ebenezer, 202, 239, 259.
——, Oliver Stearns, 328.
——, Rebecca (T.), 238, 259, 324, 328.
——, Rebecca, 328.
——, Thomas, 196, 197, 199–202, 204, 205, 207–214, 216–219, 238, 259, 328; 328.
Spear, see Speer.
Speer, Martha (R.), 326.
——, Mary (Adam), 223, 245.
——, Robert, 144, 326; 326.
Stearns, Abigail (Bellows), 245, 276, 342.
——, Abigail (Sparhawk), 239, 259, 324.
——, Abijah, 157, 164, 167, 171, 172, 176, 177, 180, 182, 185, 189, 196, 207, 237, 258.
——, Anna (B.), 238, 258, 325.
——, Anna, 325.
——, Benjamin, 168, 177, 190, 238, 258, 325, 349; 325.
——, Charles, 325.
——, Daniel, 325.
——, Rev. David, 62, 63, 76–78, 81, 82, 86, 94, 98, 102, 103, 108, 112, 116, 120, 122, 124, 127, 130, 132, 136, 139, 144, 151, 156, 161, 165, 171, 175, 179, 181, 184, 188, 191, 192, 194, 199, 245–262, 324, 349.
——, David, 239, 259, 324, 325; [2], 325.
——, Elizabeth, 202, 215, 324.
——, Elizabeth (W.), 237, 257, 306, 325, 349, 350.
——, Hannah, 324.
——, James, 325.

Stearns, Jerusha (Houghton), 231, 252, 296, 346.
——, John, 324.
——, Jonas, 238, 259, 325; 325.
——, Jonathan, 324, 349.
——, Joseph, 325, 349; 325.
——, Lucy, 324, 349.
——, Lydia (Goodridge), 250, 290, 345.
——, Lydia (T.), 324, 325, 349.
——, Lydia, 325.
——, Mary (D.), 239, 259, 310, 325.
——, Mary, 324, 349; [2], 325.
——, Moses, 238, 258.
——, Rebecca (Sparhawk), 238, 259, 324, 328.
——, Rebeckah, 325.
——, Madam Ruth (Rev. D.), 193, 194, 214, 257, 324, 349.
——, Ruth (M.), 238, 258, 296.
——, Ruth (Reddington), 237, 257, 320, 321, 324.
——, Samuel, 325.
——, Sarah (A.), 237, 258, 304.
——, Sarah, 324, 349; 324; 325.
——, Submit (Jonas), 238, 259, 325.
——, Thomas, 158, 169, 177, 324, 325, 349; [2], 324; 325.
——, Dea. William, 125, 151, 152, 156, 157, 159, 161–164, 166, 171, 180, 189, 192, 193, 196, 200, 207, 237, 257, 325, 349, 350.
——, William, Jr., 325, 350.
Stedman, Jonathan, 238, 259.
——, Tabitha (J.), 238, 259.
Steel, David, 238, 258.
——, Jennet (D.), 238, 258.
Stevens, Abigail (Gibs), 250.
——, Capt., 116.
——, Elizabeth (J.), 238, 265.
——, Jonathan, 238, 265.
——, Lydia (Randal, Pearson), 153, 170, 236, 237, 257, 265.
——, Sarah (Page), 266, 316, 348.
Steward, Abigail (W.), 238, 259, 323.
——, Abigail, 323.
——, Abraham, 322.
——, Amasa, 323.
——, Amherst, 323.
——, Anne (P.), 238, 258, 322.
——, Anne, 322.
——, Benjamin, 182, 237, 258, 322; 323.
——, Betty [2], 323.
——, Charles, 322.
——, Daniel, 204, 208, 209, 238, 258, 323; 323.
——, Elizabeth (Sol., Jr.), 238, 258, 323.

Steward, Elizabeth, 322.
—, Jacob, 239, 322.
—, John, 322; 323.
—, Margaret (W.), 257, 322.
—, Martha (S.), 322.
—, Martha [2], 322.
—, Mary (D.), 238, 258, 323.
—, Mary (Parce), 236, 257, 322.
—, Mary [2], 323.
—, Phinehas, 173, 183, 190, 238, 258, 322; 322.
—, Rebecca (B.), 237, 258, 322.
—, Rebeckah, 323.
—, Samuel Bird, 322.
—, Sarah, 323.
—, Solomon, 117, 122, 125, 130, 133, 138, 140, 141, 162, 171, 197, 322.
—, Solomon, Jr., 173, 174, 238, 258, 323.
—, Thomas, 322.
—, William, 257, 322; 238, 259, 322, 323.
Stewart, 125; see Steward.
Stickney, Mr., 184.
—, Rebekah (Hilton), 232, 253.
—, Stephen, 176, 177, 186, 196.
Stiles, Caleb, 326.
—, Charlotte, 232.
—, Hannah [2], 326.
—, Jacob, 57, 64, 96, 101, 106, 107, 108, 113, 123, 326, 350; 326.
—, Jeremiah, 326.
—, John, 326.
—, Jonathan, 326.
—, Levi, 238, 258, 326; 326.
—, Lusa, 326.
—, Lucy (Foster), 228, 249, 326.
—, Nabby (Fullam), 229.
—, Nahum [2], 326.
—, Patience (L.), 238, 258, 326, 327.
—, Patience, 326.
—, Peleg Stearns, 326.
—, Prudence, 326.
—, Sarah (Child), 225, 247.
—, Sarah (Jacob), and dau. do., 326.
—, Susanna, 239, 326.
Stimson, Rev. Daniel, 265.
Stockwell, Abigail (Divol), 227, 248.
—, Ephraim, 259.
—, Mary (Gould), 264, 293.
—, Sarah (E.), 259.
Stone, 125.
—, Edmond, 239.
—, Isaac, 14, 22, 55, 57.
—, Lydia (Pratt), 236, 257, 313.
—, Sarah (Jones), 233, 307.

Stow, Nathaniel, 15, 23, 27, 56.
—, Rev. Samuel, 25.
—, Samuel, 160.
—, Thomas, 27.
Stratton, Mary, 241.
Swan, Alexander, 238, 258.
—, Gustavus, 237, 258.
—, Isabella (G.), 237, 258.
—, John, 104.
—, Lucy (A.), 238, 258.
—, Mary (W.), 258.
—, William, 258.
Sweetland, Thomas, 239.
Symmes, Rev. William, 266.
Symonds, Abigail (W.), 259.
—, Joseph, 239.
—, Ruth (Wood), 240, 267, 332.
—, William, 259.
—, see Simonds.

Tailer, Thomas, 15, 23, 55, 56.
—, Col. William, 7, 10-12, 16-19, 21, 24-27, 30-35, 37-42, 57.
—, see Taylor.
Tarball, Eleazer, 117, 124, 127, 129, 132, 137, 141.
—, Elizabeth (Hartwell), 230, 251, 298.
—, Elizabeth, 329.
—, Mary (Z.), 239, 259, 292, 329.
—, Moley, 329.
—, Molly, 329.
—, Sarah, 329.
—, Sibel, 329.
—, Thomas, 9, 11, 15, 19, 21, 23, 56.
—, Zechariah, 239, 259, 329; 329.
Tarbell, Tarbul, see Tarball.
Taylor, Aaron, 239, 259, 329; 329.
—, Anna (Stearns), 238, 258, 325.
—, Arthur, 328.
—, Betty (David), 239, 262, 328.
—, Betty, 328.
—, Caleb, 152, 170, 172, 183, 186, 190, 203, 208, 239, 328; 328.
—, David, 168, 170, 184, 190, 196, 239, 262, 328; 329.
—, Elizabeth (Steward), 238, 258, 323.
—, Jonathan, 148; 329.
—, Martha, 328.
—, Mary, 328.
—, Matha, 329.
—, Mercy (Aaron), 239, 259, 292, 329.
—, Rebecca (Steward), 237, 258,
—, Richard, 176, 177, 181, 185, 198, 201, 203, 208, 210, 211, 213.
—, Sarah, 329.
—, Susanna (Caleb), 239, 328.

Taylor, Susannah, 328.
—, see Tailer.
Tenny, Samuel, 20.
Terrance, see Torrance.
Thaxter, Col. Samuel, 7, 12, 16, 17, 20, 21, 24–28, 31–35, 38–42, 57.
Thirston, 81, 153.
—, Daniel, 15, 22, 50, 55, 57, 67.
—, Jonathan, 15.
Thurla, Lidya (Ardeway), 223, 235.
Thurstin, Thursting, see Thirston.
Thurston, Sarah, 241.
Torrance, Margaret (McFerlin), 234, 262.
Towne, I. P., 267.
Towns, Nathan, 57.
Trowbridge, Rev. Caleb, 264.
Trull, John, 94, 329.
—, Phebe, 329.
—, Sarah (J.), 329.
—, Susannah, 329.
Turner, Jane (Henderson), 231, 252.
—, Joseph, 91.

UPTON, 121.
—, Oliver, 239.

WALKER, 125.
—, Abigail (O.), 240, 335, 336.
—, Abigail, 335.
—, Benjamin, 335.
—, Betty, 335.
—, Mary, 336.
—, Nathaniel, 336.
—, Obediah, 128, 138, 148, 168, 171, 190, 198, 240, 335, 336; 336.
—, Rebeccah, 335.
—, Samuel, 38–40.
—, Sarah, 241, 335.
Wallas, Walles, see Wallis.
Wallis, Anne, 330.
—, Benjamin, 330.
—, Benoni, 158, 168, 170, 196, 240, 260, 330.
—, Curwin, 330.
—, David [2], 330.
—, Ebenezer, 330.
—, Elizabeth (Little), 233, 261.
—, Elizabeth (Russel), 257, 329.
—, Elizabath (W.), 329, 330.
—, Frederick, 330.
—, Hannah, 330.
—, Jane (Hill), 251, 305, 329.
—, Margaret (Darrah), 226, 248, 330.
—, Martha, 329.
—, Mary (White), 260, 329, 331.
—, Molly, 330.
—, Rebecca (Benoni), 240, 260, 330.

Wallis, Samuel, 330.
—, Sarah, 330.
—, Susannah, 330.
—, William, 56, 80, 81, 111, 329, 330; 330.
Ward, Capt., 24.
Warren, Elizabeth, 337.
—, Isaac, 337.
—, Jacob, 240, 337, 350; 337.
—, John, 14, 55, 57.
—, Ensign John, 14, 22.
—, Mary (Jacob), 337, 350.
—, Matha or Meltha (Jacob), 240, 337.
—, Samuel, 57.
Warrin, see Warren.
Weatherbee, see Wetherbee.
Webb, N., 265.
Wentworth, Lydia (Robinson), 237, 267, 321.
Wetherbee, 115, 123, 125.
—, Abigail, 334.
—, Abijah, 334; 335.
—, Abraham, 334.
—, Benjamin, 240, 334.
—, Bette, 334.
—, Betty, 335.
—, Daniel [2], 335.
—, David [2], 335.
—, Elizabeth (E.), 334, 350.
—, Capt. Ephraim, 66, 68–74, 84, 87, 89, 95, 96, 99, 101, 103, 106, 108, 111, 114, 119, 122, 123, 260, 334, 350.
—, Ephraim, 335.
—, Esther, 335.
—, Hannah (P.), 240, 260, 314, 335.
—, Hannah (Thos.), 241, 335.
—, Hannah [2], 335.
—, Hephsibah, 335.
—, Hezekiah, 99, 106, 114, 126, 127, 131, 152, 334.
—, Huldah (H.), 334.
—, Isaac, 335.
—, Joab, 335.
—, Johannah (E.), 260, 334.
—, Johannah, 334.
—, John, 334.
—, Jonathan, 334.
—, Josiah, 335.
—, Lucy, 335.
—, Mary, 233, 308, 309, 334.
—, Molley, 335.
—, Patty, 335.
—, Paul, 165, 169, 180, 181, 185, 186, 197, 202, 204, 209, 212, 217, 240, 260, 335; 241, 335.
—, Phebe (Platts), 236, 256, 334.
—, Phebe, 334.

Index. 379

Wetherbee, Rachel (Putnam), 236, 256, 334.
—, Ruth (Wood), 240, 260, 332, 350.
—, Samuel, 334.
—, Sarah, 227, 334; 335.
—, Susannah, 334.
—, Thomas, 190, 241, 334, 335; 335.
Wheeler, Ebenezer, 57.
—, George, 81.
—, Jethro, 104.
—, Sarah (Holden), 263.
—, Thomas, 241.
—, William, 15, 23, 56.
 heelock, Abner, 241, 261.
—, Alice (J., Jr.), 240, 260, 315.
—, Joseph, Jr., 240, 260.
—, Mary (A.), 241, 261.
—, Olive (Broadstreet), 223, 245.
—, Phineas, 180, 186.
 hetney, Constable, 107.
 hite, Archibald, 240, 260.
—, Betty, 332.
—, Charles, 162, 177; 331.
—, David, 331.
—, Deborah (Carter), 247.
—, Elizabeth (Gilchrest), 229, 250.
—, Elizabeth, 331.
—, Jane, 240.
—, John, 172, 203, 208, 212, 218, 240, 260, 331; 331.
—, John, Jr., 260, 331, 332.
—, Jonathan, 167.
—, Lydia, 331.
—, Margaret (A.), 240, 260.
—, Mary (Grimes), 250.
— Mary (J.), 260, 329, 331.
— Jary (J., Jr.), 240, 260, 331,

—   ,d Mr., 93.
— atrick, 113, 137, 157, 162, 163,
1   180, 182, 190, 193, 215, 240.
— almon [2], 332.
— ilence (Heywood), 232.
—   isanah (Farwell), 228.
—   idow, 127.
—   illiam, 331.
Whi   , Rev. Aaron, 264.
—,   igail, 333.
—,   ier, 240, 260.
—,   guess (Ezra), 334.
—,   iraim, 133, 137, 148, 152,
1   68, 172, 180, 196, 212, 218,
      0, 334; 334.
—   [2], 334.
—   ue, 16, 23, 56.
—   d (Ephraim), 240, 260, 334.
—   . 333.
—   I 14, 22, 55, 57; 333.

Whitney, Jonathan, 16, 23, 40, 56, 64, 67, 80, 81, 90, 91, 200.
—, Jonathan, Jr., 36, 56.
—, Lewis, 264.
—, Lois (Bellows), 225, 247.
—, Lucy, 227.
—, Mary (White), 240, 260, 331, 332.
—, Mary, 333.
—, Molley, 334.
—, Moses, 334.
—, Nathaniel, Jr., 16, 20, 23, 56.
—, Rev. Phineas, 202.
—, Rebekah, 334.
—, Sarah (A.), 240, 260.
—, Sarah (Dutton), 227, 248, 333.
—, Sarah (Foster), 228, 267.
—, Sarah (Z.), 260, 273, 333.
—, Shadrik or Shadrach, 16, 23, 56.
—, Susanna, 239.
—, Webster, 265.
—, William, 9, 14, 22.
—, Zechariah, 131, 147, 153, 157, 180, 186, 190, 260, 333; 333.
Whittemore, Benjamin, 7, 9–12, 14, 16–21, 24–43, 57.
—, Nathaniel, 22, 55, 57.
Wilder, Elizabeth (Phelps), 256.
—, Joseph, Jr., 262, 263.
—, Josh Tertius, 240.
—, Mary (Boutwell), 224, 263.
—, Rezoma, 224.
—, Thomas, 167.
Willard, 115, 127.
—, Abigail (Prentice), 255, 336.
—, Abijah, 263.
—, Amity [2], 337.
—, Arathusa, 337.
—, Barzillai, 241, 261, 337.
—, Daniel, 240, 260.
—, Hannah (Col. Josiah), 336.
—, Hannah (Josiah, Jr.), 264, 336.
—, Hepsibeth (B.), 241, 261, 337.
—, Hulday, 336.
—, J., 63.
—, James Nutting, 336.
—, Jemima, 336.
—, Jeremiah, 337.
—, Ensign, Lieut., Capt. Jonathan, 57, 64, 66, 68, 70, 73, 82, 85, 87, 91, 92, 94, 95, 103, 117, 122, 124, 127, 128, 130, 131, 135, 136, 146, 150, 165, 336, 337; heirs of, 179.
—, Jonathan, 337.
—, Jonathan, Jr., 136, 157, 240, 260, 337.
—, Capt., Col. Josiah, 34–37, 39, 56, 57, 62–66, 68, 69, 71, 74, 76–78, 81–90, 94, 95, 100, 101, 127, 336.

Willard, Josiah, Jr., 79, 84, 264, 336.
—, Josiah Tersus, 336.
—, Katharine, 337.
—, Kezia (Capt. Jona.), 336, 337.
—, Keziah, 227, 337.
—, Lois, 336.
—, Lucy (D.), 240, 260.
—, Lucy, 337.
—, Madam, 56.
—, Mary (Grout), 229, 250, 336.
—, Mary [3], 337.
—, Miriam, 336.
—, Moses, 67, 96, 108, 114, 336; 336.
—, Nathan, 336.
—, Oliver, 336.
—, Pascal Paoli, 337.
—, Phebe (Jona., Jr.), 240, 260, 337.
—, Phebe, 337.
—, Prudance, 336.
—, Ruth (Farmer), 228.
—, Sampson, 336.
—, Sarah, 337.
—, Secretary, 100, 101, 135, 170.
—, Susannah (Johnson), 232, 253, 306.
—, Susanna (Moses), and dau. do., 336.
—, Susannah, 230; 336.
—, Thulah, 337.
—, Unity (Moors), 234, 255, 337.
—, Unity, 337.
—, Wilder, 336.
Williams, Rev. Mr., 216.
—, Anne (Larrabee), 233, 254.
—, Margaret (Larrabee), 233, 254.
—, Rev. William, 262.
Wilson, Isabella (Swan), 237, 258.
—, Jacob, 261.
—, Lois (Wood), 241, 261.
—, Margaret (J.), 261.
—, Mary (Houghton), 252.
Witt, Isaiah, 178, 187, 191.
Wood, 125.
—, Barnabus, 332.
—, Bette, 332; 333.
—, Bezaleel, 330.
—, Bezelial or Bezaleel, 332, 350.
—, Chloe, 235.
—, David, 138, 141, 162, 165, 168, 172, 183, 189, 196, 204, 207, 209, 240, 263, 333; 333; 332.
—, Elizabeth, 332; 333.
—, Esther, 333.
—, George, 333.
—, Hannah, 333.
—, Isaac, 333.
—, James, 241, 333.
—, Jerusha, 332.

Wood, John, 29, 56; 241, 332.
—, Capt. Jonathan, 94, 99, 121, 124, 125, 130, 133, 136, 137, 142, 144, 146, 147, 151, 153, 156, 160, 161, 167, 168, 172, 174–176, 180–182, 184, 190, 192, 193, 196, 198, 202, 203, 207, 208, 212, 217, 241, 260, 332, 350.
—, Jonathan, 332, 350; 332; 333.
—, Jonathan, Jr., 163, 183, 186, 240, 265, 333.
—, Joseph, 128, 137, 141, 157, 186, 240, 260, 267, 332, 350.
—, Joseph, Jr., 332, 350.
—, Lois (M.), 241, 261.
—, Martha (Downe), 227, 333.
—, Mary (Buss), 225, 333.
—, Mary (D.), 240, 263, 333.
—, Mary (M.), 246, 260, 333.
—, Mary, 333.
—, Mehitable (Bridge), 225, 247, 332.
—, Michael or Michal, 240, 241, 260, 261, 333.
—, Molly, 332.
—, Nathaniel, 11, 22.
—, Rachel (Jona., Jr.), 240, 265, 333.
—, Ruth (Jos.), 240, 260, 332, 350.
—, Ruth [2d], (Jos.), 240, 267, 332.
—, Sarah (Jona.), and two daus. do., 332, 350.
—, Sarah [2d], (Jona.), 241, 260, 332, 350.
—, Sarah, 333.
—, William, 14, 22, 55, 57.
—, William H., 263.
—, Zepheniah, 333.
—, see Woods.
Woodard, 101.
Woodman, Jonathan, 15, 23, 55, 56.
Woods, Elizebeth (Farmer), 264.
—, Nathaniel, 14, 17, 55, 57.
—, Nathaniel, Jr., 14, 22, 55, 57.
Woodward, Abraham, 14, 22, 55, 57.
—, Stephen, 15.
Woolley, Thomas, 15, 23, 56.
Woolson, Amos, 338.
—, Asa [2], 338.
—, Ebenezer, 338.
—, Elijah, 338.
—, Elizabeth (Asa), and dau. do., 338.
—, Joseph, 338.
—, Lois, 338.
Wright, Joseph, 38.
—, Sibil (W.), 241, 261.
—, Wincal, 241, 261.

Wyman, 119.
—, Abigail (Ezekiel), 330, 331, 350.
—, Abigail, 330, 350.
—, David, 330, 350; 331.
—, Dorrothy (Jesher), 261.
—, Elizabeth (R.), 241, 261, 331.
—, Elizabeth, 331.
—, Ezekiel, 91, 94, 96, 103, 106, 107, 111, 117, 120, 124, 128, 130, 136, 141, 157, 160, 165, 166, 168, 196, 203, 208, 330, 331, 350; 330, 331, 350.
—, Francis, 331.
—, Israel, 241, 330.
—, Jesher, 261.
—, John, 107, 120, 124, 126, 168, 180, 184, 186, 330, 350; 331.
Wyman, John, Jr., 330, 350.
—, Joseph, 241, 261, 331; 331.
—, Keziah (Jos.), 261, 331.
—, Lucy, 230, 330.
—, N., 263.
—, Oliver, 331.
—, Rebeckah (John), 330, 350.
—, Reuben, 241, 261, 330, 331.
—, Ruth, 331.
—, Sarah, 331.
—, Seth, 241, 331.
—, Silas, 330; 331.
—, Stephen, 331.
—, Susanna, 330.
—, Thomas, 331.
—, William, 331.
—, Wymon, see Wyman.

GENERAL INDEX.

ANCIENT Names of Towns, 351.
Andover, 15, 224, 225, 227, 230–232, 266.
Appletree Hill, 134.
Ashburnham, see Dorchester Canada.
Ashulot, The, 224.

BEAVER Dam, 44, 47, 48, 52, 150.
———, Pond, 48.
Benith Brook, 9.
Bennet Brook, 9.
Billerica, 233, 249, 254.
Births, 271–338.
Bolton, 228, 234, 255, 262.
Book B, 206.
Borman's Farm, 44, 46, 55.
Boston, 10, 15, 16, 20, 21, 30, 34, 39, 41, 140, 175, 179, 215, 236, 256, 350.
Boxford, 15, 226, 233, 240, 248, 254, 263.
Bradford, 15, 16, 20, 223.
Bridges, 118, 127, 128, 131, 134, 140, 142, 149, 154, 165, 169, 184, 197, 207, 209.
Brookline, 14.
Burying Place, 63, 74, 92, 150, 165, 166, 168, 190.
By-law in Reference to Pasturage, 93.

CAMBRIDGE, 18, 19, 24, 25, 27, 33, 34, 224, 285.
Carlile, 240, 241.
Cataconamog, 9, 43–47, 55.
Charlestown, N. H., 236, 256, 295.
Cheshire, 240.
Church, 75, 76, 89, 91, 195, 198, 212, 214, 216, 218, 219.
Clay Pit Meadows, 48, 49.
Committee of Town of Groton, 10, 11.
Committee to Allot and Grant Lands, 7–57, 67, 81, 99.
Common Land, 32, 45, 49, 50, 53, 54, 114, 126, 134, 187, 191.
Concord, 10–12, 14–17, 20, 21, 24–31, 42, 223, 228, 240, 248, 255.
Conditions of Settlement, 8, 13, 36.

Continental Army, 343.
Country Land, 224.
Countrey Rode, 81.
County Road, 178, 191.
Coventree, 223, 245.

DANVERS, 227.
Deaths, 341–350.
Deer, 105, 106, 111, 113, 118, 128, 131, 133, 137, 141, 148, 153, 157, 163, 168, 173, 177, 181, 183, 186, 197, 208.
Division of Town, 140, 143, 192, 206, 212, 213, 217, 218.
Dorchester, 18, 30, 38, 191.
——— Canada, 119, 120, 143, 166, 173, 187, 224, 226, 231, 234, 241, 252, 253, 311.
——— Farm, 40, 206.
Dunstable, 9, 223, 231, 235, 241, 245, 249, 252, 261.

EXCISE Bill, 166.

FALLS, The, 51.
Fast, 212, 214.
Fitchburg, 223, 225–227, 229, 230, 232, 233, 235, 236, 239, 241.
Fitzwilliam, 300.
Flat Hill, 104.
Forfeited Lots, 35, 36.
Framingham, 319.

GENERAL Court, 7, 12, 35, 40–42, 62–65, 68, 70, 71, 89, 166, 175, 204, 205, 211–213, 216, 217.
Groton, 7–12, 14–16, 18–20, 22, 25, 27, 31–34, 37, 38, 48, 67, 80, 85, 86, 114, 126, 143, 159, 170, 187, 224, 226, 228, 233, 234, 236, 237, 246, 248, 253, 254, 257, 259, 263, 264, 286, 314, 317.
——— River, 140.
——— Road, 153.

HARTWELL's Company, 127.
Harvard, 227, 228, 230, 232, 235, 248, 251, 253, 266, 278.

Harvard College Lot, 8, 18.
Hatfield, 226.
Highways, 18, 61-63, 67, 68, 72, 74, 80, 81, 85, 88, 90, 92-96, 98-101, 104, 105, 107, 108, 111, 113-115, 118-121, 123, 125-129, 131, 132, 134, 135, 138, 142, 143, 148-150, 153-160, 162, 164, 166, 167, 169, 170-172, 174, 177, 178, 181, 184, 186-188, 190, 191, 195, 197, 203, 204, 206-210.
Holding the South Town Lots, 55-57.
Horsmeat or Horsmeet Meadow, 37, 48, 55.

INTENTIONS of Marriage, 223-241.
Ipswich, 227, 264, 310-312.
—— Canada, 120, 228, 232, 234, 236, 239, 253, 256, 257, 265.
Ireland, Kingdom of, 321.

JAMAICA, W. I., 347.
Jurymen, 62, 70, 71, 152, 188.

KEENE, N. H., see Upper Ashuelot.
Kingston, 237, 257.

LANCASTER, 10, 15, 16, 23, 26, 63, 67, 83, 99, 173, 223, 224, 228, 231, 232, 234, 237-240, 245-247, 250, 255-257, 259-262, 274, 323.
Leominster, 126, 143, 167, 174, 209, 212, 217, 223, 224, 227, 235, 236, 241, 245, 247, 248, 252, 253, 256, 261, 263, 264, 331.
Lexington, 261.
Littleton, 24, 228, 239, 240, 267.
Londonderry, 238, 254, 258.
Lot for First Settled Minister, 8, 18, 57, 75.
Lower Ashuelot, 230, 231, 251, 252.
Lynn, 240, 260.

MARLBOROUGH, 14, 24, 226, 334.
Marriage, Intentions of, 223-241.
Marriages, 245-267.
Massapog, 45, 46, 55.
Meadow Lots, 25, 27, 43-54, 77.
Medfield, 20.
Meeting House, 8, 13, 18, 37, 61-63, 65, 67, 68, 72, 75, 76, 82, 84, 86, 87, 89, 90, 91, 94-96, 98-100, 102, 103, 107, 115-118, 122, 130, 134, 136-138, 146, 156, 173, 181, 184, 188, 191, 212, 217.
—— ——, New, 138, 139, 142-148, 150, 151, 154-156, 160, 161, 164, 165, 170, 181, 182, 185, 188, 198, 206, 211, 217.
—— ——, West Parish, 192.

Methuen, 237, 266.
Middlesex County, 65, 85-87.
Mills: Widow White's, 127; Josiah Dodge's, 177; Bellows', 184.
Minister's Salary, 61-64, 68, 75, 76, 78, 94, 98, 103, 108, 112, 116, 124, 127, 130, 132, 136, 139, 144, 151, 156, 161, 165, 171, 175, 179, 181, 184, 188, 192, 194, 195, 199, 214, 216, 218, 219.
Ministerial Lot, 8, 18, 48, 57, 62, 72, 77, 88, 94, 107, 122, 126.
Mohawk River, 350.
Monadnock No. 4, 320.
Monson, N. H., 225.
Monusnut Brook, 158; see Wenoosnock.
Mulpus, Mullepus or Mullipus, 50, 52, 53, 55, 93, 119, 127, 131, 184.

NARRAGANSETT No. 2, 134, 135, 140, 154, 156, 158, 164, 166, 171, 173, 174, 187, 224, 238, 241, 246, 258.
Needham, 14.
Newbery, 14, 15.
New County, 63, 65, 85-87, 216.
New Ipswich, 240.
Newton, 236, 267.
Nichawogg or Nichewoag, 317.
Nistaqualothe or Nissitissit Hill, 8.
Nistiquasit Hill, 10.
North Branch, 123, 127.
—— River, 126.
—— Town, 11, 12, 17, 20, 27, 31, 43.
Northfield Road, 62, 63, 67, 72, 88, 92, 95-97, 118, 135.
Nottingham, 226, 234, 248.
Number Four, 228, 237, 249, 258.

OLIVER'S Land, 174, 187.

PEARL HILL Brook, 67, 128, 206.
—— —— Meadow, 55.
Pearl Hills, 135.
Pepperell, 234, 238, 265.
Peterborough, 238, 258.
Petersham, 259, 264.
Poor, The, 105, 150, 160, 165, 168, 179, 207, 210.
Pound, 61, 68, 112, 116, 117, 137, 151.
Princeton, 232, 253.
Proprietors, 27, 32, 37, 77.
Proprietors' Meetings, 31, 37.
Providence, R. I., 344.
Province Land, 70.

READING, 15, 231.
River, The, 186.
Rock Meadow, 52, 53.
Rowley, 20.

Rowley Canada, 230, 232, 236, 251, 253, 256, 276, 329.

Schools, 62, 63, 77, 79, 83, 85, 86, 89, 94–96, 98, 102, 105, 108–110, 112, 113, 115, 118, 122, 124, 125, 127, 128, 129, 131–133, 135–137, 139, 141, 142, 144, 150, 155, 161–163, 165, 168, 171, 175, 179, 181, 182, 184, 185, 189, 193, 194, 199, 200, 204, 207, 209, 215.
School Lot, 8, 18, 62, 77.
Scott's Road, 187.
Secretary's Land, 197.
Sergant's Land, 126.
Shirley, 170, 225, 226, 229, 231, 232, 234, 237, 240, 247, 251, 252, 254, 259, 260, 263.
Shrewsbury, 224.
Small-pox, 179.
South Town, 7, 9, 11, 12, 16–21, 24–39, 42, 43, 55.
Spanish Expedition, 347.
Stocks, 73, 132.
Stone Bridge, 118.
Stow, 16, 23, 225, 230–232, 234, 236, 238, 251, 252, 256, 261.
Stratford, Conn., 228.
Sudbury, 229, 265.

Taxes, 63–65, 68, 70, 71, 74, 77, 82, 85, 86, 89, 90, 98, 105, 109, 110, 116, 120, 139, 142, 148, 152, 161, 166, 175, 201, 206, 207, 213, 218.
Templeton, 239, 259.
Tewksbury, 225.
Thunder Bolts, 1749, 61.
Topsfield, 237, 267, 292.
Town Meetings, 61–219.
―― ――, How Warned, 110, 130, 135, 161.

Town Records, 61–350.
―― ――, Book B, 206–219.
Townshend, 94, 127, 184, 212, 218, 228, 229, 237, 250, 258, 260, 338.
Turkey Hill Brook, 150.
―― Meadow, 55.
Turkey Hills, 7, 9, 15, 21, 27–29, 32–40, 55.
Tuxbury, 300.

Unchawalam, Unchechewalunk, or Unkechewalom Pond, 40, 45, 126.
Unimproved Lands, 70, 71, 85, 166.
Upper Ashuelot, 246.
Upton, 228, 249.
Uxbridge, 240, 265.

Wages, 86, 90, 98, 115, 120, 134, 143, 149, 154, 164, 173, 183, 187.
Walpole, 224, 246.
Watertown, 14, 15, 251.
Weights and Measures, 62, 73, 105, 156.
Wenham, 321.
Wenoosnock Brook, 169; see Monusnut.
Westminster, 238, 241, 250, 259.
Weston, 14–16, 20, 42, 229, 239, 250, 262, 267, 338.
Willard's Company, 127.
Winchendon, 265.
Winchester, 250.
Woburn, 15, 16, 20, 38, 39, 263, 294.
Woburn Farm, 38–40, 100, 101, 107, 126.
Wolves, 153.
Worcester, 70, 71, 79, 119, 166, 225, 226, 233–235, 247, 255, 261, 263, 350.
―― County, 70, 71, 73, 85–87, 166.
Work House, 171, 199.

PLATES.

First Page of Records of General Court's Committee,	frontispiece
Second Page of Same,	to face 9
Isaac Farnsworth's Copy of Rev. Andrew Gardner's Request for Dismission,	to face 75
Signatures of Town Clerks and Rev. David Stearns,	to face 220

www.ingramcontent.com/pod-product-compliance
Lightning Source LLC
Chambersburg PA
CBHW032029220426
43664CB00006B/413